HOLY WRITINGS,
LAWS OF THE PROPHET,
SONGS AND PROVERBS

HOLY WRITINGS,
LAWS OF THE PROPHET,
SONGS AND PROVERBS

AMMISHADDAI

authorHOUSE®

AuthorHouse™
1663 Liberty Drive
Bloomington, IN 47403
www.authorhouse.com
Phone: 1-800-839-8640

Published by AuthorHouse   06/29/2012

ISBN: 978-1-4634-2026-0 (sc)
ISBN: 978-1-4634-1847-2 (e)

Library of Congress Control Number: 2012910675

Any people depicted in stock imagery provided by Thinkstock are models, and such images are being used for illustrative purposes only.
Certain stock imagery © Thinkstock.

This book is printed on acid-free paper.

Because of the dynamic nature of the Internet, any web addresses or links contained in this book may have changed since publication and may no longer be valid. The views expressed in this work are solely those of the author and do not necessarily reflect the views of the publisher, and the publisher hereby disclaims any responsibility for them.

NEW CASTLE

PRODUCTION
A
Rodney D Lewis Production

authorHOUSE®

- *We Believe* -

(1) Immanuel walked among men.. Died
(crucified)
Buried and He rose again on the 3rd day According to *the Word..*

(2) We believe the Whole Book.. *16th Century King James*
(King Yahcob)
Practice and to Keep from beginning to End - Cover to Cover - not adding to.. Not subtracting from *the Word..*

All is inspired of יהוה for Correction and Reproof.. For the Way of Life..

(3) MessiYah had to leave to ascend to the Right Hand of the Abba (Father) so that He may send His Comforter.. (Holy Spirit) As Authority to give light to all men coming in to the world, the word of truth.. *Way of Life..* will lead you into All truth.. *Working on Salvation for Elect made assure..*

- *We Believe* -

The Covenant was made with His people Ysrael and Yahudah, the House of Ysrael and the Church of MessiYah, COMMANDMENT KEEPERS

We Believe..
AMMISHADDAI

1

TOPIC: *PROPHECY I..*   THUS SAYS YHWH STAND IN THE WAYS and SEE, and ASK for the OLD PATHS, where the GOOD WAY IS, and WALK IN IT; then YOU WILL FIND REST FOR YOUR SOULS..   JEREMIAH 6:16 AT THE BEGINNING of your SUPPLICATIONS the WORD WENT OUT, and I HAVE COME TO TELL YOU, for you are greatly BELOVED; therefore CONSIDER THE MATTER, and UNDERSTAND the VISION: DANIEL 9:23 Now therefore, go and I*(YHWH)* will be with your MOUTH and TEACH you what you shall say. NOW YOU SHALL SPEAK to him and put the words in HIS MOUTH. And I will TEACH you what you shall DO.. SO he shall be your SPOKESMAN TO THE PEOPLE..   EXODUS 4:12,15,16   THEN THEY WILL HEED YOUR VOICE; and you shall come, YOU and the ELDERS of YISRAEL, to the KING of EGYPT/NORTHCOUNTRY and you shall say to him, *YHWH EL(GOD) of the HEBREWS* has met with US and NOW, PLEASE, LET US GO three days journey into the WILDERNESS, that we may SACRIFICE to YHWH OUR EL...   EXODUS 3:18,19   then it will be, if they DO NOT BELIEVE you, NOR HEED the MESSAGE of the FIRST SIGN,(REVELATION 12:1) that THEY MAY BELIEVE the message of the LATTER SIGN...   EXODUS 4:8   THUS SAYS YHWH behold a people comes from the NORTHCOUNTRY, a great NATION will be raised from the FARTHEST PARTS OF THE EARTH..   They are CRUEL and shall NOT SHOW MERCY. THEREFORE HEAR THE COUNSEL OF YHWH at the taking of BABYLON the earth TREMBLES, and the cry is HEARD AMONG the NATIONS...   JEREMIAH 6:22/50:42,43,45,46 Therefore do not pray for this people, nor lift up a cry or prayer for them, nor make INTERCESSION TO ME; for I will not hear you. DO YOU NOT SEE what they do in the cities of YAHUDAH and in the streets of YAHRUSALEM?   JEREMIAH 7:16,17   I WILL GIVE POWER TO MY TWO WITNESSES, and they will PROPHESY ONE THOUSAND TWO HUNDRED and SIXTY DAYS, CLOTHED IN SACKCLOTH..

REVELATION 11:3,6

BUT *YHWH OF HOST* shall be EXALTED IN JUDGMENT, and *YHWH WHO IS HOLY* shall be HALLOWED IN RIGHTEOUSNESS. WOE TO THOSE WHO CALL EVIL GOOD, and GOOD EVIL; who put BITTER for SWEET, and SWEET for BITTER! WOE TO THOSE who are WISE in their own EYES, and PRUDENT in their own SIGHT!

ISAIAH 5:16,20,21

THOSE WHO DO WICKEDLY AGAINST THE COVENANT HE SHALL CORRUPT WITH FLATTERY; but the people who KNOW their EL(GOD) shall be STRONG, and CARRY OUT GREAT EXPLOITS... and those of the people who UNDERSTAND SHALL INSTRUCT MANY: and there shall be a time of TROUBLE, SUCH AS NEVER WAS SINCE there was a NATION, even to that time and at that time YOUR PEOPLE SHALL BE DELIVERED, many shall RUN TO and FRO, and KNOWLEDGE SHALL INCREASE.   DANIEL 11:32-45/12:1-4   ALSO violent men of your people shall EXALT THEMSELVES IN FULFILLMENT of the VISION, but they shall FALL..   DANIEL 11:14 IT WAS GRANTED TO HIM to make war with the saints and to overcome them. HE who leads into CAPTIVITY shall go into CAPTIVITY; he who KILLS with the sword MUST be KILLED with the sword. HERE IS THE PATIENCE and FAITH OF THE SAINTS...   REVELATION 13:7-10   MANY SHALL BE PURIFIED, MADE WHITE, and REFINED, but the WISE shall UNDERSTAND. And from the time that the daily sacrifice is taken away, and the ABOMINATION of DESOLATION is set up, there shall be one thousand two hundred and ninety days...   DANIEL 12:10,11   then they will deliver YOU UP to TRIBULATION and KILL you, and you will be hated by ALL NATIONS for MY NAMES SAKE.   MATTHEW 24:9   and in his PLACE shall arise a vile person, to whom they will not give the honor of royalty; but he shall come in PEACEABLY, and SEIZE THE KINGDOM BY INTRIGUE...   DANIEL 11:21   Therefore when you see the ABOMINATION of DESOLATION, "STANDING IN THE HOLY PLACE" then let those WHO ARE IN YAHUDAH FLEE to the mountains.   MATTHEW 24:15,16 THEN the WOMAN FLED into the WILDERNESS, where she has a PLACE PREPARED BY YHWH, that they should feed her THERE one thousand two hundred and sixty days(3 ½ yrs) and THEY OVERCAME HIM by the BLOOD of the LAMB and by the WORD of their TESTIMONY, and they DID NOT LOVE their lives to the DEATH. And the DRAGON WAS ENRAGED with the WOMAN, and he went to MAKE WAR with the REST of her OFFSPRING, WHO KEEP THE COMMANDMENTS OF YHWH and have the *TESTIMONY OF YAHSHUAH MESSIYAH*

REVELATION 12:6,11,12,17

BECAUSE YOU HAVE KEPT MY COMMAND to PERSEVERE, I ALSO WILL KEEP YOU from the HOUR of TRAIL which shall come upon the WHOLE WORLD, TO TEST those who dwell on the earth. REVELATION 3:10,13 three UNCLEAN spirits, coming out of the MOUTH of the DRAGON out of the MOUTH of the BEAST, and out of the MOUTH of the FALSE PROPHET which go out to the KINGS OF THE EARTH to gather them to the BATTLE OF THE GREAT DAY OF YHWH ELSHADDAI...   REVELATION 16:13-16   FOR in ONE HOUR your JUDGMENT HAS COME...   REVELATION 18:10

END TIMES MINISTRY
COMMANDMENT KEEPERS

AMMISHADDAI

TOPIC: PROPHECY II WORDS to the north country/north Americans HERE is the MIND which has WISDOM: the ten horns which you saw are ten kings who have received no KINGDOM AS YET, but they receive AUTHORITY for ONE HOUR as KINGS with the BEAST.. THESE ARE OF ONE MIND, and they will give their POWER and AUTHORITY to the BEAST.   REVELATION 17:9-18
THE beast that was, and IS not, is HIMSELF also the EIGHTH, and IS of the SEVEN, and is going to DESTRUCTION...   REVELATION 17:11

HARLOT = FORNICATION/ IMMORAL/DEFILED RELIGON/TOLARENCE of SINS

WATERS = multitude of people DIFFERENT NATIONS and tongues...

RIGHTLY DIVIDE the WORD of TRUTH.   2TIMOTHY 2:15
SURELY YHWH ELSHADDAI does nothing, UNLESS HE REVEALS HIS SECRET to HIS servants the prophets..   AMOS 3:7
THEN HE said to me, "WRITE: 'BLESSED ARE those who are called to the marriage supper of the LAMB!" and HE said to me, "THESE are the TRUE saying of YHWH EL OF HOST." WORSHIP YHWH! For the TESTIMONY of YAHSHUAH IS the SPIRIT of PROPHECY."   REVELATION 19:9,10

+ POINTS of REFFERENCE
And I heard another VOICE from HEAVEN saying, "COME OUT of HER, my people, lest you share in her SINS, and lest you RECEIVE of her PLAGUES...   REVELATION 18:4
"BABYLON the GREAT is FALLEN, is fallen, and has become a dwelling place of DEMONS, a PRISON for every FOUL SPIRIT, and a CAGE for every UNCLEAN and HATED BIRD!   REVELATION 18:2

THEREFORE SAY to the house of YISRAEL, "THUS SAYS YHWH "REPENT, turn away from your idols, and turn your (faces) away from ALL YOUR ABOMINATIONS...   EZEKIEL 14:3-7
IN the measure that SHE glorified herself and lived LUXURIOUSLY, in the same measure give her torment and sorrow; THEREFORE HER PLAGUES will come in ONE DAY - DEATH and MOURNING and FAMINE...   for STRONG IS YHWH ELSHADDAI WHO JUDGES HER   REVELATION 18:7,8
     (1) DAY
Beloved, do not forget this one thing, that with THE MOSTHIGH ONE DAY is as a thousand years, and a thousand years as ONE DAY...   YHWH IS NOT SLACK CONCERNING HIS PROMISE..
                                                                        2PETER 3:8,9

     (1) HOUR
"FOR in ONE HOUR such great riches came to nothing.' "EVERY shipmaster, all who travel by ship, sailors, and as many as trade on sea, STOOD AT A DISTANCE. FOR in ONE HOUR she is made DESOLATE...   REVELATION 18:17,18,19
"UNLESS THOSE DAYS WERE SHORTENED, (NO) FLESH would be saved; but for the ELECTS SAKE those days will be SHORTENED.   MATTHEW 24:22
I (YHWH) will also KEEP you from the HOUR OF TRAIL which shall come upon the whole world, TO TEST THOSE WHO DWELL ON THE EARTH: REVELATION 3:10
     (7) MOUNTAINS = powers

                                        PROPHETIC MESSAGE MINISTRY

     (8) DIFFERENT SYSTEMS = governments

     (10) HORNS = ruler having authority
AMMISHADDAI
   TRUE
   BELIEVER

READINGS of INSPIRATION

TOPIC: PROPHECY IV TURN FROM THE WICKED WAYS..

SO I say SO I speak today; To the leaders of the ministry for the people TRANSGRESSED more and more ACCORDING to <u>ALL ABOMINATION</u> of the NATION / USA and DEFILED the house of YHWH which HE made *HOLY in YAHRUSALEM*   (TRUE)

WARNING UNTO THEM BY HIS MESSENGERS early rising sending them because YHWH has compassion on HIS people and on HIS dwelling place. So those who escaped from the sword he carried away to Babylon for we became servants to him and his sons until the reign of the KINGDOM OF PERSIA.. seventy (years)   2CHRONICLES 36:14-21

For today we set under gentle rule.. *PONDER IN THE SCHOOL OF THOUGHT..*
Babylon / Persia / Greece and Rome / USA so now it makes me want to say DILIGENTLY (OBEY) the voice of IMMANUEL MESSIYAH to observe carefully <u>ALL HIS COMMANDMENTS</u> which I command you today. BLESSED SHALL WE BE IN THE CITY and BLESSED shall you be in the country..   DEUTERONOMY 28:1-3,10

SO all the peoples of the earth shall see you CALLED by the NAME OF YHWH and they shall be afraid of you so I say today ministers and prophets down to teachers of the land dwell within your own city to secure ISRAEL CITY BY CITY for this hour we seek to stir up the *SPIRIT of PROCLAMATION* through out the land for the KINGDOM is at HAND..

(TRUE)

FOR we are the people of this province brought INTO CAPTIVITY; so I say so we PRAY today how long will WE SLEEP and STAY CAUGHT UP in different activity did you see the distress that we lay in. So NO LONGER must we be a REPROACH, but set our hand to do this good work for the FATHER OF HEAVEN himself will prosper US; THEREFORE we his servants will RISE and BUILD CITY to CITY for truly has it come to pass, these things have come upon us being called to mind among the NATIONS / USA where YHWH have driven you so return to his voice and obey HIS COMMANDMENT that I say for your MIGHTY ONE will make you a bound in all the work of your hand, in the FRUIT OF YOUR SPIRIT and SOUL, becoming self sufficient / industry to maintain the COMMANDMENTS of the MOSTHIGH STATUES which are written in the book of the PROPHETS (LAW) providing we turn to YHWH ELSHADDAI with <u>ALL</u> your <u>HEART</u> and with <u>ALL</u> your <u>SOUL</u>

DEUTERONOMY 30:1-10

BUT even if our gospel is veiled, it is veiled to those who are PERISHING, whose minds the god of this age has BLINDED, who DO NOT BELIEVE, lest the LIGHT of the GOSPEL of the GLORY of MESSIYAH, who is the IMAGE of YHWH, should shine on them.. For it is the MOSTHIGH who COMMANDED light to shine out of darkness, who has SHONE in our HEARTS TO GIVE the LIGHT of the KNOWLEDGE of the GLORY of YHWH..

2CORINTHIANS 4:3-6

So brothers grace be given from IMMANUEL MESSIYAH YAHSHUAH with the SPIRIT of TRUTH..   AMEN

PROPHETIC MESSAGE MINISTRY
END TIMES MINISTRY
AMMISHADDAI

TOPIC: PROPHECY III   HERE IS THE MIND WHICH HAS WISDOM, for the TESTIMONY of YAHSHUAH is the SPIRIT OF PROPHECY...

" UP, UP! FLEE from the LAND of the NORTH." says YHWH; "for I YHWH have spread YOU ABROAD LIKE the four winds of heaven," says YHWH. " UP, ZION! ESCAPE, YOU WHO DWELL WITH THE DAUGHTER OF BABYLON." "SING and REJOICE, O DAUGHTER OF ZION! FOR BEHOLD, I AM COMING and I WILL DWELL IN YOUR MIDST," SAYS YHWH.   ZECHARIAH 2:6-13

"COME OUT OF HER, my people, lest you SHARE in her sins, and lest you RECEIVE OF HER PLAGUES. Therefore her plagues will come in ONE DAY - DEATH and MOURNING and FAMINE..

REVELATION 18:4,5,8

NOW it shall come to pass in the latter days, that the MOUNTAIN OF YHWH'S HOUSE SHALL BE ESTABLISHED on the top of the mountains, shall be EXALTED ABOVE THE HILLS; and ALL NATIONS SHALL FLOW TO IT. FOR out of ZION shall go forth the LAW, and the WORD OF יהוה From YAHRUSALEM   ISAIAH 2:2,3   "IN those days and in that time," says YHWH " the children of YISRAEL shall come, they and the children of YAHUDAH TOGETHER; they will ask the WAY TO ZION, saying, 'COME and let us join ourselves to YHWH in a perpetual COVENANT that will not be forgotten." my people have been lost sheep. Their shepherds have led them astray; THEY HAVE FORGOTTEN THEIR RESTING PLACE.   JEREMIAH 50:4-6   IN that day there shall be a ROOT OF JESSE, who shall stand as a BANNER to the people; for the GENTILES shall seek him, and HIS RESTING PLACE shall be glorious." it shall come to pass in that day that YHWH shall set HIS HAND AGAIN the SECOND TIME, TO RECOVER the remnant of HIS people, who are left, HE will set up a BANNER for the nations, and will ASSEMBLE THE OUTCASTS OF YISRAEL, and GATHER TOGETHER the dispersed of YAHUDAH from the four CORNERS OF THE EARTH. ISAIAH 11:10-12 YES, many peoples and strong nations shall come to seek YHWH OF HOSTS in YAHRUSALEM, and pray before THE MOST HIGH.' THUS says YHWH of HOSTS: ' IN THOSE DAYS ten men from every language of the nations shall GRASP THE SLEEVE OF A HEBREW MAN, saying, "let us go with you for we have heard that YHWH GOD IS WITH YOU."   ZECHARIAH 8:22,23   PROCLAIM, GIVE PRAISE, and SAY, 'O YHWH, SAVE YOUR PEOPLE, the remnant of YISRAEL!' BEHOLD, I (YHWH) will bring them from the north country, and gather them from the ends of the earth,

JEREMIAH 31:7,8

THEREFORE DO NOT FEAR, O MY SERVANT JACOB SAYS YHWH. 'nor be dismayed, O YISRAEL; for behold, I will SAVE YOU FROM AFAR, and your seed from the land of their captivity. JACOB shall return, have rest and be QUIET, and NO ONE shall make him AFRAID.   JEREMIAH 30:10,11 "And there will be signs in the sun, in the moon, and in the stars; and on the earth distress of nations, with perplexity, "Men's hearts failing them from fear and the expectation of those things which are coming on the earth, for the powers of the heavens will be shaken.   LUKE 21:25,26   "LET not your heart be troubled; you BELIEVE IN YHWH, believe also in ME. I GO TO PREPARE A PLACE FOR YOU.   JOHN 14:1-6   BUT, YHWH LIVES who brought up the children of YISRAEL from the land of the NORTH and from all the lands where HE HAD DRIVEN THEM. 'FOR I WILL BRING THEM BACK INTO THEIR LAND which I gave to their fathers. BEHOLD, I WILL SEND for many fishermen, says YHWH, and they shall fish them;   JEREMIAH 16:14-16   BECAUSE you have kept MY COMMAND to persevere, I also will keep you from the HOUR OF TRAIL which shall come upon the whole world, TO TEST THOSE WHO DWELL ON THE EARTH.   REVELATION 3:10   LIFT UP A BANNER ON THE HIGH MOUNTAIN, I have commanded MY sanctified ONES;   ISAIAH 13:2,3 All inhabitants of the world and dwellers on the earth: when HE lifts up a BANNER on the mountains, you see it, and when HE blows a trumpet, you HEAR IT.   ISAIAH 18:2,3   BUT the woman was given two wings of a great eagle, that she might fly into THE WILDERNESS TO HER PLACE, Then the TEMPLE OF YHWH was opened in heaven, and the ARK OF HIS COVENANT was seen in HIS TEMPLE. And there were lightnings, noises, thundering, an EARTHQUAKE, and GREAT HAIL.

REVELATION 12:6,14/11:19/14:1,5

אמקולדרא.   COMMANDMENT KEEPERS

FOR OUR EXHORTATION DID NOT COME FROM DECEIT OR UNCLEANNESS, NOR WAS IT IN GUILE.. But as we have been approved by YHWH to be ENTRUSTED with the GOSPEL, even so we speak, not as PLEASING MEN, but YHWH who TEST our hearts. For neither at any time did we USE FLATTERING WORDS, as you know, nor a cloak for COVETOUSNESS - YHWH IS WITNESS..   1THESSALONIANS 2:3-5

TOPIC: PROPHECY V For we are APPROVED by the MOSTHIGH who TESTS our hearts; So neither at any time should we use FLATTERING WORDS.   (TRUE)
For I find that a soft answer TURN AWAY harsh WRATH, but the OFFENSIVE WORD stirred up MUCH ANGER, so I would watch what I had to say. Becoming **WISER** by the day using KNOWLEDGE rightly divide **IN TRUTH** knowing sticks and stones break my bones, but WORDS OFFENSIVELY HURT ME.   PROVERBS 15:1-4

REMIND THEM to be subject to rulers and authorities, to obey to be ready for every good work showing <u>ALL</u> <u>HUMBLENESS</u> to <u>ALL</u> for we know ourselves was once FOOLISH being DECEIVED until the kindness and LOVE OF YHWH our SAVIOR toward men showed up; not by works of RIGHTEOUSNESS which we have done, but according to HIS (YHWH'S) mercy HE saved US..   (TRUE)
So I say so I speak to day; BE DILIGENT TO PRESENT YOURSELF APPROVED TO YHWH... becoming a worker who DOES NOT NEED to be ashamed *RIGHTLY DIVIDING* the WORD OF TRUTH. So I say so I speak from the HUMBLENESS of my heart CORRECTING THOSE in opposition for the MOSTHIGH MAY GRANT me repentance so that I may learn to KNOW THE TRUTH..   2TIMOTHY 2:14,25

For WISDOM is in the sight of him who has UNDERSTANDING so UNDERSTANDING becomes a wellspring of life to him who has it, For the HEART of the WISE teaches HIS MOUTH So it adds LEARNING unto HIS LIPS speaking from the *SPIRIT OF TRUTH..* PLEASANT WORDS are like a HONEYCOMB sweetness to the SOUL and HEATH to the BONES.   PROVERBS 16:22-24

SO NOW I PONDER IN SPIRIT; " And then many will be OFFENDED, will betray one another, and will hate one another.   MATTHEW 24:10
IN the last days many was OFFENDED, so the question arose? HOW long will the SIMPLE ONES ENJOY his / or hers SIMPLICITY for only FOOLS would HATE KNOWLEDGE for it is WRITTEN: COMMIT your WORKS to YHWH and your thoughts will be ESTABLISHED..   PROVERBS 16:3
The preacher was WISE, he still TAUGHT the people (ISRAEL and CHURCH) KNOWLEDGE: YES, he pondered and sought out and SET IN ORDER many proverbs. The preacher sought to FIND ACCEPTABLE WORDS; and what was WRITTEN was UPRIGHT - WORDS OF TRUTH..   ECCLESIASTES 12:9-14

READINGS of INSPIRATION
    AMMISHADDAI
        TRUE
        BELIEVER
    (1) PROPHECY (N) a divinely INSPIRED utterance, revelation, writing, teaching, etc..

Prophets in Palestine

This map is a detailed, close-up view of the land of Canaan when God was speaking through some of His earliest prophets, calling His people to repentance. The time-frame ranges from approximately 1000 B.C. to 400 B.C.

PROPHETS IN PALESTINE

Damascus

Zarephath
Elijah raises widow's son

Elisha pronounces doom on Ben-hadad

Mediterranean Sea

Elijah confronts prophets of Baal and runs to Jezreel

Mt. Carmel

Gath hepher

Sea of Galilee

Jonah's birthplace

Prophets in Samaria included Hosea, Micaiah, Oded, and possibly Amos

Jezreel

Elisha's birthplace

Abel-meholah?

Elijah's birthplace

Samaria

Tishbe?

Samuel presented to the Lord and reared here

Jonah departs for Tarshish

Amos prophesies

Shiloh

Joppa
Samuel's birthplace

Bethel

Cities in Samuel's circuit

Mizpah

Gilgal?

Nahum's birthplace

Ramah

Elkosh?

Jeremiah's birthplace

Anathoth

Jericho

Elisha raises axe head

Jerusalem

Mt. Nebo

Moresheth-gath

Tekoa

Balaam pronounces "blessing" upon Israel

Mareshah

Amos' birthplace

Dead Sea

Micah's birthplace

JUDAH

Eliezer's birthplace

Micah prophesies throughout villages and hamlets of Judah

Prophets in Jerusalem included Gad, Nathan, Isaiah, Jeremiah, Shemaiah, Hanani, Zephaniah, Haggai, Malachi, Zechariah and probably Joel; Ezekiel probably hailed from Jerusalem; Elijah translated to heaven

Obadiah prophesies against Edom

EDOM

0 ____ 30 mi.
0 ____ 40 km.

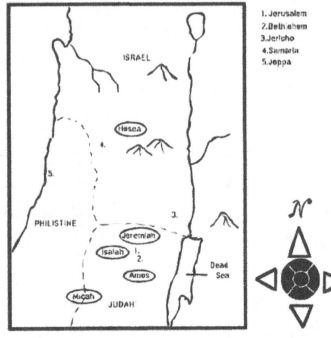

ISRAEL

Hosea

PHILISTINE

Jeremiah
Isaiah
Amos
Micah

JUDAH

Dead Sea

N

1. Jerusalem
2. Bethlehem
3. Jericho
4. Samaria
5. Joppa

Thematic Map

World Vegetation   FIRST TRUMPET : VEGETATION STRUCK
The first angel sounded: and hail and fire followed, mingled with blood, and
They were thrown to the earth.. And a <u>THIRD OF THE TREES WERE
BURN UP</u> and all green grass was burn up…   REVELATION 8 : 7

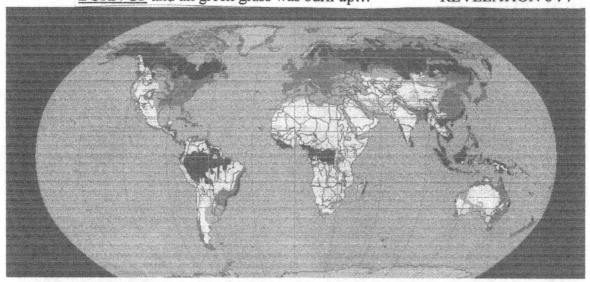

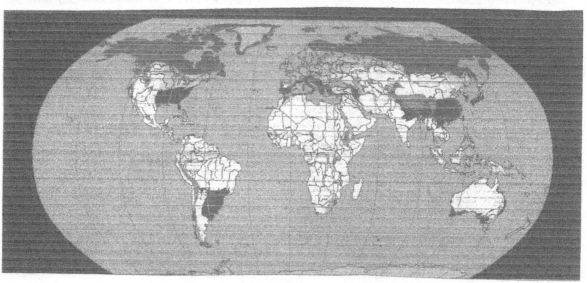

VEGETATION REGIONS

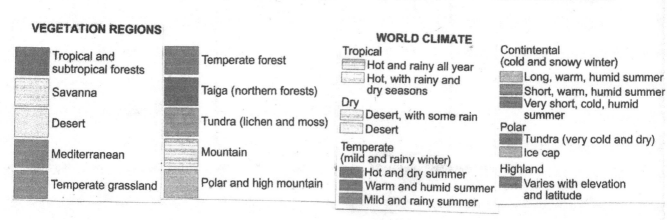

Tropical and subtropical forests	Temperate forest
Savanna	Taiga (northern forests)
Desert	Tundra (lichen and moss)
Mediterranean	Mountain
Temperate grassland	Polar and high mountain

WORLD CLIMATE

Tropical
  Hot and rainy all year
  Hot, with rainy and
  dry seasons
Dry
  Desert, with some rain
  Desert
Temperate
(mild and rainy winter)
  Hot and dry summer
  Warm and humid summer
  Mild and rainy summer

Contintental
(cold and snowy winter)
  Long, warm, humid summer
  Short, warm, humid summer
  Very short, cold, humid
  summer
Polar
  Tundra (very cold and dry)
  Ice cap
Highland
  Varies with elevation
  and latitude

8

Jerusalem-Old City

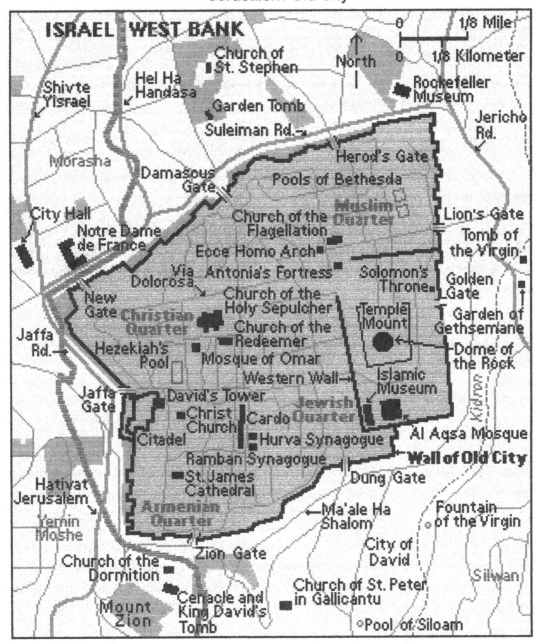

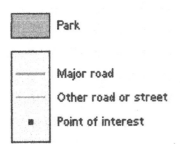

Park

Major road

Other road or street

■ Point of interest

They will fall by the edge of the sword, and led away captive into all nations. And Yahrusalem will be TRAMPLED by GENTILES until the times of the Gentiles are fulfilled..   LUKE 21:24

TOPIC: SEXUAL IMMORALITY   SO faith comes by HEARING, and HEARING by the word of YHWH..   ROMANS 10:17

You SHALL NOT LIE WITH a male as with a woman. It is a ABOMINATION.
                                            LEVITICUS 18:22,23

If a man LIES WITH A MALE as he LIES WITH A WOMAN, both of them have COMMITTED an ABOMINATION.   LEVITICUS 20:13,15

"CURSED is the one who LIES with any KIND of animal."   DEUTERONOMY 27:21

"IF I (YHWH) had NOT COME and SPOKEN to them, they would have NO SIN, but now they have NO EXCUSE for their SIN..   JOHN 15:22

"DO NOT THINK that I (YHWH) came to destroy the LAW or the PROPHETS. I did not come to destroy but to FULFILL. "For assuredly, I say to you, TILL HEAVEN and EARTH PASS AWAY, one jot or one smallest stroke will by NO MEANS PASS FROM the LAW till all is FULFILLED..   MATTHEW 5:17,18

"REMEMBER now, who ever perished being INNOCENT? Or where were the UPRIGHT ever CUT OFF? Even as I have seen those who plow INIQUITY (SIN) and sow trouble reap the same...   JOB 4:7,8

For the wrath of YHWH is revealed from heaven against ALL UNGODLINESS and UNRIGHTEOUSNESS of men, who SUPPRESS the TRUTH in UNRIGHTEOUSNESS, because what may be known of YHWH is manifest in them, for YHWH has shown it to them. For since the creation of the world HIS (YHWH) INVISIBLE ATTRIBUTES are CLEARY SEEN, being understood by the things that are made, even HIS ETERNAL POWER and DIVINE NATURE, so that they are without EXCUSE.. Because although they knew YHWH, they DID NOT GLORIFY HIM as EL (GOD) nor were thankful, but became futile in their thoughts, and their FOOLISH HEARTS were DARKENED.. PROFESSING to be wise, they became fools, therefore YHWH also gave them up to UNCLEANNESS, in the lust of their hearts, to dishonor their bodies among themselves, who EXCHANGED the TRUTH of YHWH for the LIE, and WORSHIPED and SERVED the creature rather than the CREATOR, who is BLESSED FOREVER.. AMEN   For this reason YHWH gave them up to VILE PASSIONS. For even their *WOMEN EXCHANGED the NATURAL use for what is AGAINST NATURAL..* LIKEWISE also the MEN, leaving the NATURAL USE of the woman, burned in their LUST for one another, **MEN** with **MEN COMMITTING** what is shameful, and receiving in themselves the PENALTY OF THEIR ERROR which is DUE.. Being filled with ALL UNRIGHTEOUSNESS, *SEXUAL IMMORALITY,*   ROMANS 1:18-22,24-32

DO YOU NOT KNOW that the unrighteous WILL NOT inherit the KINGDOM of YHWH? DO NOT **BE DECEIVED**. NEITHER FORNICATORS, NOR IDOLATERS, NOR ADULTERERS, NOR HOMOSEXUALS, NOR SODOMITES..   1CORINTHAIANS 6:9
PROPHETIC MESSAGE MINISTRY

AMMISHADDAI

FEAR is the topic **HEAR;** FOR as many as are led by the Spirit of YHWH, these are sons of YHWH. For you did not receive the spirit of bondage **AGAIN to FEAR,** but you received the Spirit of adoption by whom we cry out, " Abba, FATHER." the SPIRIT HIMSELF BEARS WITNESS with our spirit that we are children of YHWH..   ROMANS 8:14-16

For YHWH has not given us a spirit of **FEAR,** but of *POWER and of LOVE and of a SOUND MIND..*
                                                            2TIMOTHY 1:7

(A) Do we FEAR while performing our calling, when finding out what to do? Performing deeds in our calling?   Question

"You shall receive power when the **HOLY SPIRIT HAS COME** upon you; and you shall be **WITNESSES TO ME (YHWH)** in Yahrusalem, and in all Yahudah and Samaria, and to the END OF THE EARTH."
                                                            ACTS1:7,8

Many are called few are CHOSEN!! " You will be betrayed even by parents and brothers, relatives and friends; and they will put some of you to death.. " *BUT NOT A HAIR OF YOUR HEAD SHALL BE LOST.. " BY YOUR PATIENCE (LOVE) POSSESS YOUR SOULS:*   LUKE 21:16-19

Strengthen the WEAK; Say to those who are fearful - hearted, "Be strong, do **NOT FEAR!** Behold, your MIGHTY ONE will come with VENGEANCE, With the recompense of YHWH; HE WILL COME and SAVE YOU."   ISAIAH 35: 3,4

There is **NO FEAR IN LOVE;** but perfect LOVE cast OUT FEAR, *BECAUSE FEAR INVOLVES TORMENT..* but he who FEARS has not been made perfect in LOVE.   1JOHN 4:18

The Fear of man brings a snare, But whoever trusts in YHWH shall be **SAFE.** Justice for man comes from YHWH...   PROVERBS 29:25,26

" Whatever I tell you in the dark, speak in the light; and what you hear in the ear, PREACH on the HOUSETOPS." DO NOT FEAR those who kill the body but cannot kill the SOUL..   MATTHEW 10:27,28

" IF you do not carefully OBSERVE ALL the WORDS of this LAW that are written in this book, that you **MAY FEAR this GLORIOUS and AWESOME NAME, YHWH ELSHADDAI** Your MIGHTY ONE.." Your life shall hang in doubt before you: you shall FEAR day and night, and have no assurance of life..
                                                    DEUTERONOMY 28:58,65,66

Yes, though I walk through the valley of the shadow of death, I WILL NOT FEAR NO EVIL; you are with me; Your rod and Your staff, they COMFORT ME. You prepare a table before me in the presence of my enemies; You anoint my head with oil; My cup run over. *SURELY GOODNESS and MERCY SHALL FOLLOW ME ALL THE DAYS OF MY LIFE;* and I will dwell in the house of YHWH FOREVER..
                                                            PSALM 23:4-6

YHWH IS MY LIGHT and MY SALVATION; whom shall I FEAR? YHWH IS THE STRENGTH of my LIFE; of whom shall I be AFRAID? *MY HEART SHALL NOT FEAR;*   PSALM 27:1-3

What then shall we say to these things? *IF YHWH IS FOR US, who can be AGAINST US?*
                        ROMANS 8:31

PROPHETIC MESSAGE MINISTRY
    The Art of Studies
    KINGDOM PRICIPLES

                                                            AMMISHADDAI
                                                            TRUE
FEAR (N) a feeling of disquiet or apprehension.. AFRAID   BELIEVER

TOPIC: **LOVE, CHARITY and HOSPITALITY**... LOVE SUFFERS LONG and is KIND; LOVE DOES NOT ENVY; LOVE DOES NOT PARADE ITSELF, is not arrogant; does not behave rudely, does not seek its own, is NOT PROVOKED, thinks NO EVIL;   1CORINTHIANS 13:4,5
BUT *ABOVE ALL THINGS PUT ON LOVE*, which is the BOND OF PERFECTION. LET the peace of YHWH rule in your hearts,   COLOSSIANS 3:14,15
LET no one seek his own, but each one the other's WELL BEING.   1CORINTHIANS 10:24
BUT THIS I SAY: he who sows SPARINGLY will also REAP SPARINGLY, and he who sows BOUNTIFULLY will also reap BOUNTIFULLY. So let each one give as HE PURPOSES IN HIS HEART, not grudgingly or of necessity; for YHWH LOVES A CHEERFUL GIVER.   2CORINTHIANS 9:6,7

" *BUT WHEN YOU DO A CHARITABLE DEED*, DO NOT let your left hand know what your right hand is doing,   MATTHEW 6:1-4   "GIVE to him who asks you, and from him who wants to borrow from you do not turn AWAY.   MATTHEW 5:42   "AND you will be BLESSED, because they cannot REPAY YOU; for you shall be REPAID AT THE RESURRECTION OF THE JUST."   LUKE 14:13,14
LET BROTHERLY **LOVE CONTINUE**. DO not forget to entertain strangers, for by so doing some have UNWITTINGLY ENTERTAINED ANGELS.   HEBREWS 13:1,2
Be **HOSPITABLE** to one another without grumbling. As each one has received a gift, MINISTER it to one another, as good stewards of the MANIFOLD GRACE OF YHWH; IF anyone ministers, let him DO IT as with the ABILITY which YHWH SUPPLIES,   1PETER 4:9,10,11
DISTRIBUTING to the NEEDS of the SAINTS, given to HOSPITALITY.   ROMANS 12:13

"I HAVE SHOWN YOU IN EVERY WAY, by laboring like THIS, that you must support the WEAK. And remember the WORDS OF THE MESSIYAH YAHSHUAH, that HE said ' it is more BLESSED to give than to RECEIVE."   ACTS 20:35

BY THIS WE KNOW LOVE, because HE laid down HIS LIFE FOR US. And we also ought to lay down our lives for the brothers. But whoever HAS THIS WORLDS GOODS, and SEES his brother in NEED, and shuts up his HEART from him, how does the LOVE OF the MOSTHIGH ABIDE IN HIM? My little children, let US not LOVE IN WORD or in TONGUE, but in DEED and IN TRUTH.   1JOHN 3:16-18

BUT THE END OF ALL THINGS is at HAND; therefore be serious and WATCHFUL in your prayers. And above all things have FERVENT LOVE for one another, for " **LOVE WILL COVER A MULTITUDE OF SINS.**"   1PETER 4:8

For you brothers, have been CALLED TO LIBERTY; only do not use LIBERTY as an OPPORTUNITY for the flesh, but *THROUGH LOVE SERVE ONE ANOTHER*. For the LAW IS FULFILLED IN ONE WORD, EVEN IN THIS: " YOU shall LOVE your neighbor as yourself."   GALATIANS 5:13,14

HE who trusts in his own heart is a FOOL, but whoever WALKS WISELY will be DELIVERED, HE who gives to the poor will not LACK, but HE who hides his eyes, will HAVE MANY CURSES.
                    PROVERBS 28:27

PROPHETIC MESSAGE MINISTRY
KINGDOM PRINCIPLES

AMMISHADDAI
  TRUE
  BELIEVER

CHARITY (N) LOVE for one's fellow men.
HOSPITABLE (ADJ) FRIENDLY and concern with care toward guests.

TOPIC: SEEKING ACCESS to the MOSTHIGH.. I tell the truth in MESSIYAH, I am not lying my conscience also bearing me witness in the *HOLY SPIRIT*, who are ISRAELITES, to whom pertain the adoption, the gory the COVENANTS, the giving of the LAW the service of the MOSTHIGH, and the PROMISES; of whom are the (Elders) and from whom according to the flesh, MESSIYAH came, who is over all the *ETERNALLY BLESSED MIGHTY ONE: AMEN*   ROMANS 9:1,4,5

So also MESSIYAH did not glorify HIMSELF to become HIGH PRIEST, but it was HE who said to HIM: you are MY SON, TODAY I have begotten YOU." "YOU are a priest FOREVER according to the ORDER of MELCHIZEDEK,"   HEBREWS 5:5,6

"let not your heart be troubled; you believe in YHWH, believe also in ME, YAHSHUAH said to him, "I am the WAY, the TRUTH and the LIFE.. No one comes to the ABBA (FATHER) except through ME.   JOHN 14:1,6   LET us therefore come BOLDLY to the throne of GRACE, that we may obtain mercy and find GRACE to help in time of need.   HEBREWS 4:16

Show me your ways, O YHWH; teach me your paths. Lead me in your TRUTH and TEACH me, for your are the *MIGHTY ONE OF SALVATION;* On you I wait all the day.   PSALM 25:4,5

Therefore submit to THE MOSTHIGH. Resist the devil and he will flee from you, DRAW NEAR TO YHWH and HE will draw NEAR to you.   JAMES 4:7,8

FINALLY, my brothers, be strong in YHWH and in the POWER OF HIS MIGHT. Put on the whole ARMOR of YHWH, that you may be able to stand against the scheming and wiles of the ADVERSARY (DEVIL)   EPHESIANS 6:10,11

"BECAUSE you have kept MY COMMANDMENTS to PERSEVERE, I also will keep you from the hour of trail which shall come upon the whole world, to TEST those who dwell on the earth. "behold, I am coming QUICKLY! Hold fast what you have, that no one may take your crown.   REVELATION 3:10

YES, many peoples and strong nations shall come to *SEEK* YHWH of hosts in YAHRUSALEM, and to *PRAY BEFORE* (ACCESS) the MOSTHIGH.." "Thus says YHWH of hosts: 'In those days ten men from every language of the NATIONS shall grasp the sleeve of a *HEBREW MAN,* saying, "let us go with you, for we have heard that YHWH (GOD) is with you."   ZECHARIAH 8:22,23

PROPHETIC MESSAGE MINISTRY
KINGDOM PRINCIPLES
AMMISHADDAI

SEEK (V) to try to find or discover: search for.
ACCESS (N) a means of approaching: passage to the *KINGDOM*

HEAR, O YISRAEL: יהוה OUR EL יהוה IS (ONE)
YOU SHALL LOVE YHWH YOUR EL WITH ALL YOUR HEART, WITH ALL YOUR SOUL, and
WITH ALL YOUR STRENGTH...   DEUTERONOMY 6:4,5

TOPIC: *ABOMINABLE CUSTOMS and TRADITIONS*

THESE WORDS which I COMMAND you today shall be in your heart, you shall teach them
DILIGENTLY to your children and shall TALK OF THEM WHEN YOU SIT IN YOUR HOUSE, when
You WALK by the WAY, WHEN you lie down, and when you RISE UP.. YOU SHALL WRITE them
On the DOOR POSTS of your HOUSE and on your GATES..   DEUTERONOMY 6:6-9
You shall therefore KEEP MY STATUES and MY JUDGEMENTS and SHALL NOT COMMIT any of
These *ABOMINATIONS,* either any of your own nation, or any stranger who dwells among you...
(FOR ALL THESE ABOMINATIONS the MEN OF THE LAND HAVE DONE, WHO WERE BEFORE
YOU and THUS the LAND IS DEFILED) therefore you shall KEEP MY ORDINANCE so that you do not
COMMIT <u>ANY</u> OF THESE ABOMINABLE CUSTOMS which were COMMITTED before you, and you
Do not DEFILE YOURSELVES BY THEM: *I AM YHWH your EL*   LEVITICUS 18:26-30
HEAR THE WORD WHICH YHWH SPEAKS TO YOU, O HOUSE OF YISRAEL. THUS SAYS YHWH
DO NOT LEARN THE WAY of the GENTILES; DO NOT BE DISMAYED AT THE SIGNS OF
HEAVEN, for the GENTILES are DISMAYED AT THEM.. For the **CUSTOMS** OF THE PEOPLE ARE
FUTILE;   JEREMIAH 10:1-5
Why do you also TRANSGRESS the COMMANDMENT OF YHWH BECAUSE OF TRADITION?
THUS YOU HAVE MADE the COMMANDMENT OF YHWH OF NO EFFECT BY YOUR
TRADITION and in VAIN THEY WORSHIP ME.. TEACHING AS DOCTRINES the commandment of
MEN..   MATTHEW 15:3-9
HE WHO SAYS, "I KNOW HIM,"(*messiyah)* and does NOT KEEP HIS COMMANDMENTS, IS A LIAR
And the TRUTH IS NOT IN HIM...   1JOHN 2:4

BEWARE LEST ANYONE CHEAT YOU THROUGH

PHILOSOPHY and EMPTY DECEIT, ACCORDING TO the TRADITION OF MEN, ACCORDING TO
The BASIC PRINCIPLES OF THE WORLD, and NOT ACCORDING TO **MESSIYAH**...
                                                            COLOSSIANS 2:8
And WHEN THEY SAY TO YOU, "SEEK THOSE WHO ARE MEDIUMS and WIZARDS, WHO
Whisper and mutter," should not a people SEEK THEIR GOD? Should they seek the DEAD on behalf of
The LIVING? To the LAW and TO THE TESTIMONY! IF they do not SPEAK ACCORDING TO THIS
WORD, it is BECAUSE there is NO LIGHT IN THEM..   ISAIAH 8:19,20
THERE SHALL NOT BE FOUND AMONG YOU.. one who practices witch craft, or a soothsayer, or one
Who interprets omens, or a sorcerer or one who CONJURES SPELLS, OR A MEDIUM OR A SPIRITIST
OR ONE WHO CALLS UP THE DEAD.. For ALL who do these things are an ABOMINATION TO
YHWH and BECAUSE OF THESE ABOMINATIONS YHWH YOUR EL(GOD) drives them out from
Before you. You shall be BLAMELESS BEFORE YHWH YOUR EL for these NATIONS which you will
Dispossess LISTENED TO SOOTHSAYERS and DIVINERS; but as for you, *YHWH YOUR EL* has not
APPOINTED SUCH FOR YOU...   DEUTERONOMY 18:10-14
For when you OFFER YOUR GIFTS and MAKE YOUR SONS PASS THROUGH the fire you defile
Yourselves with ALL YOUR IDOLS, **EVEN TO THIS DAY..** what you have in your MIND SHALL
NEVER BE, when you say, 'WE WILL BE LIKE THE GENTILES, like the families in other countries,
SERVING WOOD and STONE.'   EZEKIEL 20:31,32
I RAISED MY HAND IN A OATH, THAT I **WOULD SCATTER** THEM AMONG the GENTILES and
DISPERSE THEM THROUGHOUT the COUNTRIES, BECAUSE they HAD NOT EXECUTED MY
JUDGMENTS, BUT HAD DESPISED MY STATUTES, PROFANED MY SABBATHS...
                                                            EZEKIEL 20:23-25

KINGDOM PRINCIPLES

AMMISHADDAI
   TRUE
BELIEVER

TOPIC: LYING and FALSE WITNESS.. I AM YHWH your GOD, who brought you out of the land of EGYPT, OUT OF THE HOUSE OF BONDAGE. YOU SHALL NOT bear FALSE WITNESS.

EXODUS 20: 1,2,3,16

YOU SHALL NOT STEAL, nor DEAL FALSELY, nor LIE to one another.   LEVITICUS 19:11

YOU SHALL NOT SWEAR by my NAME FALSELY, nor shall you PROFANE the NAME OF YHWH your GOD: I AM YHWH   LEVITICUS 19:12

BEHOLD YHWH'S HAND IS NOT SHORTENED that it cannot save, nor HIS EAR heavy that it cannot HEAR. But your iniquity have separated you from your EL (GOD) and your sins have hidden his FACE FROM YOU so that HE WILL NOT HEAR..   ISAIAH 59:1,2

THESE SIX THINGS YHWH HATES, YES SEVEN, are ABOMINATION TO HIM: (1) a proud look, (2) a **LYING TONGUE,** (3) hands that shed innocent blood (4) a heart that devises wicked plans, (5) feet that are swift in running to EVIL, (6) **A FALSE WITNESS** who speaks LIES.. (7) and ONE WHO sows DISCORD between brothers.   PROVERBS 6:16-19

THEREFORE, PUTTING AWAY , LYING, "let each one speak TRUTH WITH HIS NEIGHBOR, " FOR WE ARE MEMBERS OF ONE ANOTHER...   EPHESIANS 4:25

BE ANGRY, and DO NOT **SIN.** MEDITATE WITHIN your bed, and be still.. OFFER the SACRIFICES of RIGHTEOUSNESS, and put your TRUST IN YHWH.   PSALM 4:4,5

DO NOT LIE to one another, since you have put off the OLD MAN with his deeds, and have PUT ON THE NEW MAN WHO IS RENEWED IN KNOWLEDGE according to the IMAGE OF HIM (YHWH) WHO CREATED HIM..   COLOSSIANS 3:9,10

DELIVER MY SOUL, "O" YHWH, from LYING LIPS and FROM A **DECEITFUL TONGUE:** PSALM 120:2 LET the LYING LIPS BE PUT TO **SILENCE,** which speak INSOLENT things PROUDLY and CONTEMPTUOUSLY against the righteous.   PSALM 31:18

But I have TRUSTED IN YOUR MERCY; my heart shall rejoice in your SALVATION: PSALM 13:5

I rejoice at your WORD AS ONE WHO FINDS GREAT TREASURE. I HATE and **ABHOR LYING** but I LOVE your LAW, SEVEN TIMES A DAY , I PRAISE YOU, because of your RIGHTEOUS JUDGMENTS, GREAT PEACE have those who LOVE your LAW, and nothing causes them to STUMBLE.

PSALM 119:162-165

BLESSED is that man who makes YHWH HIS TRUST, and does not RESPECT the PROUD, nor such as to TURN ASIDE TO LIES.   PSALM 40:4

THE **TRUTH FULL** LIP SHALL BE ESTABLISHED **FOREVER**, but a lying tongue, is but for a moment

PROVERBS 12:19

HE WHO WORKS DECEIT SHALL NOT dwell with in MY HOUSE; HE who tell LIES, shall NOT CONTINUE IN MY PRESENCE.   PSALM 101:7,8   THE COMING OF THE lawless ONE is according to the WORKING OF SATAN, with <u>all power</u>, SIGNS, and **LYING WONDERS**

2THESSALONIANS 2:9

SPEAKING LIES IN HYPOCRISY, having their own conscience seared with a HOT IRON:

1TIMOTHY 4:2

HE WHO OVERCOMES *SHALL INHERIT ALL THINGS,* and I will be his EL (GOD) and HE shall be my SON. "BUT THE COWARDLY, and all LIARS SHALL HAVE THEIR PART IN THE LAKE which burns with FIRE and BRIMSTONE, which is the SECOND DEATH."   REVELATION 21:7,8

KINGDOM PRINCIPLES

AMMISHADDAI

(1) LIE (N) to present FALSE information, with the purpose of deceiving

(2) FALSE (ADJ) being CONTRARY to the TRUTH or FACT

TOPIC: **BEARING OTHERS BURDENS..**   INCLINE you ear and hear the WORDS OF THE WISE.   PROVERBS 22:17
BROTHERS, IF ANYONE AMONG YOU wanders from the TRUTH, and someone turns HIM BACK, let him know that he who turns a SINNER FROM THE ERROR of his way will SAVE a SOUL from death and cover a multitude of SINS.   JAMES 5:19,20
WE then who are STRONG OUGHT to **BEAR** with the *SCRUPLES* of the WEAK, and NOT to PLEASE ourselves... LET each of US please HIS neighbor for HIS GOOD, leading to EDIFICATION..   ROMANS 15:1,2
RECEIVE ONE who is WEAK in the FAITH, but not to dispute over doubtful things...
                                                   ROMANS 14:1

IF a man is overtaken in any trespass (sin) you who are SPIRITUAL restore such a ONE IN A SPIRIT of GENTLENESS, considering YOURSELF lest you also be TEMPTED, *BEAR ONE ANOTHERS BURDENS,* and so FULFILL the LAW OF MESSIYAH...   GALATIANS 6:1-5
Therefore **COMFORT EACH OTHER and EDIFY** ONE ANOTHER, just as you also are doing
                                         1THESSALONIANS 5:11
YOU also help TOGETHER in prayer for US, that thanks may be given by many persons on our behalf for the gift granted to US through many. For our boasting is this: THE TESTIMONY of our conscience that we conducted ourselves in the WORLD IN SIMPLICITY and GODLY SINCERITY, not with fleshly WISDOM but by the GRACE of YHWH and more ABUNDANTLY toward you.   2CORINTHIANS 1:11,12

Therefore I endure <u>all things</u> for the sake of the ELECT, that they also may OBTAIN THE SALVATION which is in MESSIYAH YAHSHUAH with ETERNAL GLORY
                                                   2TIMOTHY 2:10
SO then each of US, shall GIVE ACCOUNT of HIMSELF to YHWH...   THEREFORE let US not JUDGE one another ANYMORE, but rather resolve this, not to put a STUMBLING BLOCK or a cause to FALL in our brothers WAY..   ROMANS 14:12,13
BUT beware lest somehow this liberty of yours become a STUMBLING BLOCK to those who are WEAK...   BECAUSE of your KNOWLEDGE SHALL the weak brother PERISH, for whom MESSIYAH DIED? BUT when you thus SIN AGAINST the BROTHER and with their WEAK CONSCIENCE, you SIN AGAINST MESSIYAH. Therefore if food makes my brother STUMBLE, I will never again eat meat, lest I make my BROTHER STUMBLE...
                                         1CORINTHIANS 8:7-13

KNGDOM PRINCIPLES
PROPHETIC MESSAGE MINISTRY
READING of INSPIRATIONS

(1) BURDEN (N) something difficult to bear, SPIRITUALLY or physically

(2) BEAR (V) to hold up: SUPPORT..

AMMISHADDAI

COMMANDMENT KEEPERS

TOPIC: REBUKE OF FAULTS and SINS..   HARSH DISCIPLINE IS FOR HIM WHO FORSAKES THE WAY. And he who hates CORRECTION WILL DIE.   PROVERBS 15:10

NOW I myself am confident concerning you, my brothers that you also are FULL OF GOODNESS, filled with ALL KNOWLEDGE, ABLE also to ADMONISH ONE ANOTHER..   ROMANS 15:14

MOREOVER, if your brother SINS AGAINST YOU, **GO and TELL HIM HIS FAULT**, between you and HIM alone. If he hears you, you have GAINED YOUR BOTHER... BUT IF HE WILL NOT HEAR, take with YOU ONE OR TWO MORE, that by the MOUTH OF TWO OR THREE WITNESSES EVERY (WORD) may be ESTABLISHED..   MATTHEW 18:15,16

IT is the glory of the MOST HIGH TO CONCEAL A MATTER, but the glory of KINGS is to SEARCH OUT A MATTER.   PROVERBS 25:2   SO LET THE RIGHTEOUS STRIKE ME; IT SHALL BE A KINDNESS. And let HIM REBUKE ME; IT SHALL BE AS EXCELLENT OIL; LET MY HEAD NOT REFUSE IT.   PSALM 141:5   BROTHERS, if anyone among YOU wanders from the TRUTH, and SOMEONE turns him back, LET HIM KNOW that he who turns a SINNER FROM THE ERROR OF HIS WAY WILL SAVE A SOUL FROM DEATH and cover a MULTITUDE OF SINS.   JAMES 5:19,20

NOW we encourage you, brothers **WARN THOSE WHO ARE UNRULY**, COMFORT the FAINTHEARTED UPHOLD the WEAK, BE PATIENT WILL ALL.   1THESSALONIANS 5:14

He who REBUKES A MAN will find more favor after ward than he who FLATTERS WITH THE TONGUE...   PROVERBS 28:23   FOR the COMMANDMENT IS A LAMP and the LAW A LIGHT; REPROOFS OF INSTRUCTION ARE THE WAY OF LIFE.   PROVERBS 6:23

A MANS HEART PLANS HIS WAY, but YHWH directs his steps...   PROVERBS 16:9

The ear that HEARS the REBUKES OF LIFE will abide among the WISE. The FEAR of the MOST HIGH is the INSTRUCTION OF **WISDOM** and before **HONOR** is **HUMILITY**..   PROVERBS 15:31-33

A SERVANT of the MOST HIGH <u>MUST NOT QUARREL</u> but be GENTLE TO ALL, ABLE TO TEACH, PATIENTLY, IN HUMILITY **CORRECTING** THOSE WHO ARE IN OPPOSITION, if YHWH PERHAPS WILL GRANT THEM REPENTANCE, so that they may know the TRUTH...

                    2TIMOTHY 2:24-26

PREACH the WORD, BE READY IN SEASON and OUT OF SEASON. CONVINCE, REBUKE, EXHORT, with ALL LONGSUFFERING and TEACHING.   2TIMOTHY 4:2

If a man is OVERTAKEN IN ANY TRESPASS (SIN) YOU WHO ARE **SPIRITUAL** RESTORE SUCH A ONE IN A SPIRIT OF GENTLENESS, CONSIDERING YOURSELF LEST YOU ALSO BE TEMPTED...

                    GALATIANS 6:1

HE who KEEPS INSTRUCTION is in the WAY OF LIFE, but he who REFUSES CORRECTION LEADS ASTRAY.   PROVERBS 10:17   FINDING OUT what is ACCEPTABLE TO YHWH, have no fellowship with the UNFRUITFUL WORKS OF DARKNESS, but rather **EXPOSE THEM**.   EPHESIANS 5:10,11

And if anyone does not OBEY our word in this letter, NOTE THAT PERSON and do not KEEP COMPANY WITH HIM, that he may be ashamed. Yet do not count HIM as an enemy, but *WARN HIM AS A BROTHER...*   2THESSALONIANS 3:14,15

TAKE HEED TO YOURSELVES, IF your brother SINS AGAINST you, REBUKE HIM and if he REPENTS, FORGIVE HIM.   LUKE 17:3,4

AVOID FOOLISH DISPUTES, REJECT A DIVISIVE MAN after the FIRST and SECOND WARNING KNOWING that such a person is WARPED and SINNING, being SELF CONDEMNED.   TITUS 3:9-11

KINGDOM PRINCIPLES
PROPHETIC MESSAGE MINISTRY

AMMISHADDAI
  TRUE
  BELIEVER   (1) REBUKE (VT) to criticize, sharply; REPRIMAND
                                   (2) FAULT (N) a mistake: error
                                   (3) SIN (N) to commit an offense or violation

COMMANDMENT KEEPERS

TOPIC: **PATIENCE and ENDURANCE** *BLESSED BE THE MOST HIGH* FATHER OF **IMMANUEL MESSIYAH** who according to HIS abundant mercy has begotten US again to a **LIVING HOPE**, through the RESURRECTION OF IMMANUEL MESSIYAH from the dead to an INHERITANCE INCORRUPTIBLE and UNDEFILED, that does not fade away, **RESERVED IN HEAVEN** for you, WHO ARE KEPT by the power of the MOST HIGH through FAITH for SALVATION ready to be REVEALED in the LAST TIME. In this you greatly rejoice, though now for a little while, if NEED BE, you have been distress ed by **VARIOUS TRIALS.. 1PETER 1:3-6**

*I (YHWH) KNOW YOUR WORKS, YOUR LABOR, YOUR **PATIENCE**,* and that you cannot bear those who are EVIL; and you have TESTED THOSE WHO SAY they are apostles and are not, and have found them LIARS, and you have PERSEVERED and HAVE PATIENCE, and have LABORED for my names sake and HAVE NOT BECOME WEARY. REVELATION 2:2,3

The end of a thing is BETTER than its beginning; the PATIENT IN SPIRIT IS BETTER than the PROUD in spirit. ECCLESIASTES 7:8

FOR THIS IS COMMENDABLE, if because of conscience toward YHWH ONE **ENDURES** GRIEF, SUFFERING WRONGFULLY, for what CREDIT is it if, when you are beaten for your FAULTS, you take it PATIENTLY? But when you do GOOD and SUFFER, if you take it PATIENTLY, THIS IS COMMENDABLE BEFORE the MOST HIGH; for this you were called, because MESSIYAH ALSO SUFFERED FOR US, leaving US **AN EXAMPLE**, that we should follow HIS STEPS: 1PETER 2:19-22

Therefore we also, since we are surrounded by so GREAT A CLOUD OF WITNESSES, let us lay aside EVERY WEIGHT, and the SIN which so easily ENSNARES US, and let us run with **ENDURANCE** the race that is set before US. HEBREWS 12:1,2

LET LOVE BE WITHOUT HYPOCRISY... abhor what is evil. Cling to what is GOOD. Rejoicing in HOPE, PATIENT IN TRIBULATION, CONTINUING STEADFASTLY IN PRAYER. ROMANS 12:9-12

And NOT ONLY that, but we also GLORY IN TRIBULATIONS, knowing that tribulation PRODUCES, ENDURANCE, and ENDURANCE CHARACTER; and CHARACTER, HOPE. ROMANS 5:3-5

My brothers, COUNT IT ALL JOY, when you fall into various trials, knowing that the TESTING OF YOUR FAITH PRODUCES PATIENCE, but let patience have its perfect work, that you may be MATURE and COMPLETE, LACKING NOTHING. JAMES 1:2-4

HE WHO IS SLOW TO WRATH has great understanding, but he who is IMPULSIVE EXALTS FOLLY. PROVERBS 14:29

DO NOT BE RASH with your mouth, and let not your HEART UTTER ANYTHING HASTILY before YHWH because YHWH IS IN HEAVEN, and you on earth; therefore let your words BE FEW.. ECCLESIASTES 5:2

But you, O MAN of the MOST HIGH, FLEE THESE THINGS and PURSUE RIGHTEOUSNESS, GODLINESS, FAITH, LOVE PATIENCE, GENTLENESS. 1TIMOTHY 6:11,12

NOW may YHWH DIRECT YOUR HEARTS INTO THE LOVE OF THE MOST HIGH and into the **PATIENCE OF MESSIYAH** 2THESSALONIANS 3:5 THEREFORE be PATIENT, brothers, until the coming of YHWH. You also be PATIENT, ESTABLISH YOUR HEARTS, for the coming of YHWH IS AT HAND. Do not grumble against ONE ANOTHER, brothers, unlest you be CONDEMNED. Behold, the JUDGE IS STANDING AT THE DOOR! JAMES 5:7-9 but if we HOPE for what we DO NOT SEE, we EAGERLY WAIT for it with **PERSEVERANCE..** ROMANS 8:25

KINGDOM PRINCIPLES

AMMISHADDAI PROPHETIC MESSAGE MINISTRY

PATIENT (ADJ) capable of bearing ALLICTION calmly
ENDURE (V) to bear with TOLERANCE

TOPIC: **FAITH and WORKS**...   WE know as many walk according to this RULE, **PEACE and MERCY**
be upon them and upon the YAHSRAEL OF YHWH ELSHADDAI.   GALATIANS 6:16
IF MY PEOPLE who are called by MY NAME will humble themselves and pray and seek MY (WAY) and
turn from their wicked WAYS then I will hear form HEAVEN and will FORGIVE THEIR SIN and HEAL
their land. Now my eyes will be open and my ears ATTENTIVE TO PRAYERS MADE IN THIS PLACE
                                                                    2CHRONICLES 7:14,15
But he also said" more then that, *BLESSED ARE THOSE WHO HEAR the WORD OF YHWH and KEEP
IT...*   LUKE 11:28
For this is the LOVE of YHWH that we KEEP HIS COMMANDMENTS, and HIS COMMANDMENTS
are NOT burdensome.   1JOHN 5:2-5
SO IF YOU KEEP MY COMMANDMENTS you will abide in MY LOVE. Just as I have kept MY
FATHERS (ABBA'S) COMMANDMENTS and ABIDE IN HIS **LOVE**.   JOHN 15:1-17

WE truly UNDERSTAND we are NOT UNDER THE LAW of JUDGMENT, but we are to **ABIDE and
LIVE IN the LAW of LOVE**..   TRUE

KNOWING we shall love YHWH our EL with all our HEART, with all our SOUL and with all our MIND
this being the **FIRST** and the **SECOND** is like it: you shall love your NEIGHBOR AS YOURSELF,
knowing these **TWO COMMANDMENTS FULFILL ALL THE LAW** and the PROPHETS.
                                                                    MATTHEW 22:37-40
SO IT IS WRITTEN; BLESSED ARE THE UNDEFILED in the way, who walk in the law of YHWH,
blessed are those who KEEP HIS TESTIMONIES.   PSALM 119:1-10
WHO ever therefore breaks one of the least of these COMMANDMENTS and TEACHES men to DO
SO, shall be called least in the KINGDOM OF HEAVEN, but whoever does and teaches them, shall be
called GREAT IN THE KINGDOM OF HEAVEN.   MATTHEW 5:17-20

SO this is a **FAITHFUL SAYING** I TRULY want you to AFFIRM CONSTANTLY, you who BELIEVE IN
YHWH, we should be CAREFUL to **MAINTAIN GOOD WORKS**, knowing these things are GOOD and
PROFITABLE TO MEN...   TITUS 3:5-8

KNOWING ALL SCRIPTURE IS GIVEN BY INSPIRATION OF YHWH and is profitable for
DOCTRINE, for REPROOF, for CORRECTION, for TRAINING, or INSTRUCTION IN
RIGHTEOUSNESS that the man of YHWH may be COMPLETE THOROUGHLY EQUIPPED FOR EVERY
GOOD WORK   2TIMOTHY 3:16,17
IN CONCLUSION we need to abide in the law and keep our FATHERS (ABBA'S) COMMANDMENTS
BELIEVING this is THE WAY to renewing our MIND.   ROMANS 12:1,2

KNOWING whatever we ask in FAITH we receive from HIM because we KEEP HIS
COMMANDMENTS and DO THOSE THINGS that are pleasing in HIS SIGHT..   1JOHN 3:22,23
SO IN OUR MOUTH THERE IS FOUND NO DECEIT, before the throne of YHWH..   TRUE
HERE IS THE PATIENCE OF THE **SAINTS WHO KEEP** the **COMMANDMENTS OF YHWH** and the
FAITH OF YAHSHUAH MESSIYAH IMMANUEL   (AMEN)   REVELATION 14:12

COMMANDMENT (V) ORDERLY DIRECTION or LAW
LAW (N) SYSTEM of such RULES FORMED to show LOVE
                              WALKING ORDERLY   (1) FAITH
                                                          (2) WORKS

AMMISHADDAI   **PROPHETIC MESSAGE MINISTRY**
    TRUE
    BELIEVER

TOPIC: *PROPHECY I..*   THUS SAYS YHWH STAND IN THE WAYS and SEE, and ASK for the OLD PATHS, where the GOOD WAY IS, and WALK IN IT; then YOU WILL FIND REST FOR YOUR SOULS..   JEREMIAH 6:16 AT THE BEGINNING of your SUPPLICATIONS the WORD WENT OUT, and I HAVE COME TO TELL YOU, for you are greatly BELOVED; therefore CONSIDER THE MATTER, and UNDERSTAND the VISION: DANIEL 9:23 Now therefore, go and I*(YHWH)* will be with your MOUTH and TEACH you what you shall say. NOW YOU SHALL SPEAK to him and put the words in HIS MOUTH. And I will TEACH you what you shall DO.. SO he shall be your SPOKESMAN TO THE PEOPLE..   EXODUS 4:12,15,16   THEN THEY WILL HEED YOUR VOICE; and you shall come, YOU and the ELDERS of YISRAEL, to the KING of EGYPT/NORTHCOUNTRY and you shall say to him, *YHWH EL(GOD) of the HEBREWS* has met with US and NOW, PLEASE, LET US GO three days journey into the WILDERNESS, that we may SACRIFICE to YHWH OUR EL... EXODUS 3:18,19   then it will be, if they DO NOT BELIEVE you, NOR HEED the MESSAGE of the FIRST SIGN,(REVELATION 12:1) that THEY MAY BELIEVE the message of the LATTER SIGN...   EXODUS 4:8   THUS SAYS YHWH behold a people comes from the NORTHCOUNTRY, a great NATION will be raised from the FARTHEST PARTS OF THE EARTH..   They are CRUEL and shall NOT SHOW MERCY. THEREFORE HEAR THE COUNSEL OF YHWH at the taking of BABYLON the earth TREMBLES, and the cry is HEARD AMONG the NATIONS...   JEREMIAH 6:22/50:42,43,45,46 Therefore do not pray for this people, nor lift up a cry or prayer for them, nor make INTERCESSION TO ME; for I will not hear you. DO YOU NOT SEE what they do in the cities of YAHUDAH and in the streets of YAHRUSALEM?   JEREMIAH 7:16,17   I WILL GIVE POWER TO MY TWO WITNESSES, and they will PROPHESY ONE THOUSAND TWO HUNDRED and SIXTY DAYS, CLOTHED IN SACKCLOTH..

REVELATION 11:3,6

BUT *YHWH OF HOST* shall be EXALTED IN JUDGMENT, and *YHWH WHO IS HOLY* shall be HALLOWED IN RIGHTEOUSNESS. WOE TO THOSE WHO CALL EVIL GOOD, and GOOD EVIL; who put BITTER for SWEET, and SWEET for BITTER! WOE TO THOSE who are WISE in their own EYES, and PRUDENT in their own SIGHT!

ISAIAH 5:16,20,21

THOSE WHO DO WICKEDLY AGAINST THE COVENANT HE SHALL CORRUPT WITH FLATTERY; but the people who KNOW their EL(GOD) shall be STRONG, and CARRY OUT GREAT EXPLOITS... and those of the people who UNDERSTAND SHALL INSTRUCT MANY: and there shall be a time of TROUBLE, SUCH AS NEVER WAS SINCE there was a NATION, even to that time and at that time YOUR PEOPLE SHALL BE DELIVERED, many shall RUN TO and FRO, and KNOWLEDGE SHALL INCREASE.   DANIEL 11:32-45/12:1-4   ALSO violent men of your people shall EXALT THEMSELVES IN FULFILLMENT of the VISION, but they shall FALL..   DANIEL 11:14 IT WAS GRANTED TO HIM to make war with the saints and to overcome them. HE who leads into CAPTIVITY shall go into CAPTIVITY; he who KILLS with the sword MUST be KILLED with the sword. HERE IS THE PATIENCE and FAITH OF THE SAINTS...   REVELATION 13:7-10   MANY SHALL BE PURIFIED, MADE WHITE, and REFINED, but the WISE shall UNDERSTAND. And from the time that the daily sacrifice is taken away, and the ABOMINATION of DESOLATION is set up, there shall be one thousand two hundred and ninety days...   DANIEL 12:10,11   then they will deliver YOU UP TO TRIBULATION and KILL you, and you will be hated by ALL NATIONS for MY NAMES SAKE.   MATTHEW 24:9   and in his PLACE shall arise a vile person, to whom they will not give the honor of royalty; but he shall come in PEACEABLY, and SEIZE THE KINGDOM BY INTRIGUE... DANIEL 11:21   Therefore when you see the ABOMINATION of DESOLATION, "STANDING IN THE HOLY PLACE" then let those WHO ARE IN YAHUDAH FLEE to the mountains.   MATTHEW 24:15,16 THEN the WOMAN FLED into the WILDERNESS, where she has a PLACE PREPARED BY YHWH, that they should feed her THERE one thousand two hundred and sixty days(3 ½ yrs) and THEY OVERCAME HIM by the BLOOD of the LAMB and by the WORD of their TESTIMONY, and they DID NOT LOVE their lives to the DEATH. And the DRAGON WAS ENRAGED with the WOMAN, and he went to MAKE WAR with the REST of her OFFSPRING, WHO KEEP THE COMMANDMENTS OF YHWH and have the *TESTIMONY OF YAHSHUAH MESSIYAH*

REVELATION 12:6,11,12,17

BECAUSE YOU HAVE KEPT MY COMMAND to PERSEVERE, I ALSO WILL KEEP YOU from the HOUR of TRAIL which shall come upon the WHOLE WORLD, TO TEST those who dwell on the earth. REVELATION 3:10,13 three UNCLEAN spirits, coming out of the MOUTH of the DRAGON out of the MOUTH of the BEAST, and out of the MOUTH of the FALSE PROPHET which go out to the KINGS OF THE EARTH to gather them to the BATTLE OF THE GREAT DAY OF YHWH ELSHADDAI...   REVELATION 16:13-16   FOR in ONE HOUR your JUDGMENT HAS COME...   REVELATION 18:10

END TIMES MINISTRY

AMMISHADDAI   *COMMANDMENT KEEPERS*

TOPIC: PROPHECY II WORDS to the north country/north Americans HERE is the MIND which has WISDOM: the ten horns which you saw are ten kings who have received no KINGDOM AS YET, but they receive AUTHORITY for ONE HOUR as KINGS with the BEAST.. THESE ARE OF ONE MIND, and they will give their POWER and AUTHORITY to the BEAST.   REVELATION 17:9-18
THE beast that was, and IS not, is HIMSELF also the EIGHTH, and IS of the SEVEN, and is going to *DESTRUCTION...*   REVELATION 17:11

HARLOT = FORNICATION/ IMMORAL/DEFILED RELIGON/TOLARENCE of SINS

WATERS = multitude of people DIFFERENT NATIONS and tongues...

RIGHTLY DIVIDE the WORD of TRUTH.   2TIMOTHY 2:15
SURELY YHWH ELSHADDAI does nothing, UNLESS HE REVEALS *HIS SECRET* to HIS servants the prophets..   AMOS 3:7
THEN HE said to me, "WRITE: 'BLESSED ARE those who are called to the marriage supper of the LAMB!" and HE said to me, "THESE are the TRUE saying of YHWH EL OF HOST." WORSHIP YHWH! For the TESTIMONY of YAHSHUAH *IS the SPIRIT of PROPHECY."*   REVELATION 19:9,10

  + POINTS of REFFERENCE
And I heard another VOICE from HEAVEN saying, "COME OUT of HER, my people, lest you share in her SINS, and lest you RECEIVE of her PLAGUES...   REVELATION 18:4
"BABYLON the GREAT is FALLEN, is fallen, and has become a dwelling place of DEMONS, a PRISON for every FOUL SPIRIT, and a CAGE for every UNCLEAN and HATED BIRD!   REVELATION 18:2

THEREFORE SAY to the house of YISRAEL, "THUS SAYS **YHWH** "REPENT, turn away from your idols, and turn your (faces) away from **ALL YOUR ABOMINATIONS**...   EZEKIEL 14:3-7
IN the measure that SHE glorified herself and lived LUXURIOUSLY, in the same measure give her torment and sorrow; **THEREFORE HER PLAGUES** will come in ONE DAY - DEATH and MOURNING and FAMINE...   for STRONG IS YHWH ELSHADDAI WHO JUDGES HER   REVELATION 18:7,8
  (1) DAY
Beloved, do not forget this one thing, that with THE MOSTHIGH ONE DAY is as a thousand years, and a thousand years as ONE DAY...   *YHWH IS NOT SLACK CONCERNING HIS PROMISE..*
          2PETER 3:8,9

  (1) HOUR
"FOR in ONE HOUR such great riches came to nothing.' "EVERY shipmaster, all who travel by ship, sailors, and as many as trade on sea, STOOD AT A DISTANCE. FOR in ONE HOUR she is made DESOLATE...   REVELATION 18:17,18,19
"UNLESS THOSE DAYS WERE SHORTENED, (NO) FLESH would be saved; but for the ELECTS SAKE those days will be *SHORTENED.*   MATTHEW 24:22
I (YHWH) will also KEEP you from the HOUR OF TRAIL which shall come upon the whole world, **TO TEST** *THOSE WHO DWELL ON THE EARTH:*   REVELATION 3:10
    (7) MOUNTAINS = powers

          PROPHETIC MESSAGE MINISTRY

    (8) DIFFERENT SYSTEMS = governments

    (10) HORNS = ruler having authority
AMMISHADDAI
   TRUE
 BELIEVER

TOPIC: PROPHECY IV TURN FROM THE WICKED WAYS..

SO I say SO I speak today; To the leaders of the ministry for the people TRANSGRESSED more and more ACCORDING to <u>ALL ABOMINATION</u> of the NATION / USA and DEFILED the house of YHWH which HE made *HOLY in YAHRUSALEM*   (TRUE)

WARNING UNTO THEM BY HIS MESSENGERS early rising sending them because YHWH has compassion on HIS people and on HIS dwelling place. So those who escaped from the sword he carried away to Babylon for we became servants to him and his sons until the reign of the KINGDOM OF PERSIA.. seventy (years)   2CHRONICLES 36:14-21

For today we set under gentle rule.. *PONDER IN THE SCHOOL OF THOUGHT..* Babylon / Persia / Greece and Rome / USA so now it makes me want to say DILIGENTLY (OBEY) the voice of IMMANUEL MESSIYAH to observe carefully <u>ALL HIS COMMANDMENTS</u> which I command you today. BLESSED SHALL WE BE IN THE CITY and BLESSED shall you be in the country..   DEUTERONOMY 28:1-3,10

SO all the peoples of the earth shall see you CALLED by the NAME OF YHWH and they shall be afraid of you so I say today ministers and prophets down to teachers of the land dwell within your own city to secure ISRAEL CITY BY CITY for this hour we seek to stir up the *SPIRIT of PROCLAMATION* through out the land for the KINGDOM is at HAND..

(TRUE)

FOR we are the people of this province brought INTO CAPTIVITY; so I say so we PRAY today how long will WE SLEEP and STAY CAUGHT UP in different activity did you see the distress that we lay in. So NO LONGER must we be a REPROACH, but set our hand to do this good work for the FATHER OF HEAVEN himself will prosper US; THEREFORE we his servants will RISE and BUILD CITY to CITY for truly has it come to pass, these things have come upon us being called to mind among the NATIONS / USA where YHWH have driven you so return to his voice and obey HIS COMMANDMENT that I say for your MIGHTY ONE will make you a bound in all the work of your hand, in the FRUIT OF YOUR SPIRIT and SOUL, becoming self sufficient / industry to maintain the COMMANDMENTS of the MOSTHIGH STATUES which are written in the book of the PROPHETS (LAW) providing we turn to YHWH ELSHADDAI with <u>ALL</u> your <u>HEART</u> and with <u>ALL</u> your <u>SOUL</u>

DEUTERONOMY 30:1-10

BUT even if our gospel is veiled, it is veiled to those who are PERISHING, whose minds the god of this age has BLINDED, who DO NOT BELIEVE, lest the LIGHT of the GOSPEL of the GLORY of MESSIYAH, who is the IMAGE of YHWH, should shine on them.. For it is the MOSTHIGH who COMMANDED light to shine out of darkness, who has SHONE in our HEARTS TO GIVE the LIGHT of the KNOWLEDGE of the GLORY of YHWH..

2CORINTHIANS 4:3-6

So brothers grace be given from IMMANUEL MESSIYAH YAHSHUAH with the SPIRIT of TRUTH..   AMEN
PROPHETIC MESSAGE MINISTRY
END TIMES MINISTRY
AMMISHADDAI

TOPIC: PROPHECY III   HERE IS THE MIND WHICH HAS WISDOM, for the TESTIMONY of YAHSHUAH is the SPIRIT OF PROPHECY...

" UP, UP! FLEE from the LAND of the NORTH." says YHWH; "for I YHWH have spread YOU ABROAD LIKE the four winds of heaven," says YHWH. " UP, ZION! ESCAPE, YOU WHO DWELL WITH THE DAUGHTER OF BABYLON." "SING and REJOICE, O DAUGHTER OF ZION! FOR BEHOLD, I AM COMING and I WILL DWELL IN YOUR MIDST," SAYS YHWH.   ZECHARIAH 2:6-13
"COME OUT OF HER, my people, lest you SHARE in her sins, and lest you RECEIVE OF HER PLAGUES. Therefore her plagues will come in ONE DAY - DEATH and MOURNING and FAMINE..

REVELATION 18:4,5,8

NOW it shall come to pass in the latter days, that the MOUNTAIN OF YHWH'S HOUSE SHALL BE ESTABLISHED on the top of the mountains, shall be EXALTED ABOVE THE HILLS; and ALL NATIONS SHALL FLOW TO IT. FOR out of ZION shall go forth the LAW, and the WORD OF יהוה From YAHRUSALEM   ISAIAH 2:2,3   "IN those days and in that time," says YHWH " the children of YISRAEL shall come, they and the children of YAHUDAH **TOGETHER**; they will ask the WAY TO ZION, saying, 'COME and let us join ourselves to YHWH in a perpetual COVENANT that will not be forgotten." my people have been lost sheep. Their shepherds have led them astray; THEY HAVE FORGOTTEN THEIR RESTING PLACE.   JEREMIAH 50:4-6   IN that day there shall be a ROOT OF JESSE, who shall stand as a BANNER to the people; for the GENTILES shall seek him, and HIS **RESTING PLACE** shall be glorious." it shall come to pass in that day that YHWH shall set HIS **HAND AGAIN the SECOND TIME**, TO RECOVER the remnant of HIS people, who are left, HE will set up a BANNER for the nations, and will ASSEMBLE THE OUTCASTS OF YISRAEL, and GATHER TOGETHER the dispersed of YAHUDAH from the four CORNERS OF THE EARTH. ISAIAH 11:10-12 YES, many peoples and strong nations shall come to seek YHWH OF HOSTS in YAHRUSALEM, and pray before THE MOST HIGH.' THUS says YHWH of HOSTS: ' IN THOSE DAYS ten men from every language of the nations shall GRASP THE SLEEVE OF A HEBREW MAN, saying, "let us go with you for we have heard that YHWH GOD IS WITH YOU."   ZECHARIAH 8:22,23   **PROCLAIM,** GIVE PRAISE, and SAY, 'O YHWH, SAVE YOUR PEOPLE, the remnant of YISRAEL!' BEHOLD, I (YHWH) will bring them from the north country, and gather them from the ends of the earth,

JEREMIAH 31:7,8

THEREFORE DO NOT FEAR, O MY SERVANT JACOB SAYS YHWH. 'nor be dismayed, O YISRAEL; for behold, I will **SAVE** YOU FROM AFAR, and your seed from the land of their captivity. JACOB shall return, have rest and be QUIET, and NO ONE shall make him AFRAID.   JEREMIAH 30:10,11
"And there will be signs in the sun, in the moon, and in the stars; and on the earth distress of nations, with perplexity, "Men's hearts failing them from fear and the expectation of those things which are coming on the earth, for the powers of the heavens will be shaken.   LUKE 21:25,26   "LET not your heart be troubled; you BELIEVE IN YHWH, believe also in ME. **I GO TO PREPARE A PLACE FOR YOU.**   JOHN 14:1-6   BUT, YHWH LIVES who brought up the children of YISRAEL from the land of the NORTH and from all the lands where HE HAD DRIVEN THEM. 'FOR I WILL BRING THEM BACK INTO THEIR LAND which I gave to their fathers. BEHOLD, I WILL SEND for many fishermen, says YHWH, and they shall fish them;   JEREMIAH 16:14-16   BECAUSE you have kept MY COMMAND to persevere, I also will keep you from the HOUR OF TRAIL which shall come upon the whole world, TO TEST THOSE WHO DWELL ON THE EARTH.   REVELATION 3:10   LIFT UP A BANNER ON THE HIGH MOUNTAIN, I have commanded MY sanctified ONES;   ISAIAH 13:2,3 All inhabitants of the world and dwellers on the earth: when HE lifts up a BANNER on the mountains, you see it, and when HE blows a trumpet, you HEAR IT.   ISAIAH 18:2,3   BUT the woman was given two wings of a great eagle, that she might fly into THE WILDERNESS **TO HER PLACE,** Then the TEMPLE OF YHWH was opened in heaven, and the ARK OF HIS COVENANT was seen in HIS TEMPLE. And there were lightnings, noises, thundering, an EARTHQUAKE, and GREAT HAIL.

REVELATION 12:6,14/11:19/14:1,5

אכסליטמאדא.   COMMANDMENT KEEPERS

FOR OUR EXHORTATION DID NOT COME FROM DECEIT OR UNCLEANNESS, NOR WAS IT IN GUILE.. But as we have been approved by YHWH to be ENTRUSTED with the GOSPEL, even so we speak, not as PLEASING MEN, but YHWH who TEST our hearts. For neither at any time did we USE FLATTERING WORDS, as you know, nor a cloak for COVETOUSNESS - YHWH IS WITNESS..   1THESSALONIANS 2:3-5

TOPIC: PROPHECY V For we are APPROVED by the MOSTHIGH who TESTS our hearts; So neither at any time should we use FLATTERING WORDS.   (TRUE)
For I find that a soft answer TURN AWAY harsh WRATH, but the OFFENSIVE WORD stirred up MUCH ANGER, so I would watch what I had to say. Becoming **WISER** by the day using KNOWLEDGE rightly divide **IN TRUTH** knowing sticks and stones break my bones, but WORDS OFFENSIVELY HURT ME.   PROVERBS 15:1-4

REMIND THEM to be subject to rulers and authorities, to obey to be ready for every good work showing ALL HUMBLENESS to ALL for we know ourselves was once FOOLISH being DECEIVED until the kindness and LOVE OF YHWH our SAVIOR toward men showed up; not by works of RIGHTEOUSNESS which we have done, but according to HIS (YHWH'S) mercy HE saved US..   (TRUE)
So I say so I speak to day; BE DILIGENT TO PRESENT YOURSELF APPROVED TO YHWH... becoming a worker who DOES NOT NEED to be ashamed *RIGHTLY DIVIDING* the WORD OF TRUTH. So I say so I speak from the HUMBLENESS of my heart CORRECTING THOSE in opposition for the MOSTHIGH MAY GRANT me repentance so that I may learn to KNOW THE TRUTH..   2TIMOTHY 2:14,25

For WISDOM is in the sight of him who has UNDERSTANDING so UNDERSTANDING becomes a wellspring of life to him who has it, For the HEART of the WISE teaches HIS MOUTH So it adds LEARNING unto HIS LIPS speaking from the *SPIRIT OF TRUTH..* PLEASANT WORDS are like a HONEYCOMB sweetness to the SOUL and HEATH to the BONES.   PROVERBS 16:22-24

SO NOW I PONDER IN SPIRIT; " And then many will be OFFENDED, will betray one another, and will hate one another.   MATTHEW 24:10
IN the last days many was OFFENDED, so the question arose? HOW long will the SIMPLE ONES ENJOY his / or hers SIMPLICITY for only FOOLS would HATE KNOWLEDGE for it is WRITTEN: COMMIT your WORKS to YHWH and your thoughts will be ESTABLISHED..
                    PROVERBS 16:3
The preacher was WISE, he still TAUGHT the people (ISRAEL and CHURCH) KNOWLEDGE: YES, he pondered and sought out and SET IN ORDER many proverbs. The preacher sought to FIND ACCEPTABLE WORDS; and what was WRITTEN was UPRIGHT - WORDS OF TRUTH..   ECCLESIASTES 12:9-14

READINGS of INSPIRATION
     AMMISHADDAI
          TRUE
          BELIEVER
     (1) PROPHECY (N) a divinely INSPIRED utterance, revelation, writing, teaching, etc..

Prophets in Palestine

This map is a detailed, close-up view of the land of Canaan when God was speaking through some of His earliest prophets, calling His people to repentance. The time-frame ranges from approximately 1000 B.C. to 400 B.C.

PROPHETS IN PALESTINE

Damascus

Zarephath
Elijah raises widow's son

Elisha pronounces doom on Ben-hadad

Mediterranean Sea

Elijah confronts prophets of Baal and runs to Jezreel

Mt. Carmel

Gath hepher   Sea of Galilee

Jonah's birthplace

Prophets in Samaria included Hosea, Micaiah, Oded, and possibly Amos

Jezreel

Elisha's birthplace

Elijah's birthplace

Abel-meholah?

Samaria   Tishbe?

Jonah departs for Tarshish

Amos prophesies

Samuel presented to the Lord and reared here

Joppa

Shiloh   Cities in Samuel's circuit

Samuel's birthplace

Bethel   Gilgal?   Nahum's birthplace

Mizpah

Jeremiah's birthplace

Ramah   Elkosh?

Anathoth   Jericho   Elisha raises axe head

Moresheth-gath

Jerusalem   Mt. Nebo

Mareshah   Tekoa   Balaam pronounces "blessing" upon Israel

Micah's birthplace

Amos' birthplace

Eliezer's birthplace

JUDAH   Dead Sea

Micah prophesies throughout villages and hamlets of Judah

Prophets in Jerusalem included Gad, Nathan, Isaiah, Jeremiah, Shemaiah, Hanani, Zephaniah, Haggai, Malachi, Zechariah and probably Joel; Ezekiel probably hailed from Jerusalem; Elijah translated to heaven

Obadiah prophesies against Edom

EDOM

0   30 mi.
0   40 km.

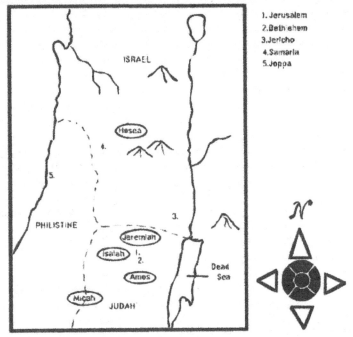

ISRAEL

Hosea

PHILISTINE

Jeremiah

Isaiah   1.
2.

Amos

Dead Sea

Micah   JUDAH

1. Jerusalem
2. Bethlehem
3. Jericho
4. Samaria
5. Joppa

N

Thematic Map

World Vegetation FIRST TRUMPET : VEGETATION STRUCK

The first angel sounded: and hail and fire followed, mingled with blood, and They were thrown to the earth.. And a <u>THIRD OF THE TREES WERE BURN UP</u> and all green grass was burn up… REVELATION 8 : 7

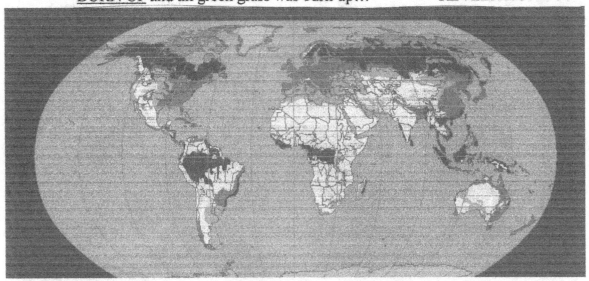

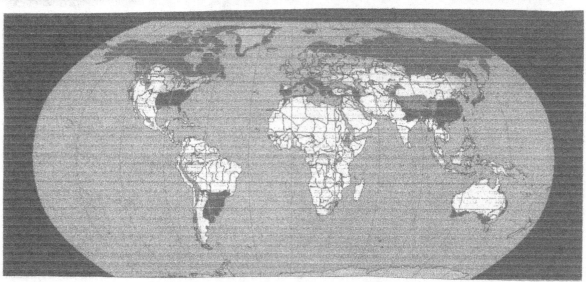

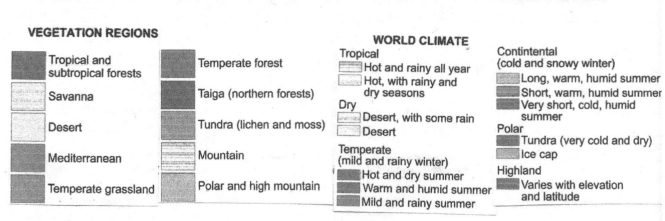

VEGETATION REGIONS

- Tropical and subtropical forests
- Savanna
- Desert
- Mediterranean
- Temperate grassland
- Temperate forest
- Taiga (northern forests)
- Tundra (lichen and moss)
- Mountain
- Polar and high mountain

WORLD CLIMATE

Tropical
- Hot and rainy all year
- Hot, with rainy and dry seasons

Dry
- Desert, with some rain
- Desert

Temperate
(mild and rainy winter)
- Hot and dry summer
- Warm and humid summer
- Mild and rainy summer

Contintental
(cold and snowy winter)
- Long, warm, humid summer
- Short, warm, humid summer
- Very short, cold, humid summer

Polar
- Tundra (very cold and dry)
- Ice cap

Highland
- Varies with elevation and latitude

26

Jerusalem-Old City

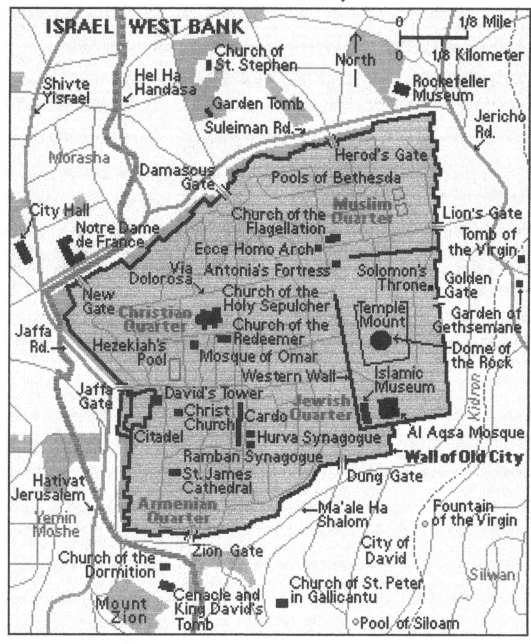

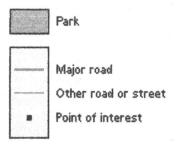

Park

———— Major road

———— Other road or street

■ Point of interest

They will fall by the edge of the sword, and led away captive into all nations. And Yahrusalem will be TRAMPLED by GENTILES until the times of the Gentiles are fulfilled.. LUKE 21:24

TOPIC: SEXUAL IMMORALITY SO faith comes by HEARING, and HEARING by the word of YHWH..   ROMANS 10:17

You SHALL NOT LIE WITH a male as with a woman. It is a ABOMINATION.
                                                      LEVITICUS 18:22,23

If a man LIES WITH A MALE as he LIES WITH A WOMAN, both of them have COMMITTED an ABOMINATION.   LEVITICUS 20:13,15

"CURSED is the one who LIES with any KIND of animal."   DEUTERONOMY 27:21

"IF I (YHWH) had NOT COME and SPOKEN to them, they would have NO SIN, but now they have NO EXCUSE for their SIN..   JOHN 15:22

"DO NOT THINK that I (YHWH) came to destroy the LAW or the PROPHETS. I did not come to destroy but to FULFILL. "For assuredly, I say to you, TILL HEAVEN and EARTH PASS AWAY, one jot or one smallest stroke will by NO MEANS PASS FROM the LAW till all is FULFILLED..   MATTHEW 5:17,18

"REMEMBER now, who ever perished being INNOCENT? Or where were the UPRIGHT ever CUT OFF? Even as I have seen those who plow INIQUITY (SIN) and sow trouble reap the same...   JOB 4:7,8

For the wrath of YHWH is revealed from heaven against ALL UNGODLINESS and UNRIGHTEOUSNESS of men, who SUPPRESS the TRUTH in UNRIGHTEOUSNESS, because what may be known of YHWH is manifest in them, for YHWH has shown it to them. For since the creation of the world HIS (YHWH) INVISIBLE ATTRIBUTES are CLEARY SEEN, being understood by the things that are made, even HIS ETERNAL POWER and DIVINE NATURE, so that they are without EXCUSE.. Because although they knew YHWH, they DID NOT GLORIFY HIM as EL (GOD) nor were thankful, but became futile in their thoughts, and their FOOLISH HEARTS were DARKENED.. PROFESSING to be wise, they became fools, therefore YHWH also gave them up to UNCLEANNESS, in the lust of their hearts, to dishonor their bodies among themselves, who EXCHANGED the TRUTH of YHWH for the LIE, and WORSHIPED and SERVED the creature rather than the CREATOR, who is BLESSED FOREVER.. AMEN For this reason YHWH gave them up to VILE PASSIONS. For even their *WOMEN EXCHANGED the NATURAL use for what is AGAINST NATURAL..* LIKEWISE also the MEN, leaving the NATURAL USE of the woman, burned in their LUST for one another, MEN with MEN COMMITTING what is shameful, and receiving in themselves the PENALTY OF THEIR ERROR which is DUE.. Being filled with ALL UNRIGHTEOUSNESS, *SEXUAL IMMORALITY,*   ROMANS 1:18-22,24-32

DO YOU NOT KNOW that the unrighteous WILL NOT inherit the KINGDOM of YHWH? DO NOT BE DECEIVED. NEITHER FORNICATORS, NOR IDOLATERS, NOR ADULTERERS, NOR HOMOSEXUALS, NOR SODOMITES..   1CORINTHAIANS 6:9
                    PROPHETIC MESSAGE MINISTRY

AMMISHADDAI

FEAR *is the topic* **HEAR;** FOR as many as are led by the Spirit of YHWH, these are sons of YHWH. For you did not receive the spirit of bondage **AGAIN to FEAR,** but you received the Spirit of adoption by whom we cry out, " Abba, FATHER." the SPIRIT HIMSELF BEARS WITNESS with our spirit that we are children of YHWH..   ROMANS 8:14-16

For YHWH has not given us a spirit of **FEAR,** but of *POWER and of LOVE and of a SOUND MIND..*
                    2TIMOTHY 1:7

(A) Do we FEAR while performing our calling, when finding out what to do? Performing deeds in our calling?   Question

"You shall receive power when the **HOLY SPIRIT HAS COME** upon you; and you shall be **WITNESSES TO ME (YHWH)** in Yahrusalem, and in all Yahudah and Samaria, and to the END OF THE EARTH."
                    ACTS1:7,8

Many are called few are CHOSEN!! " You will be betrayed even by parents and brothers, relatives and friends; and they will put some of you to death.. " *BUT NOT A HAIR OF YOUR HEAD SHALL BE LOST.. " BY YOUR PATIENCE **(LOVE)** POSSESS YOUR SOULS:*   LUKE 21:16-19

Strengthen the WEAK; Say to those who are fearful - hearted, "Be strong, do **NOT FEAR!** Behold, your MIGHTY ONE will come with VENGEANCE, With the recompense of YHWH; HE WILL COME and SAVE YOU."   ISAIAH 35: 3,4

There is **NO FEAR IN LOVE;** but perfect LOVE cast OUT FEAR, **BECAUSE FEAR INVOLVES TORMENT..** but he who FEARS has not been made perfect in LOVE.   1JOHN 4:18

The Fear of man brings a snare, But whoever trusts in YHWH shall be **SAFE.** Justice for man comes from YHWH...   PROVERBS 29:25,26

" Whatever I tell you in the dark, speak in the light; and what you hear in the ear, PREACH on the HOUSETOPS." DO NOT FEAR those who kill the body but cannot kill the SOUL..   MATTHEW 10:27,28

" IF you do not carefully OBSERVE ALL the WORDS of this LAW that are written in this book, that you **MAY FEAR this GLORIOUS and AWESOME NAME, YHWH ELSHADDAI** Your MIGHTY ONE.." Your life shall hang in doubt before you: you shall FEAR day and night, and have no assurance of life..
                    DEUTERONOMY 28:58,65,66

Yes, though I walk through the valley of the shadow of death, I WILL NOT FEAR NO EVIL; you are with me; Your rod and Your staff, they COMFORT ME. You prepare a table before me in the presence of my enemies; You anoint my head with oil; My cup run over. **SURELY GOODNESS and MERCY SHALL FOLLOW ME ALL THE DAYS OF MY LIFE;** and I will dwell in the house of YHWH FOREVER..
                    PSALM 23:4-6

YHWH IS MY LIGHT and MY SALVATION; whom shall I FEAR? YHWH IS THE STRENGTH of my LIFE; of whom shall I be AFRAID? **MY HEART SHALL NOT FEAR;**   PSALM 27:1-3

What then shall we say to these things? **IF YHWH IS FOR US, who can be AGAINST US?**
                    ROMANS 8:31

PROPHETIC MESSAGE MINISTRY
    The Art of Studies
    KINGDOM PRICIPLES

                    AMMISHADDAI
                    TRUE
FEAR (N) a feeling of disquiet or apprehension.. AFRAID   BELIEVER

TOPIC: **LOVE, CHARITY and HOSPITALITY**... LOVE SUFFERS LONG and is KIND; LOVE DOES NOT ENVY; LOVE DOES NOT PARADE ITSELF, is not arrogant; does not behave rudely, does not seek its own, is NOT PROVOKED, thinks NO EVIL;   1CORINTHIANS 13:4,5

BUT *ABOVE ALL THINGS PUT ON LOVE*, which is the BOND OF PERFECTION. LET the peace of YHWH rule in your hearts,   COLOSSIANS 3:14,15

LET no one seek his own, but each one the other's WELL BEING.   1CORINTHIANS 10:24

BUT THIS I SAY: he who sows SPARINGLY will also REAP SPARINGLY, and he who sows BOUNTIFULLY will also reap BOUNTIFULLY. So let each one give as HE PURPOSES IN HIS HEART, not grudgingly or of necessity; for YHWH LOVES A CHEERFUL GIVER.   2CORINTHIANS 9:6,7

" *BUT WHEN YOU DO A **CHARITABLE DEED**,* DO NOT let your left hand know what your right hand is doing,   MATTHEW 6:1-4   "GIVE to him who asks you, and from him who wants to borrow from you do not turn AWAY.   MATTHEW 5:42   "AND you will be BLESSED, because they cannot REPAY YOU; for you shall be REPAID AT THE RESURRECTION OF THE JUST."   LUKE 14:13,14

LET BROTHERLY **LOVE CONTINUE**. DO not forget to entertain strangers, for by so doing some have UNWITTINGLY ENTERTAINED ANGELS.   HEBREWS 13:1,2

Be **HOSPITABLE** to one another without grumbling. As each one has received a gift, MINISTER it to one another, as good stewards of the MANIFOLD GRACE OF YHWH; IF anyone ministers, let him DO IT as with the ABILITY which YHWH SUPPLIES,   1PETER 4:9,10,11

DISTRIBUTING to the NEEDS of the SAINTS, given to HOSPITALITY.   ROMANS 12:13

"I HAVE SHOWN YOU IN EVERY WAY, by laboring like THIS, that you must support the WEAK. And remember the WORDS OF THE MESSIYAH YAHSHUAH, that HE said ' it is more BLESSED to give than to RECEIVE."   ACTS 20:35

BY THIS WE KNOW LOVE, because HE laid down HIS LIFE FOR US. And we also ought to lay down our lives for the brothers. But whoever HAS THIS WORLDS GOODS, and SEES his brother in NEED, and shuts up his HEART from him, how does the LOVE OF the MOSTHIGH ABIDE IN HIM? My little children, let US not LOVE IN WORD or in TONGUE, but in DEED and IN TRUTH.   1JOHN 3:16-18

BUT THE END OF ALL THINGS is at HAND; therefore be serious and WATCHFUL in your prayers. And above all things have FERVENT LOVE for one another, for " **LOVE WILL COVER A MULTITUDE OF SINS.**"   1PETER 4:8

For you brothers, have been CALLED TO LIBERTY; only do not use LIBERTY as an OPPORTUNITY for the flesh, but *THROUGH LOVE SERVE ONE ANOTHER.* For the LAW IS FULFILLED IN ONE WORD, EVEN IN THIS: " YOU shall LOVE your neighbor as yourself."   GALATIANS 5:13,14

HE who trusts in his own heart is a FOOL, but whoever WALKS WISELY will be DELIVERED, HE who gives to the poor will not LACK, but HE who hides his eyes, will HAVE MANY CURSES.
PROVERBS 28:27

PROPHETIC MESSAGE MINISTRY
KINGDOM PRINCIPLES

AMMISHADDAI
   TRUE
   BELIEVER

CHARITY (N) LOVE for one's fellow men.
HOSPITABLE (ADJ) FRIENDLY and concern with care toward guests.

TOPIC: SEEKING ACCESS to the MOSTHIGH.. I tell the truth in MESSIYAH, I am not lying my conscience also bearing me witness in the *HOLY SPIRIT,* who are ISRAELITES, to whom pertain the adoption, the gory the COVENANTS, the giving of the LAW the service of the MOSTHIGH, and the PROMISES; of whom are the (Elders) and from whom according to the flesh, MESSIYAH came, <u>who is over all</u> the *ETERNALLY BLESSED MIGHTY ONE: AMEN*   ROMANS 9:1,4,5

So also MESSIYAH did not glorify HIMSELF to become HIGH PRIEST, but it was HE who said to HIM: you are MY SON, TODAY I have begotten YOU." "YOU are a priest FOREVER according to the ORDER of MELCHIZEDEK,"   HEBREWS 5:5,6

"let not your heart be troubled; you believe in YHWH, believe also in ME, YAHSHUAH said to him, "I am the WAY, the TRUTH and the LIFE.. No one comes to the ABBA (FATHER) except through ME.   JOHN 14:1,6   LET us therefore come BOLDLY to the throne of GRACE, that we may obtain mercy and find GRACE to help in time of need.   HEBREWS 4:16

Show me your ways, O YHWH; teach me your paths. Lead me in your TRUTH and TEACH me, for your are the *MIGHTY ONE OF SALVATION;* On you I wait all the day.   PSALM 25:4,5

Therefore submit to THE MOSTHIGH. Resist the devil and he will flee from you, DRAW NEAR TO YHWH and HE will draw NEAR to you.   JAMES 4:7,8

FINALLY, my brothers, be strong in YHWH and in the POWER OF HIS MIGHT. Put on the whole ARMOR of YHWH, that you may be able to stand against the scheming and wiles of the ADVERSARY (DEVIL)   EPHESIANS 6:10,11

"BECAUSE you have kept MY COMMANDMENTS to PERSEVERE, I also will keep you from the hour of trail which shall come upon the whole world, to TEST those who dwell on the earth. "behold, I am coming QUICKLY! Hold fast what you have, that no one may take your crown.   REVELATION 3:10

YES, many peoples and strong nations shall come to *SEEK* YHWH of hosts in YAHRUSALEM, and to *PRAY BEFORE* (ACCESS) the MOSTHIGH.." "Thus says YHWH of hosts: 'In those days ten men from every language of the NATIONS shall grasp the sleeve of a *HEBREW MAN,* saying, "let us go with you, for we have heard that YHWH (GOD) is with you."   ZECHARIAH 8:22,23

PROPHETIC MESSAGE MINISTRY
KINGDOM PRINCIPLES
AMMISHADDAI

SEEK (V) to try to find or discover: search for.
ACCESS (N) a means of approaching: passage to the *KINGDOM*

The ART of STUDIES
KINGDOM PRICIPLES

HEAR, O YISRAEL: יהוה OUR EL יהוה IS (ONE)

YOU SHALL LOVE YHWH YOUR EL WITH ALL YOUR HEART, WITH ALL YOUR SOUL, and
WITH ALL YOUR STRENGTH...   DEUTERONOMY 6:4,5

TOPIC:*ABOMINABLE CUSTOMS and TRADITIONS*

THESE WORDS which I COMMAND you today shall be in your heart, you shall teach them
DILIGENTLY to your children and shall TALK OF THEM WHEN YOU SIT IN YOUR HOUSE, when
You WALK by the WAY, WHEN you lie down, and when you RISE UP.. YOU SHALL WRITE them
On the DOOR POSTS of your HOUSE and on your GATES..   DEUTERONOMY 6:6-9

You shall therefore KEEP MY STATUES and MY JUDGEMENTS and SHALL NOT COMMIT any of
These *ABOMINATIONS,* either any of your own nation, or any stranger who dwells among you...
(FOR ALL THESE ABOMINATIONS the MEN OF THE LAND HAVE DONE, WHO WERE BEFORE
YOU and THUS the LAND IS DEFILED) therefore you shall KEEP MY ORDINANCE so that you do not
COMMIT <u>ANY</u> OF THESE ABOMINABLE CUSTOMS which were COMMITTED before you, and you
Do not DEFILE YOURSELVES BY THEM: *I AM YHWH your EL*   LEVITICUS 18:26-30

HEAR THE WORD WHICH YHWH SPEAKS TO YOU, O HOUSE OF YISRAEL. THUS SAYS YHWH
DO NOT LEARN THE WAY of the GENTILES; DO NOT BE DISMAYED AT THE SIGNS OF
HEAVEN, for the GENTILES are DISMAYED AT THEM.. For the **CUSTOMS** OF THE PEOPLE ARE
FUTILE;   JEREMIAH 10:1-5

Why do you also TRANSGRESS the COMMANDMENT OF YHWH BECAUSE OF TRADITION?
THUS YOU HAVE MADE the COMMANDMENT OF YHWH OF NO EFFECT BY YOUR
TRADITION and in VAIN THEY WORSHIP ME.. TEACHING AS DOCTRINES the commandment of
MEN..   MATTHEW 15:3-9

HE WHO SAYS, "I KNOW HIM,"*(messiyah)* and does NOT KEEP HIS COMMANDMENTS, IS A LIAR
And the TRUTH IS NOT IN HIM...   1JOHN 2:4

BEWARE LEST ANYONE CHEAT YOU THROUGH
PHILOSOPHY and EMPTY DECEIT, ACCORDING TO the TRADITION OF MEN, ACCORDING TO
The BASIC PRINCIPLES OF THE WORLD, and NOT ACCORDING TO **MESSIYAH**...
                                                      COLOSSIANS 2:8

And WHEN THEY SAY TO YOU, "SEEK THOSE WHO ARE MEDIUMS and WIZARDS, WHO
Whisper and mutter," should not a people SEEK THEIR GOD? Should they seek the DEAD on behalf of
The LIVING? To the LAW and TO THE TESTIMONY! IF they do not SPEAK ACCORDING TO THIS
WORD, it is BECAUSE there is NO LIGHT IN THEM..   ISAIAH 8:19,20

THERE SHALL NOT BE FOUND AMONG YOU.. one who practices witch craft, or a soothsayer, or one
Who interprets omens, or a sorcerer or one who CONJURES SPELLS, OR A MEDIUM OR A SPIRITIST
OR ONE WHO CALLS UP THE DEAD.. For ALL who do these things are an ABOMINATION TO
YHWH and BECAUSE OF THESE ABOMINATIONS YHWH YOUR EL(GOD) drives them out from
Before you. You shall be BLAMELESS BEFORE YHWH YOUR EL for these NATIONS which you will
Dispossess LISTENED TO SOOTHSAYERS and DIVINERS; but as for you, *YHWH YOUR EL* has not
APPOINTED SUCH FOR YOU...   DEUTERONOMY 18:10-14

For when you OFFER YOUR GIFTS and MAKE YOUR SONS PASS THROUGH the fire you defile
Yourselves with ALL YOUR IDOLS, **EVEN TO THIS DAY..** what you have in your MIND SHALL
NEVER BE, when you say, 'WE WILL BE LIKE THE GENTILES, like the families in other countries,
SERVING WOOD and STONE.'   EZEKIEL 20:31,32

I RAISED MY HAND IN A OATH, THAT I **WOULD SCATTER** THEM AMONG the GENTILES and
DISPERSE THEM THROUGHOUT the COUNTRIES, BECAUSE they HAD NOT EXECUTED MY
JUDGMENTS, BUT HAD DESPISED MY STATUTES, PROFANED MY SABBATHS...
                                                      EZEKIEL 20:23-25

KINGDOM PRINCIPLES

AMMISHADDAI
  TRUE
BELIEVER

TOPIC: LYING and FALSE WITNESS.. I AM YHWH your GOD, who brought you out of the land of EGYPT, OUT OF THE HOUSE OF BONDAGE. YOU SHALL NOT bear FALSE WITNESS.

EXODUS 20: 1,2,3,16

YOU SHALL NOT STEAL, nor DEAL FALSELY, nor LIE to one another.   LEVITICUS 19:11

YOU SHALL NOT SWEAR by my NAME FALSELY, nor shall you PROFANE the NAME OF YHWH your GOD: I AM YHWH   LEVITICUS 19:12

BEHOLD YHWH'S HAND IS NOT SHORTENED that it cannot save, nor HIS EAR heavy that it cannot HEAR. But your iniquity have separated you from your EL (GOD) and your sins have hidden his FACE FROM YOU so that HE WILL NOT HEAR..   ISAIAH 59:1,2

THESE SIX THINGS YHWH HATES, YES SEVEN, are ABOMINATION TO HIM; (1) a proud look, (2) a **LYING TONGUE,** (3) hands that shed innocent blood (4) a heart that devises wicked plans, (5) feet that are swift in running to EVIL, (6) **A FALSE WITNESS** who speaks LIES.. (7) and ONE WHO sows DISCORD between brothers.   PROVERBS 6:16-19

THEREFORE, PUTTING AWAY , LYING, "let each one speak TRUTH WITH HIS NEIGHBOR, " FOR WE ARE MEMBERS OF ONE ANOTHER...   EPHESIANS 4:25

BE ANGRY, and DO NOT **SIN.** MEDITATE WITHIN your bed, and be still.. OFFER the SACRIFICES of RIGHTEOUSNESS, and put your TRUST IN YHWH.   PSALM 4:4,5

DO NOT LIE to one another, since you have put off the OLD MAN with his deeds, and have PUT ON THE NEW MAN WHO IS RENEWED IN KNOWLEDGE according to the IMAGE OF HIM (YHWH) WHO CREATED HIM..   COLOSSIANS 3:9,10

DELIVER MY SOUL, "O" YHWH, from LYING LIPS and FROM A **DECEITFUL TONGUE:** PSALM 120:2

LET the LYING LIPS BE PUT TO **SILENCE,** which speak INSOLENT things PROUDLY and CONTEMPTUOUSLY against the righteous.   PSALM 31:18

But I have TRUSTED IN YOUR MERCY; my heart shall rejoice in your SALVATION: PSALM 13:5

I rejoice at your WORD AS ONE WHO FINDS GREAT TREASURE. I HATE and **ABHOR LYING** but I LOVE your LAW, SEVEN TIMES A DAY , I PRAISE YOU, because of your RIGHTEOUS JUDGMENTS, GREAT PEACE have those who LOVE your LAW, and nothing causes them to STUMBLE.

PSALM 119:162-165

BLESSED is that man who makes YHWH HIS TRUST, and does not RESPECT the PROUD, nor such as to TURN ASIDE TO LIES.   PSALM 40:4

THE **TRUTH FULL** LIP SHALL BE ESTABLISHED **FOREVER,** but a lying tongue, is but for a moment

PROVERBS 12:19

HE WHO WORKS DECEIT SHALL NOT dwell with in MY HOUSE; HE who tell LIES, shall NOT CONTINUE IN MY PRESENCE.   PSALM 101:7,8   THE COMING OF THE lawless ONE is according to the WORKING OF SATAN, with <u>all power</u>, SIGNS, and **LYING WONDERS**

2THESSALONIANS 2:9

SPEAKING LIES IN HYPOCRISY, having their own conscience seared with a HOT IRON:

1TIMOTHY 4:2

HE WHO OVERCOMES *SHALL INHERIT ALL THINGS,* and I will be his EL (GOD) and HE shall be my SON. "BUT THE COWARDLY, and all LIARS SHALL HAVE THEIR PART IN THE LAKE which burns with FIRE and BRIMSTONE, which is the SECOND DEATH."   REVELATION 21:7,8

KINGDOM PRINCIPLES

AMMISHADDAI

(1) LIE (N) to present FALSE information, with the purpose of deceiving

(2) FALSE (ADJ) being CONTRARY to the TRUTH or FACT

TOPIC: **BEARING OTHERS BURDENS..**   INCLINE you ear and hear the WORDS OF THE WISE.   PROVERBS 22:17
BROTHERS, IF ANYONE AMONG YOU wanders from the TRUTH, and someone turns HIM BACK, let him know that he who turns a SINNER FROM THE ERROR of his way will SAVE a SOUL from death and cover a multitude of SINS.   JAMES 5:19,20
WE then who are STRONG OUGHT to **BEAR** with the *SCRUPLES* of the WEAK, and NOT to PLEASE ourselves... LET each of US please HIS neighbor for HIS GOOD, leading to EDIFICATION..   ROMANS 15:1,2
RECEIVE ONE who is WEAK in the FAITH, but not to dispute over doubtful things...
                                                ROMANS 14:1

IF a man is overtaken in any trespass (sin) you who are SPIRITUAL restore such a ONE IN A SPIRIT of GENTLENESS, considering YOURSELF lest you also be TEMPTED, *BEAR ONE ANOTHERS BURDENS,* and so FULFILL the LAW OF MESSIYAH...   GALATIANS 6:1-5
Therefore **COMFORT EACH OTHER and EDIFY** ONE ANOTHER, just as you also are doing
                                          1THESSALONIANS 5:11
YOU also help TOGETHER in prayer for US, that thanks may be given by many persons on our behalf for the gift granted to US through many. For our boasting is this: THE TESTIMONY of our conscience that we conducted ourselves in the WORLD IN SIMPLICITY and GODLY SINCERITY, not with fleshly WISDOM but by the GRACE of YHWH and more ABUNDANTLY toward you.   2CORINTHIANS 1:11,12

Therefore I endure all things for the sake of the ELECT, that they also may OBTAIN THE SALVATION which is in MESSIYAH YAHSHUAH with ETERNAL GLORY
                                              2TIMOTHY 2:10
SO then each of US, shall GIVE ACCOUNT of HIMSELF to YHWH...   THEREFORE let US not JUDGE one another ANYMORE, but rather resolve this, not to put a STUMBLING BLOCK or a cause to FALL in our brothers WAY..   ROMANS 14:12,13
BUT beware lest somehow this liberty of yours become a STUMBLING BLOCK to those who are WEAK...   BECAUSE of your KNOWLEDGE SHALL the weak brother PERISH, for whom MESSIYAH DIED? BUT when you thus SIN AGAINST the BROTHER and with their WEAK CONSCIENCE, you SIN AGAINST MESSIYAH. Therefore if food makes my brother STUMBLE, I will never again eat meat, lest I make my BROTHER STUMBLE...
                                          1CORINTHIANS 8:7-13

KNGDOM PRINCIPLES
PROPHETIC MESSAGE MINISTRY
READING of INSPIRATIONS

(1) BURDEN (N) something difficult to bear, SPIRITUALLY or physically

(2) BEAR (V) to hold up: SUPPORT..

AMMISHADDAI

COMMANDMENT KEEPERS

TOPIC: REBUKE OF FAULTS and SINS..   HARSH DISCIPLINE IS FOR HIM WHO FORSAKES THE WAY. And he who hates CORRECTION WILL DIE.   PROVERBS 15:10

NOW I myself am confident concerning you, my brothers that you also are FULL OF GOODNESS, filled with ALL KNOWLEDGE, ABLE also to ADMONISH ONE ANOTHER..   ROMANS 15:14

MOREOVER, if your brother SINS AGAINST YOU, **GO and TELL HIM HIS FAULT**, between you and HIM alone. If he hears you, you have GAINED YOUR BOTHER... BUT IF HE WILL NOT HEAR, take with YOU ONE OR TWO MORE, that by the MOUTH OF TWO OR THREE WITNESSES EVERY (WORD) may be ESTABLISHED..   MATTHEW 18:15,16

IT is the glory of the MOST HIGH TO CONCEAL A MATTER, but the glory of KINGS is to SEARCH OUT A MATTER.   PROVERBS 25:2   SO LET THE RIGHTEOUS STRIKE ME; IT SHALL BE A KINDNESS. And let HIM REBUKE ME; IT SHALL BE AS EXCELLENT OIL; LET MY HEAD NOT REFUSE IT.   PSALM 141:5   BROTHERS, if anyone among YOU wanders from the TRUTH, and SOMEONE turns him back, LET HIM KNOW that he who turns a SINNER FROM THE ERROR OF HIS WAY WILL SAVE A SOUL FROM DEATH and cover a MULTITUDE OF SINS.   JAMES 5:19,20

NOW we encourage you, brothers **WARN THOSE WHO ARE UNRULY**, COMFORT the FAINTHEARTED UPHOLD the WEAK, BE PATIENT WILL ALL.   1THESSALONIANS 5:14

He who REBUKES A MAN will find more favor after ward than he who FLATTERS WITH THE TONGUE...   PROVERBS 28:23   FOR the COMMANDMENT IS A LAMP and the LAW A LIGHT; REPROOFS OF INSTRUCTION ARE THE WAY OF LIFE.   PROVERBS 6:23

A MANS HEART PLANS HIS WAY, but YHWH directs his steps...   PROVERBS 16:9

The ear that HEARS the REBUKES OF LIFE will abide among the WISE. The FEAR of the MOST HIGH is the INSTRUCTION OF **WISDOM** and before **HONOR** is **HUMILITY**..   PROVERBS 15:31-33

A SERVANT of the MOST HIGH <u>MUST NOT QUARREL</u> but be GENTLE TO ALL, ABLE TO TEACH, PATIENTLY, IN HUMILITY **CORRECTING** THOSE WHO ARE IN OPPOSITION, if YHWH PERHAPS WILL GRANT THEM REPENTANCE, so that they may know the TRUTH...   2TIMOTHY 2:24-26

PREACH the WORD, BE READY IN SEASON and OUT OF SEASON. CONVINCE, REBUKE, EXHORT, with ALL LONGSUFFERING and TEACHING.   2TIMOTHY 4:2

If a man is OVERTAKEN IN ANY TRESPASS (SIN) YOU WHO ARE **SPIRITUAL** RESTORE SUCH A ONE IN A SPIRIT OF GENTLENESS, CONSIDERING YOURSELF LEST YOU ALSO BE TEMPTED...   GALATIANS 6:1

HE who KEEPS INSTRUCTION is in the WAY OF LIFE, but he who REFUSES CORRECTION LEADS ASTRAY.   PROVERBS 10:17   FINDING OUT what is ACCEPTABLE TO YHWH, have no fellowship with the UNFRUITFUL WORKS OF DARKNESS, but rather **EXPOSE THEM**.   EPHESIANS 5:10,11

And if anyone does not OBEY our word in this letter, NOTE THAT PERSON and do not KEEP COMPANY WITH HIM, that he may be ashamed. Yet do not count HIM as an enemy, but *WARN HIM AS A BROTHER...*   2THESSALONIANS 3:14,15

TAKE HEED TO YOURSELVES, IF your brother SINS AGAINST you, REBUKE HIM and if he REPENTS, FORGIVE HIM.   LUKE 17:3,4

AVOID FOOLISH DISPUTES, REJECT A DIVISIVE MAN after the FIRST and SECOND WARNING KNOWING that such a person is WARPED and SINNING, being SELF CONDEMNED.   TITUS 3:9-11

KINGDOM PRINCIPLES
PROPHETIC MESSAGE MINISTRY

AMMISHADDAI
  TRUE
  BELIEVER

(1) REBUKE (VT) to criticize, sharply; REPRIMAND
(2) FAULT (N) a mistake: error
(3) SIN (N) to commit an offense or violation

TOPIC: **PATIENCE and ENDURANCE** *BLESSED BE THE MOST HIGH* FATHER OF **IMMANUEL MESSIYAH** who according to HIS abundant mercy has begotten US again to a **LIVING HOPE**, through the RESURRECTION OF IMMANUEL MESSIYAH from the dead to an INHERITANCE INCORRUPTIBLE and UNDEFILED, that does not fade away, **RESERVED IN HEAVEN** for you, WHO ARE KEPT by the power of the MOST HIGH through FAITH for SALVATION ready to be REVEALED in the LAST TIME. In this you greatly rejoice, though now for a little while, if NEED BE, you have been distress ed by **VARIOUS TRIALS**..   1PETER 1:3-6

I (YHWH) KNOW YOUR WORKS, YOUR LABOR, YOUR PATIENCE, and that you cannot bear those who are EVIL; and you have TESTED THOSE WHO SAY they are apostles and are not, and have found them LIARS, and you have PERSEVERED and HAVE PATIENCE, and have LABORED for my names sake and HAVE NOT BECOME WEARY.   REVELATION 2:2,3

The end of a thing is BETTER than its beginning; the PATIENT IN SPIRIT IS BETTER than the PROUD in spirit.   ECCLESIASTES 7:8

FOR THIS IS COMMENDABLE, if because of conscience toward YHWH ONE **ENDURES** GRIEF, SUFFERING WRONGFULLY, for what CREDIT is it if, when you are beaten for your FAULTS, you take it PATIENTLY? But when you do GOOD and SUFFER, if you take it PATIENTLY, THIS IS COMMENDABLE BEFORE the MOST HIGH; for this you were called, because MESSIYAH ALSO SUFFERED FOR US, leaving US **AN EXAMPLE**, that we should follow HIS STEPS: 1PETER 2:19-22

Therefore we also, since we are surrounded by so GREAT A CLOUD OF WITNESSES, let us lay aside EVERY WEIGHT, and the SIN which so easily ENSNARES US, and let us run with **ENDURANCE** the race that is set before US.   HEBREWS 12:1,2

LET LOVE BE WITHOUT HYPOCRISY... abhor what is evil. Cling to what is GOOD. Rejoicing in HOPE, PATIENT IN TRIBULATION, CONTINUING STEADFASTLY IN PRAYER.   ROMANS 12:9-12

And NOT ONLY that, but we also GLORY IN TRIBULATIONS, knowing that tribulation PRODUCES, ENDURANCE, and ENDURANCE CHARACTER; and CHARACTER, HOPE.   ROMANS 5:3-5

My brothers, COUNT IT ALL JOY, when you fall into various trials, knowing that the TESTING OF YOUR FAITH PRODUCES PATIENCE, but let patience have its perfect work, that you may be MATURE and COMPLETE, LACKING NOTHING.   JAMES 1:2-4

HE WHO IS SLOW TO WRATH has great understanding, but he who is IMPULSIVE EXALTS FOLLY.   PROVERBS 14:29

DO NOT BE RASH with your mouth, and let not your HEART UTTER ANYTHING HASTILY before YHWH because YHWH IS IN HEAVEN, and you on earth; therefore let your words BE FEW..   ECCLESIASTES 5:2

But you, O MAN of the MOST HIGH, FLEE THESE THINGS and PURSUE RIGHTEOUSNESS, GODLINESS, FAITH, LOVE PATIENCE, GENTLENESS.   1TIMOTHY 6:11,12

NOW may YHWH DIRECT YOUR HEARTS INTO THE LOVE OF THE MOST HIGH and into the **PATIENCE OF MESSIYAH** 2THESSALONIANS 3:5 THEREFORE be PATIENT, brothers, until the coming of YHWH. You also be PATIENT, ESTABLISH YOUR HEARTS, for the coming of YHWH IS AT HAND. Do not grumble against ONE ANOTHER, brothers, unlest you be CONDEMNED. Behold, the JUDGE IS STANDING AT THE DOOR!   JAMES 5:7-9   but if we HOPE for what we DO NOT SEE, we EAGERLY WAIT for it with **PERSEVERANCE**..   ROMANS 8:25

KINGDOM PRINCIPLES

AMMISHADDAI   PROPHETIC MESSAGE MINISTRY

PATIENT (ADJ) capable of bearing ALLICTION calmly
ENDURE (V) to bear with TOLERANCE

TOPIC: **FAITH and WORKS**...   WE know as many walk according to this RULE, **PEACE and MERCY** be upon them and upon the YAHSRAEL OF YHWH ELSHADDAI.   GALATIANS 6:16

IF MY PEOPLE who are called by MY NAME will humble themselves and pray and seek MY (WAY) and turn from their wicked WAYS then I will hear form HEAVEN and will FORGIVE THEIR SIN and HEAL their land. Now my eyes will be open and my ears ATTENTIVE TO PRAYERS MADE IN THIS PLACE

                                                                         2CHRONICLES 7:14,15

But he also said" more then that, *BLESSED ARE THOSE WHO HEAR the WORD OF YHWH and KEEP IT...*   LUKE 11:28

For this is the LOVE of YHWH that we KEEP HIS COMMANDMENTS, and HIS COMMANDMENTS are NOT burdensome.   1JOHN 5:2-5

SO IF YOU KEEP MY COMMANDMENTS you will abide in MY LOVE. Just as I have kept MY FATHERS (ABBA'S) COMMANDMENTS and ABIDE IN HIS **LOVE**.   JOHN 15:1-17

WE truly UNDERSTAND we are NOT UNDER THE LAW of JUDGMENT, but we are to **ABIDE and LIVE IN the LAW of LOVE**..   TRUE

KNOWING we shall love YHWH our EL with all our HEART, with all our SOUL and with all our MIND this being the **FIRST** and the **SECOND** is like it: you shall love your NEIGHBOR AS YOURSELF, knowing these **TWO COMMANDMENTS FULFILL ALL THE LAW and the PROPHETS.**

                                                                       MATTHEW 22:37-40

SO IT IS WRITTEN; BLESSED ARE THE UNDEFILED in the way, who walk in the law of YHWH, blessed are those who KEEP HIS TESTIMONIES.   PSALM 119:1-10

WHO ever therefore breaks one of the least of these COMMANDMENTS and TEACHES men to DO SO, shall be called least in the KINGDOM OF HEAVEN, but whoever does and teaches them, shall be called GREAT IN THE KINGDOM OF HEAVEN.   MATTHEW 5:17-20

SO this is a **FAITHFUL SAYING** I TRULY want you to AFFIRM CONSTANTLY, you who BELIEVE IN YHWH, we should be CAREFUL to MAINTAIN **GOOD WORKS**, knowing these things are GOOD and PROFITABLE TO MEN...   TITUS 3:5-8

KNOWING ALL SCRIPTURE IS GIVEN BY INSPIRATION OF YHWH and is profitable for DOCTRINE, for REPROOF, for CORRECTION, for TRAINING, or INSTRUCTION IN RIGHTEOUSNESS that the man of YHWH may be COMPLETE THOROUGHLY EQUIPPED FOR EVERY **GOOD WORK**   2TIMOTHY 3:16,17

IN CONCLUSION we need to abide in the law and keep our FATHERS (ABBA'S) COMMANDMENTS **BELIEVING** this is THE WAY to renewing our MIND.   ROMANS 12:1,2

KNOWING whatever we ask in FAITH we receive from HIM because we KEEP HIS COMMANDMENTS and DO THOSE THINGS that are pleasing in HIS SIGHT..   1JOHN 3:22,23

SO IN OUR MOUTH THERE IS FOUND NO DECEIT, before the throne of YHWH..   TRUE

HERE IS THE PATIENCE OF THE **SAINTS WHO KEEP the COMMANDMENTS OF YHWH** and the FAITH OF YAHSHUAH MESSIYAH IMMANUEL   (AMEN)   REVELATION 14:12

COMMANDMENT (V) ORDERLY DIRECTION or LAW
LAW (N) SYSTEM of such RULES FORMED to show LOVE
                          WALKING ORDERLY   (1) FAITH
                                                                   (2) WORKS

AMMISHADDAI   **PROPHETIC MESSAGE MINISTRY**
   TRUE
   BELIEVER

TOPIC: COMMUNICATIONS DO NOT BE HASTY with your mouth, AND LET NOT your heart utter anything HASTILY BEFORE YHWH, for the MOST HIGH IS IN HEAVEN and you on EARTH; therefore let your words be FEW..   ECCLESIASTES 5:2

SO DO NOT GO HASTILY TO CONTROVERSY for what will you do in the END, when your neighbor has put you to SHAME? **DEBATE your CASE** with your neighbor himself and DO NOT DISCLOSE the SECRET TO ANOTHER; lest HE who HEARS IT expose your shame and your REPUTATION BE RUINED..   PROVERBS 25:8-10

SO AVOID FOOLISH DISPUTES, GENEALOGIES, CONTROVERSY and STRIVINGS about the LAW; for they are **UNPROFITABLE and USELESS..** (REJECT) A DIVISIVE MAN AFTER the FIRST and SECOND ADMONITION knowing that such a person is WARPED and SINNING being SELF CONDEMNED.   TITUS 3:9-11

SO a FOOLS LIP enter into CONTROVERSY and HIS MOUTH CALLS FOR BLOWS.   PROVERBS 18:6

THEREFORE the beginning of STRIFE is like releasing water **STOP CONTROVERSY** before a QUARREL STARTS   PROVERBS 17:14

A SOFT ANSWER TURNS AWAY WRATH, BUT A HARSH WORD STIRS UP ANGER, the tongue of the WISE USES KNOWLEDGE RIGHTLY, but the mouth of fools pours forth FOOLISHNESS
                                           PROVERBS 15:1,2

IF ANYONE TEACHES OTHERWISE and DOES NOT CONSENT TO **WHOLESOME WORDS**, the words of our IMMANUEL YAHSHUAH and to the DOCTRINE which is ACCORDING TO GODLINESS he is proud, knowing nothing but is OBSESSED with DISPUTES AND ARGUMENTS OVER words from which COME ENVY, STRIFE, REVILING, EVIL SUSPICIONS, USELESS WRANGLINGS of MEN of CORRUPT MINDS, and DESTITUTE OF THE TRUTH, from such **WITHDRAW YOURSELF**...
                                           1TIMOTHY 6:3-5

And **AVOID FOOLISH and IGNORANT DISPUTES**, knowing that they generate (STRIFE) and a servant of the MESSIYAH MUST NOT QUARREL, but be GENTLE TO ALL able to teach PATIENT in HUMILITY CORRECTING those who are in OPPOSITION, IF YHWH PERHAPS will grant them REPENTANCE so they may KNOW THE TRUTH..   2TIMOTHY 2:23-26

READINGS OF INSPIRATION
HE WHO HAS EAR, LET HIM HEAR WHAT THE
SPIRIT SAYS TO THE CHURCHES
PROPHETIC MESSAGE MINISTRY

AMMISHADDAI
     TRUE
     BELIEVER

COMMUNICATIONS (N) the exchange of THOUGHTS, messages, or INFORMATION.

Lord Jesus Christ/ IMMANUEL YAHSHUAH MESSIYAH
MIGHTY GOD with US/ YAHSaviour
ANOINTED   (SON)

THE ART OF STUDIES the process of studying: THE PURSUIT OF KNOWLEDGE
WISDOM and UNDERSTANDING by reading OBSERVATION (PLUS) RESEARCH.
TOPIC: **OATHS, CONTRACTS and VOWS..**

DO NOT be QUICK with your mouth and DO NOT let your heart UTTER anything HASTILY
Before YHWH because YHWH is in HEAVEN and you on EARTH, so therefore allow your
WORDS to be FEW...   ECCLESIASTES 5:2

SO now I make you SWEAR by YHWH the MOSTHIGH OF HEAVEN and the HOLY ONE of
the EARTH.   GENESIS 24:3

YOU SHALL FEAR YHWH your MIGHTY ONE and SERVE HIM and SHALL TAKE OATHS
IN HIS (NAME)   DEUTERONOMY 6:13

IF a man makes a **VOW** to YHWH OR SWEAR to an **OATH** or binds himself to some
AGGREEMENT he shall NOT BREAK his WORD, he shall DO ACCORDING TO ALL that is
said from HIS MOUTH...   NUMBERS 30:2

SO let your **YES** be **YES** and your **NO** be **NO** for WHATEVER MORE then it is from the
EVIL (ONE)   MATTHEW 5:37

YOU SHALL NOT SWEAR by YHWH'S NAME *FALSELY* nor shall you PROFANE THE NAME
of your HOLY ONE: I AM YHWH ELSHADDAI   LEVITICUS 19:12

"WHEN you make a VOW to YHWH your EL (GOD) you shall NOT DELAY to PAY IT;

BUT IF YOU **ABSTAIN** from VOWING, it shall NOT be SIN unto you, but with that which

HAS GONE FROM your LIPS YOU SHALL KEEP and PROFORM:
                                          DEUTERONOMY 23:21,22,23

LET A MANS WORD, BE HIS BOND, and COVENANT BEFORE יהוה ..

PROPHETIC MESSAGE MINISTRY
COMMANDMENT KEEPERS

AMMISHADDAI
 TRUE
 BELIEVER

TOPIC: **HONESTY and SINCERITY**.. IT is honorable for a man to STOP STRIVING, since ANY FOOL can start a QUARREL.. PROVERBS 20:3

ONLY LET YOUR CONDUCT BE WORTHY of the GOSPEL OF MESSIYAH, so that whether I come and see you or am absent, I may hear of your affairs, that you stand fast in ONE SPIRIT, with ONE MIND striving together for the FAITH of the GOSPEL. And not in any way terrified by your ADVERSARIES, which is to them a PROOF OF PERDITION, but to YOU OF SALVATION, and that from YHWH. FOR to you it has been GRANTED ON BEHALF OF MESSIYAH, not only to **BELIEVE IN HIM**, but also to SUFFER FOR HIS SAKE.. PHILIPPIANS 1:27-29

THAT YOU ASPIRE TO LEAD A QUIET LIFE, to mind your OWN BUSINESS, and to work with your own hands, as we COMMAND YOU, that you may walk PROPERLY toward those who are OUTSIDE, and that you **MAY LACK NOTHING..** 1THESSALONIANS 4:11,12

AND this I pray, that your LOVE may ABOUND still more and more in KNOWLEDGE and ALL DISCERNMENT, that you may approve the things that are excellent, that you may be SINCERE and without OFFENSE till the DAY OF MESSIYAH, being filled with the FRUITS OF RIGHTEOUSNESS which are by YAHSHUAH MESSIYAH, to the GLORY and PRAISE OF THE **YHWH ELSHADDAI.** PHILIPPIANS 1:9-11

FOR OUR EXHORTATION did NOT come from *ERROR OR UNCLEANNESS,* nor was it in DECEIT, but as we have been APPROVED BY YHWH to be entrusted with the GOSPEL, even so we speak, not AS pleasing men, but YHWH WHO TEST OUR HEARTS. For neither at anytime did we use FLATTERING WORDS, AS YOU KNOW, nor a cloak for covetousness - YHWH IS WITNESS.. Nor did we seek GLORY from men, either from you or from others, when we might have made demands as APOSTLES OF MESSIYAH... 1THESSALONIANS 2:3-6

I PRAY TO YHWH THAT YOU DO NO EVIL, not that we should appear approved, but that you should do what is HONORABLE, though we may seem DISQUALIFIED. For we can do NOTHING AGAINST the TRUTH, but for the TRUTH. 2CORINTHIANS 13:7,8
PROVIDING **HONORABLE** THINGS, NOT ONLY IN THE SIGHT OF YHWH, but also in the SIGHT OF MEN. 2CORINTHIANS 8:21

PRAY FOR US; for we are confident that we have a good conscience, in all things **DESIRING TO LIVE HONORABLY...** HEBREWS 13:18

FINALLY, BROTHERS, WHATEVER things are **TRUE**, whatever things are **NOBLE**, whatever things are **JUST**, whatever things are **LOVELY**, whatever things are of **GOOD REPORT**, IF THERE in any virtue and if there is anything PRAISE WORTHY - *MEDITATE ON THESE THINGS..* THE things which you learned and received and heard and saw in me, THESE DO, and YHWH OF PEACE will be with you. PHILIPPIANS 4:8,9
YOU ARE THE LIGHT OF THE WORLD. A CITY THAT IS SET ON A HILL WHICH CANNOT BE HIDDEN.. Let your light (SO) SHINE BEFORE MEN, that they may see your **GOOD WORKS and GLORIFY** your FATHER (ABBA) in heaven. MATTHEW 5:14,16

KINGDOM PRINCIPLES
AMMISHADDAI   PROPHETIC MESSAGE MINISTRY
                    THE ART OF STUDIES

(1) HONEST (ADJ) marked by integrity and truth
(2) SINCERE (ADJ) presenting no false appearance: HONEST

KINGDOM PRINCIPLES
THE ART OF STUDIES...

BELOVED WHILE I WAS VERY DILIGENT TO WRITE YOU CONCERNING OUR COMMNON
SALVATION...   JUDE 1:3
TOPIC *FAITH AND BELIEF...*

NOW *FAITH* IS THE SUBSTANCE OF THINGS HOPED FOR, THE CONFIDENCE OF THINGS
NOT SEEN...   HEBREWS 11:1

Faith comes by HEARING THE WORD.. ROMANS 10:16-17 since we have the same SPIRIT OF
FAITH according to what is written, I believed and therefore I spoke we also believe and therefore SPEAK.
2CORINTHIANS 4:13

FAITH TRIUMPHS IN TROUBLE.. ROMANS 5:1-5 TEST ALL THINGS.. 1THESSALONIANS 5:21

FOR if you believed MOSES, you would believe me; for he wrote about me (*messiah*) but if you do not
BELIEVE HIS WRITINGS HOW WILL YOU BELIEVE MY WORDS?   JOHN 5:46,47

That you may be mindful of the words which were SPOKEN before by the HOLYPROPHET and THE
COMMANDMENT OF US THE APOSTLES OF YHWH and YAHSHUAH...   2PETER 3:2

ONLY LET YOUR CONDUCT BE WORTHY OF THE GOSPEL OF MESSIAH: that you stand fast in
ONE SPIRIT WITH ONE MIND STRIVING TOGETHER FOR THE FAITH OF THE GOSPEL...
PHILLIPPIANS 1:27

IF ANY OF YOU LACKS WISDOM, LET HIM ASK OF YHWH BUT LET HIM ASK IN **FAITH,**
WITH NO DOUBTING...   JAMES 1:2-8

MOREOVER, BROTHERS, I declare to you the GOSPEL which I preached to you. Which you stand, by
Which also you are **SAVED,** IF YOU HOLD FAST THAT WORD WHICH I PREACHED TO YOU
UNLESS YOU BELIEVED IN VAIN. FOR I DELIVERED TO YOU FIRST OF ALL THAT WHICH I
ALSO RECEIVED: THAT MESSIAH DIED FOR OUR SINS ACCORDING TO THE SCRIPTURES...
And THAT HE WAS BURIED, and HE ROSE AGAIN THE THIRD DAY ACCORDING TO THE
SCRIPTURES..   1CORINTHIANS 15:1-4

but DO YOU WANT TO KNOW, O FOOLISH MAN,
THAT *FAITH WITHOUT WORKS IS DEAD?*   JAMES 2:20

AMMISHADDAI
  True   3 FOLD MINISTRY (KEYS) OF THE KINGDOM

BELIEVER   OF יהוה...

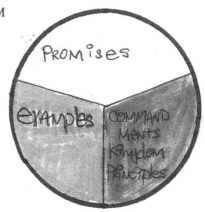

DEFINED:
(1) HOPE (N) feeling that ones (prayer) or needs will come (true)

(2) BELIEF (N) thing believed: TRUST; confidence: HAVE FAITH

The ART of STUDIES, the PROCESS of STUDYING: the PURSUIT of KNOWLEDGE, **WISDOM and UNDERSTANDING** by READING OBSERVATION (PLUS) RESEARCH.

TOPIC: SALVATION and ELECTION MADE SURE..

(1) STUDY YOURSELF APPROVED

We being more noble minded then those in Thessalonica in that we received the WORD with ALL READINESS and **SEARCHED the SCRIPTURES DAILY** to find out whether these things were so.   ACTS 17:10-12

(2) THE TEST OF KNOWING YHWH EL (GOD) OF YISRAEL

Now by this we know that we know HIM if we **KEEP HIS COMMANDMENTS** whoever says I KNOW HIM and does NOT KEEP HIS commandments is a LIAR and the TRUTH IS NOT IN him..   1JOHN 2:3,4

(3) BECOME A WITNESS to our ANOINTED ONE OF YISRAEL

No one has ascended to heaven but HE WHO CAME DOWN FROM HEAVEN which is the SON OF MAN who is in heaven therefore whoever **BELIEVE IN HIM** SHALL NOT PERISH but have eternal life for our FATHER so loved the world that HE GAVE HIS ONLY BEGOTTEN SON that whoever BELIEVES IN HIM should NOT PERISH but have everlasting LIFE.   JOHN 3:13-16

(4) FAITH with EFFORT to WALKING IN THE SPIRIT

IF we believe in the spirit, let us also WALK IN THE SPIRIT, because those who belong to MESSIYAH have CRUCIFIED the FLESH with its PASSIONS and DESIRES for the FRUIT OF THE SPIRIT IS **LOVE, JOY, PEACE, LONGSUFFERING, KINDNESS, GOODNESS, FAITHFULNESS, GENTLENESS, and SELF - CONTROL..**   GALATIANS 5:22-26

SO the things that you read and find (ONLY) to be TRUE IN SCRIPTURE shall we teach and preach to others for this is the CALLING and DUTY OF ALL SAINTS. (TRUST) in the MOST HIGH FOREVER for in YAH the mighty ONE **IS EVERLASTING STRENGTH.**   ISAIAH 26:4

PROPHETIC MESSAGE MINISTRY

AMMISHADDAI
    TRUE
    BELIEVER

COMMANDMENT KEEPERS

TOPIC: **ALL SCRIPTURE** is **GIVEN** by *INSPIRATION* of the **MOSTHIGH**, and **IS** *PROFITABLE for DOCTRINE, for REPROOF, for CORRECTION, for INSPIRATION IN RIGTEOUSNESS...*   2TIMOTHY 3:16
Every word of YHWH is PURE; HE is a SHIELD TO THOSE WHO PUT THEIR TURST IN HIM... DO NOT add to HIS WORDS...   PROVERBS 30:5,6

THIS IS HIS COMMANDMENT: that we believe on the name of HIS SON YAHSHUAH MESSIYAH (JOHN 3:16) and love one another; as HE GAVE US COMMANDMENT..
                    1JOHN 3:23

Having been born again, NOT of CORRUPTIBLE seed but Incorruptible THROUGH the word of the MOSTHIGH which lives and abides FOREVER..   1PETER 1:23

CIRCUMCISION is NOTHING and UNCIRCUMCISION is NOTHING, but KEEPING the COMMANDMENTS of the MOSTHIGH IS WHAT MATTERS.   1CORINTHIANS 7:19
FEAR THE MOSTHIGH and KEEP HIS COMMANDMENTS for this is mans ALL
                    ECCLESIASTES 12:13

Be DILIGENT to present yourself APPROVED to the MOSTHIGH; a worker who does not need be ashamed, rightly **DIVIDING the WORD OF TRUTH..**   2TIMOTHY 2:15
By the **MERCIES** of the MOSTHIGH, you present your BODIES A LIVING SACRIFICE, HOLY, ACCEPTABLE to the MOSTHIGH which is your REASONABLE SERVICE...
                    ROMANS 12:1,2

NO one is good but ONE, that is YHWH (ROMANS 3:23) but if you want to ENTER INTO LIFE, **KEEP the COMMANDMENTS..**   MATTHEW 19:17

WHOEVER therefore breaks one of the LEAST of these COMMMANDMENTS and TEACHES men to do so, SHALL BE CALLED LEAST in the KINGDOM of HEAVEN;
                    MATTHEW 5:19
He who says, I KNOW HIM, (YHWH) and does NOT KEEP HIS COMMANDMENTS, is a liar; and the TRUTH IS NOT IN HIM.   1JOHN 2:4-6

FOR I DELIVERED TO YOU (FIRST) of all that which I also RECEIVED: that MESSIYAH DIED for our SINS according to the SCRIPTURES, and that HE was BURIED, and that HE ROSE AGAIN the THIRD DAY according to the SCRIPTURES...   1CORINTHIANS 15:1-4

KINGDOM PRINCIPLES
PROPHETIC MESSAGE MINISTRY
The ART of STUDIES

AMMISHADDAI
  TRUE
BELIEVER

TOPIC: *HYPOCRISY*.. HOLD your PEACE with me, and let me SPEAK, then let come on me what may! Though he slay me, yet will I TRUST HIM (YHWH) HE also shall be my SALVATION, for a **HYPOCRITE** could not come before HIM...   JOB 13:13-16

For the company of HYPOCRITES will be barren and *FIRE* will consume the TEMPLES OF BRIBERY.   JOB 15:34

The RIGHTEOUS is delivered from TROUBLE, and it comes to the WICKED INSTEAD. the HYPOCRITE with his mouth destroys his neighbor, but through KNOWLEDGE the RIGHTEOUS WILL BE DELIVERED...   PROVERBS 11:8,9

"the MASTER of that servant will come on a day, when he is not looking for HIM and at A HOUR that he is not AWARE OF, and will cut him in two and appoint him his portion with the HYPOCRITES. There shall be WEEPING and GNASHING OF TEETH".. MATTHEW 24:50,51

BEWARE OF THE LEAVEN of the Pharisees, which is HYPOCRISY. For there is nothing covered that will not be revealed, nor hidden that will NOT BE KNOWN. Therefore whatEVER you have spoken in the DARK will be heard in the LIGHT, and what you HAVE SPOKEN in the ear in inner ROOMS, will be PROCLAIMED on the housetops.   LUKE 12:1-3

SO the HYPOCRITE should not reign, lest the people be ENSNARED.   JOB 34:30

NOW THE SPIRIT EXPLICITLY SAYS, that in latter times (some) will depart from the FAITH, giving HEED to DECEIVING SPIRITS and DOCTRINES of DEMONS speaking lies in HYPOCRISY having their OWN CONSCIENCE seared with a hot iron..   1TIMOTHY 4:1,2

Therefore, lay aside ALL MALICE, ALL DECEIT, **HYPOCRISY**, ENVY and ALL EVIL SPEAKING, as new born babes, desire the PRUE MILK of the WORD, that you may grow thereby.   1PETER 2:1-3

WOE to you, scribes and Pharisees, HYPOCRITES for you shut up the KINGDOM OF HEAVEN AGAINST MEN; for you neither go in yourselves, nor do you ALLOW those who are entering in to go..   MATTHEW 23:13

WOE to you, scribes and Pharisees, HYPOCRITES for you are like white washed tombs which indeed APPEAR BEAUTIFUL OUT WARDLY, but inside are full of DEAD MENS BONES and ALL UNCLEANNESS...   even so you also OUTWARDLY APPEAR RIGHTEOUS to men, but indeed you are full of HYPOCRISY and LAWLESSNESS.   MATTHEW 23:27,28

And I say to you, my friends, do not be afraid of those who KILL the body, and after that have NO MORE that they can do. But I will show you WHOM you SHOULD FEAR: FEAR HIM WHO, after HE has KILLED, and has power to CAST into HELL; *YES, I SAY TO YOU, FEAR HIM.*   LUKE 12:4,5

SERPENTS, BROOD of VIPER! how can you ESCAPE the COMDEMNATION OF HELL?
MATTHEW 23:33
PROPHETIC MESSAGE MINISTRY

AMMISHADDAI
   TRUE
   BELIEVER
(1) HYPOCRISY (N) the practice of expressing, BELIEFS, feelings and virtues that one does not PRACTICE or KEEP:

The ART of STUDIES

TOPIC: the value of DILIGENCE.. I call to remembrance my song in the night; I meditate within my HEART, and my spirit makes DILIGENT SEARCH..   PSALM 77:6

THE lazy man does not roast what he took in hunting, but DILIGENCE IS MANS PRECIOUS POSSESSION.   PROVERBS 12:27

PURSUE PEACE with ALL people, and HOLINESS, without which no one will see YHWH; looking DILIGENTLY less anyone FALL SHORT of the GRACE of YHWH; lest any root of bitterness springing up cause trouble, and by this MANY BECOME DEFILED;

                    HEBREWS 12:14,15

LET US therefore be DILIGENT to enter that REST, lest anyone fall according to the same EXAMPLE OF DISOBEDIENCE. For the WORD of YHWH IS LIVING and POWERFUL, and sharper that any TWO - EDGED SWORD, piercing even to the DIVISION of SOUL and SPIRIT, and of joints and marrow, and is a DISCERNER of the THOUGHTS and INTENTS of THE HEART. And there is no creature hidden from HIS SIGHT, but all things are NAKED and OPEN to the eyes of HIM to WHOM we must give account.   HEBREWS 4:11-13

REJOICE, O YOUNG MAN, IN YOUR YOUTH, and let your heart cheer you in the days of your YOUTH; walk in the ways of your heart, and as YOU SEE BEST but KNOW that for all these YHWH will bring you INTO JUDGEMENT. Therefore remove sorrow from your heart, and PUT AWAY EVIL from your FLESH, for childhood and youth are VANITY.

                    ECCLESIASTES 11:9,10

REMEMBER (NOW) your CREATOR, in the days of your YOUTH, before the DIFFICULT DAYS COME, and the years draw near when you say, I have NO PLEASURE IN THEM...

                    ECCLESIASTES 12:1

Cast your bread upon the waters, so you will find it after many days. Give a serving to seven, and also to eight, for you do not know what EVIL WILL BE ON the earth. HE who observes the wind will not sow, and he who regards the clouds will not reap. AS you do not know what is the way of the spirit, or how the bones grow in the womb of her who is with child, so you do not know the WORKS of the MOSTHIGH WHO MAKES EVERYTHING. In the morning sow your seed, and in the evening do not withhold your hand; for you do not know which will PROSPER, EITHER THIS OR THAT, or WHETHER BOTH ALIKE will be GOOD...

                    ECCLESIASTES 11:1,2,4-6

NOW I REJOICE, not that you were made sorry, but that your SORROW LED TO REPENTANCE... FOR you were made sorry in a GODLY MANNER, that you might suffer loss From US in NOTHING. For GODLY SORROW PRODUCES REPENTANCE, LEADING TO SALVATION, not to be REGRETTED; but the sorrow of the world produces DEATH. For OBSERVE THIS VERY THING, that you sorrowed in a GODLY MANNER; what DILIGENCE IT PRODUCED IN YOU, what clearing of yourselves, what indignation, what fear, what vehement desire, what zeal, what vindication! IN ALL THINGS YOU PROVED YOURSELVES TO BE CLEAR IN THIS MATTER...   2CORINTHIANS 7:9-11

BUT as you abound in EVERYTHING - IN FAITH, IN SPEECH, IN KNOWLEDGE, IN ALL DILIGENCE, and in your LOVE for US, see that you abound in GRACE ALSO. I SPEAK not by commandment, but I am testing the SINCERITY OF YOUR LOVE by the DILIGENCE of others..   2CORINTHIANS 8:7,8

AMMISHADDAI   KINGDOM PRINCIPLES

(1) DILIGENCE (N) persistent application to ones work: unceasing EFFORT

TOPIC: **KINDNESS and COURTESY...**   INCLINE your ear and HEAR the words of the wise.   PROVERBS 22:17

LET (LOVE) be with out HYPOCRISY, abhor what is EVIL.. CLING to what is GOOD. Be kindly affectionate to one another; not lagging in DILIGENCE, fervent in SPIRIT, SERVING YHWH.   ROMANS 12:9-11   by PURITY, by KNOWLEDGE, by LONGSUFFERING, by KINDNESS, by the HOLYSPIRIT, by SINCERE LOVE.. 2CORINTHIANS 6:6   SO DO NOT GRIEVE the HOLY SPIRIT OF THE MOSTHIGH by whom (YOU) were SEALED for the day of redemption.. Let ALL BITTERNESS, WRATH, ANGER, LOUD QUARRELING and EVIL SPEAKING be put AWAY from you, with ALL MALICE. BE *KIND* to one another, TENDERHEARTED, FORGIVING one another, even as the MESSIYAH FORGAVE you...
EPHESIANS 4:30-32

Therefore, as the ELECT of YHWH, HOLY and BELOVED, put on tender mercies KINDNESS, HUMILITY, MEEKNESS, LONGSUFFERING, BEARING with ONE ANOTHER, and FORGIVING ONE ANOTHER, if anyone has a complaint against another, even as MESSIYAH FORGAVE you (so) you must do...   COLOSSIANS 3:12,13

FINALLY, ALL of you be on ONE MIND, having compassion for one another love as brothers, be tender hearted, be *COURTEOUS;*   1PETER 3:8

BUT also for this very REASON, giving all diligence, ADD TO your FAITH VIRTUE, to VIRTUE KNOWLEDGE, to KNOWLEDGE SELF - CONTROL, to SELF - CONTROL PERSEVERANCE, to PERSEVERANCE GODLINESS, to GODLINESS brotherly KINDNESS, and to brotherly KINDNESS (LOVE) therefore, brothers, be even more DILIGENT to make your CALL and ELECTION SURE, for if you do these things you will never stumble; so an entrance will be supplied to you abundantly into the everlasting KINGDOM OF THE MOSTHIGH and SAVIOR IMMANUEL MESSIYAH...   2PETER 1:5-11

FOR we OUSELVES were also ONCE FOOLISH, DISOBEDIENT, DECEIVED, serving VARIOUS LUSTS and PLEASURES, living in malice and envy, HATEFUL and hating one another.. BUT when the KINDNESS and the LOVE of IMMANUEL OUR SAVIOUR toward man APPEARED, not by works of righteousness which WE HAVE DONE, but ACCORDING TO HIS MERCY HE SAVED US THROUGH the washing of REGENERATION and RENEWING of the HOLY SPIRIT whom he POURED OUT on us abundantly through YAHSHUAH MESSIYAH our SAVIOUR... this is a FAITHFUL SAYING, and these things I want you to AFFIRM CONSTANTLY, that those who have BELIEVED in YHWH should BE CAREFUL TO MAINTAIN GOOD WORKS. These things ARE GOOD and PROFITABLE to men...
TITUS 3:3-8

KINGDOM PRINCIPLES

AMMISHADDAI   PROPHETIC MESSAGE MINISTRY
   TRUE   the ART of STUDIES
  BELIEVER

(1) KIND (N) friendly, generous, or tenderhearted in spirit.

(2) COURTEOUS (ADJ) marked by consideration toward and respect for another..

46

The ART/Of STUDIES

TOPIC : OBEDIENCE.. For I am not ashamed of the GOSPEL Of MESSIYAH, for it is the POWER Of YHWH to SALVATION for every one who believes, (JOHN 3:16) For the HEBREW first and also for the GENTILE. For in it the RIGHTEOUSNESS Of YHWH is revealed from FAITH to FAITH; as it is written, the just shall live by faith. Which HE promised before through HIS prophets in the HOLY SCRIPTURES, concerning HIS SON YAHSHUAH MESSIYAH who was born of the seed of DAVID according to the flesh, and declared to be the SON Of YHWH with POWER according to the SPIRIT Of HOLINESS by the RESSURRECTION from the DEAD. Through HIM we have received GRACE and APOSTLESHIP for OBEDIENCE to the faith among all NATIONS for HIS NAME. But HE (MESSIYAH) said, more than that, BLESSED are those who hear the WORD Of YHWH and KEEP IT!!

ROMANS 1:16,17 / 1:2-6 / LUKE 11:28

But <u>be doers Of the WORD, and not hearers ONLY</u>, Deceiving yourselves, for if anyone is a hearer of the WORD and NOT a DOER, he is like a man observing his natural face in a mirror; for he observes himself, goes away and immediately forgets what kind of man he was. But he who looks into the perfect LAW Of LIBERTY and CONTINUES IN IT, and is not a forgetful hearer but a doer of the work, this one will be blessed in what he does. Therefore, to him who knows to DO GOOD and DOES NOT DO IT, to him it is SIN..

JAMES 1:22-25 / 4:17

Therefore BE IMITATORS Of YHWH as dear children. Let NO ONE DECEIVE you with empty words, for because of these things the WRATH Of YHWH comes upon the SONS OF DISOBEDIENCE therefore DO NOT BE PARTAKERS with them. Circumcise yourselves to YHWH, and take away the foreskins of your hearts. And KEEP the CHARGE of YHWH your EL; to walk in HIS WAYS, to keep HIS STATUTES, HIS COMMANDMENTS, HIS JUDGMENTS, and HIS TESTIMONIES, as it is written in the LAW Of Moses, that you may prosper in all that you do and wherever you turn; Now therefore, amend your ways and your doings and OBEY the VOICE Of YHWH your EL; then YHWH will relent concerning the DOOM that HE has pronounced against you..

EPHESIANS 5:1,6,7 / JEREMIAH 4:4 / 1KINGS2:3 / JEREMIAH 26:13

Nevertheless they were DISOBEDIENT, and REBELLED against you, cast your LAW behind their backs and killed your prophets, who TESTIFIED AGAINST them to turn them to yourself; and they worked great provocations. Therefore you delivered them into the hand of their enemies, who oppressed them; and in the time of their trouble, when they cried to YOU, you heard from heaven; and according to your abundant mercies you gave them deliverers who saved them from the hand of their enemies. But after they had rest, they again DID EVIL before you. Therefore you left them in the hand of their enemies, so that they had dominion over them; yet when they returned and cried out to you, you heard from heaven; and many times you delivered them according to your mercies, and testified against them, that you might <u>bring them back to your LAW</u>.. Yet they acted PROUDLY, and did not heed YOUR COMMANDMENTS but SIN against YOUR JUDGMENTS, which if a man does, he shall live by them. Nevertheless in YOUR GREAT MERCY you did not utterly consume them nor forsake them: For YOU ARE EL (GOD),

NEHEMIAH 9:26-31

TOPIC: **GOSSIP and MEDDLING..** he who HEEDS the WORD wisely will find GOOD, and WHOever trusts in the MOSTHIGH, **HAPPY is HE**   PROVERBS 16:20   for we hear that there are some who walk among you in a DISORDERLY MANNER, not working at ALL, but are busy bodies...
2THESSALONIANS 3:11

FOR I FEAR UNLEST, WHEN I COME, I SHALL NOT FIND you such as I wish, and I shall be found by you such as you do not WISH; unless there BE CONTENTIONS, JEALOUSIES, OUTBURSTS of WRATH, SELFISH AMBITIONS, BACKBITINGS, WHISPERINGS, CONCEITS, TUMULTS.
2CORINTHIANS 12:20

It is **HONORABLE** for a man to STOP STRIVING, since any FOOL CAN START A QUARREL.
PROVERBS 20:3

HAVING condemnation because they have cast OFF their FIRST FAITH.. And besides they learn to be IDLE, WANDERING ABOUT from house to house and not only idle but also **GOSSIPS** and BUSYBODIES, saying things which they OUGHT NOT...   1TIMOTHY 5:12,13   HE who covers a TRANSGRESSION SEEKS LOVE, but he who repeats a MATTER SEPARATES FRIENDS..
PROVERBS 17:9

A perverse man sows STRIFE, and a *WHISPERER SEPARATES* the best of friends. PROVERBS 16:28 HE who goes about as a TALEBEARER, REVEALS SECRETS; therefore do not ASSOCIATE WITH ONE who flatters with his lips...   PROVERBS 20:19   WHERE there is no wood, the fire goes out; and where there is NO GOSSIP, STRIFE CEASES..   PROVERBS 26:20   WHO EVER guards his mouth and tongue KEEPS HIS SOUL *FROM TROUBLES..*   PROBERBS 21:23   HE who PASSES BY and **MEDDLES IN** a QUARREL not his own, is like one who takes a DOG by the EARS...
PROVERBS 26:17

MY SON, *FEAR the MOSTHIGH* and the KING; do not **ASSOCIATE** with those given to change; for their CALAMITY will rise SUDDENLY, and who knows the ruin those two can bring?
PROVERBS 24:21,22

AND even as they do not like to RETAIN YHWH in their KNOWLEDGE, YHWH GAVE them over to a DEBASED MIND, to do those things which are NOT FITTING; being filled with ALL unrighteousness, who knowing the righteous JUDGMENT of the MOSTHIGH, that those who PRATICE SUCH THINGS are deserving of DEATH, not only those who do the same, but also APPROVE OF THOSE WHO PRACTICE THEM..   ROMANS 1:28-32

BUT let none of you SUFFER AS A MURDERER, A THIEF, and EVILDOER, or as a *MEDDLER* in other peoples MATTERS, yet if anyone suffers as a BELIEVER, LET HIM NOT BE ASHAMED, but let HIM GLORIFY YHWH IN THIS MANNER.   FOR the time has come for JUDGMENT TO BEGIN at the HOUSE of YHWH; and if it BEGINS with US FIRST, what will be the END of THOSE who DO NOT OBEY the gospel of the MOSTHIGH?   1PETER 4:15-17

KINGDOM PRINCIPLES
PROPHETIC MESSAGE MINISTRY
The ART of STUDIES

AMMISHADDAI
  TRUE
  BELIEVER

(1) GOSSIP (N) one who HABITUALLY repeats intimate or private rumors.

(2) MEDDLE (V) to intrude in OTHER peoples BUSINESS or affairs; interfere..

READINGS of INSPIRATION
The ART of STUDIES..
TOPIC: *PLEASURES and LUSTS...* INCLINE YOUR EAR and HEAR the words of the wise.
                                                              PROVERBS 22:17
(SO) we have spent enough of our past time in doing the will of the GENTILES - when we walked in LEWDNESS, LUST, DRUNKENNESS, REVELRIES, DRINKING PARTIES, and ABOMINABLE IDOLATRIES..   1PETER 4:3
THE night is far spent, the day is at hand therefore let us CAST OFF the WORKS OF DARKNESS, and let us put on the *ARMOR OF LIGHT..* let us WALK PROPERLY, as in the day, not in REVELRY and DRUNKENNESS, not in LEWDNESS and **LUST**, NOT IN STRIFE and ENVY.   ROMANS 13:12,13   BETTER is the poor who walks in his INTEGRITY, then one perverse in his ways, THOUGH HE BE RICH.   PROVERBS 28:6   CHOOSING rather to suffer AFFLINCTION with the people of YHWH then enjoy the TEMPORARY PLEASURES OF SIN...   HEBREWS 11:25

BUT KNOW THIS, that in the last days PERILOUS TIMES WILL COME: for men will be LOVERS of THEMSELVES, LOVERS of MONEY, BOASTERS, PROUD, BLASPHEMERS, LOVERS of **PLEASURE** rather then lovers of YHWH. Having a FORM OF EL(GOD) but DENYING HIS POWER... *FROM SUCH PEOPLE TURN AWAY...*   2TIMOTHY 3:1-5

  YOU HAVE LIVED ON THE EARTH in PLEASURE and LUXURY; you have FATTENED your hearts as in a day of slaughter..   JAMES 5:5
YOU will say to your soul, SOUL, you have many goods laid up for many years; TAKE YOUR EASE; eat, drink, and BE MERRY... but YHWH said, FOOL! This night your soul will be REQUIRED of YOU; then whose will those things be which you have provided? (SO) is he who lays up treasure for himself, and is not RICH TOWARD YHWH...   LUKE 12:19-21
DO not overwork to be RICH; because of your own understanding, cease!   PROVERBS 23:4

HE WHO LOVES PLEASURE will be a poor man; he who loves WINE and OIL will not be rich..   PROVERBS 21:17
DO NOT love the world or the things in the world. IF ANYONE LOVES the WORLD the LOVE of the MOSTHIGH is not in him.. FOR all that is in the world - the *LUST* of the FLESH, the LUST of the EYES, and the PRIDE of LIFE - is NOT OF THE MOSTHIGH but is of the world...   1JOHN 2:15,16
THERFORE do not let SIN REIGN in your mortal body, that you should OBEY it in its LUST..
                                                              ROMANS 6:12
        BUT he who LIVES IN PLEASURE is DEAD while HE LIVES...   1TIMOTHY 5:6
                        KINGDOM PRINCIPLES
AMMISHADDAI   the ART of STUDIES...
   TRUE
   BELIEVER

(1) PLEASURES (N) a source of enjoyment, gratification or delight.

(2) LUST (N) an overwhelming craving...

TOPIC: *PRIDE and HAUGHTINESS..*   THE WICKED IN HIS PROUD COUNTENANCE
DOES NOT SEEK YHWH, YHWH IS IN NONE OF HIS THOUGHTS...   PSALM 10:4
THESE THINGS I HAVE WRITTEN TO YOU CONCERNING THOSE WHO TRY TO DECEIVE YOU
But the ANOINTING which you have received from him (YHWH) abides in YOU, and YOU DO NOT
NEED THAT *ANYONE TEACH YOU;* but as the same ANOINTING TEACHES YOU CONCERNING
ALL THINGS..   1JOHN 2:26,27   the **PRIDE** OF YOUR HEART HAS DECEIVED YOU, YOU
WHO DWELL IN THE CLEFTS OF THE ROCK, whose habitation is high; you who say in your heart,
Who will bring me down to the ground? Though you set your nest among the STARS, FROM THERE I
WILL BRING YOU DOWN, SAYS YHWH...   OBADIAH 1:3,4   TALK NO MORE SO VERY
PROUDLY; LET NO ARROGANCE COME FROM YOUR MOUTH, for YHWH IS THE MIGHTY
ONE of KNOWLEDGE; and BY HIM ACTIONS ARE WEIGHED...   1SAMUEL 2:3
WHOEVER GUARDS HIS MOUTH and TONGUE KEEPS HIS SOUL from TROUBLES...
                                                                   PROVERBS 21:23
PRIDE GOES BEFORE DESTRUCTION and A **HAUGHTY SPIRIT** BEFORE A FALL...
                                                                   PROVERBS 16:18
A HAUGHTY LOOK, A PROUD HEART, and THE plowing of the WICKED are SIN PROVERBS 21:4

I (YHWH) WILL PUNISH THE WORLD for its EVIL, and the WICKED for their INIGUITY; I will halt
The ARROGANCE of the PROUD, and WILL LAY LOW the HAUGHTINESS OF THE TERRIBLE
                                                                   ISAIAH 13:11

THESE SIX THINGS YHWH HATES, YES, SEVEN ARE AN ABOMINATION TO HIM..A PROUD
LOOK, A LYING TONGUE, HANDS THAT SHED INNOCENT BLOOD   PROVERBS 6:16-19
The proud looks of man shall be humbled the haughtiness of man shall be bowed down and YHWH
ALONE SHALL BE EXALTED IN THAT DAY...   ISAIAH2:11
YOU will save the humble people; but your eyes are on the HAUGHTY, that you may bring them down
                                                                   2 SAMUEL 22:28
BEHOLD, I AM AGAINST YOU, O MOST HAUGHTY ONE! SAYS YHWH EL OF HOSTS; for your
Day has come, the TIME THAT I WILL PUNISH YOU.. The MOST PROUD SHALL STUMBLE and
FALL, and NO ONE WILL RAISE HIM UP; I WILL KINDLE A FIRE IN HIS CITIES, and IT WILL
DEVOUR ALL AROUND HIM...   JEREMIAH 50:31,32
YHWH OF HOST has purposed it, to bring to DISHONOR the PRIDE OF ALL GLORY.. ISAIAH 23:9
The rich mans WEALTH is his STRONG CITY, and like a HIGH WALL in his OWN ESTEEM...
                                                                   PROVERBS 18:11
EVERY ONE PROUD IN HEART IS AN ABOMINATION TO YHWH...   PROVERBS16:5
AFTER ALL THIS, if you do not OBEY ME, (YHWH) then I will PUNISH YOU SEVEN TIMES more
For your SINS, I will break the PRIDE OF YOUR POWER and your STRENGTH shall be spent in VAIN
                                                                   LEVITICUS 26:18-20
THE LABOR OF THE RIGHTEOUS LEADS TO LIFE, the wages of the wicked (to) sin BUT HE who
REFUSES CORRECTION goes astray...   PROVERBS 10:16,17
THE RIGHTEOUS WILL NEVER BE REMOVED, BUT the wicked will not INHABIT THE EARTH
The mouth of the RIGHTEOUS BRINGS FORTH WISDOM, but the perverse TONGUE WILL BE CUT
OUT... THE lips of the RIGHTEOUS KNOWS WHAT IS ACCEPTABLE..   PROVERBS 10:30-32
                         READINGS OF INSPIRATION

AMMISHADDAI
   TRUE
   BELIEVER
HAUGHTY (A) proud; arrogant; disdainful
PROUD (A) SELF-RESPECTING: ARROGANT

TOPIC: BIBLICAL WORK ETHIC; IN the sweat of your face you shall eat bread..

GENESIS 3:19

For you yourselves know how you ought to follow us, for we were NOT DISORDERLY among you; NOR did we eat anyone's bread FREE of CHARGE, but worked with **LABOR and TOIL** night and day, that we might not be a burden to any of you, for even when we were with you, we *COMMANDED YOU THIS:* IF anyone will not work, neither shall he eat.

2THESSALONIANS 3:7-10

That you also *ASPIRE TO LEAD A QUIET LIFE,* to mind your own business, and to work with your own hands, as we COMMANDED you, that you may walk properly toward those who are outside, and that you may lack nothing.   1THESSALONIANS 4:11,12   I therefore, the prisoner of YHWH, beseech you to **WALK WORTHY** of the **CALLING** with which you were CALLED..

EPHESIANS 4:1

" And as you go, PREACH, saying ' THE KINGDOM OF HEAVEN IS AT HAND.' "Heal the sick, CLEANSE the lepers, raise the dead, CAST OUT DEMONS. Freely you HAVE RECEIVED, freely GIVE. For a **WORKER IS WORTHY OF HIS FOOD.**   MATTHEW 10:7-10

Let the elders who RULE WELL be counted WORTHY OF DOUBLE HONOR, *ESPECIALLY THOSE WHO LABOR IN THE WORD and DOCTRINE..* for the Scripture says, " You shall NOT muzzle an ox while it treads out the grain," and " *THE LABORER IS WORTHY OF HIS WAGES."*

1TIMOTHY 5:17,18

DO WE HAVE NO RIGHT TO EAT AND DRINK? Do we have NO right to take along a BELIEVING wife, who ever goes to war at his own EXPENSE? Who plants a vineyard and does NOT eat of its FRUIT? Or who tends a flock and does NOT drink of the MILK of the FLOCK? Do I say these things as a mere man? Or does not the **LAW say the same ALSO?** For it is written in the LAW of Moses, " YOU SHALL NOT MUZZLE AN OX WHILE IT TREADS OUT THE GRAIN." *IS IT OXEN YHWH IS CONCERNED ABOUT?* Or does HE say it ALTOGETHER for our SAKES? IF we have sown SPIRITUAL THINGS for you, is it a great thing if we REAP your MATERIAL THINGS?   1CORINTHIANS 9:4,5,7-11

HERE is what I have seen: it is good and fitting for one to eat and drink, and to enjoy the good of <u>ALL HIS LABOR</u> in which he TOILS under the sun all the days of his life which YHWH gives him; for it is HIS HERITAGE..   ECCLESIASTES 5:18

And also that every man should eat and drink and enjoy the GOOD OF ALL HIS LABOR - it is the GIFT OF YHWH.   ECCLESIASTES 3:13

NOTING IS BETTER FOR A MAN THAN that he should eat and drink, and that his soul should ENJOY GOOD in his **LABOR.** This also, I saw, was from the HAND OF the MOSTHIGH;   ECCLESIASTES 2:24

PROPHETIC MESSAGE MINISTRY
   AMMISHADDAI

TOPIC: FLATTERY; let ME NOT, I pray show partiality to anyone; NOR let me **FLATTER**, any man.   JOB 32:21,22

These are grumblers, complainers, walking according to their own LUST; and they mouth GREAT swelling words, **FLATTERING** people to gain ADVANTAGE;   JUDE 1:16

They speak IDLY everyone with HIS NEIGHBOR; with FLATTERING LIPS and a inconsistent MIND they speak, may the MOSTHIGH cut off all FLATTERING lips, and the TONGUE that SPEAKS PROUD things,   PSALM 12:2,3

For our exhortation did NOT come form ERROR or UNCLEANNESS, NOR was it in DECEIT, so we SPEAK NOT PLEASING men, but THE MOSTHIGH who test our hearts. Neither at any time did we use FLATTERING WORDS - YHWH IS WITNESS..
                                                    1THESSALONIANS 2:3-5

For you are NOT the EL (GOD) who takes pleasure in wickedness, *YOU HATE ALL WORKERS OF INIQUITY..* FOR there is no UPRIGHTNESS and FAITHFULNESS in their mouth; their inward part is DESTRUCTION; they FLATTER with their TONGUE. PRONOUNCE THEM GUILTY, O YHWH! Let them fall by their own COUNSELS;
                                                      PSALM 5:4-6,9,10

A men who FLATTERS his neighbor spreads a net for his feet. By transgression (SIN) an EVIL man is SNARED,   PROVERBS 29:5,6

Whoever digs a pit will fall into it, and he who rolls a stone will have it roll BACK ON HIM, A LYING TONGUE hates those who are crushed by it, and a **FLATTERING** mouth works RUIN..   PROVERBS 26:28

For you have hidden their heart form UNDERSTANDING; HE who speaks FLATTERY to his friends, even the eyes of his children will fail..   JOB 17:4,5

NOW I URGE YOU, BROTHERS, NOTE THOSE who cause divisions and offenses, contrary to the DOCTRINE which you LEARNED, and AVOID THEM: For those who are such DO NOT serve our IMMANUEL MESSIYAH YAHSHUAH, but their own belly, and by smooth words and FLATTERING speech DECEIVE the hearts of the simple;
                                                      ROMANS 16:17,18

PROPHETIC MESSAGE MINISTRY
   KINGDOM PRINCIPLES

AMMISHADDAI
   TRUE
   BELIEVER

        FLATTER (V) compliment or praise insincerely; DISPLAY to advantage..

TOPIC: *FRAUD and DECEIT..* THE REMNANT OF ISRAEL shall do NO unrighteousness, and speak NO LIES, NOR shall a **DECEITFUL TONGUE** be found in their mouth;
ZEPHANIAH 3:13

For " he who would love life and see good days, let him REFRAIN his tongue form EVIL, and his lips from speaking **DECEIT**. let him turn away from evil and do GOOD; let him seek peace and PURSUE IT..
1PETER 3:10,11

He who works DECEIT shall NOT DWELL within my house; he who TELLS LIES shall not continue in MY PRESENCE.
PSALM 101:7

The wicked in his PROUD countenance does NOT SEEK YHWH; YHWH is in NONE of his THOUGHTS.. His mouth is FULL OF CURSING and **DECEIT** and OPPRESSION; under his tongue is TROUBLE and iniquity (SIN)
PSALM 10:4,7

For those who are such, DO NOT SERVE our *IMMANUEL MESSIYAH YAHSHUAH..*
ROMANS 16:18

Hold me up, and I shall be SAFE, and I shall OBSERVE your STATUES <u>continually</u>: you reject all those who stray form you r statues, for their *DECEIT IS FALSEHOOD..*
PSALM 119:118

Bread gained by DECEIT IS SWEET to a man, afterward his mouth will be FILLED with gravel; DO NOT be a WITNESS AGAINST your neighbor without CAUSE, for would you DECEIVE with your lips?
PROVERBS 20:17/24:28

For you (YHWH) are NOT the EL (GOD) who takes pleasure in WICKEDNESS, NOR shall evil dwell with you. You HATE workers of iniquity (SIN) you shall destroy those who speak FALSEHOOD; for there is NO FAITHFULNESS in their mouth;
PSALM 5:4-6,9,10

" *TAKE HEED THAT NO ONE DECEIVES YOU,* "   MARK 13:5,6

Let no one CHEAT you of your REWARD, taking delight in **FALSE** humility and worship of angels, intruding into those things which he has NOT SEEN,
COLOSSIANS 2:18

IN CONCLUSION: can any one HIDE himself in SECRET PLACES. So I shall not SEE him? "says YHWH; " DO I NOT FILL heaven and earth?" says YHWH: " I have heard what the prophets have said who PROPHESY **LIES** IN MY NAME, saying, 'I have dreamed, I have dreamed!' " How long will this be in the heart of the prophets who PROPHESY LIES? Indeed they are prophets of **DECEIT** of their own heart, " Who try to make MY people FORGET MY NAME by their dreams which everyone tells his neighbor as their forefathers forgot MY NAME for Baal (Jesus, Jehovah, Allah, Buddha, Hail Mary, master farad Mohammad, and many more PAGAN DEITIES)
JEREMIAH 23:23-27

Who is the man who DESIRES LIFE, and loves many days, that he may SEE GOOD? Keep your tongue from EVIL, and your lips from speaking **DECEIT**.. *DEPART FROM EVIL and DO GOOD; SEEK PEACE and PURSUE IT..*
PSALM 34:12-14

PROPHETIC MESSAGE MINISTRY
   KINGDOM PRINCIPLES

AMMISHADDAI

FRAUD (N) deceit, trickery; DECEPTION;
DECEIT (N) fraud; dishonest action; TRICK

TOPIC: KNOWING the WILL of הוהי EL (GOD) of YISRAEL; WE must be RENEWED of the mind spiritually FILLED BELIEVERS of the word who desires to know and do the PERFECT WILL OF YHWH, allowing the MOSTHIGH to take control of our LIFE and make us COMPLETE IN EVERY GOOD WORK to do HIS WILL, because YHWH has a plan for our life, he did not give you HOPE of SALVATION, to let you go your way and make your own DECISIONS ACCORDING to your carnal NATURE, but on the CONTRARY HE gives the BELIEVER A RENEWING of the mind, to COMBAT the old NATURE of our sinful (WAYS) through HIS DIVINE POWER through KNOWLEDGE of HIM WHO CALLED US by glory and virtue;   2PETER 1:3,4

But to the natural man who does NOT BELIEVE cannot RECEIVE the things of the SPIRIT OF the MOSTHIGH, for they are FOOLISHNESS to him, nor can he know because they are SPIRITUAL **RIGHT and WRONGS..**   1CORINTHIANS 2:13,14

Sort of speak, sort of say to the ONES WHO ARE PERISHING, SPIRITUAL THINGS are FOOLISHNESS;   TRUE   SO the question must be ANSWERED how do we know the PERFECT WILL OF the MOSTHIGH for our life? YOU MUST SINCERELY DESIRE to do our ABBA'S WILL knowing this becomes an act of **FAITH IN HIS WORDS**, therefore the JUST SHALL LIVE BY FAITH, but if anyone draws back, the MOSTHIGH HAS NO PLEASURE in him.   HEBREWS 10:38,39

"SO THIS LEAVES US WITH THE CONCLUSION TO A FACT"

(1) WE must search the scriptures from beginning to end if we are to know the MOSTHIGH'S WILL for our life, with READINESS IN RECEIVING HIS WORD seeking daily to find out if these things are so;   ACTS 17:11,12

Through the studies of HIS (YHWH'S) WORD, will equip us to know and live out his PERFECT PLAN and CALLING FOR OUR LIFE.   TRUE

(2) IF you indeed SINCERELY DESIRE to know the WILL OF YHWH, you must RECOGNIZE the teaching and ministry of the INDWELLING HOLY SPIRIT, for HE COMMUNICATES with our SPIRIT always in HARMONY WITH SCRIPTURES assuring us that we are the children of the MOSTHIGH
                                                                          ROMANS 8:15,16

BECAUSE when were not sure of the MOSTHIGH'S WILL in our daily decisions we can ALL WAYS **TRUST the INDWELLING HOLY SPIRIT** to reveal his perfect will because he INTERCEDES for the BELIEVER according to the WILL OF YHWH...   ROMANS 8:26-28

KNOWING when HE the SPIRIT OF TRUTH has come HE will guide you into ALL TRUTH, for HE will not speak on his own AUTHORITY but will speak whatever he hears and will tell you things to come.
                                                                          JOHN 16:13

THROUGH the SCRIPTURES the HOLY SPIRIT also leads us into ALL TRUTH, we need to know about YHWH'S will for our lives, the HOLY SPIRIT OF YHWH REVEALED in the SCRIPTURES having made known to us the MYSTERY of HIS WILL according to his GOOD PLEASURE which HE PURPOSED IN HIMSELF   EPHESIANS 1:9

(3) IN CLOSING, we MUST READ the outward signs of the MOSTHIGH'S PROVIDENCE knowing if an individual is living in the MOSTHIGH'S PERFECT PLAN, YHWH'S WILL open doors of SERVICE, that no one can close or HE WILL CLOSE DOORS that no one can OPEN.   2CORINTHIANS 2:12

For the MOSTHIGH does use outward CIRCUMSTANCES to REVEAL HIS WILL to us, because if you truly DESIRE to serve YHWH in a job, or business of choice and the door is CLOSED don't try to FORCE IT OPEN, yet learn to wait on OUR SAVIOR, and HE SHALL DIRECT our path;
                                                                          PROVERBS 3:5,6

BECAUSE the MOSTHIGH WILL CAUSE ever thing to work together for our SPIRITUAL GOOD in the END.   ROMANS 8:28

PROPHETIC MESSAGE MINISTRY
AMMISHADDAI   COMMANDMENT KEEPERS

TOPIC: I AM (YHWH) in the midst of YISRAEL..
WE are one in the spirit we are one in the blood YES they KNOW WE ARE HEBREWS by
YHWH'S LOVE.   JOEL 2:27-32

SEMITIC/PROPHETIC STYLE OF RHYME

Having the NATURE of PROPHECY these have the least possible degree of STYLISTIC change. With short sentences and simple coordinating conjunctions, modern day (HEBREWS) shall contribute impart to forming a VIVID DESCRIPTION or to make KNOWN with the words that we SPEAK as a REPRESENTATION for modern day EVENTS...

THESE FEATURES SHALL INCLUDE: PARALLELISM and RHYTHMS with special constructions; together with **PARABLES** will become a large extent in modern day (HEBREW) POETRY as found in the PSALMS/LAW of the prophets (OT) sort of speak sort of say for in the last day the prophet would give a VIVID EXPRESSION that would be STRIKINGLY EFFECTIVE when TEACHING through the **SEMITIC/PROPHETIC** style of rhyme.

What shall I profit you UNLESS I SPEAK to you either by REVELATION, by KNOWLEDGE, by PROPHESYING, or by TEACHING?   1CORINTHIANS 14:6

MY SOUL clings to the dust for revive me, according to the WORD was a must. I think about my ways but then I turn my mind SPIRIT and **SOUL** to YHWH'S TESTIMONIES OF OLD, BEFORE MY AFFLICTION I went ASTRAY with out the **TRUE WAY**, but now I have kept your word for my AFFLICTION has become very MUCH revive me "O" MOSTHIGH according to your WORD for it is my (CLUCTH) this is my comfort IN AFFLICTION for YHWH'S WORD has given me LIFE WITHOUT ADDICTION. You are the extent of my ALL "O" MOSTHIGH today I CRIE, for I keep your WORDS OF YOUR **LAW** until the day I DIE, AWAITING, LOOKING SOON, to new birth MEDITATION to the HEAVENS, SKYS ABOVE the earth.

YET HEAR NOW, O YISRAEL MY SERVANT, and YAHUDAH
WHOM I HAVE CHOSEN..   ISAIAH 44:1

KNOWING WE ARE ONE IN THE SPIRIT WE ARE ONE IN THE BLOOD, YES THEY KNOW WE ARE HEBREWS BY YHWH'S LOVE...

COMMANDMENT KEEPERS
READING of INSPIRATIONS

AMMISHADDAI
   TRUE
  BELIEVER

GRACE to you and peace from YHWH the MOSTHIGH FATHER (ABBA) of our MESSIYAH IMMANUEL who gave HIS SON for our SINS, that HE might DELIVER us from this PRESENT EVIL AGE, according to the will of the MOSTHIGH our FATHER to whom GLORY BE **FOREVER and EVER..**

TOPIC: A **CURSED** PEOPLE, **PROMISED TO BE RESTORED**   Our skin was black as an oven because of the FAMINE.   LAMENTATIONS 5:10   WE shall fall by the edge of the sword and be led away CAPTIVE INTO ALL NATIONS and YAHRUSALEM will be trampled by GENTILES until times of the GENTILES are COMPLETE.   LUKE 21:24   AND the MOSTHIGH will take you back to BONDAGE AGAIN with ships by the way of which I say to you and the MOSTHIGH will SCATTER you among ALL PEOPLES and AMONG THOSE NATIONS you will find no rest while your LIFE WILL HANG IN DOUBT...   DEUTERONOMY 28:64-68   A NATION whom you have not known shall eat the FRUIT of your LAND and the produce of your LABOR and you shall be only **OPPRESSED and CURSED CONTINUALLY.**   DEUTERONOMY 28:33   The MOSTHIGH will make the MEMORY OF YOU to cease from among MEN;   DEUTERONOMY 32:26   FOR IT IS WRITTEN: **CURSED** IS EVERYONE who hang from a tree.   GALATIANS 3:13
NOW your APPEARANCE IS BLACKER THEN SOOT; we got our bread at the RISK OF OUR LIFE..
OUR forefather sinned but now are NO MORE, so we bear THEIR INIQUITIES (SINS)
                                 LAMENTATIONS 4:8/5:7,9
BUT THIS IS US, a people robbed and plundered; all of us are snared in holes, and we are hidden in PRISON HOUSES for plunder and NO ONE says " **RESTORE.**"   ISAIAH 42:22

THE MOSTHIGH KNOWS YOUR WORKS, TRIBULATIONS and POVERTY, but you are RICH; the MOSTHIGH KNOWS the BLASPHEMY of those who say they are JEWS (HEBREWS) but are NOT.
                                 REVELATIONS 2:9
LOOK AND BEHOLD OUR REPROACH! our inheritance has BEEN TURNED OVER TO ALIENS and our HOUSES TO FOREIGNERS;   LAMENTATIONS 5:1,2
Sort of speak, sort of say; ALL THESE CURSES SHALL COME UPON US and PURSUE and OVERTAKE US until we are destroyed, because we did not OBEY THE VOICE OF the MOSTHIGH your EL (GOD) To keep HIS COMMANDMENTS and HIS STATUTES which HE COMMANDED US and it shall be upon US FOR A **SIGN and a WONDER** and on our DESCENDANTS FOREVER   DEUTERONOMY 28:45,46

NOW when IT COMES to pass when ALL these things come upon you the **BLESSING** and the **CURSE** and you CALL them to MIND among all the NATIONS where the MOSTHIGH your EL has driven you and YOU RETURN to the MOSTHIGH your EL (GOD) and OBEY HIS VOICE you and your children with ALL YOUR HEART and all your SOUL that the MOSTHIGH your EL will BRING YOU BACK from CAPTIVITY and have COMPASSION ON YOU and gather you AGAIN from all the nations where THE MOSTHIGH your EL HAS SCATTERED you...   DEUTERONOMY 30:1-3
SO **DILIGENTLY OBEY** the VOICE of the MOSTHIGH to **OBSERVE CAREFULLY** ALL HIS COMMANDMENTS so HE will set you HIGH ABOVE ALL NATIONS of the earth and all the BLESSINGS SHALL COME UPON YOU and overtake you, because you OBEY THE VOICE OF THE MOSTHIGH EL OF YISRAEL;   DEUTERONOMY 28:1,2

PROPHETIC MESSAGE MINISTRY
READING of INSPIRATION
COMMANDMENT KEEPERS

AMMISHADDAI
  TRUE
  BELIEVER

   The ART of STUDIES: the PROCESS of STUDYING, the PURSUIT of KNOWLEDGE, WISDOM and UNDERSTANDING by READING OBSERVATION PLUS RESEARCH; he who has ear let him hear.. *BLESSED IS HE WHO READS and THOSE WHO LISTEN to the WORD OF THIS PROPHECY and KEEP THOSE THINGS WHICH ARE WRITTEN:*

JAMES 5:7,8

For if we sin willfully after we have RECEIVED the KNOWLEDGE of the **TRUTH** there NO LONGER REMAIN A SACRIFICE for SINS..   HEBREWS 10:26

For YHWH is not the AUTHOR OF CONFUSION but of **PEACE** as in all the churches of the SAINTS, let all things be DONE DECENTLY and in ORDER..   1CORINTHIANS 14:40

The prophet DANIEL shut up the word and sealed the book UNTIL THE TIME OF THE END, many shall run to and fro and KNOWLEDGE SHALL BE INCREASED.   DANIEL 12:4

REVELATION of YAHSHUAH MESSIYAH which the MOSTHIGH gave HIM to show HIS servants things which must SHORTLY TAKE PLACE;   REVELATION 1:1-3

THEN HE said unto me, DO NOT seal the words of this **PROPHECY** of the book for the TIME IS AT HAND..   REVELATION 22:9,10

SO what shall I profit you UNLESS I speak to you either by REVELATION by KNOWLEDGE by PROPHESYING or by TEACHING?   1CORINTHIANS 14:6

THIS is the TESTIMONY: that the MOSTHIGH has given us for ETERNAL LIFE this LIFE is within HIS SON moreover who ever has HIS SON HAVE LIFE..   1JOHN 5:10-12

Now he who would KEEP YHWH'S COMMANDMENTS abides in HIM and YHWH in him, by this we know that YHWH ABIDES in US by the SPIRIT whom HE has given us, so mighty beloved DO NOT BELIEVE EVERY SPIRIT, but test that SPIRIT whether they are of the MOSTHIGH, for look around many FALSE PROPHETS have gone out in the world..

1JOHN 3:24/4:1,2

READINGS of INSPIRATION
YAHUDAH IN TODAY'S TIME, PROPHETIC MESSAGE MINISTRY

AMMISHADDAI
   TRUE
   BELIEVER

MOREOVER you shall select from ALL the people ABLE MEN, such as FEAR YHWH, men of **TRUTH**, HATING COVETOUSNESS; and place SUCH over them to be RULERS; and let them JUDGE the people at all times. " IF you do this thing, and YHWH so COMMANDS you, then you will be able to ENDURE, and all this people will also go to THEIR PLACE IN PEACE."   EXODUS 18:21-23

   TOPIC: *NATION COMING OUT FROM UNDER A NATION;* DISTRIBUTION OF POWER LEVELS OF **AUTHORITY** NEED BE ESTABLISHED..   DEUTERONOMY 1:13-15
To bring us back to YHWH EL (GOD) of our forefathers then we must SET JUDGES in the land, throughout to STRENGTHEN and SECURE the HOUSE OF YISRAEL city by city;
                                                  2CHRONICLES 19:4,5
With the **LAWS of YHWH** to READ and AGREED upon in PUBLIC ADDRESSES BY ELDERS (ZAKEN) JUDGES/OFFICERS to direct this course of government;   JOSHUA 8:34,35   THUS shall we build on the ROCK   LUKE 6:46-49   THE rebuilding of the city, then can it only manifest through the FIRST and SECOND LAW of them ALL.   MATTHEW 22:34-40   AND then shall the mountains drip with SWEET WINE an all the hills shall flow with it..   AMOS 9:11-15   SO today we are BLESSED with NEW WINE so now it is time to get a NEW BOTTLE so all who BELIEVE WILL FOLLOW   (TRUE)   SO wake up, an understand for no longer can we stay asleep not willing to take the NECESSARY STEPS to cover all area's and LAWS OF THE MOSTHIGH, first and foremost we most LOVE YOUR NEIGHBOR AS YOURSELF   (TRUE)   You shall not hate your brother in your HEART;   LEVITICUS 19:17,18   BUT put him as yourself in your start to INVEST or PUT TO EFFECT the establishment of the LOWER STRUGGLING brother FIRST financially or economically to GATHER WITH SELF the work of TRUTH that needs to be done to REBUILD the CITY..
   STATE
    REGIONAL
     NATIONAL..
AND then shall the eyes of the blind be opened an the ears of the DEATH SHALL BE UNSTOPPED.
                                                  ISAIAH 35:5-10
So then we are TOGETHER IN THE AREAS OF AGREEMENT to AGREE
    EDUCATION --- *LEADERSHIP*
    HEALTH --- *ECONOMICS*
BECOME self sufficient to the COMMUNITY and to our self...   Question? Who profits from these areas? the NATION OF YISRAEL and the CHURCH IN MESSIYAH... And those whom come UP WITH THE BLESSED IDEAS to come together as ONE WHOLE;   1CORINTHIANS 1:10,11

NOW ALL WHO **BELIEVE** ARE TOGETHER, having all things in COMMON, DIVIDING AMONG ALL, as anyone having need..   CONTINUE DAILY WITH ONE ACCORD   ACTS 2:44-47
IN HARMONY with ONE MIND and ONE PURPOSE, SO for now we as a people NEED to FORTIFY the cities being the proper ORDER to working our way up, so I say in the SPIRIT OF FAITH and LOVE in 3 DAYS can the city be built.   (TRUE)   PEACE TO THE BROTHERS and LOVE WITH FAITH from the MOSTHIGH and IMMANUEL YAHSHUAH. GRACE be with all those who LOVE our MESSIYAH in sincerity   AMEN

PROPHETIC MESSAGE MINISTRY

     AMMISHADDAI
        TRUE
     BELIEVER

TOPIC: **PROPHECY, PROPAGATION and OBSERVATION** to the end of the AGE, and the SIGNS of the TIMES; SO the world now WORSHIPED the DRAGON who gave AUTHORITY to the BEAST and they WORSHIPED the BEAST, saying who is like the beast? Who is able to make war with HIM? He is given AUTHORITY TO CONTINUE for FORTY - TWO months (3yrs 5mths) IT was also granted to him, to MAKE WAR with the saints and to overcome THEM and authority was also given him over every tribe TONGUE and NATION all who dwell on the earth will worship him whose NAME HAVE NOT BEEN WRITTEN IN THE BOOK OF LIFE of the LAMB slain from the foundation of the world.

REVELATION 14:3-17

And then the MOSTHIGH will give power to HIS TWO **WITNESSES** so they shall PROPHESY one thousand two hundred and sixty days (3yrs 4mths) clothed in sackcloth these are the TWO OLIVE TREES and the TWO LAMP STANDS STANDING BEFORE the god of the earth, these TWO HAVE **POWER** to shut heaven up so no rain falls in the days of their PROPHECY and to STRIKE the EARTH with ALL PLAGUES as often as they DESIRE;

REVELATION 11:3-14

Now a GREAT SIGN APPEARED IN HEAVEN: a woman clothed with the SUN with the MOON under HER feet, and on HER head a garland of TWELVE STARS SHE bore a male child who was to RULE ALL NATIONS with a rod of iron and her child was caught up to YHWH and HIS THRONE, then the woman FLED INTO the WILDERNESS where she has a place PREPARED by YHWH that HE should feed HER there one thousand two hundred and sixty days (3yrs 4mths) Woe to the inhabitants of the earth and the sea for the DEVIL HAS COME having great wrath, because he knows that he has a SHORT TIME!! But the WOMAN is given TWO WINGS OF A GREAT EAGLE so she may FLY into the WILDERNESS to her place where she is NOURISHED FOR A TIME and TIMES and HALF A TIME from the PRESENCE of the serpent so the dragon being ENRAGED with the woman went to make war with the rest of her offspring WHO KEEP THE COMMANDMENTS OF YHWH and have the **TESTIMONY of IMMANUEL**   REVELATION 12:1-6/12:13-17

WORD to the WISE, SOUL FOOD for THOUGHT KNOWING if anyone worship the beast and his image and receives HIS MARK on his forehead or in his hand HE HIMSELF shall also drink of the WINE OF THE WRATH OF YHWH, he shall be tormented with FIRE and BRIMSTONE in the presence of the HOLY ANGELS and in the presence of the LAMB and the smoke of their torment ascends FOREVER and EVER and they have NO REST day or night who worship the BEAST AND HIS IMAGE and whoever receives the MARK OF HIS NAME, here is the **PATIENCE** of the saints who KEEP THE COMMANDMENTS OF YHWH the MOSTHIGH and the FAITH OF IMMANUEL   REVELATION 14:1-12

SO we see the unclean SPIRITS coming out of the mouth of the DRAGON, out of the mouth of the BEAST, and out of the mouth of the FALSE PROPHET for they are SPIRITS OF DEMONS performing signs which go out to the KINGS OF THE WHOLE WORLD to gather them to the battle of the GREAT DAY OF THE MOSTHIGH ELSHADDAI to the place called in HEBREW, ARMAGEDDON;   REVELATION 16:13-16

PROPHETIC MESSAGE MINISTRY

אממסמאלדא

TOPIC: **the ART of STUDIES**; the PROCESS of STUDING, the PURSUIT of KNOWLEDGE, WISDOM and UNDERSTANDING by READING, OBSERVATION (PLUS) RESEARCH, he who has ear let him hear. NOW he who would KEEP YHWH COMMANDMENTS, abides in HIM and YHWH in him by this WE KNOW that YHWH ABIDES in US by the SPIRIT whom HE has given US so mighty beloved DO NOT BELIEVE every SPIRIT but TEST the SPIRIT whether they are of the MOSTHIGH, for look around *MANY FALSE PROPHETS,* have gone out in the world..   1JOHN 3:24/4:1,2

FOR there is a remnant of certain (HEBREWS) who DO NOT SERVE your gods, or worship the GOLDEN IMAGES   DANIEL 3:12,13

NEVER AGAIN, depend on him who DEFEATED you for the REMNANT will return YES THE REMNANT OF YAHCOB (YISRAEL) to the MIGHTY YHWH   ISAIAH 10:20,21

FOR THE TESTIMONY of YAHSHUAH is the SPIRIT OF PROPHESY. WORSHIP YHWH
REVELATION 19:10
THIS is the TESTIMONY: that the MOSTHIGH has given US for **ETERNAL LIFE** this LIFE IS WITHIN HIS SON sort of speak sort of say WHO EVER HAS HIS SON have LIFE..
1JOHN 5:10-12
SO what shall I profit you unless I speak to you either by **REVELATION** by **KNOWLEDGE** by **PROPHESYING** or by **TEACHING**..   1CORINTHIANS 14:6

BUT the prophet DANIEL shut up the word and SEALED the BOOK until the time of the END many shall RUN to and FRO and KNOWLEDGE SHALL BE INCREASED.   DANIEL 12:4

THEN HE SAID UNTO ME, do not SEAL the WORDS of this PROPHESY of the book for the TIME IS AT HAND.   REVELATION 22:9,10

REVELATION of YAHSHUAH MESSIYAH which the MOSTHIGH GAVE HIM to show HIS servants things which MUST SHORTLY TAKE (PLACE)   REVELATION 1:1-3

BLESSED IS HE WHO READS and those who LISTEN to the WORD OF THIS PROPHECY and KEEP THOSE THINGS which are WRITTEN IN IT; for the time is near therefore be patient brothers until the coming of the LAMB is at hand ESTABLISH your HEARTS.   JAMES 5:7,8

FOR IF WE SIN WILLFULLY after WE have received the KNOWLEDGE of the TRUTH there (NO) LONGER remain a SACRIFICE for SINS   HEBREWS 10:26

FOR YOU ALL CAN PROPHESY ONE by ONE that all may learn and all may be encouraged
1CORINTHIANS 14:31
SO IF ANYONE thinks HIMSELF to be a prophet or spiritual let him ACKNOWLEDGE that the things which I write to you **BE TRUE**, the COMMANDMENTS of YHWH   1CORINTHIANS 14:37

FOR YHWH is NOT the AUTHOR OF CONFUSION, but of PEACE as in all the CHURCHES OF THE SAINTS let all things be done decently and IN ORDER   1CORINTHIANS 14:40
SO remind them of these things, CHARGE THEM BEFORE YHWH not to strive about WORDS for it is no PROFIT and a ruin to the HEARERS   2TIMOTHY 2:14,15

AMMISHADDAI   PROPHETIC MESSAGE MININSTY
TRUE
BELIEVER

TOPIC: TO MINISTER IN A NATION OF MINISTERS..

The MYSTERY OF 7 STARS an 7 LAMPSTANDS. The 7 STARS are ANGELES OF the 7 CHURCHES
and the 7 LAMPSTANDS ARE 7 CHURCHES...   REVELATION 1:20

SO THUS we find to be TRUE, we are the BODY OF MESSIYAH membered INDIVIDUALLY (YHWH)
has APPOINTED these in the CHURCH, first **APOSTLES**, second **PROPHETS**, third **TEACHES**,
*AFTER THAT MIRACLES, then GIFTS of HEALINGS, HELPS, ADMINISTRATIONS, VARIETIES OF
TONGUES...*   1CORINTHIANS 12:27-31

SO TODAY the SPIRIT OF TRUTH leads me to say TO THE WISE.. "O" CHURCH OF
PHILADELPHIA for have you not little strength yet keep the FATHERS WORD and have NOT DENIED
HIS SONS NAME. ALL may learn an be ENCOURAGED to let all things be done for EDIFICATION
                    1CORINTHIANS 14:26-40

SO I SAY, SO I SPEAK today let US get all THINGS DONE DECENTLY IN ORDER. To verify our
PATH and ESTABLISHING you and me (ONE) way BIBLICALLY with out FALSE DOCTRINE, for
many are afflicted and the same befall the RIGHTEOUS, BUT YHWH DELIVERS US OUT OF ALL.
FOR HE guards all my bones; not one of them were BROKEN for I see evil would be slayed with the
WICKED who was around and to all WHO HATE TO DO THE RIGHT THING would also be
CONDEMNED. SO here it is WRITTEN that YHWH IMMANUEL redeems the soul of his SERVANTS
for not one who **TRUST IN HIM** shall be condemned   PSALM 34:19-22

I BESEECH YOU to set back and allow the SPIRIT TO OPEN YOUR HEART and SOUL listening to the
teacher **INTERPRET (V)** to exsplain or clarify the meaning of the **PROPHESY (V)** to reveal by DIVINE
BLESSING to do what is GOOD / RIGHT and TRUE before YHWH OUR FATHER in SPIRIT and
TRUTH...   2CHRONICLES 31:20,21

SO I SAY, SO I SPEAK to another brother today with THIS IN MIND   MATTHEW 11:10-19

"From THIRTY YEARS OLD and ABOVE, even to FIFTY YEARS OLD, all who ENTER the SERVICE
To do the work in the TABERNACLE OF MEETING: NUMBERS 4:3

PEACE and BLESSING OF FAITH to BELIEVE IN the **LOVE OF THE MOSTHIGH** and service to
YAHSHUAH in sincerity..   *AMEN*

PROPHETIC MESSAGE MINISTRY
READING of INSPIRATION

AMMISHADDAI
TRUE
BELIEVER

BUT let US who are of the DAY be SOBER, putting on the BREASTPLATE OF FAITH and LOVE and as a HELMET the HOPE of SALVATION.   1THESSALONIANS 5:8

SUPER NATURAL: (GOAL) edification for the CHURCH
                    (A) learn and teach what is SCRIPTUAL = resource only (bible)
                    (B) learn and teach what is LAWFULL = resource only (bible)

NATURAL... IN order to be COMPLETE AS AMBASSADORS of YHWH. WE must be willing to OBSTAIN from ANYTHING which STUMBLES another when AFFIRMING SCRIPTURE or LAW among the church/temple/nation of people..   BOAST IN THE MOSTHIGH ANCIENT of DAYS praise YAHSHUAH for glory be to our FATHER. I CHARGE you therefore before YHWH and YAHSHUAH MESSIYAH who will JUDGE the LIVING and **DEAD** at HIS APPEARING and HIS KINGDOM: "PREACH the WORD" be ready IN SEASON and OUT of SEASON **CONVICE, REBUKE, EXHORT** and **ALL LONGSUFFERING** and **TEACHING** for the time will come when they will not ENDURE SOUND DOCTRINE but according to their OWN DESIRES because they have ITCHING EARS they shall heap up for themselves TEACHERS. They will turn their ears away from the (TRUTH) being turned ASIDE TO FABLES...   but YOU be WATCHFULL in all things ENDURE AFFLICTION do the work of AN EVANGELIST.   FULFILL YOUR MINISTRY...   2TIMOTHY 4:1-8

TEN COMMANDMENTS..

YOU SHALL HAVE NO OTHER GODS BEFORE ME..   EXODUS 20:3
YOU SHALL NOT MAKE CARVED IMAGES FOR YOURSELF..   EXODUS 20:4
YOU SHALL NOT TAKE THE NAME OF YHWH YOUR GOD IN VAIN.   EXODUS 20:7
REMEMBER THE SABBATH DAY, TO KEEP IT HOLY..   EXODUS 20:8
HONOR your FATHER and your MOTHER.   EXODUS 20:12

YOU SHALL NOT MURDER..   EXODUS 20:13
YOU SHALL NOT COMMIT ADULTERY.   EXODUS 20:14
YOU SHALL NOT STEAL.   EXODUS 20:15
YOU SHALL NOT BEAR FALSE WITNESS OPPOSITE to your neighbor...   EXODUS 20:16
YOU SHALL NOT COVET YOUR NEIGHBORS HOUSE.   EXODUS 20:17

MAY YHWH DELIVER YOU from every evil work and PRESERVE YOU for HIS HEAVENLY KINGDOM to HIM BE GLORY FOREVER and EVER..   AMEN

PROPHETIC MESSAGE MINISTRY
COMMANDMENT KEEPERS

AMMISHADDAI
    TRUE
    BELIEVER

THREE TIMES YOU SHALL KEEP A FEAST TO ME IN THE YEAR: EXODUS 23:14
TOPIC: FEAST and HIGH HOLY DAYS.

Six Days shall work be done, but the SEVENTH (DAY) is a SABBATH of solemn (Rest)
A HOLY CONVOCATION.. You shall do NO WORK ON IT; it is the SABBATH of יהוה in <u>All</u>
<u>your dwellings</u>   LEVITICUS 23:1-3

THESE are the FEAST of יהוה; *HOLY CONVOCATIONS* which you shall **PROCLAIM** at
their APPOINTED TIMES: LEVITICUS 23:4-44

HOLY DAY	MONTH / DAY		DURATION
PASSOVER	1	14	1DAY
FEAST OF UNLEAVENED BREAD	1	15-21	7DAYS
FIRST FRUITS	1	22	1DAY
FEAST OF WEEKS (PENTECOST) **ACTS 2:1**	3	14	1DAY
FEAST OF TRUMPETS	7	1	1DAY
DAY OF ATONEMENT (YOM KIPPUR)	7	10	1DAY
FEAST OF TABERNACLES	7	15-21	7DAYS
FEAST OF DEDICATION (HANUKKAH) **JOHN 10:22**	9	25	8DAYS
FEAST OF PURIM	12	14,15	2DAYS

ESTHER 9:18-32
" FAST DAYS "

   THE WORD *of* יהוה of HOST came to me saying: thus says יהוה of HOST..
The FAST of the FOURTH MONTH
The FAST of the FIFTH
The FAST of the SEVENTH
The FAST of the TENTH
**SHALL BE JOY and GLADNESS and CHEERFUL FEAST FOR THE HOUSE OF
YAHUDAH,** therefore LOVE, TRUTH and PEACE..   ZECHARIAH 8:18,19
In conclusion, SO it is WRITTEN: it shall be a statue FOREVER throughout your generations
<u>in all of your dwellings</u>..   LEVITICUS 23:31
                    PROPHETIC MESSAGE MINISTRY

CONVOCATION (N) A sacred assembly
STATUE (N) A form or likeness, sculpted modeled or carved.

TOPIC: *the DAY of ATONEMENT* This shall be an EVERLASTING STATUE for YOU... as we meditate on the COVENANT ORDER which YHWH LAID down in the OLD TESTAMENT being a STATUE FOREVER through out our generations in ALL OUR DWELLINGS.. (TODAY) we the HOUSE of YAHSRAEL fall on our knees in a NEW MANNER, or FORM of OLD to WORSHIP YHWH to beg HIS FORGIVENESS, to SEEK HIS APPROVAL, to await HIS sending us forth, and to expect HIS COMING BLESSING.. We enter the COURT of HIS TABERNACLE, having HIS PRAISES on our lips and MESSIYAH as our LAMB with out BLEMISH..

AMEN

THIS shall be a STATUE FOREVER for you.. In the SEVENTH MONTH, on the TENTH DAY of the month, you shall AFFLICT your souls, and DO NO work at all... IT shall be a HOLY CONVOCATION for you..   LEVITICUS 16:29

IT shall be to you a SABBATH of solemn REST, and you shall AFFLICT your souls; on the NINTH DAY of the MONTH AT EVENING, from EVENING to EVENING you shall OBSERVE your SABBATH...   LEVITICUS 23:32

AND the priest (KOHEN) who is *ANOINTED* and *CONSECRATED to minister as priest IN HIS FATHERS PLACE, shall make ATONEMENT* and put on the LINEN CLOTHES, the HOLY GARMENTS (1THESSALONIANS 5:8) then he shall make ATONEMENT for the HOLY SANCTUARY, and he shall make ATONEMENT for the TABERNACLE of MEETING and for the ALTAR and he shall make ATONEMENT for the PRIEST and for ALL the people of the ASSEMBLY... this shall be an *EVERLASTING STATUE* for you to make ATONEMENT for the children of YAHSRAEL, for ALL SINS, once a year...   LEVITICUS 16:32-34

LET your light so shine before men, that they may SEE YOUR GOOD WORKS and **GLORIFIY** your FATHER IN HEAVEN. *DO NOT THINK,* I (YAHSHUAH) came to destroy the LAW or the PROPHETS.. I did not come to destroy but to FULFILL..

MATTHEW 5:16-18

GRACE, MERCY and PEACE be with Y.O.U. from the MOSTHIGH the ABBA YAH SHALOM and from IMMANUEL YAHSHUAH MESSIYAH, BELOVED and HOLY SON of YAH, in TRUTH and LOVE..

LET US PRAY face the east!

AMMISHADDAI   PROPHETIC MESSAGE MINISTRY
   true   KINGDOM PRICNIPLES
BELIEVER

(THE) ART (OF) STUDIES

The WORD paints the picture (thus) the ART of LISTENING becomes the HIGHEST LEVEL of ART (for) in the beginning was the WORD...   JOHN 1:1

THEN you shall KNOW that I AM in the midst of YAHSRAEL. FOR young men DO SEE (VISIONS) thus the WORD paints the PICTURE.   JOEL 2:27,28

AND your DREAMS become clearer and clearer.

TOPIC: OBSERVING the month of ABIB and KEEPING the PASSOVER (to) IMMANUEL YOUR SAVIOUR for in the month of ABIB IMMANUEL YOUR SAVIOUR brought you out of EGYPT by night...   DEUTERONOMY 16:1

ON the 14th day of the first month is the PASSOVER OF IMMANUEL and on the 15th day of this month is the (FEAST) UNLEAVENED BREAD on the first day you shall have a HOLY CONVOCATION..   NUMBERS 28:16-18

And IMMANUEL said to MOSES and AARON this is the ORDINANCE of the PASSOVER: NO outSIDER shall eat of it but when you have become CIRCUMCISED of the heart then he may eat of it in ONE HOUSE it shall be eaten. ALL the congregation of YAHSRAEL SHALL KEEP IT so when the stranger wants to keep the PASSOVER to YHWH let his males be circumcised of the heart and then let him come near and keep it. ONE LAW shall be for NATIVE - BORN and for the stranger AMONG YOU.   EXODUS 12:43-50

THUS ALL THE CHILDREN OF YAHSRAEL DID... for these are the FEAST OF IMMANUEL HOLY CONVACATIONS which you PROCLAIM at their APPOINTED TIMES. ON the FIRST DAY you shall have a HOLY CONVOCATION: you shall do no customary work on it but shall OFFER an OFFERING TESTED by FIRE to IMMANUEL for seven days the SEVENTH DAY shall be a HOLY CONVOCATION   LEVITICUS 23:4-8

SEVEN DAYS you shall eat UNLEAVENED BREAD and on the seventh day there shall be a FEAST TO IMMANUEL UNLEAVENED BREAD shall be eaten seven days and TELL your SONS in that DAY THIS IS DONE BECAUSE of what IMMANUEL DID FOR ME when I came UP FROM EGYPT it shall BE A SIGN TO YOU AS A MEMORIAL between your eyes that YHWHS LAW MAY BE IN YOUR MOUTH; for with a strong hand IMMANUEL BROUGHT YOU OUT OF EGYPT. You shall therefore KEEP THIS ORDINANCE IN its season from year to year   EXODUS 13:6-10

BEHOLD the VIRGIN SHALL BE WITH CHILD and BEAR A SON and they shall call HIS NAME IMMANUEL...   MATTHEW 1:23

SO DO NOT THINK I CAME TO DESTROY the LAW OR the PROPHETS, I DID NOT COME TO DESTROY BUT TO FULFILL   MATTHEW 5:17,18

THEN CAME THE DAY OF UNLEAVED BREAD WHEN THE PASSOVER MUST BE KILLED   LUKE 22:7-20

HE WHO HAS AN EAR, LET HIM HEAR WHAT THE SPIRIT SAYS TO THE CHURCHES
PROPHETIC MESSAGE MINISTRY

AMMISHADDAI
  TRUE
  BELIEVER

The ART of STUDIES: the pursuit of KNOWLEDGE, WISDOM and UNDERSTANDING by
READING, OBSERVATION (PLUS) RESEARCH..   TRUE

TOPIC: הוהי BLESSED the SEVENTH DAY and SANCTIFIED IT;
Because in it HE RESTED from ALL HIS work which YHWH had CREATED and MADE so the
heavens and the earth were FINISHED and on the *SEVENTH DAY* YHWH ENDED HIS
WORK which HE had DONE, so HE rested on the *SEVENTH DAY* from all HIS WORK which
had been DONE.   GENESIS 2:1-3

SIX DAYS shall your work be done but the SEVENTH DAY is a *SABBATH* of solemn rest a
HOLY CONVOCATION; you shall do NO WORK on it for it is the *SABBATH OF THE
MOSTHIGH* in all your dwellings   LEVITICUS 23:3

SPEAK ALSO TO THE CHILDREN OF ISRAEL; saying surely the MOSTHIGH SABBATH
you SHALL KEEP for this is a SIGN BETWEEN ME and YOU throughout your generations
that you may KNOW that I AM the MOSTHIGH EL (GOD) *WHO SANCTIFIES Y.O.U.*
                                                           EXODUS 31:13
Thus says YHWH take heed to yourselves and bear NO BURDEN on the SABBATH NOR
CARRY A BURDEN out of your HOUSES on the SABBATH NOR do any work but HALLOW
the SABBATH DAY as I COMMANDED your forefathers   JEREMIAH 17:21,22

So the MOSTHIGH HAS GIVEN you the SABBATH; therefore HE gives you the SIXTH
DAY BREAD FOR TWO DAYS   EXODUS 16:29
So you can CALL THE SABBATH a delight, the HOLYDAY of YHWH honorable and shall
HONOR HIM NOT DOING your own ways NOR finding your own PLEASURE NOR
SPEAKING your own words, then you shall DELIGHT yourself in the MOSTHIGH and HE
shall cause you to ride on the HIGH HILLS of the earth and feed you with the *HERITAGE
OF YAHCOB* (ISRAEL) your father, for the mouth of YHWH HAS SPOKEN
                                                           ISAIAH 58:13,14
        The SON OF MAN IS *the ANOINTED* even of the SABBATH   MATTHEW 12:8

        ORDER OF THE DAY for the HOLY DAY of SABBATH: (3) BASIC STEPS

(1) DIVINE WORSHIP to be a time for holy convocation;   EZEKIEL 46:1-3

(2) LAW OF THE PROPHETS and HOLY WRITINGS/SCRIPTURES are to be read on holy
Sabbath;   ACTS 13:14,15

(3) *TO DO GOOD, TO SAVE LIFE, TO GIVE CHARITY IS LAWFUL ON SABBATH;*
                                                           LUKE 6:6-11
FOR IT IS WRITTEN: the SABBATH WAS MADE for man and NOT man for THE
SABBATH..   MARK 2:25-28

PROPHETIC MESSAGE MINISTRY
        AMMISHADDAI

TOPIC : RELIGION and ORGANIZATIONS Of FALSE TEACHING.. Moreover you shall say to them. Thus says YHWH; why has this people slidden back (YES) YAHRUSALEM in a perpetual backsliding they hold FAST to DECEIT. They <u>refuse to return</u> I listened and heard, they DO NOT SPEAK A RIGHT.. No man repented of his wickedness saying what have I done? Everyone turn to his own course like a horse rushing into battle (even) the stork in the heavens knows her APPOINTED TIMES; the turtledove, the swift and the swallow observe the time of their coming.. But my people do not know the JUDGEMENT Of YHWH.. I would comfort myself in sorrow, my heart is faint in me. LISTEN! the cry of the DAUGHTER Of my people from a far country; is not YHWH in ZOIN? Is not her KING in her? Why have they provoked YHWH to ANGER with their CARVED IMAGES with FOREIGN IDOLS..

                                                    JEREMIAH 8: 4-13 / 18-20

Oh I had in the wilderness a lodging place for travelers; that I might leave my people and go from them. Because they are all adulterers an ASSEMBLEY Of TREACHEROUS MEN. <u>Like the bow they have bent their tongues for lies</u> they are not bold for the TRUTH ON EARTH.. For they proceed from evil to evil and they do not know me says YHWH everyone take heed to his neighbor and do not trust any brother every neighbor will walk with slanderers everyone will deceive his neighbor and will not speak the TRUTH.. They have taught their tongue to speak lies, exhaust themselves to commit iniquity (SIN) your dwelling place is in the midst of deceit, through deceit they refuse to know me says YHWH Of Hosts. Behold I will refine them and test them so how shall I deal with the DAUGHTER Of my people? Their tongue is an arrow shot out; it speaks deceit one speaks peaceably to his neighbor with his mouth but in his heart he lies in wait.. *Shall I not AVENGE MYSELF ON SUCH A NATION AS THIS??* Moreover YHWH says <u>because they have forsaken MY LAW</u> WHICH I SET BEFORE THEM.. And have not obeyed my voice nor walked according to it. <u>But have walked according to the understanding of their own hearts</u> and after the BAALS which their fore parents taught them. Therefore YHWH Of Hosts EL Of YSRAEL says behold I will feed them with bitterness and give them poisonous water of gall to drink and will also SCATTER THEM AMONG the GENTILES.. and I will send a sword after them until I have consumed them. HEAR THE WORD which YHWH speaks to you " O " house Of YSRAEL thus says YHWH : <u>do not learn the WAY Of the Gentiles</u> do not be dismayed at the signs Of heaven because the Gentiles are dismayed at them. <u>The CUSTOMS Of the people are USELESS</u>..

                                          JEREMIAH 9:2-9,13-16 / 10:2-8

(SOUL) Food for thought WORD to the WISE.. Worthless Doctrines is liken to a wooden IDOL. *EXAMINE YOURSELVES* as to whether you are in the faith, TEST yourselves KNOW for yourselves that IMMANUEL IS IN YOU? Unless indeed you be DISQUALIFIED..   (HERESY)   *Check the Hidden Facts :*

        HOLLOWEEN   ST. VALENTINES DAY   THANKSGIVING
CHRISTMAS   EASTER   GOODFRIDAY   PALM SUNDAY

COMMENT: the ORIGINAL **HEBREW WORD** for (CHURCH) DENOTES A NUMBER OF PERSONS CALLED TOGETHER FOR ANY SPIRITUAL PURPOSE, of AN ASSEMBLY OF ANY KIND, CIVIL or SPIRITUAL. The (WORD) FREQUENTLY OCCURS IN THE SENSE OF AN ASSEMBLY OF (BELIEVERS) CALLED TOGETHER FOR יהוה PURPOSE. Which is certain DUTIES and RESPONSIBILITIES. A CHURCH MAY REFER TO AN ASSEMBLY OF PERSONS AT A PARTICULAR PLACE, OR A GROUP WHICH MEETS ANYWHERE, APPOINTED BY THE MOST HIGH, as in some ONES HOME. (ACTS 2:46) this is REGARDED AS A UNIVERSAL SUPERNATURAL SENSE.. The CHURCH OF MESSIYAH or the CHURCH OF THE MOST HIGH in which every BELIEVER IS A MEMBER OF and HAS a FUNCTION IN THAT BODY or CHURCH. (ONE) FUNCTION IS THE (SERVICE) or MINISTRY which can render to the WHOLE. THUS having CHARACTERISTICS and RESPONSIBILITIES..
(FRUITS and WORKS)

(NOW) he who plants and he who waters are (ONE) we are YHWH'S FELLOW WORKERS; you are YHWH'S FIELD, you are YHWH'S BUILDING..   1CORINTHIANS 3:8,9

DO YOU NOT KNOW that you are the **TEMPLE OF** יהוה and that the **SPIRIT OF** יהוה **DWELLS IN YOU?**   1CORINTHIANS 3:16,17

For as the body is ONE and has MANY MEMBERS but ALL THE MEMBERS of that ONE BODY, BEING MANY, are ONE BODY so ALSO is MESSIYAH the CHURCH.
FOR in fact the BODY is NOT ONE MEMBER but MANY.   1CORINTHIANS 12:12-14
NOW you are the BODY of MESSIYAH and MEMBERS INDIVIDUALLY and YHWH HAS APPOINTED THESE IN THE CHURCH: FIRST **APOSTLES**, SECOND **PROPHETS**, THIRD **TEACHERS**, AFTER THAT MIRACLES, THEN GIFTS OF HEALINGS, HELPS, ADMINISTRATIONS, VARIETIES OF TONGUES..   1CORINTHIANS 12:27-31

GO STAND IN THE TEMPLE and SPEAK TO THE PEOPLE (ALL) THE WORDS OF THIS LIFE.   ACTS 5:20   I WRITE so that you may KNOW HOW YOU OUGHT TO CONDUCT YOURSELF IN THE HOUSE OF YHWH, which is the CHURCH OF THE LIVING MOST HIGH GOD OF YISRAEL the FOUNDATION and MAINSTAY OF **THE TRUTH**..
                    1TIMOTHY 3:15
ENDEAVOR TO KEEP THE UNITY OF THE SPIRIT, IN THE BOND OF PEACE.
                    EPHESIANS 4:3-6
BUT one and the SAME SPIRIT WORKS ALL, distributing to each one individually as HE WILLS...   1CORINTHIANS 12:11   FOR WE, THOUGH MANY, ARE ONE BREAD and ONE BODY; for we all partake of that ONE BREAD. **OBSERVE YISRAEL AFTER the FLESH:** ARE NOT THOSE WHO EAT OF THE SACRIFICES FELLOW SHIPPERS OF the ALTAR?
                    1CORINTHIANS 10:17-22
SO we being MANY, are ONE BODY IN MESSIYAH, and individually members of ONE ANOTHER having the GIFTS DIFFERING ACCORDING to the GRACE which is given to us, let us USE THEM: if PROPHECY, let us PROPHESY in proportion to our FAITH;
                    ROMANS 12:4-8
FOR YOU CAN ALL PROPHESY ONE BY ONE, that all may LEARN and all may be ENCOURAGED for YHWH IS NOT THE AUTHOR OF CONFUSION BUT OF PEACE, as in all the **CHURCHES OF THE SAINTS**...   1CORINTHIANS 14:26-40

TOPIC : PURPOSE Of DUTY in the CHURCH.. Let us hear the conclusion of the whole matter: *FEAR YHWH and KEEP HIS COMMANDMENTS*, for this is mans all. For YHWH will bring every work into judgment, including every secret thing, whether GOOD or EVIL. The Preacher sought to find ACCEPTABLE WORDS; and what was written was UPRIGHT WORDS Of TRUTH..   ECCLESIASTES 12:12-14

But if I am delayed, I write so that you may know how you ought to conduct yourself in the HOUSE Of YHWH, which is the CHURCH Of the LIVING EL (GOD) the PILLAR and GROUND Of the TRUTH. Without CONTROVERSY great is the hidden TRUTH Of Godliness: Knowing this first, that NO PROPHECY Of SCRIPTURE is Of any PRIVATE INTERPRETATION..

                    1 TIMOTHY 3:14-16 / 4:1,2 / 2 PETER 1:19-21

ALL SCRIPTURE IS GIVEN BY INSPIRATION Of YHWH, and is profitable for DOCTRINE, for REPROOF, for CORRECTION, for INSRUTION in RIGHTEOUSNESS, that the man Of YHWH may be complete, thoroughly EQUIPPED for every Good Work..   2 TIMOTHY 3:16,17   You worship what you DO NOT KNOW; we KNOW what we (worship) for Salvation is of the HEBREWS.. But the hour is coming, and now is when the TRUE WORSHIPPERS will WORSHIP the ABBA (Father) In SPIRIT and TRUTH; the ABBA is seeking such to WORSHIP HIM. YHWH IS SPIRIT, and those who worship HIM must worship in SPIRIT and TRUTH..   JOHN 4:22-24   For this is the LOVE Of YHWH, that we KEEP HIS COMMANDMENTS, and HIS COMMANDMENTS are NOT BURDENSOME. This is HE who came by water and blood - YAHSHUAH MESSIYAH; not only by water, but by water and blood. And it is the SPIRIT WHO BEARS WITNESS, because the SPIRIT IS TRUTH. For there are THREE that bear witness on earth: the SPIRIT, the WATER, and the BLOOD; and these THREE AGREE AS ONE..   1 JOHN 5:3,6-8

For I say, through the GRACE GIVEN to me, to everyone who is among you NOT TO THINK Of himself more HIGHLY than he ought to think but to THINK SOBERLY as YHWH has dealt to each one a measure of FAITH.. So we being many, are ONE BODY in MESSIYAH (CHURCH) and INDIVIDUALLY members Of one another. He who exhorts, in exhortation; he who gives, with LIBERALITY; he who LEADS, with DILIGENCE; he who SHOWS MERCY, with CHEERFULNESS. Let love be without HYPOCRISY.. Abhor what is EVIL. Cling to what is GOOD. I speak as to wise men; JUDGE for yourselves what I say. OBSERVE YSRAEL AFTER THE FLESH: by ONE SPIRIT we are all baptized into ONE BODY - whether HEBREWS or GENTILES whether slaves or free - and have all been made to drink into ONE SPIRIT. That there should be no division in the body (CHURCH)

                    ROMANS 12:3-9 / 1CORINTHIANS 10:15-22 / 12:12-14,25-31

TOPIC : PURPOSE Of DUTY in the CHURCH.. Indeed I (YHWH) will cast her (CHURCH) into a sickbed, and those who commit ADULTERY with her into GREAT TRIBULATION, unless they repent of their deeds. I will KILL HER CHILDREN with DEATH, and all the CHURCHES shall know that I am HE WHO SEARCHES the minds and hearts. And I will give to each one of you according to your works. For I earnestly exhorted your fore parents in the day I (YHWH) brought them up out of the land Of EGYPT, until this day, rising early and exhorting saying " OBEY MY VOICE " because you have kept my COMMAND to persevere, I also will keep you from the HOUR Of TRAIL which shall come upon the whole world, to TEST THOSE who dwell on the earth behold I am COMING QUICKLY!! I know your works, that you are neither COLD or HOT. I could wish you were COLD nor HOT, I will vomit you out of MY MOUTH..

REVELATION 2:22,23 / JEREMIAH 11:7 / REVELATION 3:10-13,15,16
HONOR WIDOWS WHO ARE REALLY WIDOWS, but if any widow has children, or Grandchildren, let them first learn to show piety at home and to repay their parents; this is GOOD and ACCEPTABLE (JAMES 1:27) before YHWH. If any believing man or woman has widows, let them GIVE AID TO THEM, and do not let the church be burdened, that it may give aid to those who are really widows..   1 TIMOTHY 5:3-5,16

GO, STAND IN THE TEMPLE and SPEAK TO the PEOPLE ALL the WORDS, Of this LIFE..   ACTS 5:20
Yet in the CHURCH I would rather speak five words with understanding, that I may TEACH others also, to me who am less than the least of all the SAINTS, this GRACE WAS GIVEN, that I should PREACH AMONG the GENTILES the unseachable riches Of MESSIYAH, for this reason I bow my knees to the FATHER Of IMMANUEL YAHSHUAH MESSIYAH, from whom the whole family in heaven and earth is NAMED, that HE would GRANT you, according to the riches Of HIS GLORY, to be strengthened with might through HIS SPIRIT in the inner man, to know the LOVE Of MESSIYAH, which passes KNOWLEDGE; that you may be filled with all fullness of YHWH.. This is a GREAT MYSTERY, but I speak concerning MESSIYAH and the CHURCH praying always with all prayer and supplication in the SPIRIT, being watchful to this end with all perseverance and supplication for all SAINTS..
1 CORINTHIANS 14:19 / EPHESIANS 3:8,11-19 / 6:16-20

PROPHETIC MESSAGE MINISTRY
The ART Of STUDIES
READINGS OF INSPIRATION

PROPHETIC MESSAGE MINISTRY
TOPIC: WE ARE OF THE MOSTHIGH HE WHO KNOWS THE MOSTHIGH HEARS US; HE WHO IS NOT
OF THE MOSTHIGH DOES NOT HEAR US... BY THIS WE KNOW THE SPIRIT OF TRUTH and THE
SPIRIT OF ERROR...   1JOHN 3:24/4:1-6
  STEP (1) MOREOVER, brothers I DECLARE TO YOU THE GOSPEL which I PREACH TO YOU WHICH
ALSO YOU RECEIVED and IN WHICH YOU STAND... FOR I DELIVERED TO YOU FIRST OF ALL THAT
WHICH I ALSO RECEIVED... that CHRIST DIED FOR OUR SINS ACCORDING TO THE SCRIPTURES, and
THAT HE WAS BURIED and HE ROSE AGAIN the THIRD DAY ACCORDING TO THE SCRIPTURES...
                                                                    1CORINTHIANS 15:1-4
NOW FAITH IS the REALITY OF THINGS HOPED FOR, the CONFIDENCE OF THINGS NOT SEEN... FOR
BY THIS the ELDERS OBTAINED A GOOD TESTIMONY BY FAITH WE UNDERSTAND THAT THE
WORLD WAS FRAMED BY THE WORD OF THE MOSTHIGH... SO THAT THE THINGS WHICH ARE
SEEN WERE NOT MADE OF THINGS WHICH ARE VISIBLE... HEBREWS 11:1 HAVING DISARMED
PRINCIPALITIES and POWERS (HE) MADE A PUBLIC SPECTACLE OF THEM TRIUMPHING OVER THEM
IN IT... COLOSSIANS 2:15 FOR WE DO NOT WRESTLE AGAINST FLESH and BLOOD BUT AGAINST
PRINCIPALITIES, AGAINST POWERS, AGAINST the RULERS OF THE DARKNESS OF THIS AGE...
AGAINST SPIRITUAL HOST OF WICKEDNESS...   EPHESIANS 6:12
  STEP (2) YHWH IS NOT SLACK CONCERNING HIS PROMISE AS (SOME) COUNT SLACKNESS BUT IS
LONGSUFFERING TOWARD US NOT WILLING THAT ANY ONE SHOULD PERISH BUT THAT ALL
SHOULD COME TO REPENTANCE... 2PETER 3:9 the TIME IS FULFILLED and THE KINGDOM OF
YHWH GOD OF ISRAEL IS AT HAND... REPENT and BELIEVE IN THE GOSPEL...   MARK 1:14-15
BUT WHEN THE FULLNESS OF THE TIME HAD COME YHWH SENT FORTH HIS SON BORN OF A
WOMAN BORN UNDER the LAW... TO REDEEM THOSE WHO WERE UNDER THE LAW that (WE)
MIGHT RECEIVE the ADOPTION AS SONS... GALATIANS 4:4-5 OR DO YOU DESPISE THE RICHES OF
HIS GOODNESS, FORBEARANCE and LONGSUFFERING NOT KNOWING THAT THE GOODNESS OF
THE MOSTHIGH LEADS YOU TO REPENTANCE?   ROMANS 2:4
  STEP (3) AND EVEN AS THEY DID NOT LIKE TO RETAIN YHWH IN THEIR KNOWLEDGE YHWH
GAVE THEM OVER TO A REPROBATED MIND TO DO THOSE THINGS WHICH ARE NOT FITTING...
                                                                    ROMANS 1:28
LET NO ONE DECEIVE YOU WITH EMPTY WORDS FOR BECAUSE OF THESE THINGS THE WRATH OF
THE MOSTHIGH COMES UPON THE SONS OF DISOBEDIENCE THEREFORE DO NOT BE PARTAKERS
WITH THEM... EPHESIANS 5:6-7 ** SOUL FOOD FOR THOUGHT WORD TO THE WISE** SEARCH

the SCRIPTURES DAILY TO FIND OUT WHETHER THESE THINGS ARE SO...   ACTS 17:11

A FEW DO'S and DO NOT'S
EPHESIANS 4:10-32/ ROMANS 1:29-32

EXAMINE YOURSELVES AS TO WHETHER YOU ARE IN THE FAITH... TEST YOURSELVES DO YOU
NOT KNOW YOURSELVES THAT CHRIST IMMANUEL IS IN YOU? UNLESS INDEED YOU BE
DISQUALIFIED... 2CORINTHIANS 13:5-6 ELDERS LISTEN UP... FOR THERE ARE MANY ...
INSUBURDINATE , BOTH IDLE TALKERS and DECEIVERS, WHOSE MOUTHS MUST BE STOPPED WHO
SUBVERT WHOLE HOUSEHOLDS TEACHING THINGS WHICH THEY OUGHT NOT... THEY PROFESS
TO KNOW THE MOSTHIGH BUT IN WORKS THEY DENY HIM, BEING ABOMINABLE, DISOBEDIENT
and DISQUALIFIED FOR EVERY GOOD WORK... TITUS 1:10-16 CAN TWO WALK TOGETHER,
UNLESS THEY ARE AGREED? YOU WILL KNOW THEM BY THEIR FRUITS EVEN SO EVERY GOOD
TREE BEARS GOOD FRUIT BUT A BAD TREE BEARS BAD FRUIT EVERY TREE THAT DOES NOT BEAR
GOOD FRUIT IS CUT DOWN and THROWN INTO THE FIRE... THEREFORE BY THEIR FRUITS YOU
WILL KNOW THEM... NOT EVERYONE WHO SAYS TO ME CHRIST JESUS SHALL ENTER THE
KINGDOM OF HEAVEN BUT HE WHO DOES THE WILL OF MY FATHER IN HEAVEN... and then I will
DECLARE TO THEM I NEVER KNEW YOU DEPART FROM ME YOU WHO PRATICE LAWLESSNESS...
                                                                    MATTHEW 7:16-23
FOR THERE IS NO PARTIALITY WITH YHWH NOT THE HEARERS OF THE LAW ARE JUST IN THE
SIGHT OF THE MOSTHIGH BUT THE DOERS OF THE LAW WILL BE JUSTIFIED... ROMANS 2:11-13
HERE IS WISDOM LET HIM WHO HAS UNDERSTANDING, UNDERSTAND...
PRESS ON TO A GOOD TESTIMONY: GOOD INTENT DOES NOT EQUAL = OBEDIENCE...
1JOHN 5:7-8

STEP (1) FAITH/ SPIRIT
STEP (2) REPENT/ WATER
STEP (3) OBEDIENCE/ BLOOD

AMMISHADDAI
TRUE
BELIEVER

TOPIC: THE KINGDOM OF יהוה IS NOT IN WORD, BUT IN POWER..

What do you want? Shall I come to you with a ROD, or with LOVE in the SPIRIT OF
GENTLENESS?   1 CORINTHIANS 4:20,21

Therefore DO NOT be UNWISE, but UNDERSTAND what the will of יהוה IS.
                                                    EPHESIANS 5:17

Sort of speak, sort of say if your brother SINS against you, GO and tell him his FAULT
between you and him ALONE, if he HEARS you, you have gained a brother but if he will NOT
HEAR, take with you one or two more that by the mouth of two or three WITNESSES (so)
Every word may be ESTABLISHED..   MATTHEW 18:15-17

Now I myself am confident concerning my brothers, You who also are FULL of GOODNESS
Filled with (all) KNOWLEDGE also able to admonish one another.   ROMANS 15:14

UNDERSTAND JUDGE NOT and you will NOT be JUDGED with the Judgment you Judge..
You will be Judged; and with what MEASURE YOU USE, it will BE MEASURED BACK TO
YOU..   MATTHEW 7:1

BROTHERS if a man is overtaken in ANY TRESPASS you who are SPIRITUAL RESTORE
such a one in the SPIRIT OF GENTLENESS considering yourself, UNLESS you ALSO be
TEMPTED..   GALATIANS 6:1

IN HUMILITY CORRECT THOSE WHO ARE IN OPPOSITION, IF יהוה PERHAPS will
grant them REPENTANCE so that they may KNOW THE TRUTH,   2 TIMOTHY 2:24-26

AVOID FOOLISH DISPUTES, REJECT A DIVISIVE man after the FIRST and SECOND
WARNING knowing that such a person is WARPED and SINNING, being self - condemned..
                                                    TITUS 3:10,11

SPEAK these things, EXHORT, and REBUKE with ALL AUTHORITY, let no one despise You.
                                                    TITUS 2:15

PREACH the WORD! be ready IN SEASON and OUT OF SEASON. *CONVINCE REBUKE,*
EXHORT with (all) longsuffering and teaching..   2 TIMOTHY 4:2-4

TO THE TWELVE TRIBES WHICH ARE SCATTERED ABROAD:
COUNT IT ALL JOY when you fall into VARIOUS TRAILS, KNOWING that the TESTING
OF YOUR FAITH PRODUCES *ENDURANCE and PATIENCE*..   JAMES 1:1-5

PROPHETIC MESSAGE MINISTRY
אממסהאדדא.   COMMANDMENT KEEPERS
תר.
בלשׁךּ

COMMANDMENT KEEPERS

TOPIC: He who dwells in the *SECRET PLACE OF* יהוה shall ABIDE UNDER the SHADOW OF יהוה my GOD in HIM I will TRUST..   PSALM 91:1,2

The Kingdom of יהוה is NOT in Word but In power..   1 CORINTHIANS 4:20

WHAT SHALL WE DO? That we may work the works of יהוה ? MESSIYAH ANSWERED: THIS is the work of יהוה hat you BELIEVE in HIM whom HE sent.   JOHN 6:28,29

Being confident of this very thing that HE who has begun a good work in YOU, will complete it until the day of MESSIYAH IMMANUEL.   PHILIPPIANS 1:6

Not that I have already obtained it or already perfected it but I press on that I lay hold of that which MESSIYAH has also laid HOLD of ME, but one thing I do. Forgetting those things which are behind and reaching forward to those things which are ahead I press toward the GOAL for the PRIZE of the UPWARD CALL of the MOSTHIGH in MESSIYAH IMMANUEL.   PHILIPPIANS 3:12-16

Holding fast the *WORD OF LIFE,* so that we may REJOICE in the DAY OF IMMANUEL that We have not run in vain or LABORED IN VAIN..   PHILIPPIANS 2:16

DO NOT be DECEIVED: evil company corrupts good habits.   1 CORINTHIANS 15:33

IF a household is worthy let your PEACE COME UPON IT, but if it is NOT worthy let your PEACE RETURN to you. And whoever will NOT receive you NOR your WORDS, when you depart from that house or city. SHAKE OFF THE DUST from your feet..
                    MATTHEW 10:11,14

CAN TWO WALK TOGETHER, UNLESS THEY ARE AGREED...   AMOS 3:3

EVERYONE who is CALLED by my NAME, whom I have CREATED for my GLORY I have formed him, YES I HAVE MADE HIM, therefore you are my WITNESSES says יהוה that I am GOD THE MOSTHIGH..   TRUE   Do not remember the former things nor consider the things of old, behold I will do a NEW THING now it shall SPRING FORTH, will you NOT KNOW IT?   ISAIAH 43:18,19

Therefore behold the days are coming says יהוה that it shall NO MORE be said IMMANUEL LIVES who brought up the children of YISRAEL from the land of the NORTH and from ALL THE LANDS where HE has driven them (behold) I will send for <u>many Fisherman</u> says יהוה and they SHALL FISH THEM..   JEREMIAH 16:14-18

Because I give WATERS IN THE WILDERNESS and RIVERS IN THE DESERT to give drink to my people, my CHOSEN the people I have FORMED for MYSELF they shall *DECLARE MY PRAISE.* For I will pour MY SPIRIT on your descendants and MY BLESSING on your offspring..   ISAIAH 43:20,21 / 44:3

As the sash clings to the waist of a man, so I have caused the whole HOUSE of YISRAEL and the whole HOUSE of YAHUDAH to cling to ME says יהוה that they may become my people, for RENOWN, for PRAISE and for GLORY.. But they do not hear.. JEREMIAH 13:11

PROPHETIC MESSAGE MINISTRY

אממסאדדאהרא.

PROPHETIC MESSAGE MINISTRY
the ART of STUDIES...
STRICTLY FOR ??? WITNESSES

TOPIC: HEAVEN and HELL.
I WRITE TO YOU IN FEW WORDS... SOUL FOOD for THOUGHT WORD to the WISE... THAT WHICH IS BORN OF THE FLESH IS FLESH and THAT WHICH IS BORN OF the SPIRIT IS SPIRITUAL... JOHN 3:6

ACCORDING TO THE WORD OF THE MOSTHIGH THERE ARE THREE HEAVENS... the prophet APOSTLE PAUL SAID I KNOW A MAN IN MESSIAH who fourteen years AGO WHETHER IN BODY I DO NOT KNOW... WHETHER OUT OF BODY I DO NOT KNOW... YHWH KNOWS- SUCH A ONE WAS CAUGHT UP TO THE THIRD HEAVEN also I KNOW SUCH A MAN WHOM WAS CAUGHT UP IN TO PARADISE and HEARD INDESCRIBABLE WORDS WHICH IS NOT LAWFUL FOR A MAN TO UTTER... 2 CORINTHIANS 12:2-6

IN THE HOLY SPIRIT understand REASON, SINCE THERE IS A THIRD HEAVEN THERE ALSO MUST BE A FIRST and SECOND HEAVEN... IN IMMANUELS LETTER TO THE CHURCH AT EPHESUS HE SAID HE WHO HAS AN EAR LET HIM HEAR WHAT THE SPIRIT SAYS TO THE CHURCH... TO HIM WHO OVERCOMES I WILL GIVE TO EAT FROM THE TREE OF LIFE WHICH IS IN THE MIDST OF THE PARADISE OF YHWH... REVELATION 2:7

HEAR IS WISDOM LET HIM WHO HAS UNDERSTANDING... UNDERSTAND the BOOK of INSTRUCTION BEFORE LIVING ETERNALLY... IT has MORE to say about HELL then it does about HEAVEN and TO DENY THE FACT OF HELL IS TO DENY THE INFALLIBLE WORD OF THE MOSTHIGH... IF ANYONE WORSHIPS the BEAST and HIS IMAGE and RECEIVES HIS MARK ON HIS FOREHEAD OR ON HIS HAND HE HIMSELF WILL ALSO DRINK OF THE WINE OF THE WRATH OF YHWH... WHICH IS POURED OUT (FULL) STRENGTH INTO THE CUP OF HIS INDIGNATION and HE SHALL BE TORMENTED WITH FIRE and BRIMSTONE IN THE PRESENCE OF THE HOLY ANGELS and IN THE PRESENCE OF THE LAMB... the SMOKE of their TORMENT ASCENDS FOREVER and EVER; and THEY HAVE NO REST DAY OR NIGHT WHO WORSHIP THE BEAST AND HIS IMAGE AND WHOEVER RECEIVES the MARK OF HIS NAME... REVELATION 14:9-12
AND ANYONE NOT FOUND WRITTEN IN THE BOOK OF LIFE WILL BE CAST INTO THE LAKE OF FIRE...REVELATION 20:12-15 ALSO the COWARDLY, UNBELIEVING, ABOMINABLE, MURDERERS, SEXUALLY IMMORAL, SORCERERS, IDOLATERS and (ALL) LIARS WILL HAVE THEIR PART IN THE LAKE WHICH BURNS WITH FIRE and BRIMSTONE, WHICH IS THE SECOND DEATH...   REVELATION 21:5-8   HELL IS A BIBLICAL FACT... NOT A RELIGIOUS FABLE USED TO SCARE the WICKED INTO BECOMING GOOD CITIZENS. FOR EXAMPLE the SON of THE MOSTHIGH HIMSELF said IF YOUR EYE CAUSES YOU TO SIN, PLUCK IT OUT... IT IS BETTER FOR YOU TO ENTER THE KINGDOM OF YHWH with ONE EYE, RATHER THEN HAVING TWO EYES TO BE CAST INTO HELL FIRE." WHERE THEIR WORM DOES NOT DIE and THE FIRE IS NOT QUENCHED" MARK 9:43-48

(MOREOVER) TO DENY THAT THERE IS A SUPERNATURAL ETERNAL HELL IS TO ALSO DENY THE DEITY OF CHRIST IMMANUEL... IF WE CANNOT EXCEPT and BELIEVE WHAT HE SAID ABOUT HELL, THEN HOW CAN WE BELIEVE ANY-THING HE TAUGHT? IF THERE IS NO HELL, THEN CHRIST IMMANUEL IS NOT "THE WAY, THE TRUTH, and THE LIFE "... JOHN 14:1-6
IN CONCLUSION I TELL YOU THE TRUTH IN MESSIAH IM NOT LYING MY CONSCIENCE ALSO BEARING ME WITNESS IN THE HOLY SPIRIT... OUR SAVIOR SAID, " FOR JUDGMENT I HAVE COME INTO THIS WORLD, THAT THOSE WHO DO NOT SEE MAY SEE... and TO THOSE WHO SEE MAY BE MADE BLIND " then some of the PHARISEES WHO WERE with HIM HEARD THESE WORDS, SAID TO HIM " ARE WE BLIND ALSO? " IMMANUEL SAID IF YOU WERE BLIND YOU WOULD HAVE NO SIN; BUT NOW YOU SAY, WE SEE... THEREFORE YOUR SIN REMAINS... JOHN 9:38-41
PROPHETIC MESSAGE MINISTRY

AMMISHADDAI
TRUE
BELIEVER

COMMANDMENT KEEPERS

TOPIC: LESSONS ON PRAYER

Prayer is one of the PILLARS of a SPIRITUAL LIFE.. it's the Privilege to take (all) Burdens, Requests and Praise to יהוה our FATHER in PRAYER. In prayer We Praise HIM (YHWH) and Thank HIM - be anxious for nothing but in everything Pray with Supplication and with THANKSGIVING let your Request be made known to יהוה and the *PEACE of the MOSTHIGH* which Surpasses (all) Understanding will guard your Heart and Mind through MESSIYAH IMMANUEL..   PHILIPPIANS 4:6-7

When We Pray, We Communicate with our HEAVENLY FATHER.. יהוה Yahshuah Son of the MOSTHIGH Taught his disciples to Not Pray like the Hypocrites or Do Not use VAIN repetitions as the Heathen does. Thinking that they will be heard for the many words they speak but when you pray go into your Room, *Shut Your Door,* Pray to your FATHER who is in SECRET and your FATHER who *SEES IN SECRET, WILL REWARD YOU OPENLY...* Understand your FATHER Knows the things you have Need of before you ASK HIM.
                                                    MATTHEW 6:5-15

HOW EVER also if we make our Request known to יהוה our FATHER with THANKSGIVING The indwelling *SPIRIT OF TRUTH* will GUIDE US into (all) *TRUTH AS WE PRAY..* HE will COMFORT US, STRENGTHEN US, and ENCOURAGE US, in the *WAY OF RIGHTEOUSNESS* Before יהוה our FATHER..   JOHN 16:13-15

(6) *BASIC STEPS TO PRAYER..*

(1) *PRAY AS THE MESSIYAH PRAYED*   MATTHEW 6:5-15

(2) *PRAY WITHOUT DOUBT / UNBELIEF*   MATTHEW 21:21,22

(3) *PRAY IN יהוה NAME..*   JOHN 16:23,24

(4) *PRAY ACCORDING TO יהוה WILL*   1 JOHN 5:14,15

(5) *PRAY IN THE HOLY SPIRIT*   JUDE 20,21

(6) *PRAY WITH OUT CEASING*   1 THESSALONIANS 5:17,18

In Conclusion: BLESSED IS HE WHO READS and THOSE WHO HEAR THE WORDS OF THIS *PROPHECY*, and KEEP those things which are *WRITTEN IN IT;* For the TIME IS NEAR. If you FORGIVE men of their SINS. Your HEAVENLY FATHER יהוה will also FORGIVE You, But if you DO NOT FORGIVE men of their SINS, Neither will your FATHER FORGIVE Your SINS..   *TRUE*

PROPHETIC MESSAGE MINISTRY

אממסהאדרא.
תר.
בלשׁכ

The ART of STUDIES
READING of INSPIRATION

TOPIC: *INSTRUCTION IN PRAYER*

BASIC STEPS to PRAYER and FASTING.. Also best times for SUPPLICATIONS

*NIGHT TIME HOURS*_____ *DAY TIME HOURS*

1ST HOUR at SUNSET   1ST HOUR at SUNRISE

10TH HOUR **SPECIAL** PRAYER   7TH HOUR AROUND NOON

12TH HOUR JUST BEFORE SUNRISE   12TH HOUR at SUNDOWN

INSTRUCTION to PRAYER, FASTING and BEST SUPPLICATION TIME:

MATTHEW 6:5-15 / DANIEL 9:16-19 / 1KINGS 8:28-31 / PSALM 51:1-19

-- WHILE FASTING --

PROVIDE that IF you have FAITH as a mustard seed, nothing will BE IMPOSSIBLE for you.
HOWEVER this kind does not go out EXCEPT by PRAYER and FASTING..

MATTHEW 17:20,21

ORDER of the DAY for FASTING: 6 BASIC STEPS

(1) wash yourself

(2) ANOINT yourself with OIL   VIRGIN OIL (OLIVE)

(3) CONTINUE in PRAYER with MEDITATION of YHWH'S WORD   PSALM 119 (ALL)

(4) profess your SINS and your FOREFATHERS SINS

(5) REQUEST your needs as OFTEN as you like

(6) AND last but not least, GIVE AS MUCH CHARITY AS POSSIBLE during your **FAST**, for
that will COVER the MUTITUDE of SINS

For it is WRITTEN: man shall NOT LIVE BY BREAD ALONE, but by EVERY WORD that
PROCEEDS from the MOUTH OF THE MOSTHIGH..   MATTHEW 4:4

AMMISHADDAI
   TRUE
   BELIEVER

I pray to יהוה EL (GOD) of HEAVEN.. "O" GREAT and AWESOME GOD. We who keep your COVENANT and MERCY with those who love YOU and OBSERVE your COMMANDMENTS.. Please let YOUR EAR BE ATTENTIVE and YOUR EYES OPEN that YOU hear the prayer of YOUR servant which I pray BEFORE YOU NOW.. DAY and NIGHT so the children of ISRAEL, YOUR servants and I CONFESS the SINS OF THE CHILDREN OF ISRAEL which we have SINNED AGAINST YOU both my fathers house and I have SINNED..   NEHEMIAH 1:6

We have acted very CORRUPTLY AGAINST YOU and have NOT KEPT the COMMANDMENTS the STATUTES NOR the ORDINANCES which YOU COMMANDED YOUR SERVANT MOSES..
                                                          DEUTERONOMY 28:15

" REMEMBER" (IF) YOU ACT TREACHEROUSLY UNFAITHFUL.. *I WILL SCATTER YOU AMONG the NATIONS* but (IF) you return to ME and KEEP MY COMMANDMENTS and DO THEM.. EVEN THOUGH SOME OF US ARE CAST OUT TO THE FARTHEST PART of the heavens.. יהוה will gather us from here and BRING US to the place which HE has CHOSEN as a dwelling for HIS NAME.. Now these are YOUR SERVANTS and YOUR PEOPLE whom YOU shall REDEEM BY YOUR *GREAT POWER and BY YOUR STRONG HAND..*   TRUE

" O " יהוה I PRAY.. PLEASE LET YOUR EAR BE ATTENTIVE TO THE PRAYER OF YOUR SERVANT PLUS the PRAYER of YOUR SERVANTS who desire to FEAR YOUR NAME; and let YOUR SERVANT PROSPER THIS DAY..   *NOW I PRAY*   NEHEMIAH 1:5-11

" O " יהוה IN HEAVEN,

HOLY BE YOUR NAME.. YOUR KINGDOM COME..

Now YOUR WILL BE DONE ON EARTH as it is
IN HEAVEN
GIVE US THIS DAY.. OUR DAILY BREAD..

FORGIVE US OUR DEBTS AS WE FORGIVE OUR DEBTORS

And DO NOT LEAD US INTO TEMPTATION, but DELIVER US FROM

The EVIL ONE.. For YOURS IS THE KINGDOM and THE POWER and THE GLORY

FOREVER... AMEN   MATTHEW 6:5-15

PROPHETIC MESSAGE MINISTRY
The ART of STUDIES

AMMISHADDAI
TRUE
BELIEVER

COMMANDMENT KEEPERS

TOPIC: יהוה IS GRACIOUS and ABUNDANT IN MERCY..

Therefore not excepting HIS LOVE and HIS RIGHTEOUS STANDARD I CHARGE YOU...
HIS people with REFUSAL and STUBBORNNESS of the NECK to FORSAKE your former
Ways, WITHHOLDING tithes and offerings from your HEART giving your <u>all without doubt</u>
Stop robbing our GOD.. You have gone away from HIS *ORDINANCES and HAVE NOT KEPT
THEM.*   MALACHI 3:7

IN SPITE of your SINS יהוה still LOVES his creation; and is WILLING TO FORGIVE you
HIS sinful people. Bring the PRIESTHOOD TO A HIGHER LEVEL in MESSIYAH, through a
fulfilling CONCEPT OF יהוה with stern RESPONSIBILITY in performing your DUTIES.
Understand *SPIRITUAL LEADERS..* what's going WRONG in the community, in the church
and the problems WE SEE are DUE to POOR EXAMPLE and POOR CONCEPT of יהוה and
HIS RIGHTEOUS REQUIREMENTS.   ECCLESIASTES 12:13

       SOUL FOOD FOR THOUGHT, WORD TO THE WISE.. DO NOT destroy
PROPHETIC inspiration teaching with the LAW. For it is TOTALLY DIFFERENT then
PROPHECY teaching UNDER THE LAW.. Return to ME and I will return to you says יהוה of
HOST...   TRUE

With POOR CONCEPTS of יהוה and HIS REQUIREMENTS RELIGION in theses days NEED
MANY ADJUSTMENTS. Causing CONFUSION with DEFECTIVE CONDUCT in human
RELATIONSHIPS produced among one another having NO CHOICE but to see it in today's
SOCIETY we have LOST SIGHT OF DIVINE PURPOSE and SERVICES, a truth that must
have been FORGOTTEN BY HIS PEOPLE.   LAMENTATIONS 2:6

EXAMINE YOURSELVES TO WHETHER YOU ARE IN THE FAITH.. TEST YOURSELVES
DO you know yourselves, that *SAVIOR ANOINTED IMMANUEL* is in you? Unless indeed
you are DISQUALIFIED...   But I trust you KNOW we are NOT DISQUALIFIED.
                                                          2 CORINTHIANS 13:5

FINALLY, brothers become COMPLETE, be of ONE MIND, live IN PEACE and יהוה of LOVE
And PEACE will be with you..   2 CORINTHIANS 13:11
So assuredly I say to you also, *UNTIL HEAVEN AND EARTH PASS AWAY* not even the
smallest stroke will by NO MEANS PASS from the LAW *UNTIL ALL IS COMPLETED..*
                                                             AMEN

PROPHETIC MESSAGE MINISTRY

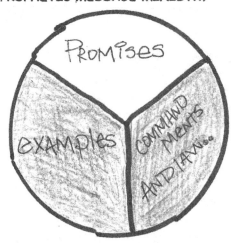

PROPHETIC MESSAGE MINISTRY

WORK ASSIGNMENTS

SU   M   TU   W   TH   F

She opens HER mouth with WISDOM and on HER TONGUE is the LAW of KINDNESS, she watches over the WAYS of HER HOUSEHOLD and does not eat the bread of IDLENESS;   PROVERBS 31:26,27

Therefore LAY up these words of mine in you HEART, and in your soul and bind them as a SIGN ON YOUR HAND, you shall TEACH THEM to your CHILDREN, speaking of them when you sit in your HOUSE and you shall write them on the DOORPOSTS of your HOUSE and on your GATES.
                                                                                DEUTERONOMY 11:18-20

For YHWH ESTABLISHED A TESTIMONY IN YAHCOB and APPOINTED A LAW IN YISRAEL, which HE COMMANDED our forefathers THAT they should make them KNOWN to their children.
                                                                                PSALM 78:5

2THESSALONIANS 3:10 WE COMMAND YOU THIS: IF anyone will NOT WORK, neither shall HE EAT;

DAILY ACTIVITY --- BREAKFAST BEFORE 10:00 AM

                                                            LUNCH SERVED AT   2:00 PM

                                                            DINNER SERVED AT   6:00 PM

          (NOTE) ALL ASSIGNMENTS MUST BE DONE BETWEEN 11:00 AM THRU 5:30 PM ALSO ONE (1) CHAPTER of BIBLE MUST BE READ ON for the days TOPIC which will be DISCUSSED ON SABBATH'S NIGHT or SABBATH'S DAY...

WORK DETAILS BREAK DOWN:

(1) CLEAN ROOM   (2) CLEAN BATHROOM   (3) DISHES / CLEAN KITCHEN

DETAILS TO #1
Sweep/ straiten up clothes/ empty trash / make up bed

DETAILS TO #2
Clean sink and toilet area / clean up tub/ sweep and mop/ empty trash

DETAILS TO #3
Wash dishes/ wash off tables and counter tops /sweep and mop

HONOR YOUR FATHER and YOUR MOTHER as the MOSTHIGH your MIGHTY ONE HAS COMMANDED you, that your days may be LONG and that it may BE WELL WITH YOU;
                                                                                DEUTERONOMY 5:16

WORK ASSIGNMENTS

(1) DAY   (2) DAY   (3) DAY   (4) DAY   (5) DAY   (6) DAY

PROPHETIC MESSAGE MINISTRY
KINGDOM PRINCIPLES..

YHWH SAID SEE I HAVE GIVEN YOU EVERY HERB THAT YIELDS SEED WHICH IS ON THE FACE OF ALL THE (EARTH) and EVERY TREE WHOSE FRUIT YIELDS SEED; TO YOU IT SHALL BE FOR FOOD... GENESIS 1:29 THEREFORE DO NOT BE UNWISE BUT UNDERSTAND WHAT THE WILL OF YHWH IS... EPHESIANS 5:17 (NOW) **YHWH SPOKE:** SPEAK TO THE CHILDREN OF YISRAEL and SAY THESE ARE THE ANIMALS WHICH YOU **MAY EAT** AMONG ALL THE ANIMALS THAT ARE ON THE EARTH: LEVITICUS 11:1-3 THESE YOU **MAY EAT** OF ALL THAT ARE IN THE WATER: LEVITICUS 11:9 ALL CLEAN BIRDS YOU **MAY EAT** DEUTERONOMY 14:11-21 YET THESE YOU **MAY EAT** OF EVERY FLYING INSECT THAT CREEPS ON ALL FOURS LEVITICUS 11:21,22 **THIS IS THE LAW CONCERNING THE ANIMALS and THE BIRDS and EVERY LIVING CREATURE** THAT MOVES IN THE WATERS, and OF EVERY CREATURE THAT CREEPS ON THE EARTH; TO DISTINGUISH BETWEEN THE ANIMAL THAT MAY BE EATEN and THE ANIMAL THAT MAY NOT BE EATEN""... LEVITICUS 11:46,47

TOPIC: LOW FAT (K) MENU

DAY (1)
Dinner: REDBEANS AND RICE WITH SWEETPOTATO or SIRION STEAK WITH MUSHROOMS/SALAD
Breakfast: 1cup STRAWBERRIES, 1CUP OATMEAL WITH HONEY/MILK
Lunch: HEBREW SALAD
Snack: 2 pears; 1TANGERINE

DAY(2)
Dinner: GRILLED FISH WITH LEMON; 1BAKED POTATO WITH BUTTER; STEAMED SPINACH..
Breakfast: WATERMELON SECTIONS
Lunch: CHEFS SALAD WITH SHREDDED LETTUCE TOPPED WITH CHEESE, OLIVES and TOMATO
Snack: 1APPLE, 1ORANGE

DAY(3)
Dinner: GRILLED TURKEY or CHICKEN; HEBREW SALAD
Breakfast: 1LARGE GRAPEFRUIT, WITH BOWL CERAL:
Lunch:GRILLED VEGGIES
Snack: 1banana, 2PEARS

DAY(4)
Dinner: GRILLED FISH WITH LEMON; DINNER SALAD WITH RED WINE
Breakfast: 2CUPS PINEAPPLE; 1WHEAT TOAST WITH HONEY
Lunch: SWEET POTATO WITH BUTTER; STEAMED CARROTS
Snack: 10 nuts; 2PEACHES

DAY(5)
Dinner: TURKEY, LETTUE, TOMATO SANDWHICH WITH CHIPS or SPINACH DIP
Breakfast: ½ LARGE CANTALOUPE: WITH BRAIN MUFFINS
Lunch: FRESH FRUIT PLATE WITH YOGURT...
Snack:1apple, 1BANANA

DAY(6)
Dinner: GRILLED SKINLESS CHICKEN BREAST; STEAMED BROCCOLI WITH LEMON ,GREEN SALAD
Breakfast: GRAPEFRUIT JUICE; 1SLICE WHEAT TOAST
Lunch:GRILLED VEGGIES / SNACKS: 1NONFAT YOGURT;1CUP STRAWBERRIES

SABBATH FEAST: MENUE
ROAST LAMB, BROWN RICE, COOKED WITH BROTH, STEAMED BROCCOLI,WITH HEBREW SALAD FRESH FRUIT WITH YOGURT SERVED WITH RED WINE...

REMEMBER YHWH YOUR GOD LED YOU ALL THE WAY THESE FORTY YEARS IN THE WILDERNESS TO HUMBLE YOU and TEST YOU, TO KNOW WHAT WAS IN YOUR HEART, WHETHER YOU WOULD KEEP HIS COMMANDMENTS OR NOT... DEUTERONOMY 8:1-3 IT IS WRITTEN, MAN SHALL NOT LIVE BY BREAD ALONE, BUT BY EVERYWORD THAT PROCEEDS FROM THE MOUTH OF THE MOSTHIGH'' MATTHEW 4:4

PROPHETIC MESSAGE MINISTRY

FOR KNOWLEDGE IS THE KEY...   SO DON'T STAY LOCKED OUT

(1) B I B L E

(2) national Sunday law
(3) gospels of barnabas
(4) Egypt to canaan
(5) the gospel raw and uncut..

ITS NOTHING WRONG with reading material out side of the LAW of the PROPHETS and the HOLY WRITINGS.. Sorter speak sorter say out side of the WORD OF YHWH as LONG as it RETURNS to become COMFORMATION, WITNESSING to TESTIFY of the TRUTH. Set WITHIN our FATHERS WORD..

YAHSHUAH MESSIYAH and HIS SPIRIT WHO BEARS WITNESS because the SPIRIT IS TRUTH for there are THREE which BEAR WITNESS IN HEAVEN, the **FATHER** the **WORD** and the **HOLYSPIRIT** and these THREE ARE **ONE**   1JOHN 5:6-8

SO he who BELIEVES in the SON OF THE MOSTHIGH.. Has the WITNESS IN HIMSELF; this is the TESTIMONY that YHWH has given US *ETERNAL LIFE* this life is in HIS **SON IMMANUEL.**   1JOHN 5:11,12

SO to put a CONCLUSION to this MATTER; we must understand the putting TOGETHER OF MANY BOOKS there IS NO END. *MUCH STUDY IS WEARISOME TO THE FLESH..* (NATURALLY) SO let US hear a solution to the whole MATTER: FEAR YHWH and KEEP HIS COMMANDMENTS for this is mans ALL   ECCLESIASTES 12:12-14

BECAUSE those who do wickedly against the covenant shall be POLLUTED with FLATTERY but our people who know their EL (GOD) YHWH shall be STRONG and carry out GREAT EXPLOITS. BECAUSE we understand, WE shall INSTRUCT MANY.   DANIEL 11:32-34

Rightly **DIVIDE** the WORD of TRUTH. **SEARCH the SCRIPTURES DAILY** to find out whether these THINGS ARE SO.   ACTS 17:11

PROPHETIC MESSAGE MINISTRY
COMMANDMENT KEEPERS
READINGS of INSPIRATION

FOR KNOWLEDGE IS THE KEY..   SO DON'T STAY LOCKED OUT

AMMISHADDAI
    TRUE
    BELIEVER

TOPIC: The DEITY of MESSIYAH IMMANUEL.. Therefore יהוה Himself will give you a SIGN; behold the virgin SHALL CONCEIVE and BEAR A SON.. And shall call HIS name IMMANUEL.   ISAIAH 7:14

יהוה who at VARIOUS TIMES and VARIOUS WAYS spoke in times past, to the fore parents by the PROPHETS.. Has in these last days spoken to us by HIS SON whom HE has APPOINTED HEIR OF (ALL) THINGS. Through whom also HE made the Worlds; who being the BRIGHTNESS of HIS GLORY and the EXPRESS IMAGE of HIS person and upholding ALL THINGS by the WORD OF HIS POWER when HE had purged our sins, sat down at the RIGHT HAND of the MAJESTY ON HIGH. Having become so much better than the ANGELS as he has by INHERITANCE OBTAINED a more EXCELLENT NAME than they. So To the SON *HE SAYS:* your THRONE "O" GOD (MIGHTY ONE) is forever and ever, a RULERS STAFF of RIGHTEOUSNESS is the scepter of your KINGDOM.. You have LOVED RIGHTEOUSNESS and HATED LAWLESSNESS; therefore GOD (MIGHTY ONE) your GOD The MOSTHIGH יהוה has ANOINTED YOU.. With the oil of GLADNESS more then your companions.   HEBREWS 1:1-14

AND THE WORD BECAME FLESH and DWELT AMONG US and we beheld HIS GLORY as of the ONLY BEGOTTEN of the FATHER יהוה, full of GRACE and TRUTH. I can of MYSELF DO NOTHING. As I hear, I judge; and MY judgment is RIGHTEOUS, because I DO NOT SEEK MY OWN WILL, but the WILL of the FATHER יהוה who sent me... The FATHER HIMSELF who sent ME has TESTIFIED OF ME, you have NEITHER HEARD HIS VOICE at any time nor SEEN HIS FORM. YOU SEARCH the scriptures for in them you think you have ETERNAL LIFE; and these are they which TESTIFY OF ME. JOHN 1:14 / 5:30-46

ON OCCASION the Pharisees, Herodians and Sadducees who had NOTHING IN COMMON, but a Religious HATRED FOR THE MESSIYAH. They came to HIM with questions DESIGNED TO ENTANGLE HIM in HIS teaching to try to EXPOSE MESSIYAH as a fraud..
                                                                        MATTHEW 22:15-40

Because they DID NOT KNOW or would NOT ACCEPT the Biblical TRUTH ABOUT MESSIYAH IMMANUEL in the LAW, they were *SPIRITUALLY BLIND* to the LAW of MESSIYAH; they only saw the LAW as they WRONGLY INTERPRETED IT.. But they DID NOT RECOGNIZE the LAWGIVER who came to complete the LAW. And All the prophecies That Pertained to HIS FIRST COMING. However when MESSIYAH IMMANUEL RETURNS, HE *WILL COMPLETE ALL THOSE RELATED TO HIS SECOND COMING..*
                                                                        MATTHEW 5:17-20

YAHsavior as IMMANUEL, is Davids GOD (MIGHTY ONE) YAHsavior as MESSIYAH is Davids SON, (man) again YAHSavior said I AM the ROOT and OFFSPRING of DAVID, the BRIGHT and MORNING STAR.   REVELATION 22:16   HE IS THE TRUE LIGHT which gives LIGHT to every man coming into the world. HE was in the world, and the world DID NOT KNOW HIM. He came to HIS OWN PEOPLE and HIS OWN did not receive HIM. But as many who RECIVE HIM, to them HE gave the right to become children of יהוה: TO those who *BELIEVE* IN HIS NAME: For יהוה so loved the world that HE gave HIS only begotten SON that whoever believes in HIM SHOULD NOT PERISH, but have everlasting LIFE..   JOHN 1:6-13 / 3:16   HE who has an ear, let HIM hear what the SPIRIT says to the churches, GRACE to you PEACE from HIM who is and who was and who is to come. MESSIYAH IMMANUEL the FAITHFUL WITNESS... *The FIRSTBORN FROM THE DEAD.*

TOPIC: YHWH IS SPIRIT AND THOSE WHO WORSHIP HIM.. MUST WORSHIP IN SPIRIT AND TRUTH...   JOHN 4:23,24

MEN AND BROTHERS (SONS) OF THE FAMILY AND STOCK OF ABRAHAM AND THOSE AMONG YOU WHO *FEAR THE MOST HIGH..* TO YOU THE WORD OF THIS SALVATION HAS BEEN SENT: ACTS 13:26
AFTER THE READING OF THE LAW AND THE PROPHETS LET THE ELDERS AND RULERS OF THE *SYNAGOGUE* SPEAK TO THEM SAYING MEN AND BROTHERS IF YOU HAVE <u>ANY WORDS</u> OF ENCOURAGEMENT SPEAK ON...   ACTS 13:15

AND I APPEAL TO YOU BROTHERS BEAR WITH THE WORD OF EXHORTATION FOR I HAVE WRITTEN TO YOU IN FEW WORDS...   HEBREWS 13:22

TWO FORMS OF TRUE WORSHIP..

(1) *WORSHIP IN THE SYNAGOGUE*
     A. THE WORD SYNAGOGUE IS SIMPLY A GREEK WORD FOR CONGREGATION.

     B. CONGREGATION A GATHERING OF THE PEOPLE: ASSEMBLY..

I BESEECH YOU ELDERS AND RULERS OF THE SYNAGOGUE...   LED THE WORSHIP.. OUR FATHER(ABBA) IS *SPIRIT* AND THOSE WHO WORSHIP HIM.. <u>MUST WORSHIP</u> IN *SPIRIT AND TRUTH.* ESPECIALLY IN TEACHING THE LAW CONDUCTING SERVICES OF PRAYER WERE SCRIPTURE IS READ AND EXPOUNDED ON BY MEN OF THE CONGREGATION...   AMEN

(2) *CHURCH WORSHIP..*
     A. ITS ELEMENTS OR ESPECIALLY SUITED TO WORSHIP IN SPIRIT AND TRUTH...
         1 CORINTHIANS 3: 11-17
     B. SO IT MUST BE PRIORITY IN ALL OUR THOUGHTS, BECAUSE IT'S THE MOST IMPORTANT THING WE DO AS BELIEVERS..

     C. PRAYER BECOMES VITAL TO BELIEVERS GROWTH AND POWER IN THE HOLY SPIRIT..

     D. READING SCRIPTURES MOTIVATE WORSHIP

     E. USE MUSIC TO ENHANCE WORSHIP FOR SONGS OF PRAISE.. PSALM 150:3-6

UNDERSTAND THERE ARE ONLY TWO WAYS TO WORSHIP..

IN SPIRIT AND TRUTH..   TELL ME WHAT YOU THINK AND I WILL TELL YOU

WHAT YOU ARE. FOR AS A MEN THINKS IN HIS HEART, SO IS HE.. PROVERBS23:7

PROPHETIC MESSAGE MINISTRY
KINGDOM PRINCIPLES
COMMANDMENT KEEPERS

AMMISHADDAI
    TRUE
    BELIEVER

COMMANDMENT KEEPERS
The ART of STUDIES

SPIRIT	MIND	SOUL
3 FAITH	3 KNOWLEDGE	3 READING
6 LOVE	6 WISDOM	6 OBSERVATION
0 HOPE of SALVATION	0 UNDERSTANDING	0 RESEARCH

HEBREW ONE YEAR DAILY BIBLE READING SCHEDULE

TOTAL NUMBER of CHAPTERS IN THE BIBLE IS (1189)

LAW OF the PROPHETS   **HOLY WRITINGS**

OLD TESTAMENT (929)   NEW TESTAMENT (260)

TO COMPLETE A READING OF THE BIBLE IN ONE HEBREW YEAR, STARTING IN THE

FIRST MONTH OF ABIB to the END OF THE YEAR...

(3) chapters READ DAILY on FIRST DAY, SECOND DAY, THIRD DAY, FIFTH DAY
    and SIXTH DAY of the week.

(4) chapters READ DAILY on FOURTH DAY (ALSO) FAST that day.

(5) chapters READ ON SABBATH..

(3) chapters READ on the LAST FOURTH DAY OF THE YEAR (ALSO) FAST that day.

(7) chapters READ on the LAST SABBATH OF THE YEAR.

THIS BIBLE STUDY SCHEDULE is CHRONOLOGICAL FROM GENESIS THRU
REVELATION...

PROPHETIC MESSAGE MINISTRY

AMMISHADDAI
   TRUE
   BELIEVER

PROPHETIC MESSAGE MINISTRY the ART of STUDIES, the PROCESSES of STUDYING: the PURSUIT of KNOWLEDGE, WISDOM and UNDERSTANDING by reading, observation (PLUS) research...   (FACT)

FOUR BASIC, MUST READ and STUDY ITEMS;

(1) HOW TO PRAY   MUST READ and STUDY   MATTHEW 6:6-15

(2) HOW TO TEST THE SPIRIT OF TRUTH, and the spirit of ERROR;   1JOHN 3:24/4:1-6
                MUST READ and STUDY

(3) TEACH NO OTHER DOCTRINE (**BIBLE**)   1TIMOTHY 1:3-8
                MUST READ and STUDY

(4) TEACH and INSTRUCT the WHOLE DUTY of a man: ECCLESIASTES 12:9-14
                MUST READ and STUDY

The things that WE READ and FIND ONLY to be **TRUE IN SCRIPTURE** shall we teach and preach, to others for this is OUR **CALLING and DUTY..** BE WISE, use your TALENTS and BLESSING to bring fourth your teaching and preaching to the MASTERS PLAN, ANOINTED KING OF ISRAEL; to expand the MOSTHIGH'S GOOD NEWS.   (TRUST) in the MOSTHIGH (FOREVER) FOR IN YHWH, the MIGHTY ONE is everlasting STRENGTH.   ISAIAH 26:4

PROPHETIC MESSAGE MINISTRY

THE ART OF STUDIES

AMMISHADDAI

    TRUE

    BELIEVER

TOPIC: *HOW GOOD and HOW PLEASANT IT IS, FOR BROTHERS TO DWELL TOGETHER IN UNITY...*   PSALM 133:1   ENDEAVOR to keep the UNITY OF THE SPIRIT in the bond of PEACE... TILL we all come to the **UNITY OF THE FAITH** and the KNOWLEDGE of the SON OF THE MOSTHIGH, to become a perfect man to the measure of the stature of the fullness of MESSIYAH;

EPHESIANS 4:3,13

"O" HOUSE OF YAHSRAEL, REPENT, REPENT, PROCLAMATION TO A NATION;

Now it will come to pass. When all these things come upon us the BLESSING and the CURSE which YHWH have set before us and we call them to mind among all nations where YHWH your ELOHIM DRIVES YOU and to you, RETURN TO YHWH your ELOHIM and OBEY HIS VOICE ACCORDING to all that I COMMAND YOU TODAY, you and your children with ALL YOUR HEART and with all your SOUL, so that YHWH your ELOHIM will bring Y.O.U. back from CAPTIVITY and have COMPASSION ON YOU and GATHER YOU AGAIN from all the NATIONS where YHWH YOUR ELOHIM HAS SCATTERED you. If any of you are DRIVEN OUT to the FARTHEST PARTS UNDER HEAVEN, from there YHWH our EL (GOD) will gather us and from there HE will bring US.   DEUTERONOMY 30:1-4

When your people YAHSRAEL ARE DEFEATED before the enemy because we have SINNED against you and when we TURN BACK to YOU and CONFESS YOUR NAME, and PRAY and MAKE SUPPLICATION TO YOU in this TEMPLE. Whatever prayer whatever supplication is made by ANYONE, OR BY ALL your people YAHSRAEL, when each one knows the PLAGUE OF HIS OWN HEART, and spreads out his hands toward this TEMPLE: "then hear in HEAVEN YOUR DWELLING PLACE, "O" YHWH and **FORGIVE,** and ACT, and GIVE TO EVERYONE ACCORDING TO ALL HIS WAYS whose heart YOU KNOW.   1KINGS 8:33,38,39

CAN TWO WALK TOGETHER, UNLESS THEY ARE AGREED?   AMOS 3:3

TWO ARE BETTER THAN ONE, because they have a good reward for their LABOR;

ECCLESIASTES 4:9-12

But, speaking the TRUTH IN LOVE, may grow up in ALL THINGS UNTO HIM who is the HEAD - MESSIYAH - from whom the whole body, joined and knit together by what every joint SUPPLIES, according to the EFFECTIVE WORKING by which every part does its share, causes growth of the BODY FOR THE EDIFYING of ITSELF IN **LOVE.**   EPHESIANS 4:15,16   THAT their hearts may be ENCOURAGED being KNIT **TOGETHER** IN LOVE, and attaining to all riches of the FULL ASSURANCE of UNDERSTANDING to the KNOWLEDGE of the MYSTERY OF THE MOSTHIGH and of MESSIYAH in whom are HIDDEN ALL the TREASURES OF WISDOM and KNOWLEDGE.

COLOSSIANS 2:2,3

YHWH IS FAITHFUL by whom you were CALLED into the FELLOWSHIP of HIS SON YAHSHUAH MESSIYAH of NAZARETH, by the NAME OF SAVIOUR ANOINTED, LET us all speak the SAMETHING and that there be NO DIVISIONS AMONG US, but that we be perfectly JOINED TOGETHER in the same MIND and in the same JUDGMENT.   1CORINTHIANS 1:9,10

EACH ones work will become CLEAR; for the day will declare it because it will be revealed by fire; and the FIRE WILL TEST EACH ONES WORK of what sort it is, if anyones work which he has built on it ENDURES, HE WILL RECEIVE A REWARD. If anyones work is BURNED HE WILL SUFFER LOSS; but he himself will be SAVED yet so as through fire. Do you know that you are the TEMPLE OF YHWH and that the SPIRIT OF YHWH DWELLS IN YOU   1CORINTHIANS 3:8-17   THE LAW OF YHWH is perfect converting the SOUL; the TESTIMONY OF YAHSHUAH OF NAZARETH is sure, making WISE the SIMPLE   PSALM 19:7   AS for the MOSTHIGH, *HIS WAY IS PERFECT;* the word of YHWH IS PROVEN. He is a shield to ALL WHO TRUST IN HIM..   PSALM 18:30

TO CONCLUDE: I URGE Y.O.U. note those who CAUSE DIVISIONS and OFFENSESES, CONTRARY to the DOCTRINE which you learned, and AVOID THEM.   ROMANS 16:17-20

COMMANDMENT KEEPERS

PROPHETIC MESSAGE MINISTRY

AMMISHADDAI

TOPIC: HISTORICALLY DEALING with PAGAN RELIGION and CULTURES..

The ISRAELITES CAME INTO CONTACT with Canaanites, Egyptians, Babylonians and Romans who worshiped FALSE GODS. YHWH WARNED HIS people, yet the ISRAELITES disOBEYED HIM;   DEUTERONOMY 28:2-68   A WORLD from which ISRAEL was called to be *RADICALLY DIFFERENT BOTH ethically and ideologically..*

DEUTERONOMY 28:1-3

ANCIENT people felt that some sort of RELIGION was NECESSARY, this is true with modern SOCIETY OF TODAY; we should also realize that in these MODERN TIMES and LAST DAYS we live in a PLURALISTIC SOCIETY in which every person is FREE to BELIEVE or DISBELIEVE as he chooses; but RELIGION is everywhere it is the HEART OF SOCIETY a person worship the DEITIES of his TOWN, city or civilization certain FEATURES ARE COMMON they all partake of the SAME WORLD VIEW which are centered on LOCALITY and PRESTIGE the differences between BABYLONIAN and GREEK RELIGION or between THE ROMANS and modern day AMERICAN RELIGIONS or MARGINAL, the idea of ONE GOD is the same JUST cultural wrapping is DIFFERENT; so one culture could ABSORB the RELIGION OF ANOTHER with out changing stride or breaking step with ONLY MINOR CHANGES; another COMMON TRAIT of today's PAGAN RELIGION and CULTURE is the making of IMAGES or Totems which in fact: ALL of these RELIGIONS and CULTURES worship IDOLS or HOLD IN HIGH ESTEEM IMAGES pertaining to the DEITIES OF TOWNS, CITIES or CIVILIZATIONS; Moreover these PAGAN GOD'S of today are merely AMPLIFIED human beings of DIFFERENT DEGREE'S, today's gods are humans made BIGGER THAN LIFE often projections of the city or township which are a *DIRECT ENMITY* to the COMMANDMENTS OF THE MOSTHIGH; you shall have NO OTHER GODS before ME and you shall NOT MAKE for yourselves CARVED IMAGES;   EXODUS 20:3,4

WHILE IN ANCIENT ROME OFFICIAL RELIGION was ORIENTED to its states while POPULAR RELIGION was ORIENTED to geographical LOCALE while RELIGION has become a COMMON PRACTICE in today's CULTURE WORLD WIDE..   TRUE

I BESEECH you ISRAEL by the MERCIES of YHWH that you present your bodies a LIVING SACRIFICE, *HOLY ACCEPTABLE TO YHWH ELSHADDAI* which is your RESPONSIBILITY NOT TO BE CONFORMED to this world, but be TRANSFORMED BY *THE RENEWING OF YOUR MIND*, that you may PROVE what is **GOOD and PERFECT** through the WILL OF YHWH...   ROMANS 12:1,2

SO I SAY, SO I SPEAK TODAY; ISRAEL we must remain absolutely **UNIQUE** being **RADICALLY DIFFERENT** from our PAGAN NEIGHBORS not allowing TRADITIONS, RELIGIONS and CULTURAL PRACTICE to remain above THE MOSTHIGH'S COMMANDMENTS and PRINCIPLES; he who has an ear let him hear what the SPIRIT says to the churches, SOJOURNING in the PAGAN CULTURES and SOCIETY, to the TWELVE TRIBES SCATTERED ABROAD *AMONG the NATIONS..*   AMEN

PROPHETIC MESSAGE MINISTRY
        AMMISHADDAI

TOPIC: CHRIST-LIKE Gentiles bond by REASONABLE service; even <u>ALL THE GENTILES</u> who are called by MY NAME, " therefore I judge that we should not trouble those from among the Gentiles who are TURNING TO the MOSTHIGH, "but that we write to them to ABSTAIN FROM things polluted by IDOLS, from SEXUAL IMMORALITY, from things STRANGLED, and from BLOOD. Being read in the synagogues every SABBATH."

ACTS 15:19-21

I beseech you therefore, brothers, by the MERCIES of YHWH, that you present your bodies a living sacrifice, holy ACCEPTABLE to YHWH, which is your *REASONABLE SERVICE...* Do not be conformed to this world, but be transformed by the RENEWING of your MIND, that you may PROVE what is that GOOD and ACCEPTABLE and PERFECT WILL OF THE MOSTHIGH.. ROMANS 12:1,2 MESSIYAH has redeemed us from the **CURSE OF THE LAW**; having become a curse for us, that the *BLESSING OF ABRAHAM* might come upon the GENTILES IN MESSIYAH YAHSHUAH, that WE (ISRAEL) might receive the promise of the SPIRIT THROUGH FAITH.. GALATIANS 3:13,14 That HE (YHWH) might present HER (CHURCH) to HIMSELF a glorious church, not having SPOT or WRINKLE or a ANY SUCH THING, but that she should be HOLY and WITHOUT BLEMISH. EPHESIANS 5:27 REMIND them of these things, charging them before YHWH NOT TO STRIVE about words to NO PROFIT, to the ruin of the hearers. Be DILIGENT to present yourself approved to YHWH, a worker who does not need to be ashamed, RIGHTLY DIVIDING the WORD OF TRUTH. 2TIMOTHY 2:14,15

DO WE THEN MAKE VOID the LAW THROUGH FAITH? Certainly NOT! On the contrary, we ESTABLISH the LAW.. ROMANS 3:31 Therefore the LAW IS HOLY, and the COMMANDMENT HOLY and JUST and GOOD. ROMANS 7:12 "For this is the COVENANT that I will make with the house of ISRAEL after those days says YHWH: I will put MY LAWS in their MIND and WRITE THEM on their HEARTS; and I will be their EL (GOD) and they shall be MY people." HEBREWS 8:10

I say then, has YHWH CAST AWAY HIS people? Certainly NOT! For I also am an ISRAELITE, of the seed of ABRAHAM, of the tribe of BENYAMIN: even so then, at this PRESENT TIME there is a REMNANT according to the election of GRACE. What then? ISRAEL has not obtained what it seeks; but the ELECT have obtained it, and the REST were BLINDED. Just as it is WRITTEN: " YHWH has given them a SPIRIT of stupor, *TO THIS VERY DAY."* For IF the first fruit is holy, the lump is also holy; and if the root is holy, so are the branches. You will say then, "braches were broken off that I might be GRAFTED IN." Well said. Because of UNBELIEF they were broken off, and you stand by FAITH. Do not be haughty, but FEAR. ROMANS 11:1,5,7,8,11, 16-20 FEAR YHWH and KEEP HIS COMMANDMENTS, for this is man's all. ECCLESIASTES 12:13,14 IT seemed good to us, being assembled with ONE ACCORD, for it seemed GOOD to the HOLY SPIRIT, and to us, to lay upon you NO GREATER BURDEN than these NECESSARY THINGS: that you ABSTAIN from things OFFERED TO IDOLS (false worship) FROM BLOOD (traditions of man) FROM THINGS STRANGLED (unclean meats) and FROM SEXUAL IMMORALITY. If you KEEP yourselves from THESE, you will do well.. (FAREWELL) ACTS 15:25,28,29
AMMISHADDAI

TOPIC: A SCATTERED PEOPLE

DISOBEDIENCE RESULTED IN **CAPTIVITY**... I (YHWH) raised My hand in an **OATH** to those in the wilderness, that I would *SCATTER* them among the GENTILES and DISPERSE them throughout the countries, " because they had not executed MY judgments, but had despised MY STATUTES, PROFANED MY SABBATHS, Therefore I also gave them up to statutes that were NOT GOOD, and judgments by which they could NOT LIVE;   EZEKIEL 20:23-25

" Therefore it happened, that just as He proclaimed and they would NOT HEAR, so they called out and I would NOT LISTEN," says the MOSTHIGH of hosts.. " BUT I **SCATTERED** them (ISRAEL) with a whirlwind among all the nations which they had not known. Thus the land became desolate after them,
                    ZECHARIAH 7: 11-14

" And they will fall by the edge of the sword, *and BE LED AWAY CAPTIVE* into all NATIONS. And YAHRUSALEM will be TRAMPLED by GENTILES until the times of the GENTILES are fulfilled
                    LUKE 21:24

WARNING to THE PASTORS /PRIEST/ MINISTER/ and ever day street teacher..
" WOE to the shepherds who destroy and scatter the sheep of MY PASTURE! "   *(ISRAEL and CHURCH)*
Therefore thus says YHWH MIGHTY ONE OF ISRAEL against the shepherds who feed MY people:
" You have scattered MY flock, driven them away, and NOT attended to them. *BEHOLD,* I will attend to you for the EVIL of your doings, '' says YHWH .. I (YHWH) will set up SHEPHERDS over them who will FEED them; and they shall FEAR NO MORE, nor be dismayed nor shall they be lacking, " says YHWH...   JEREMIAH 23:1- 4

YAHUDAH	dispersed thru out LAND of the NORTH (GREAT AMERICA)
BENYAHMIN	dispersed thru out WEST INDIES
LEVI	dispersed thru out HAITIES
SIMEON	dispersed thru out DOMINICAN REBULIC
ZEBULON	dispersed thru out PANAMA
EPHRAIM / YOSEPH	dispersed thru out PUERTO RICO
MANASSEH	dispersed thru out CUBA
GAD	dispersed thru out NATIVE peoples of the NORTH COUNTRY
REUBEN	dispersed thru out SEMINOLE INDIANS of the NORTH COUNTRY
ASHER	dispersed thru out COLUMBIA to URUGUAY
NAPTHALI	dispersed thru out ARGENTINA and CHILE
ISSACHAR	dispersed thru out MEXICO

And many more NATIONS and CULTURES have been INFLUNCED by the ALMIGHTY (ELSHADDAI) and HIS people (ISRAEL)..   YOU are the LIGHT OF THE WORLD.. MATTHEW 5:14

HE (YHWH) was moved with compassion for them, because they were **WEARY and SCATTED,** like sheep having NO SHEPHERD.. *THE HAVEST TRULY IS PLENTIFUL, but THE LABORERS are FEW*...
                    MATTHEW 9:36-38
"ISRAEL is like **SCATTERED** sheep; FIRST the king of Assyria devoured him; NOW at last this Nebuchadnezzar king of Babylon has broken his bones." THUS says YHWH MOSTHIGH of hosts: " The children of ISRAEL were oppressed, Along with the children of YAHUDAH; All who took them captive have held them fast; They have refused to let them go.. ISRAELS REDEEMER IS STRONG; YHWH MOSTHIGH of hosts is HIS NAME.. " Against the inhabitants of Babylon, A sword is against the soothsayers, and they will be fools. And against all the mixed peoples who are in her midst; A sword is against her treasures, and they will be robbed. A drought is against her waters, and they will be dried up.. For the land of carved IMAGES; and they are insane with their IDOLS..   JEREMIAH 50:17,33-38
AMMISHADDAI   *PROPHETIC MESSAGE MINISTRY*
                    (1) DISPERSED (VT) CAUSE to break up and scatter..

AFTER THE CAPTIVITY OF THE ISRAELITES.. And the RETURN OF ,7717' Chosen people going back to the land of YAHRUSALEM and YAHUDAH, Now in the first year of Cyrus king of Persia, that the Word of ,7717' by the mouth of Jeremiah might be fulfilled, ,7717' stirred up the Spirit of Cyrus King of Persia, so that he made a proclamation throughout all his Kingdom, WHO is among you of all HIS people? May his GOD (YHWH) be With him, and let him go up to YAHRUSALEM which is in YAHUDAH, and build the HOUSE OF ,7717' GOD OF ISRAEL (HE IS GOD) which is in YAHRUSALEM..   EZRA 1 : 11 / 2 : 1

   The Babylonian names of the Month, was more often used. The following is a list of the TWELVE HEBREW months, their modern Equivalents, the Characteristic, the Weather at the time, and the Agricultural activity, undertaken during them and there Seasons..

HEBREW NAME of MONTHS

(1) ABIB - (MARCH-APRIL) *ABIB* - Spring (latter) rains coupled with melting mountain snows filled streams and rivers.

(2) ZIV - (APRIL-MAY) *BALNE* - The dry season begins. Barley harvesting is completed in the month of ZIV.

(3) SIVAN - (MAY-JUNE) *MISRI* - Hot winds from southern deserts blow across the trans-Jordan area. Almonds begin to ripen. Wheat was harvested & honey gathered.

(4) TAMMUZ - (JUNE-JULY) *TOT* - Heavy dews in the morning were followed by extremely hot days. Barley figs begin to ripen.

(5) AB - (JULY-AUGUST) *HATOR* - Weather continues as the month of TAMMUZ. Walnuts, grapes and olives ripen and are harvested.

(6) ELUL - (AUGUST-SEPTEMBER) *KYAK* - heat continues with brief storms of little or no rain. Grapes, figs, and olives were processed. Winemaking is started. Summer figs and dates ripen. Pomegranates begin to ripen and are Harvested.

(7)ETHANIM - (SEPTEMBER-OCTOBER) *TOBE* - Early Fall, days shortens and nights become colder. Fields are plowed and barley and wheat is sown.

(8) BUL - (OCTOBER-NOVEMBER) *MASHIR* - Rainy season is full swing. Wheat and barley sowing is finished early in the month of HESHVAN to take advantage of the rains. Winter figs were harvested.

(9) KISLEV (CHISLEV) - (NOVEMBER-DECEMBER) *BURANT* - Weather cold with intense rainstorms. Flocks were moved down to plains from mountains to take advantage of recent growth of grasses and avoid the mountain snows.

(10) TEBETH - (DECEMBER-JANUARY) *BABNE* - Rains continue with snow and hail in the mountains. TEBETH is the coldest month of the year, and no agricultural activity is pursued.. People exist on stored and processed foods.

(11) SHEBAT - (JANUARY-FEBRUARY) *BASHAW* - Gradual warming from the Winter mouths to mild Spring. Almond and peach trees blossom.

(12) ADAR - (FEBRUARY-MARCH) *HESHVAN* Mild, pleasant days, cool nights. Light, Spring rains begin CITRUS FRUITS RIPEN and are HARVESTED:

AMMISHADDAI

| | New Moon | First Quarter | Full Moon | Last Quarter |

NEW MOON
FIRST QUARTER
FULL MOON
LAST QUARTER

" Behold, the days are coming, says יהוה when I will make a New Covenant with the house of YISRAEL and with the house of YAHUDAH " not according to the Covenant that I made with heir fathers in the day that I took them by the hand to lead them out of the land of EGYPT, My Covenant which they broke, In that HE says, " A New Covenant, " HE has made the first obsolete and growing old is ready to vanish away.. JEREMIYAH 31:31-34 / HEBREWS 8:7-13

YAHSAVIOR MESSIYAH
c.6 BC–c.AD 30
Central figure of Christianity

The central figure of the Christian faith, Jesus of Nazareth was named by his followers "Christ," deriving from the Greek meaning "Anointed One." Raised as the son of a carpenter, he was hailed as the Son of God, and continues to be recognized as such by Christians all over the world. His life is described in the four Gospels of the New Testament, written by his disciples to spread Christianity.

Christ lived in obscurity for much of his life, training as a carpenter. Not until he was 30 did he become known as a radical preacher. With a band of 12 disciples, he traveled through Galilee, proclaiming the coming of the kingdom of God and emphasizing the importance of charity, humility, and love over strict observance of Jewish ritual. The Gospels state that he also performed miracles.

He attracted many followers, and was seen as a threat by the Jewish authorities, who, in Jerusalem, had him arrested and crucified for blasphemy. According to the Gospels he rose from the dead three days after his death. His disciples went on to preach the New Covenant, winning many converts.

ARK OF THE COVENANT

Ark of the Covenant was a sacred wooden chest described in the Bible as representing God's presence. It was called the Ark of the Covenant because it symbolized the *covenant*, a special agreement that the Israelites made with God at Mount Sinai.

Model of the ark of the covenant. The ark was a rectangular box of acacia wood that contained the tables of the Ten Commandments, a pot of manna, and Aaron's rod. The lid, or "mercy seat," was a gold plate surrounded by golden cherubim with outstretched wings. The ark was the symbol of God's presence among His people.

Hebrew Letter Charts

NAME	BOOK	CURSIVE	BOLD	RASHI	HAND	NUMBER	Sound	Literal Meaning	Symbolic Meaning
Aleph	א					1	a	ox, bull	strength, leader, first
Bet /Vet	ב					2	b/v	tent, house	household in, into
Gimel	ג					3	g	camel	pride, to lift up
Dalet	ד					4	d	door	pathway, to enter
He	ה					5	h	window, fence	"the", to reveal
Vav	ו					6	u	nail	"and", add, secure, hook
Zayin	ז					7	z	weapon	cut, to cut off
CHet	ח					8	CH	fence, hedge, chamber	private, to separate
Tet	ט					9	t	to twist, a snake	to surround
Yud	י					10	i	closed hand	deed, work, to make
Kaf/ Chaf	כ					20	j	arm, wing open hand	to cover, allow, strength
Lamed	ל					30	l	cattle goad, staff	prod, go toward, tongue
Mem	מ					40	m	water	massive, overpower chaos
Nun	נ					50	n	fish (moving)	activity, life
Samech	ס					60	x	a prop	support, turn
Ayin	ע					70	o	eye	see, know, experience
Pe/Fe	פ					80	p/f	mouth	speak, open, word
Tzadi	צ					90	c	fish-hook	harvest, desire
Kof	ק					100	q	back of the head	behind, the last, least
Resh	ר					200	r	head	person, head highest
Sin/ Shin	ש					300	s/sh	teeth	consume, destroy
Tau	ת					400	t	sign, cross	covenant, to seal

5/3/2002

CHRONOLOGY OF ISRAELITE CIVILIZATION

MOSES LED THE CHILDREN OF ISRAEL OUT OF EGYPT

YAHSHUAH THE SON OF NUN, LED ISRAEL INTO CANAAN

The PERIOD of the JUDGES
YAHSHUAH
OTHNIEL
EHUD
DEBORAH
GIDEON
AHIMELECH
JEPHTHATH
IBZAN
ELON
ABDON
SAMSON
MICAH
The DANITES
The LEVITE
The ISRAELITE CONFEDERATION AGAINST BENYAHMIN
BOAZ
ELI
SAMUEL

The PERIOD of the MONARCHY

KING SAUL
KING DAVID
KING SOLOMON

19 KINGS OF YAHUDAH   20 KINGS OF ISRAEL
1QUEEN

THE DESTRUCTION OF ISRAEL IN 721 B. C .E.

THE DESTRUCTION OF YAHUDAH IN 586 B. C. E.

CAPTIVITY AND RISE OF GENTILE POWERS

BABYLON
PERSIA
GREECE
DIVIDED GREEK EMPIRE
ROME
EAST and WEST ROMAN EMPIRE
EAST and WEST EUROPE
THE USA, EURO, UN, G - 7, CHINA - JAPAN, ARABS

ISRAEL IN CAPTIVITY AMONG NATIONS

KINGS AND QUEENS OF ISRAEL
KINGS OF UNITED ISRAEL

SAUL	1042-1000 BC
DAVID	1000-961 BC
SOLOMON	961-922 BC

KINGS AND QUEENS OF SOUTHERN KINGDOM (YAHUDAH)

REHOBOAM	922-915 BC
ABIYAH	915-913 BC
ASA	913-873 BC
YEHOSHAPHAT	873-849 BC
YEHORAM	849-842 BC
AHAZIAH	842 BC
QUEEN ATHALIAH	842-837 BC
YOASH	837-800 BC
AMAZIAH	800-783 BC
UZZIAH/AZARIAH	783-742 BC
YOTHAM	742-735 BC
AHAZ	735-715 BC
HEZEKIAH	715-687 BC
MANASSEH	687-642 BC
AMON	642-640 BC
YOSIAH	640-609 BC
YEHOAHAZ	609 BC
YEHOIAKIM	609-598 BC
YEHOIACHIN	598-597 BC
ZEDEKIAH	597-587 BC

KINGS OF NORTHERN KINGDOM (ISRAEL)

YEROBOAM I	922-901 BC
NADAB	901-900 BC
BAASHA	900-877 BC
ELAH	877-876 BC
ZIMRI	876 BC
OMRI	876-869 BC
AHAB	869-850 BC
AHAZIAH	850-849 BC
YORAM	849-842 BC
YEHU	842-815 BC
YEHOAHAZ	815-801 BC
YEHOASH	801-786 BC
YEROBOAM II	786-746 BC
ZECHARIAH	746-745 BC
SHALLUM	745 BC
MENAHEM	745-738 BC
PEKAHIAH	738-737 BC
PEKAH	737-732 BC
HOSHEA	732-722 BC

PROPHETIC MESSAGE MINISTRY

AMMISHADDAI

CHART of the EMPIRES

Based on DANIEL 2: 1-49 & 7: 1-28
REVELATION 17: 1-18

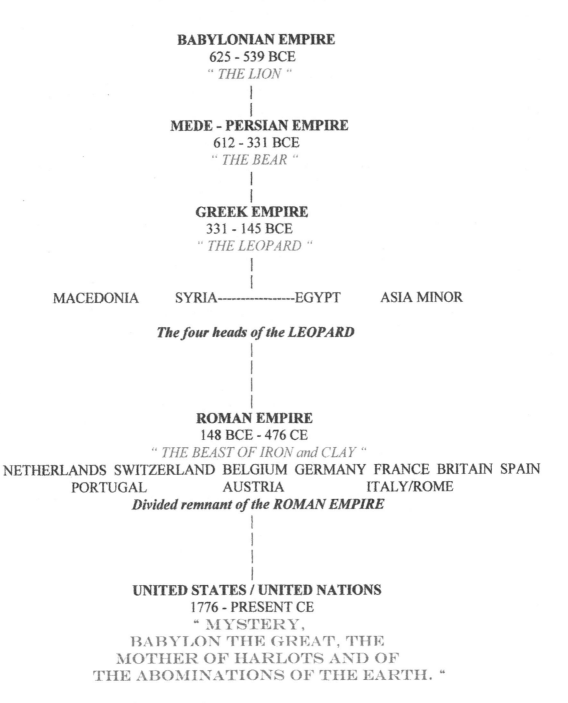

BABYLONIAN EMPIRE
625 - 539 BCE
" THE LION "

MEDE - PERSIAN EMPIRE
612 - 331 BCE
" THE BEAR "

GREEK EMPIRE
331 - 145 BCE
" THE LEOPARD "

MACEDONIA   SYRIA-----------------EGYPT   ASIA MINOR

The four heads of the LEOPARD

ROMAN EMPIRE
148 BCE - 476 CE
" THE BEAST OF IRON and CLAY "

NETHERLANDS SWITZERLAND BELGIUM GERMANY FRANCE BRITAIN SPAIN
PORTUGAL   AUSTRIA   ITALY/ROME
Divided remnant of the ROMAN EMPIRE

UNITED STATES / UNITED NATIONS
1776 - PRESENT CE
" MYSTERY,
BABYLON THE GREAT, THE
MOTHER OF HARLOTS AND OF
THE ABOMINATIONS OF THE EARTH. "

PROPHETIC MESSAGE MINISTRY

AMMISHADDAI
TRUE
BELIEVER

TOPIC : WHO'S (MIGHTY ONE) GOD is TRUE ??

" Your name shall NO LONGER be called YAHCOB, but YISRAEL (Prince with YAH) for you have struggled with YHWH and with men, and have PREVAILED."   GENESIS 32:27,28

YHWH will establish you as a HOLY people to HIMSELF, just as HE has sworn to you, *IF YOU KEEP THE COMMANDMENTS OF YHWH AND WALK IN HIS WAYS.. "* Then all peoples of the earth shall see that you are called by the name of YHWH, and they shall be AFRAID Of YOU.   DEUTERONOMY 28:9,10

QUESTION ? What does the HEBREW or YISRAELITE, have to do with SALVATION ?

(A) " You worship what you do not know; we know what we worship, for SALVATION IS Of The HEBREWS.. " But the hour is coming, and now is, when the TRUE WORSHIPERS will WORSHIP the ABBA (FATHER) in SPIRIT and TRUTH; for the ABBA is seeking such to WORSHIP HIM.. YHWH is SPIRIT, and those who worship HIM MUST WORSHIP in Spirit and Truth."   JOHN 4:20-24

(B) I Say then, *HAS YHWH CAST AWAY HIS PEOPLE ?* Certainly NOT! For I also am an YISRAELITE, of the seed of ABRAHAM, of the tribe of BENYAHMIN.. YHWH HAS NOT CAST AWAY HIS PEOPLE whom HE foreknew..   ROMANS 11:1-8

(C) For if the FIRSTFRUIT is HOLY, the lump is also HOLY; and if the ROOT is HOLY, so are the BRANCHES. Do not boast against the branches. Remember that you do not support the root, but the root supports you. You will say then, " BRANCHES were broken off that I might be grafted in." Well said. Because of UNBELIEF they were broken off, and you stand by FAITH. DO NOT BE HAUGHTY, but fear. *OTHERWISE YOU ALSO WILL BE CUT OFF* And they also, if they DO NOT CONTINUE in unbelief, will *BE GRAFTED IN,* for YHWH is able to GRAFT THEM IN AGAIN.. And so all YISRAEL will be SAVED, as it is written :
          ROMANS 11:13-27

(D) Who are YISRAELITES, to whom pertain the adoption, the glory, the *COVENANTS,* the *GIVING Of The LAW, (COMMANDMENTS) The SERVICE Of YHWH, And The PROMISES;* from whom, according to the flesh, MESSIYAH CAME, who is over all, the eternally blessed GOD (MIGHTY ONE) AMEN..   ROMANS 9:4,5

QUESTION ? Whom did YHWH MAKE A NEW COVENANT with ??

" For this is the COVENANT that I will make with the HOUSE Of YISRAEL after those days, says YHWH: I WILL PUT MY LAWS IN THEIR MINDS and WRITE THEM ON THEIR HEARTS; and I will be their GOD (MIGHTY ONE) and they shall be MY PEOPLE. In that HE says, *A NEW COVENANT,* " He has made the first obsolete.   HEBREWS 8:7-13

PROPHETIC MESSAGE MINISTRY
. אמתסמאדדאהמא

TOPIC : TEACHING AS DOCTRINES THE COMMANDMENTS OF MEN..

" Why do you also TRANSGRESS the COMMANDMENT of YHWH because of your TRADITION? ' Thus you have *MADE THE COMMANDMENT OF YHWH OF NO EFFECT BY YOUR TRADITION.*. ISAIAH prophesy of you HYPOCRITES, as it is written: This people honors ME (YHWH) with their lips, But their heart is far from ME. And in VAIN they WORSHIP ME, Teaching as doctrines the commandments of men.' " For laying aside the COMMANDMENT OF YHWH, you hold the TRADITION of men - and many other such things you do." ALL TOO WELL you REJECT (set aside) the COMMANDMENT OF YHWH, that you may keep your TRADITION.   MATTHEW 15:3,6 / MARK 7:6-9

" <u>Therefore by their fruits you will know them</u>. " Not everyone who says to ME, " YHWH, YHWH,' shall enter the KINGDOM OF HEAVEN, but he who does the will of MY FATHER in HEAVEN. " Many will say to ME in that day, YHWH, YHWH have we not prophesied in YOUR NAME, and done many wonders in YOUR NAME?' " And then I will declare to them, I never knew you; depart from ME, you who practice lawlessness!' " For they bind heavy burdens, hard to bear, and lay them on men's shoulders; but they themselves will not move them with one of their fingers. " <u>But all their works they do to be seen by men</u> " They love the place of honor at the feasts, the best seats in the synagogues, EVEN SO you also outwardly appear righteous to men, but inside you are full of HYPOCRISY and LAWLESSNESS..
                    MATTHEW 7:20-23 / MATTHEW 23:4-6,28

Therefore YHWH said: " Inasmuch as these people draw near with their mouths And honor ME (YHWH) with their lips, But have removed their hearts far from ME, <u>And their fear toward ME is taught by the commandment of men</u>, SURELY YOU HAVE THINGS TURNED AROUND!   ISAIAH 29:13,16

LET NO ONE CHEAT YOU OF YOUR REWARD, taking delight in **FALSE HUMILITY and WORSHIP** of Angels, intruding into those things which he has seen, vainly puffed up by his fleshly mind, and NOT HOLDING FAST to the Head (MESSIYAH) from whom all the body, nourished and knit together by joints and ligaments, grows with the INCREASE that is from YHWH.. Therefore, if you died with MESSIYAH from the basic principles of the world, why as though living in the world, do you subject yourselves to regulations - ACCORDING to the COMMANDMNETS and DOCTRINES of men? These things indeed have an appearance of wisdom in self - imposed religion, FALSE HUMILITY, and NEGLECT of the body, BUT ARE OF NO VALUE against the indulgence of the flesh.   COLOSSIANS 2:18-23

THIS TESTIMONY IS TRUE.. Therefore rebuke them sharply, that they may be sound in the faith, not giving heed to JEWISH FABLES and commandments of men who turn from the TRUTH. They profess to KNOW YHWH, but in works they DENY HIM (YHWH) being abominable, disobedient, and disqualified for every good work..   TITUS 1:13,14,16

PROPHETIC MESSAGE MINISTRY
אמכמאודדא .

TOPIC : YAHSAVIOR, DO YOU REALLY KNOW HIM (HIS) WAY ?

In the beginning was the WORD, And the WORD was with YHWH, And the WORD was YHWH. HE was in the beginning with YHWH. In HIM was LIFE, and the LIFE was the LIGHT OF MEN. And the WORD became FLESH And DWELT among US, and we beheld HIS GLORY, the GLORY as of the ONLY BEGOTTEN OF the FATHER, full of grace and truth..

JOHN 1:1-5,14

(B) BORN INTO THE WORLD SENT TO THE HOUSE OF ISRAEL.

" I was not sent except to the LOST SHEEP OF THE HOUSE OF YISRAEL." " It is NOT GOOD to take the children's bread and throw it to the little dogs..

MATTHEW 15:24,28

AND HE (YAHSAVIOR) will reign over the house of YAHCOB FOREVER, and of HIS KINGDOM there will be no end."

LUKE 1:33

(C) The Customs of RELIGIONS are Use - Less. (Christmas , Easter, Lent, Halloween ect.)

DO NOT LEARN the way of the Gentiles; DO NOT be dismay at the signs of heaven.. For the CUSTOMS OF the peoples are FUTILE;

JEREMIAH 10:1-5

(D) YAHSAVIOR DIED FOR OUR SINS ON PASSOVER; Which represents HIM..

For indeed MESSIYAH, Our PASSOVER, was sacrificed for US. Therefore keep the FEAST, with the unleavened bread of sincerity and truth.

1 CORINTHIANS 5:7,8

(E) DID NOT DIE ON GOOD FRIDAY.. OR RESURRECT ON EASTER SUNDAY..

" FOR as YONAH was three days and three nights in the belly of the great fish, so will the SON OF MAN be three days and three nights in the heart of the earth.

MATTHEW 12:40

The KINGDOMS of this world have become the KINGDOMS of YHWH and of HIS MESSIYAH, and HE shall reign FOREVER and EVER!"

REVELATION 11:15

(F) MANY THINK THEY KNOW the CREATOR, BUT INSTEAD THEY DON'T BELIEVE the CREATOR;

For if he who comes preaches another YAHSAVIOR whom we have not preached, or if you receive a different SPIRIT which you have NOT RECEIVED, or a DIFFERENT GOSPEL which you have NOT ACCEPTED..

2 CORINTHIANS 11:4-15

REPENT AND CHANGE YOUR WAY BEFORE ITS TO LATE! Many will say to ME in that day, LORD, LORD have we not prophesied in YOUR NAME, cast out demons in YOUR NAME, and done many wonders in YOUR NAME?" And then I will decalare to them, I never knew you; depart from ME, you who practice lawlessness!'

MATTHEW 7:21-23

PROPHETIC MESSAGE MINISTRY

אכמסהאודא.

Which Day Is The Sabbath Day?

Every Sunday, millions upon millions of people all over the world attend church services without given their actions a second thought. It probably would seem blasphemous for these people to change their day of worship. After all, this is the way of the world. Nevertheless...

Revelation 12:9 And the great dragon was cast out, that old serpent, called the Devil, and Satan, WHICH DECEIVETH THE WHOLE WORLD: he was cast out into the earth...

One way that Satan has deceived the world is through the neglect (or change) of the weekly sabbath day.

Many theologians teach that Saturday is the JEWISH sabbath, and Sunday is the Christian sabbath. When Yahweh instituted the sabbath there was neither Jew nor Christian around.

Genesis 2:2-3 And on the seventh day Elohim ended his work which he had made.
And Elohim BLESSED THE SEVENTH DAY, AND SANCTIFIED IT: because that in it HE rested from all his work which Elohim created and made.

The sabbath observance is so important that YAHWEH listed it in the Ten Commandments!

Exodus 20:8-11 Remember the sabbath day, to keep it holy.
Six days shall thy labor and do all thy work: But the seventh day is the sabbath of Yahweh thy Elohim: in it thou shalt not do any work, thou, nor thy son, nor thy daughter, thy manservant, nor thy maidservant, nor thy cattle, nor thy stranger that is within thy gates:
For in six days Yahweh made heaven and earth, the sea, and all that in them is, and rested the SEVENTH day: wherefore YAHWEH BLESSED the sabbath day, and HALLOWED it.

On the sabbath we refrain from work and we have a holy gathering.

Leviticus 23:3 Six days shall work be done: but the seventh day is the sabbath of rest, an HOLY CONVOCATION; ye shall do NO work therein: it is the sabbath of YAHWEH in all your dwellings.

Yahshua gave us some very important info here in

Matthew 15:5,7-9 3 But he answered and said unto them, Why do ye also transgress the commandment of Elohim by your tradition?......Ye hypocrites, well did Isaiah prophesy of you, saying, This people draweth nigh unto me with their mouth, and honoureth me with their lips; but their heart is far from me.

But in vain they do worship me, teaching for doctrines the commandments of men.

The true Messiah taught us to do the will of the Father (YAHWEH) by keeping his commandments. Churches are not teaching people the message of REPENTENCE and HOLINESS!

Acts 13:42 And when the Jews were gone out of the synagogue, the Gentiles besought that these words might be preached to them the next SABBATH day.

The apostle Paul observed the sabbath!:

Acts 18:4 And he reasoned in the synagogue every SABBATH, and persuaded the Jews and the Greeks.

Yahshua observed the sabbath!

Luke 4:16 ...and as his (Yahshua's) custom was, he went into the synagogue on the SABBATH day to read.

All the servants of YAH observed his laws, statutes, and ordinances.

Isaiah 24:5-6 The earth also is defiled under the inhabitants thereof; because they have transgressed the laws, changed the ordinance, broken the everlasting covenant.

Therefore hath the curse devoured the earth, and they that dwell therein are desolate: therefore the inhabitants of the earth are burned, and few men left.

Colossians 2:8 Beware lest any man spoil you through philosophy and vain deceit, after the tradition of men, after the rudiments of the world, and not after Messiah.

Learn the truth of the scriptures!

Meet us every sabbath (Saturday) @ noon @

Regency Square Library
9900 Regency Sq Blvd.
Jacksonville, Fl

Isaiah 56:6-8 Also the sons of the stranger, that join themselves to YAHWEH, to serve him, and to love the name of YAHWEH, to be his servants, EVERYONE THAT KEEPETH THE SABBATH FROM POLLUTING IT, AND TAKETH HOLD OF MY COVENANT;
Even them will I bring to my holy mountain, and make them joyful in my house of prayer: their burnt offerings and their sacrifices shall be accepted upon my altar; for mine house shall called an HOUSE OF PRAYER FOR ALL PEOPLE.

www.yahshuah.com

Article courtesy of "The Gospel: Raw, Uncut & Unheard!

8/3/2003

TOPIC : WARNINGS and TAKING HEED.. O Dry bones, hear the WORD Of YHWH.
" Son of man, I have made you a watchman for the house of YISRAEL; therefore hear a word from MY mouth, and give them **WARNING** for ME; When I say to the wicked, You shall surely die, and you give him NO WARNING, nor speak to warn the wicked from his wicked way, to save his life, that same wicked man shall die in his iniquity; but his blood I will require at your hand. " Yet, if you warn the wicked, and he DOES NOT turn from his wickedness, nor from his wicked way, he shall die in his iniquity; but you have delivered your soul. Again, when a righteous man turns from his righteousness and commits iniquity, and I lay a stumbling block before him, he shall die; because you DID NOT give him WARNING, he shall die in his sin, and his righteousness which he has done shall NOT BE REMEMBERED; but his blood I will require at your hand. " Nevertheless if you WARN the righteous man that the righteous should NOT SIN, and he does not sin, he shall surely live because he **TOOK WARNING**; also you will have delivered your soul."   EZEKIEL 3:17-21

Now upon you I will soon pour out MY FURY, and spend MY ANGER upon you; I will judge you according to you ways, and I will repay you for all your ABOMINATIONS.. MY eye will not spare, nor will I have pity; I will repay you according to your ways, and your abominations will be in your midst. Then you shall know that I am YHWH who strikes.   EZEKIEL 7:8,9
" And you shall know that I am YHWH; for you have NOT WALKED in MY STATUES nor executed MY JUDGMENTS, but have done according to the CUSTOMS OF THE GENTILES which are all around you." But if a man is just and does what is lawful and right; nor lifted up his eyes to the idols of the house of YISRAEL, nor defiled his neighbor's wife, if he has not oppressed anyone, has robbed NO ONE BY VIOLENCE, but has given his bread to the hungry and covered the naked with clothing; if he has not exacted usury nor taken any increase, but has withdrawn his hand from iniquity and EXECUTED TRUE JUDGMENT between man and man; if he has walked in MY STATUES and KEPT MY JUDGMENTS faithfully - he is just; he shall surely live!" says YHWH MIGHTY ONE..
                    EZEKIEL 11:12 / 18:5-9

" But when a righteous man turns away from his righteousness and commits iniquity, and does according to all the abominations that the wicked man does, shall he live? All the righteousness which he has done shall not be remembered; because of the unfaithfulness of which he is guilty and the sin which he has committed, because of them he shall die. When a righteous man turns away from his righteousness, commits iniquity, and dies in it, it is because of the iniquity which he has done that he dies.. " Because they HAD NOT executed MY JUDGMENTS but had despised MY STATUES, profaned MY SABBATHS, and their eyes were fixed on their fathers idols (traditions) therefore I also gave them up to statutes that were NOT GOOD, and judgments by which they could not live; and I pronounced them UNLCEAN because of their RITUAL GIFTS, Nevertheless if you warn the wicked to turn from his way, and he does not turn from his way, he shall die in his iniquity; but you have delivered your soul. " Say to them: as I live, says YHWH MIGHTY ONE, I have no pleasure in the death of the wicked, but that the wicked turn from his way and live. *TURN, FROM YOUR EVIL WAYS! FOR WHY SHOULD YOU DIE,* O HOUSE Of YISRAEL? EZEKIEL 18:24-26 / 2 PETER 2:19-22 / EZEKIEL 20:23-26 / EZEKIEL 33:7-9,11
                    MYTH : ONCE SAVED ALL WAYS SAVED   REVELATION 22:19
AMMISHADDAI

TOPIC : PRACTICAL WISDOM.. Happy is the man who finds WISDOM, And the man who gains understanding; Her WAYS are WAYS Of pleasantness, And all her PATHS ARE PEACE She is a TREE Of LIFE to those who take hold of her. And happy are ALL WHO RETAIN HER.. (WISDOM)
PROVERBS 3:4-6,13,17,18

WISDOM is a defense (PROTECTIVE SHADE) as money is a defense, But the EXCELLENCE Of KNOWLEDGE is that WISDOM gives LIFE to those who have it.. ECCLESIASTES 7:12

GIVE INSTRUCTION to a WISE man, and he will be still WISER; Teach a JUST man, and he will INCREASE in LEARNING.. The *FEAR Of the MOSTHIGH is the BEGINNING Of WISDOM*, And the KNOWLEDGE Of the HOLYONE is UNDERSTANDING.. PROVERBS 9:9-12

WISDOM is the principal thing; Therefore get WISDOM. And in all your getting, get UNDERSTANDING.. EXALT HER, and she will promote you; She will bring you HONOR, when you EMBRACE Her. She will place on your head and ornament of grace; A CROWN Of GLORY She will deliver to you." And the years of your LIFE will be MANY. I have taught you in the WAY OF WISDOM;
PROVERBS 4:1,2,4-11

WISDOM strengthens the WISE more then ten rulers of the city. For there is NOT a JUST man on earth who DOES GOOD And does NOT SIN .. ALSO do not take to heart everything people say. For many times, also your own heart has KNOWN that even you have cursed others. All this I have PROVED (TESTED) BY WISDOM.. I applied my heart to know, to search and seek out WISDOM and the REASON OF THINGS, ECCLESIASTES 7:19-26

WISDOM is better than STRENGTH. Nevertheless the poor mans WISDOM is despised, and his WORDS are not heard. Words of the wise, spoken quietly, should be heard rather than the shout of a ruler of fools. WISDOM is better than weapons of war; but ONE SINNER destroys much good."
ECCLESIASTES 9:13-18

Through WISDOM a House is Built, And by UNDERSTANDING it is ESTABLISHED; A WISE man is strong, (KEN) YES, a man of KNOWLEDGE INCREASES STRENGTH; For by WISE COUNSEL you will wage your own war, And in a multitude of counselors there is safety. PROVERBS 24:2,3,5,6

WARNING.. AVOID WORLDLY WISDOM..

Let NO ONE deceive himself. If anyone among you seems to be WISE in this AGE, let him become a fool that HE MAY become WISE. For the WISDOM OF THIS WORLD (SECULAR) is foolishness with יהוה for it is written, " HE catches the wise in their own craftiness. " 1 CORINTHIANS 3:18-23

For our boasting is this : the TESTIMONY Of our conscience that we conducted ourselves in the world in SIMPLICITY and YHWH SINCERITY, Not with Fleshly wisdom but by the GRACE Of יהוה and more abundantly toward you. For we are not writing any other things to you than what you READ or UNDERSTAND. Now I TRUST YOU will UNDERSTAND, even to the end in the day of *IMMANUEL YAHSAVIOR..* YAH BLESS.. Shalom.. 2 CORINTHIANS 1:12,13

PROPHETIC MESSAGE MINISTRY
אמםאדראמא .

TOPIC : MALE and FEMALE SERVANTS..

Among the YISRAELITES, involuntary SERVITUDE and SLAVE TRADING was PROHIBITED, and to guard against such PRACTICES, יהוה promulgated this ORDINANCE :

(EXODUS 21:16 / DEUTERONOMY 24:7)

The SERVICE or SERVITUDE that existed with the YISRAELITES was either VOLUNTARY or JUDICIALLY IMPOSED by the LAW OF יהוה as a form of RETRIBUTION. These conditions or service were never to exceed SIX YEARS and during the period of INDENTURE the servant was to be treated as a HIRED SERVANT :   (LEVITICUS 25:39-42 / EXODUS 22:2-4)   The LAW gave the HIRED SERVANT and even the INDENTURED SERVANT many rights and privileges which his EMPLOYER or MASTER was bond to RESPECT..   (TRUE)

You shall NOT OPPRESS a hired servant who is poor and needy, whether one of your brothers or one of the foreigners who is in your land within your gates. " Each day you shall give him his WAGES, and not let the sun go down on it, for he is poor and has set his heart on it; lest he cry out against you to YHWH, and it be SIN TO YOU.. WOE to him who builds his house by unrighteousness and his chambers by injustice, who uses his neighbor's service without wages and gives him nothing for his work,   DEUTERONOMY 24:14,15 / JEREMIAH 22:22:13   FOR THE SCRIPTURE SAYS, " You SHALL NOT muzzle an ox while it treads out the grain" and " THE LABORER IS WORTHY OF HIS WAGES." You SHALL NOT cheat your neighbor, nor rob him. The wages of him who is HIRED shall not remain with you all night until morning..   1 TIMOTHY 5:18 / LEVITICUS 19:13

Masters (Employer) give your bondservants what is JUST and FAIR, knowing that you also have a MASTER IN HEAVEN.. Bondservants, be OBEDIENT to those who are you masters according to the flesh, with fear and trembling, in SINCERITY OF HEART, as to MESSIYAH. With good will doing SERVICE, as to YHWH and NOT to men, knowing that whatever GOOD anyone does, he will receive the same from YHWH, whether he is a SLAVE or FREE..   COLOSSIANS 4:1 / EPHESIANS 6:5-9

Indeed the wages of the LABORES who mowed your fields, which you kept back by fraud, cry out; and the cries of the reapers have reached the ears of YHWH of SABAOTH (PEACE) You SHALL NOT rule over him with RIGOR, but you shall FEAR your GOD (MIGHTY ONE) And as for your male and female slaves whom you may have - from the NATIONS (foreigners) around you, from them YOU MAY BUY male and female SLAVES..   JAMES 5:4 / LEVITICUS 25:43,44   IF your brother, a HEBREW man, or a HEBREW woman, is sold to you and SERVES you SIX YEARS, then in the seventh year you shall LET HIM GO FREE from you. And when you send him away free from you, you shall NOT LET HIM GO AWAY EMPTY - HANDED: " you shall supply him liberally, from your flock, from what YHWH has BLESSED you with, you shall give to him. A WISE servant will rule over a son who causes shame, and will share an inheritance among the brothers.. DEUTERONOMY 15:12-18 / PROVERBS 17:2

" If you buy a HEBREW SERVANT, he shall serve SIX YEARS; and in the seventh he shall go out FREE and pay nothing. If he comes in by himself, he shall go out by himself; if he comes in married, then his wife shall go out with him. " But if the servant plainly says, I love my master, my wife, and my children; I will NOT GO OUT FREE," " Then his master shall bring him to the JUDGES. He shall also bring him to the door, or to the doorpost, and his master shall pierce his ear with an awl; and he shall serve him forever.. " if he takes another wife, he shall NOT DIMINISH her food, her clothing, and her MARRIAGE RIGHTS.. And if he does not do these three for her, then she shall go out free,

EXODUS 21:1-6

PROPHETIC MESSAGE MINSTRY
      AMMISHADDAI   PAGE 1 OF 2

TOPIC : MALE and FEMALE SERVANTS..

NOW THESE ARE THE ORDINANCES WHICH YOU SHALL SET BEFORE THEM :

Moreover you may buy the children of the strangers who dwell among you, and their families who are with you, which they beget in your land; and they shall become your property.. And you may take them as an INHERITANCE for your children after you, to inherit them as a possession; they shall be your PERMANENT SLAVES (SERVANTS) But regarding your brothers, the children of YISRAEL, you shall not rule over one another with RIGOR. Now if a SOJOURNER or STRANGER close to you becomes RICH, and one of your brothers who dwells by him becomes poor, and sells himself to the stranger or sojourner close to you or to a member of the strangers family, after he is sold he may be REDEEMED again. One of his brothers may redeem him; or his uncle or his uncles son may redeem him; Or anyone who is near of kin to him in his family may redeem him; or if he is able he may redeem himself. THUS he shall RECKON with him who bought him: he shall be with him as a yearly hired servant, and he shall NOT RULE with rigor over him in your sight..   LEVITICUS 25:45-54

" You SHALL NOT give back to his master the slave who has escaped from his master to you. " He may dwell with you in your midst, in the place which he chooses within one of your gates, where it seems best to him; you shall NOT OPPRESS him.   DEUTERONOMY 23:15,16

" And if a man beats his MALE or FEMALE servant with a rod, so that he dies under his hand, he shall surely be PUNISHED.. " Notwithstanding, if he remains alive a day or two, he shall not be punished; for he is his PROPERTY.. And if he knocks out the tooth of his MALE or FEMALE servant, he shall let him go FREE for the sake of his tooth..   EXODUS 21:20,21

Let as many bondservants as are under the yoke count their own masters worthy of all honor, so that the NAME Of יהוה and HIS DOCTRINE may NOT BE BLASPHEMED.. And those who have BELIEVING masters, let them NOT DESPISE them because they are brothers, but rather SERVE them because those who are benefited are BELIEVERS and beloved. Teach and exhort these things.   1 TIMOTHY 6:1,2

Bondservants, OBEY in all things your master according to the flesh, not with eye service, as men - pleasers, but in SINCERITY Of HEART, FEARING YHWH.. And whatever you do, do it heartily, as to YHWH and not to men. Knowing that from YHWH you will receive the REWARD OF THE INHERITANCE; for you serve IMMANUEL MESSIYAH.. But he who does wrong will be REPAID for what he has done, and there is NO PARTIALITY.. Masters (Employers) give your bondservants what is JUST and FAIR, knowing that you also have a MASTER IN HEAVEN..   COLOSSIANS 3:22-25 / 4:1

Exhort bondservants to BE OBEDIENT to their own masters, TO BE WELL PLEASING in all things, not answering back.. Not thieving, but showing all good fidelity, that they may adorn the doctrine of YHWH our SAVIOR in all things..   TITUS 2:9,10

PROPHETIC MESSAGE MINISTRY
    אמסמאחרא .

TOPIC : PROPHECY the INGATHERING Of HIS People.. Now when the sun was going down, a deep sleep fell upon ABRAM; and behold, horror and great darkness fell upon him. Then HE (YHWH) said to Abram; " KNOW CERTAINLY that your descendants will be strangers in a land that is NOT THEIRS, and will SERVE THEM, and they will afflict them four hundred years. " And also the NATION whom they SERVE I will JUDGE; afterward they shall come out with great possessions. On the same day YHWH made a covenant with Abram, saying: to your descendants I have given this land, from the river of EGYPT to the great river, the RIVER EUPHRATES -   GENESIS 15:12-14

They shall not hurt nor destroy in all MY HOLY MOUNTAIN, for the earth shall be full of the KNOWLEDGE Of the MOSTHIGH As the waters cover the sea.. In that day there shall be a ROOT OF JESSE, who shall stand as a BANNER to the people; for the Gentiles shall seek Him, And His resting place shall be Glorious." It shall come to pass in that day that YHWH shall set HIS HAND AGAIN the second time to RECOVER the REMNANT of HIS people who are left, HE will set up a banner for the NATIONS, And will ASSEMBLE (GATHER) the outcasts of YISRAEL, And GATHER together the DESPERSED of YAHUDAH from the FOUR CORNERS of the earth..   ISAIAH 11:9-12
" I will strengthen the HOUSE Of YAHUDAH, And I will save the HOUSE Of YOSEPH (ISRAEL) I will bring them back, Because I have MERCY on them. They shall be as though I had NOT CAST them aside; For I am YHWH their MIGHTYONE, And I will hear them. I will WHISTLE for them and GATHER THEM, For I will REDEEM THEM; And they shall increase as they once increased. I will scatter (SOW) them AMONG the peoples, And they shall remember ME in FAR COUNTRIES; they shall live, together with their children, And they shall return. I will also bring them back from the land of EGYPT, And GATHER THEM from Assyria. Until NO more room is found for them.
                                                                ZECHARIAH 10:6-10
     And it shall come to pass in that day From the channel of the RIVER EUPHRATES to the Brook of EGYPT; And you will be GATHERED ONE by ONE, O you children of YISRAEL. So it shall be in that day; the GREAT TRUMPET will be blown; they will come, who are about to perish in the land of Assyria. And they who are OUTCASTS in the land of EGYPT (BONDAGE) and shall worship YHWH in the HOLY mount at YAHRUSALEM.. " Therefore thus says YHWH, who redeemed Abraham, concerning the house of YAHCOB : " YAHCOB shall not now, BE ASHAMED, Nor shall his face now, GROW PALE; But when he sees his children, the work of MY (YHWH) HANDS, in his midst, they will HALLOW the HOLY ONE Of YAHCOB (IMMANUEL) And FEAR the MIGHTY ONE OF YISRAEL. These also who erred in spirit will come to understanding, And those who complained will learn doctrine." Thus says YHWH, the HOLY ONE OF YISRAEL and HIS MAKER : Ask Me of things to come concerning My sons; And concerning the work of My Hands, you command Me. I have raised him up in RIGHTEOUSNESS, And I will direct all his ways; He shall build My city And let My EXILES GO FREE. Not for price nor reward." SAYS THE MOSTHIGH OF HOSTS..   ISAIAH 27:12,13 / 29:22-24 / 45:11-13

NOW A GREAT SIGN APPEARED IN HEAVEN: then the woman fled into the wilderness, where she has a place prepared by YHWH, But the woman was given two wings of a GREAT EAGLE, that she might fly into the wilderness to her place, where she is nourished for a time and times and half a time, from the presence of the serpent. These are the ones who were NOT DEFILED with women (FAKE RELIGION) for they are virgins. These are the ones who follow the LAMB wherever He goes. These were REDEEMED from AMONG MEN, being first fruits to YHWH and to the LAMB.. And in their mouth was found NO DECEIT, for they are WITHOUT FAULT before the throne of YHWH. For all have sinned and fall short of the glory of YHWH, being JUSTIFIED FREELY by His grace through the redemption that is in MESSIYAH. And that the Gentiles might GLORIFY YHWH for His mercy, as it is written: "Rejoice, O Gentiles, with His people!" There shall be a root of JESSE; And He who shall rise to reign over the Gentiles, In Him the Gentiles shall hope."
                              REVELATIONS 12:6,14 / 14:4,5 / ROMANS 3:23-26 / 15:9-13
AMMISHADDAI   PROPHETIC MESSAGE MINISTRY

TOPIC : BAPTIZING..   For MESSIYAH also suffered once for SINS, the JUST for the UNJUST, that HE might bring us to YHWH, being put to death in the flesh but made alive by the SPIRIT, by whom also HE went and preached to the spirits in prison, who formerly were disobedient, when once the DIVINE LONGSUFFERING waited in the days of NOAH, while the ark was being prepared, in which a few, that is, eight SOULS, were save through water. There is also an antitype which now SAVES US - BAPTISM (not the removal of the filth of the flesh, but the ANSWER OF A GOOD CONSCIENCE TOWARD YHWH) through the resurrection of YAHSHUAH MESSIYAH, who has gone into heaven and is at the right hand of YHWH, angels and authorities and powers having been made subject to HIM..   1 PETER 3:18-22   And HE said to them, GO into all the world and preach the gospel to every creature. " HE who believes and is BAPTIZED will be SAVED; but he who does not believe will be CONDEMNED.   MARK 16:15,16

For with the heart ONE BELIEVES unto righteousness, and with the mouth CONFESSION is made unto salvation. REPENT, AND LET EVERY ONE OF YOU BE BAPTIZED in the NAME OF YAHSHUAH MESSIYAH for the remission of SINS; and you shall receive the gift of the HOLY SPIRIT. For the promise is to you and to your children, and to ALL WHO ARE AFAR OFF, as many as YHWH our MIGHTY ONE will call. Then those who gladly received his word were BAPTIZED; and that day about three thousand souls were added to them. For you will be HIS WITNESS to all men of what you have seen and heard. And now why are you waiting? Arise and be BAPTIZED, and wash away your sins, calling on the NAME OF YHWH..
                              ROMANS 10:10 / ACTS 2:38,39,41 / 22:15,16
Let us draw near with a TRUE HEART in full assurance of FAITH, having our hearts sprinkled from an evil conscience and our bodies washed with PURE WATER. Moreover, brothers, I do not want you to be UNAWARE that all our fathers were under the cloud, all passed through the sea, all were BAPTIZED into MOSES in the cloud and in the sea, all ate the same SPIRITUAL FOOD, and all drank the same spiritual drink. For they drank of that SPIRITUAL ROCK that followed them, and that ROCK WAS MESSIYAH.. For by ONE SPIRIT we were ALL BAPTIZED into one body - whether HEBREW or GENTILE whether SLAVES or FREE - and have all been made to drink into ONE SPIRIT.
                              HEBREWS 10:22 / 1 CORINTHIANS 10:1-7 / 12:13
For you are all sons of YHWH through FAITH in MESSIYAH YAHSHUAH. For as many of you as were BAPTIZED into MESSIYAH have put on MESSIYAH (ANNOINTED) this is HE of whom I said, after me comes a Man who is higher than I, for HE was before me. " I did not know HIM; but that HE should be revealed to YISRAEL, therefore I came BAPTIZING WITH WATER. " I did not know HIM, but HE who sent me to BAPTIZE with water said to me, UPON WHOM YOU SEE THE SPIRIT DESCENDING, and remaining on HIM, this is HE WHO BAPTIZES WITH THE HOLY SPIRIT.' And I have seen and testified that this is the SON OF YHWH..   GALATIANS 3:26-28 / JOHN 1:30,31,33,34

" GO THERFORE and MAKE DISCIPLES OF ALL THE NATIONS, BAPTIZING THEM IN THE NAME OF THE FATHER and OF THE SON and OF THE HOLY SPIRIT, teaching them to observe all things that I have commanded you; and lo, I am with you always, even to the end of the age." AMEN..   MATTHEW 28:19,20
אבמסמןאודדא.   PROPHETIC MESSAGE MINISTRY

TOPIC : STUMBLING BLOCKS and STUMBLING.. My brothers, let not many of you become teachers, knowing that we shall receive a stricter judgment.. For <u>we all stumble in many things</u>.. But NO MAN CAN TAME the TONGUE, it is a UNRULY EVIL, (for there is no one who does not sin) For whoever shall keep the whole law, and yet **STUMBLE** in ONE point, he is guilty of all. But whoever causes one of these little ones who believe in ME (YAHSHAUAH) to STUMBLE, it would be better for him if a millstone were hung around his neck, and he were thrown into the sea.

JAMES 3:1,2 / 1 KINGS 8:46 / JAMES 2:10 / MARK 9:42

Then HE said to the disciples, " It is IMPOSSIBLE that NO OFFENSES (stumbling blocks) Should come, but WOE TO HIM through whom they do come! It would be better for him if a millstone were hung around his neck, and he were thrown into the sea, than that he should OFFEND one of these little ones. " <u>Take heed to yourselves</u>, if your brother sins against you, rebuke him; and if he REPENTS, FORGIVE him. " And if he <u>sins against you seven times </u>in a day, and <u>seven times in a day returns</u>. To you, saying, I repent, you <u>SHALL FORGIVE HIM</u>."

LUKE 17:1-4

But you have departed from the way; You have caused many to **STUMBLE** at the law. You have corrupted the covenant of LEVI," Says יהוה OF HOSTS..   MALACHI 2:8

The way of the WICKED is like darkness; They DO NOT KNOW what makes them STUMBLE. So then each of us shall give account of himself to יהוה Therefore let us NOT JUDGE one another anymore, but rather resolve this, not to put a **STUMBLING BLOCK** or a cause to fall in our brothers way. Therefore let us pursue the things which make for peace and the things by which one may EDIFY another. It is good neither to eat meat nor drink wine nor DO ANYTHING by which your brother STUMBLES or is OFFENDED or is MADE WEAK. But beware lest some how this liberty of yours become a STUMBLING BLOCK to those who are weak. Therefore, if food makes my brother STUMBLE, I will never again eat meat, lest I make my brother STUMBLE..

PROVERBS 4:19 / ROMANS 14:12,13,21 / 1 CORINTHIANS 8:9,13

You shall not curse the deaf, <u>nor put a stumbling block before the blind</u>, O YISRAEL, return to the MOSTHIGH your MIGHTY ONE, for you have STUMBLED because of your iniquity; " Are there not twelve hours in the day? If anyone walks in the day, he does NOT STUMBLE, because he sees the light of this world. " But if one walks in the night, he STUMBLES, because the light is NOT IN HIM."

LEVITICUS 19:14 / HOSEA 14:1 / JOHN 11:9,10

PROPHETIC MESSAGE MINISTRY

COMMANDMENT KEEPERS
אממסהאדדא.

TOPIC : MYTH, ONCE SAVED ALL WAYS SAVED??

CAN A MAN LOOSE HIS SALVATION??

I lay down and slept; I awoke, for YHWH sustained me. SALVATION BELONGS TO YHWH. Your blessing is upon your people..   PSALM 3:5,8

But YISRAEL shall be SAVED by YHWH with an everlasting SALVATION; You shall not be ashamed or disgraced FOREVER and EVER.. " Look to ME, and be SAVED, All you ends of the earth! For I am YHWH, and there is NO OTHER.   ISAIAH 45:17,22

" Heal the sick, cleanse the lepers, raise the dead, cast out demons. Freely you have received, freely give.   MATTHEW 10:8

Being confident of this very thing, that He who has begun a good work in you will complete it until the day of YAHSHUAH MESSIYAH; Therefore, my beloved, as you have always obeyed, not as in my presence only, but now much more in my absence, work out your own SALVATION with fear and trembling; for it is YHWH who works in you both to will and to do for HIS GOOD PLEASURE. Holding fast the WORD OF LIFE, so that I may rejoice in the day of MESSIYAH that I have not run in vain or labored in vain..
PHILLIPPIANS 1:6 / 2:12,13,16-18

** WARNING **

" Again, when a RIGHTEOUS man turns from his righteousness and commits iniquity, and I lay a stumbling block before him, he shall die; because you did not give him warning, he shall die in his sin, and his RIGHTEOUSNESS which he has done shall not be remembered; but his blood I will require at your hand. " But when a righteous man turns away from his righteousness and COMMITS INIQUITY (sin) and does according to all the ABOMINATIONS that the wicked man does, shall he LIVE?? All the righteousness which he has done shall not be remembered; because of the UNFAITHFULNESS of which he is guilty and the SIN which he has committed, because of them HE SHALL DIE. " Yet you say, the way of YHWH is not fair.' HEAR NOW O house of YISRAEL, is it not MY WAY WHICH IS FAIR, and your ways which are not fair?? " When a righteous man turns away from his RIGHTEOUSNESS, commits iniquity, and dies in it, it is because of the iniquity which he has done that he dies. " Again, when a wicked man turns away from the wickedness which he committed, and does what is LAWFUL and RIGHT, he preserves himself alive. Because he considers and turns away from all the transgressions which he committed, he shall surely live; he shall not die.. " For I have NO PLEASURE in the DEATH of one who dies." says YHWH MIGHTY ONE. " Therefore TURN and LIVE!" When I say to the righteous that he shall surely live, but he trusts in his own righteousness and commits iniquity, none of his righteous works shall be remembered; but because of the iniquity that he has committed, he shall die..   EZEKIEL 3:20 / 18:24-27 / 33:13,14,16,17

PROPHETIC MESSAGE MINISTRY
AMMISHADDAI
TRUE
BELIEVER

TOPIC : EVIL COMPANY.. <u>Do Not Be Deceived</u> : " EVIL company corrupts Good Habits. "   I wrote to you in my letter NOT TO KEEP COMPANY with SEXUALLY IMMORAL people. But now I have written to you not to KEEP COMPANY with anyone named a brother, who is SEXUALLY IMMORAL, or COVETOUS, or an IDOLATER, or a REVILER, or a DRUNKARD, or an EXTORTIONER - not even to eat with such a person.. <u>Therefore put away from yourselves</u> the EVIL PERSON. "   1 CORINTHIANS 15:33 / 5: 9-13

He is PROUD, knowing nothing, but is OBSESSED with DISPUTES and ARGUMENTS over words, from which come envy, strife, reviling, EVIL suspicions, useless wrangling of men of CORRUPT MINDS and destitute of the truth, who suppose that godliness is a means of gain. <u>From such withdraw yourself</u>..
                    1 TIMOTHY 6:4,5

NOW I URGE YOU, brothers, note those who cause DIVISIONS and OFFENSES, contrary to the doctrine which you learned, and <u>Avoid them</u>..   ROMANS 16:17

But as for you, brothers, DO NOT GROW WEARY in doing good. And if anyone does NOT OBEY our word in this letter, note that person and <u>do not KEEP COMPANY with him</u> , that he may be ashamed. Yet do not count him as an enemy, but ADMONISH (warn) him as a brother..   2 THESSALONIANS 3:13-15

" Moreover if your brother sins against you, go and tell him his FAULT between you and him alone. If he hears you, you have gained your brother. " But if he will not hear, take with you ONE or TWO more, that by the mouth of TWO or THREE witnesses every word may be established. " And if he refuses to hear them, tell it to the church. But if he refuses even to hear the church, let him be to you like a <u>heathen and a tax collector</u>.. But we command you, brothers, in the name of IMMANUEL YAHSHUAH MESSIYAH, that you <u>withdraw from every brother who walks disorderly</u> and not according to the custom which he received from us..
                    MATTHEW 18: 15-17 / 2 THESSALONIANS 3:6
Brothers, if anyone among you wanders from the truth, and someone turns him back. Let him know that he who turns a sinner from the ERROR of his way will save a soul from DEATH and cover a MULTITUDE of sins..   JAMES 5:19,20

PROPHETIC MESSAGE MINISTRY

אממסהאדדאבאיניאהדאה

TOPIC : SELF - EXAMINATION..

Know what you are TALKING ABOUT before you SPEAK, and give ATTENTION to your HEALTH before you get sick. EXAMINE YOUR CONSCIENCE before YHWH judges you; then when that time comes, HE WILL FORGIVE YOU.. Humble yourself before you are PUNISHED with SICKNESS. When you have sinned, show repentance. If you make a promise to the MOSTHIGH, keep it as soon as you can. Don't wait until you are about to DIE to set things STRAIGHT.. But before you make such a promise, be prepared to KEEP IT. Don't try to TEST the MOSTHIGH'S patience. THINK!! Do you want HIM to be angry with you on the day you die? When you face HIS JUDGEMENT, do you want HIM to turn HIS back on you? When you have all you want, think what it is like to be hungry, what it is to be poor. Things CAN CHANGE in a single day; YHWH can act very quickly. If you are wise, you will be careful in everything you do. When sin is all around you, be especially careful that you do not become guilty. Every intelligent person can recognize WISDOM and WILL HONOR ANYONE who shows it. If you appreciate WISDOM when you hear it, you will become WISE yourself, and your words will be a source of WISDOM for others..   SIRACH 18: 19 - 29

WORDS OF WISDOM..

COMMANDMENT KEEPERS
AMMISHADDAI
PROPHETIC MESSAGE MINISTRY

KINGDOM PRINCIPLES..

TOPIC : LOOSE TALK!! AVOID IDLE TALK, and you will AVOID a lot of trouble. Never REPEAT what you hear, and you will have NO REGRETS. Don't tell it to your friends or your enemies <u>unless it would be sinful</u> to keep it to yourself. Whoever hears you will take note of it, And sooner or later will hate you for it. Have you heard a rumor? Let it DIE WITH YOU.. **BE BRAVE!** it won't make you explode. A foolish person trying to keep a secret suffers like a woman in labor. Any time he hears a secret, it's like an arrow stuck in his leg. If you hear that a friend has done something wrong, ask him about it. Maybe it isn't true. If it is true, he won't do it again. If you hear that a neighbor has said something he shouldn't, ask him about it. Maybe he didn't say it. If he did, he won't say it again. If you hear something bad about a friend, ask him about it. It might be a lie. Don't believe everything you hear. <u>A person may say something carelessly</u> and <u>not really mean it</u>. Everyone has SINNED in this way <u>at one time or another</u>. If you hear something that makes you angry with your neighbor, ask him about it before you threaten him.. Leave the MATTER to the LAW Of the MOSTHIGH..

SIRACH 19:6-19

WORDS of WISDOM..
PROPHETIC MESSAGE MINISTRY
אממסהאדדא.
COMMANDMENT KEEPERS

TOPIC : **KNOWING WHEN TO TALK** A person can be rebuked in the WRONG WAY; it may be WISER to KEEP QUIET then to SPEAK. But it is much better to REBUKE the person than to keep your anger bottled up. Admit when you are wrong, and you will AVOID EMBARRASSMENT. Using force to get a point across is like a castrated man trying to rape a young woman. Some people are thought to be wise because they don't talk much; others are disliked because they TALK TOO MUCH.. Some people keep quiet because they don't have anything to say; others keep quiet because they KNOW the RIGHT TIME to SPEAK. A wise person will not speak until the right moment, but a BRAGGING FOOL DOESN'T KNOW when that time is. No one can stand a person who TALKS TOO LONG and will not give others a chance to SPEAK..

SIRACH 20: 1-8

12/10/03

TOPIC : **INAPPROPRIATE TALK** A slip of the tongue is worse than a slip on the pavement; the wicked will go to ruin just as suddenly as a person slips and falls. An impolite person is like one of those off-color stories that ignorant people are always telling.. NOBODY TAKES A PROVERB SERIOUSLY when some fool quotes it at the WRONG TIME. If a person is too poor to afford SIN, he can rest without a guilty conscience. You can lose all your self-respect by being reluctant to speak up in the presence of stupidity. If you promise a friend something because you are to bashful to say NO, you're NEEDLESSLY making an enemy. Lying is an UGLY BLOT on a person's character, but ignorant people do it all the time. A thief is better than a HABITUAL LIAR, but both are headed for ruin. A liar has NO HONOR. He lives in constant disgrace.

SIRACH 20: 18-26

WORDS OF WISDOM..

AMMISHADDAI
   TRUE
   BELIEVER

TOPIC : FILTHY TALK There is ONE WAY of speaking that is LIKE DEATH itself - may NO YISRAELITE (believer) ever be guilty of it !! DEVOUT PEOPLE do not wallow in such SIN, and they will <u>keep away from such BEHAVIOR</u>. Don't fall into the HABIT OF COARSE, PROFANE TALK; it is SINFUL. You might forget yourself while in the company of important people and make a fool of yourself with some FOUL WORD that comes to you NATURALLY. Think how your parents would feel! You would curse the day you were born and wish you were dead! If you fall into the HABIT OF USING OFFENSIVE LANGUAGE, you will never break yourself of it as long as you live.

SIRACH 23: 12-15

(A) PROFANE (adj) Showing irreverence or contempt toward YHWH or sacred things : BLASPHEMOUS..

12/15/03

TOPIC : FOOLISH TALK When DEVOUT people talk, what they say always makes sense, but FOOLISH people are always CONTRADICTING themselves. When you find yourself with STUPID people, <u>look for some excuse to leave</u>, but when you are with SERIOUS - MINDED people, stay as LONG AS YOU CAN. The stories that foolish people tell are OFFENSIVE, and they <u>make jokes about the worst kinds</u> of SIN. When such people CURSE, it is enough to make your hair stand on end, and when they <u>start arguing among themselves</u>, all you can do is to stop up your ears. It is PAINFUL to listen to them INSULT each other, and such blustering can lead to VIOLENCE..

SIRACH 27: 11-15

(B) CURSE (N) An appeal for evil or injury to befall someone or something. (profane oath)

(C) CURSING (VT) to invoke evil, upon : afflict.

WORDS of WISDOM..
AMMISHADDAI
TRUE
BELIEVER

TOPIC : INTERPRETING the LAW (TANAKH) If you FEAR YHWH, you will ACCEPT HIS correction. He will bless those who get up early in the morning to pray. STUDY HIS LAW, and you will MASTER IT. Unless you are insincere about it, in which case you will fail. If you FEAR the MOSTHIGH, you will know what is right, and you will BE FAMOUS for your FAIRNESS. Sinners have NO USE for correction, and will INTERPRET the LAW to suit themselves. SENSIBLE PEOPLE will consider every option, but ARROGANT PEOPLE will let nothing stand in their way. Never do anything without thinking it through, and once you have done something, don't look back and wish you had done something else. Don't take a course of action that is dangerous, and don't make the same mistake twice. DON'T BE TOO SURE OF YOURSELF, even when the way looks easy.. Always watch where you are going. Whatever you do be careful; THIS IS KEEPING YHWH'S COMMANDMENTS.. BELIEVING IN THE LAW MEANS KEEPING YHWH'S COMMANDS. If you TRUST in YHWH, you cannot lose. NO EVIL WILL EVER COME to a person who FEARS YHWH; however often DANGER COMES, YHWH will come to RESCUE. A person who has no use for the LAW (TANAKH) doesn't have good SENSE, and anyone who is insincere about it is going to be tossed about like a boat in a storm. IF YOU ARE WISE, you will believe in the LAW; you will find it as reliable as the SACRED LOTS. Prepare what you are going to say and people will listen to you. Use what you have learned before you start talking. A foolish person's mind works like a cartwheel, going around and round in circles. A sarcastic friend is like a wild horse that neighs no matter who tries to ride him.   SIRACH 32:14-24 / 33:1-6

(A) OPTION (N) An act of choosing : Freedom of choice.
(B) OPINION (N) A belief or idea held with confidence in spirit; but not substantiated by direct proof in TANAKH.
(C) NEIGHS (N) The long, high - pitched sound made by a house.

WORDS OF WISDOM..

אממסהאדדא

TOPIC : *SPEECH REFLECTS TRUE FEELINGS..* Your talk shows your faults; it is like a <u>sifter that separates out the rubbish</u>.. The WAY YOU THINK SHOWS your character just as surely as <u>the OVEN SHOWS any flaws </u>in the pottery being FIRED.. You can tell how well a tree has been cared for by the fruit it bears, and you can tell a person's FEELINGS by the WAY HE EXPRESSES HIMSELF. Never praise anyone before you hear him talk; *that is the real test.*   SIRACH 27: 4-7

11/28/03

TOPIC : *HOME and HOSPITALITY* The necessities of life are water, FOOD, CLOTHING, and a HOME were you can have PRIVACY. It is better to be poor and live under your own crude roof than to enjoy lavish banquets in other people's homes.. <u>BE HAPPY with what you have</u>, even if it isn't very much, and don't listen to anyone who would insult your HOME AND FAMILY.. (2) GOING FROM HOUSE to HOUSE is a miserable way to live. <u>Anywhere you go, you don't dare speak.</u> You welcome the guest and pure the drinks, and nobody thanks you. Instead, people HUMILIATE YOU by saying things like : "STRANGER! Come here and set the table! I want to eat what you've got there! Give it here! Go away, STRANGER! I've got an important guest! My brother is coming to visit, and I need the room!" <u>BEING DENIED HOSPITALITY</u> or having a moneylender hound you - these are hard things for any SENSITIVE person to endure.   SIRACH 29:21-28

(A) STRANGER (N) A newcomer, foreigner, or outsider. A visitor : Guest..

WORDS of WISDOM..

אמממסהאאדדא.

TOPIC : SICKNESS and MEDICINE .. Give doctors the honor they deserve, for יהוה gave them their work to do. Their SKILL CAME from the MOSTHIGH, and Kings REWARD them for it. Their KNOWLEDGE gives them a Position of Importance, and powerful people hold them in high regard. יהוה created medicines from the earth, and a sensible person will not hesitate to use them. Didn't a tree once make bitter water fit to drink, so that יהוה power might be known? HE gave medical KNOWLEDGE to human beings, so that we would PRAISE HIM for the MIRACLES HE performs. The herbalist (druggist) mixes these medicines, and the DOCTOR will use them to cure diseases and ease pain. There is NO END to the activities of יהוה, who GIVES HEALTH to the people of the world. My child, when you get sick, don't ignore it. PRAY TO יהוה and he will make you well. CONFESS all your sins and determine that in the future you will live a RIGHTEOUS LIFE. Offer incense and a grain OFFERING, as fine as you can afford. Then call the DOCTOR - for יהוה created him - and keep him at your side; you need him. There are times when you have to depend on his skill. The doctor's prayer is that יהוה will make him able to EASE his patients' pain and make them well again. As for the person who sins against his CREATOR, he deserves to be sick..

SIRACH 38:1-15

(A) MEDICINE (n) The science of DIAGNOSING, treating, or preventing disease or damage to the body or mind (spirit)

(B) PHARMACY (n) The art of preparing and dispensing drugs

(C) DRUG (n) A herbal substance used as medicine in the treatment of illness or disease.   WORDS Of WISDOM..

AMMISHADDAI

TOPIC : CAUTION IN TAKING ADVICE.. Anyone can GIVE ADVICE, but some people do so only in their own interest. Be careful when somebody offers you advice. Find out first what his interest in the matter is, because you can be sure that he is thinking primarily of himself. Why should he come out on top instead of you? He will assure you that things look good, and then stand back to watch what happens to you. Don't ask advice of anyone who doesn't trust you, and don't GIVE ADVICE to anyone who is jealous of you. Don't ask a woman for advice about a rival of hers,

A coward about war,

A merchant about a bargain,

A buyer about selling,

A stingy person about charity,

A cruel person about kindness,

A lazy person about work,

A casual worker about finishing a job,

A lazy servant about a difficult task.

PAY NO ATTENTION TO ANY ADVICE THEY MAY GIVE.. Instead, rely on someone who is SPIRITUAL and KNOWN to KEEP YHWH'S COMMANDS, someone who is SYMPATHETIC with you, who will be sorry to see you fail. And TRUST YOUR OWN JUDGMENT; no one's advice is more reliable. Sometimes your own INTUITION can tell you more than SEVEN WACTHMEN on a high tower. ABOVE ALL, PRAY to the MOSTHIGH that HE will show you the RIGHT THING to do..

WORDS OF WISDOM..   SIRACH 37 : 7-15

AMMISHADDAI

TRUE

BELIEVER

WHO ARE ISRAELITES? To whom PERTAIN the ADOPTION, the GLORY, the COVENANTS, the giving of the LAW, the service of YHWH, and the PROMISE; according to the FLESH, MESSIYAH came, who is OVER ALL, eternally blessed MIGHTY ONE.. AMEN

ROMANS 9:1-5

In that HE SAYS, " A NEW COVENANT, " HE has made the FIRST OBSOLETE. Now what is becoming obsolete and growing old is ready to vanish away.. And for this reason: HE is the MEDIATOR of the NEW COVENANT, by means of death, for the redemption of the transgressions under the FIRST COVENANT, that those who are called may receive the promise of the eternal inheritance. HEBREWS 8:7-13 / 9:1-5,11-21

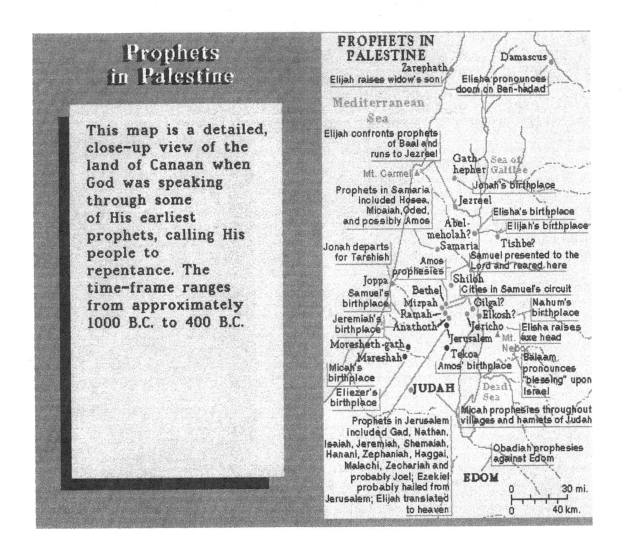

Prophets in Palestine

This map is a detailed, close-up view of the land of Canaan when God was speaking through some of His earliest prophets, calling His people to repentance. The time-frame ranges from approximately 1000 B.C. to 400 B.C.

PROPHETS IN PALESTINE

Damascus
Zarephath
Elijah raises widow's son
Elisha pronounces doom on Ben-hadad
Mediterranean Sea
Elijah confronts prophets of Baal and runs to Jezreel
Mt. Carmel
Gath hepher
Sea of Galilee
Jonah's birthplace
Prophets in Samaria included Hosea, Micaiah, Oded, and possibly Amos
Jezreel
Elisha's birthplace
Abel-meholah?
Elijah's birthplace
Jonah departs for Tarshish
Samaria
Tishbe?
Amos prophesies
Samuel presented to the Lord and reared here
Joppa
Shiloh
Cities in Samuel's circuit
Samuel's birthplace
Bethel
Gilgal?
Nahum's birthplace
Mizpah
Elkosh?
Ramah
Jericho
Elisha raises axe head
Jeremiah's birthplace
Anathoth
Jerusalem
Mt. Nebo
Moresheth-gath
Tekoa
Balaam pronounces "blessing" upon Israel
Mareshah
Amos' birthplace
Micah's birthplace
JUDAH
Dead Sea
Eliezer's birthplace
Micah prophesies throughout villages and hamlets of Judah
Prophets in Jerusalem included Gad, Nathan, Isaiah, Jeremiah, Shemaiah, Hanani, Zephaniah, Haggai, Malachi, Zechariah and probably Joel; Ezekiel probably hailed from Jerusalem; Elijah translated to heaven
Obadiah prophesies against Edom
EDOM
0   30 mi.
0   40 km.

kaduri.jpg kaak.jpg

Reb Moshe

rmsale.jpg rbmoshe.jpg

rbmoshe2.jpg rebba.jpg

3:9 "BEHOLD, I WILL MAKE THEM OF THE SYNAGOGUE OF SATAN, WHICH SAY
THEY ARE YISRAEL AND ARE NOT, BUT DO LIE, BEHOLD, I WILL MAKE THEM TO
COME AND WORSHIP BEFORE YOUR FEET, AND TO KNOW THAT I HAVE LOVED
YOU."

EDOM AND THE KHAZARS

ARTHUR KOESTLER
THE THIRTEENTH TRIBE

'The large majority of surviving Jews in the world are of Eastern European descent - and thus perhaps mainly of Khazar origin. If so, this would mean that their ancestors came not from the Jordan but from the volga, not from Canaan but from the Caucasus, once believed to be the cradle of the Aryan race; and that genetically they are more closely related to the Hun, uigur, and Magyar tribes than to the seed of Abraham, Isaac, and Jacob".

" And יהוה will take you back to Egypt in ships, by the way of which I said to you, ' You shall never see it again.' And there you shall be offered for sale to your enemies as male and female slaves, but no one will buy you."

DEUTERONOMY 28:68

TOPIC : DEATH (DEATH) The very thought of it is bitter to someone who is prosperous, living peacefully with his possessions, FREE OF WORRIES, and still able to enjoy his food. DEATH! <u>Its sentence is welcome to someone living in poverty</u>, with FAILING HEATH, very old, <u>burdened with worries</u>, blind, and without hope. DO NOT BE AFRAID OF DEATH'S DECREE. (ORDER) Remember that it came to those before you and will come to those after you. יהוה has decreed it for every living creature. Who are you to OBJECT to what the MOSTHIGH wishes?? In the world of the dead NO ONE WILL CARE whether you lived ten years, a hundred, or a thousand.   SIRACH 41:1-4

TOPIC : the Fate Of the Wicked.. the children of sinners, brought up in UNGODLY SURROUNDINGS, turn out to be HATEFUL people. <u>They will lose whatever they inherit</u>, and their OWN DESCENDANTS will live in permanent disgrace. The children will put the BLAME for their DISGRACE on their UNGODLY parents. <u>You are doomed</u>, you NONSPIRITUAL people who have ABANDONED the LAW OF the MOSTHIGH GOD.. When you have children, disaster will strike them and you will be left with NOTHING but SORROW. There will be great joy whenever you stumble, and even after your death <u>you will be cursed</u>. What comes into being from nothing will return to nothing; so it will be with the godless, <u>doomed to extinction</u>. A person's body amounts to nothing, but a good reputation will last FOREVER. Protect your reputation; it will outlive you and last longer than a thousand treasures of gold. A good life lasts only so long, but a good reputation will last Forever..   SIRACH 41:5-13

My son, if you receive my words, and treasure my commands within you, so that you incline your ear to wisdom, and apply your heart to understanding; yes if you cry out for discernment, and lift up your voice for understanding, <u>and search for her as for hidden treasures</u>; Then you will understand the FEAR Of יהוה and find the knowledge of יהוה for the MOSTHIGH gives wisdom; from his mouth knowledge and understanding;   PROVERBS 2:1-12
WORDS OF WISDOM..   AMMISHADDAI

KINGDOM PRINCIPLES

TOPIC : MOURNING For the DEAD.. My child, when someone dies, you should mourn. Weep and wail to show how deeply you feel the loss. Prepare the body in the proper way, and be present at the burial. Weep bitterly and passionately; <u>observe the proper period of mourning for the person.</u> MOURN for a whole day or maybe two, to keep people from talking, but then pull yourself together and reconcile yourself to the loss. <u>Grief can undermine your health</u> and even lead to your own death. Grief lingers on after the death of a loved one, but it is not wise to let it lead you into poverty. <u>Don't lose yourself in sorrow; drive it away.</u> Remember that we must all die sometime. There is no way to bring the DEAD person back. All your sorrow does him NO GOOD, and it hurts you. Don't forget that. You will die, just as he did. Today it was his turn; tomorrow it will be yours. When the dead have been laid to rest, let the memory of them fade. ONCE THEY ARE GONE, TAKE COURAGE..   SIRACH 38:16-23

Now HE who has prepared us for this very thing is YHWH, who also has given us the SPIRIT as a guarantee. So we are always confident, knowing that while we are at home in the body we are absent from YHWH. For we walk by FAITH, NOT BY SIGHT. We are CONFIDENT, yes, well pleased rather to be ABSENT from the body and to be PRESENT with YHWH. Therefore we make it our aim, whether PRESENT or ABSENT, <u>to be well pleasing to HIM</u>..

                    2 CORINTHIANS 5:5-10 / PHILIPPIANS 1:21-24

TOPIC : The Results Of Evil nothing that comes from bribery or injustice will last, but the EFFECTS of LOYALTY will REMAIN FOREVER. Wealth that has been obtained dishonestly is like a stream that runs full during a thunderstorm. Tumbling rocks along as it flows, but then suddenly goes dry. The children of UNGODLY people will not leave large families; they are like plants trying to take root on rock, like reeds along a river bank, withering before any other plant. <u>Acts of kindness and charity are as LASTING as ETERNITY</u>...

                              SIRACH 40:12-17

WORDS Of WISDOM
   AMMISHADDAI

TOPIC : RESENTMENT Anger and a hot temper are horrible things, but SINNERS have both. YHWH is taking NOTE of your SINS, and if you take VENGEANCE on someone, YHWH will take VENGEANCE on you. But if you FORGIVE someone who has wronged you, your SINS will be forgiven when you pray. You cannot expect YHWH to pardon you while you are holding a grudge against someone else. You yourself are A SINNER, and if you won't FORGIVE another person, you have not right to pray that YHWH will FORGIVE your SINS.. If you cannot get rid of your ANGER, you have NO HOPE OF FORGIVENESS - you are only a human being. Think about it! Some day you will die, and your body will decay. So give up HATE and Live by YHWH'S COMMANDS, the Commands in the Covenant of the MOSTHIGH. Instead of getting upset over your neighbor's faults, OVERLOOK THEM..

SIRACH 27:30 / 28:1-7

TOPIC : יהוה IS JUDGE the MOSTHIGH is always aware of what people do; there is NO WAY to hide from HIM. He gave each nation its own ruler, but YISRAEL is YHWH'S own possession. YHWH is always watching what people do; everything they do is as clear as day to HIM. None of their SINS are hidden from HIM; HE is aware of them all. When we give to the poor, YHWH considers it as precious as a valuable ring. Human KINDNESS is as precious to Him as life itself. Later HE will JUDGE the wicked and punish them; they will get what they deserve. But YHWH will allow those who repent to return to him. He always gives encouragement to those who are losing hope..

SIRACH 17:15-24

WORDS of WISDOM..
   AMMISHADDAI

123

TOPIC : PRIDE.. Don't be angry with someone for every little thing he does wrong. Don't do anything out of injured pride. <u>Arrogance and injustice are hated by both YHWH and people.</u> Injustice, Arrogance, and Wealth cause Nations to fall from power, and others then rise to take their place. We are only dust and ashes; <u>what have we got to be proud of</u>?? Our body decays even while we are alive. A long illness puzzles the doctor. Even a king may be alive today and dead tomorrow. When a person dies, all he then possesses is worms, flies, and maggots. <u>Pride has its beginning when a person abandons YHWH</u>, his maker (Creator) Pride is like a fountain pouring out sin, and <u>whoever persist in it</u> will be full of WICKEDNESS.. That is why YHWH brought terrible punishments on some people and completely destroyed them. YHWH has overthrown kings and put humbler people in their place. YHWH has pulled up Nations by the roots and established humbler ones in their place. YHWH has overthrown empires and completely devastated their lands. HE DESTROYED SOME so completely that they are not even remembered any more. The CREATOR never intended for human beings to be arrogant and violent..   SIRACH 10:6-18

TOPIC : SENSE OF PRIDE.. On the other hand, it is possible to sin by giving in to other people too much. Here are some things you should not be ashamed of : *The LAW of the MOSTHIGH AND HIS COVERNANT,*
Judging even godless people fairly,
SHARING expenses with a business partner or a traveling companion,
Sharing and inheritance, using accurate weights and measures,
Making a profit, whether great or small, bargaining with a merchant,
Discipline your children often, beating a disloyal slave until blood flows.
It is wise to lock things up if you can not trust your wife or if too many people are around. Keep an accurate record of any deposits you make or of anything you give or receive. <u>Don't hesitate to correct someone</u> who is <u>acting foolishly</u> or and old man who goes around with prostitutes. All of this is worthwhile advice, and if you follow it, everyone will approve of your behavior..   SIRACH 42:1-8
WORDS OF WISDOM
   AMMISHADDAI

TOPIC : APPEARANCES Do not compliment a person on his good looks. On the other hand, do not look down on someone who is unattractive. Compared to most flying things, a bee is very small, but the honey it makes the sweetest of foods. Don't make fun of someone who has fallen on hard times and is dressed in rags. YHWH does wonderful <u>things that human beings never notice</u>. Many are the kings who have ended their careers sitting on the ground, while their crowns were worn by those no one had heard of before. Many are the rulers who have suffered disgrace. Many are the famous people who have fallen into the power of others. Before you start criticizing, get your facts straight and think the matter through. Don't take part in decisions that are being made by sinners.   SIRACH 11:2-9

TOPIC : SUDDEN CHANGES OF FORTUNE.. Bad fortune can sometimes lead to success, <u>and a stroke of good fortune can sometimes lead to loss</u>. Generosity will sometimes do you no good, but at <u>other times it will repay you double</u>. Honor can be followed by disgrace, but there are people who have risen from obscurity to places of honor. Sometimes <u>what seems like a real bargain</u> can turn out to be a very <u>expensive mistake</u>. When a person with good judgment speaks, he wins friends. A stupid person, though, can shower compliments on everybody, it won't help him a bit. If such a person gives you something, it won't do any good; it wont be as valuable as he thinks it is. He isn't as generous with anything but criticism, which he will shout for all the world to hear. If he lends you something today, he'll want it back tomorrow. (do you hate people like that?) then that fool will say, " Nobody likes me. Nobody appreciates what I do for them. They'll take what I give them, but then talk about me behind my back." And he's right - he's a constant joke to everyone..   SIRACH 20:9-17

WORDS OF WISDOM..

AMMISHADDAI

TOPIC : Giving to the Poor; Giving to the poor can make up for SIN, just as water can put out a blazing fire. Anyone who responds to others with <u>acts of kindness is thinking of the future</u>, because he will find help if he ever falls on hard times. My child, don't prevent the poor from making a living, or keep them waiting in their need. Never give a hungry person any cause for resentment or anger. Don't add to the troubles of someone who is already desperate. If he is in need, don't put off giving to him. <u>Don't refuse to help a beggar who is in distress.</u> Don't turn your back on a poor person or give him any reason to curse you. If he becomes so bitter that he does curse you, his CREATOR will hear his prayer. Make yourself popular in the synagogue. Bow your head to men of authority. Listen to what the poor have to say, and answer them politely. Protect people from those who want to wrong them, and be firm in your judgments. <u>Be like a father to orphans</u>, and <u>provide widows with the help</u> their husbands can no longer give them. (JAMES 1:27) Then you will be like a child of the MOSTHIGH, and he will love you more than your own mother does..   SIRACH 3:30,31 / 4:1-10

TOPIC : GENEROSTIY.. Nevertheless, be understanding with those who are poor. Don't keep them waiting for your generosity. YHWH has commanded us to help the poor; don't refuse them the help they need. It is better to lose your money by helping a relative or a friend than to lose it by letting it rust away under a rock somewhere. Use your wealth as the MOSTHIGH has commanded; this will do you more good then keeping your money for yourself. Count among your treasures the fact that you give to the poor. <u>It will save you from all kinds of trouble</u> and will be a better defense against your enemies than the strongest shield or stoutest spear. (or biggest Gun)   SIRACH 29:8-13

TOPIC : BEGGING My child, don't live the life of a beggar; it is better to die than to beg. If you have to depend on someone else for your food, you are not really living your own life. You pollute yourself by accepting food from another. Begging is torture to the soul of any sensitive person. A shameless person can make begging sound sweet, but <u>something inside him burns</u>.   SIRACH 40:28-30

AMMISHADDAI   WORDS OF WISDOM

TOPIC : HEALTH It is better to be poor, but strong and healthy, than to be rich, but in poor health. A sound, healthy body and a cheerful attitude are more valuable then gold and jewels. Nothing can make you richer or give you <u>greater happiness then those two things</u>. It would be better to be dead, asleep forever, then to live in the misery of chronic illness. The finest food means nothing if you are too sick to eat it; it might as well be offered to an idol. But there is no point in offering food to an idol; it can't eat it or smell it. It is just the same with someone whom YHWH has afflicted. He looks at his food and sighs, like a castrated man hugging a young woman.   SIRACH 30:14-20

TOPIC : CHEERFULNESS and SADNESS.. Don't deliberately torture yourself by giving in to depression. Happiness makes for a long life and makes it worth living. Enjoy yourself and be happy; don't worry all the time. <u>Worry never did anybody any good</u>, and it has destroyed many people. <u>It will make you old before your time</u>. Jealousy and anger will shorten your life. A cheerful person with a good attitude will have a good appetite and enjoy his food.   SIRACH 30:21-25

TOPIC : CONTROLLING the APPETITE My child, as you go through life, <u>keep your appetite under control</u>, and don't eat anything that you know is bad for you. All food doesn't agree with everyone, and everyone doesn't like the same kinds of food. Don't feel that you just have to have all sorts of fancy food, and don't be a glutton over any food. If you eat too much, you'll get sick; if you do it all the time, you'll always have stomach trouble. Gluttony has been the death of many people. AVOID IT and LIVE LONGER..   SIRACH 37:27-31

COMMANDMENT KEEPERS

WORDS OF WISDOM..

AMMISHADDAI

82. Jesus' true relatives

Matthew

12:46 While he yet talked to the people, behold, his mother and his brethren stood without, desiring to speak with him. **47** Then one said unto him, Behold, thy mother and thy brethren stand without, desiring to speak with thee. **48** But he answered and said unto him that told him, Who is my mother? and who are my brethren? **49** And he stretched forth his hand toward his disciples, and said, Behold my mother and my brethren! **50** For whosoever shall do the will of my Father which is in heaven, the same is my brother, and sister, and mother.

Mark

3:31 There came then his brethren and his mother, and, standing without, sent unto him, calling him. **32** And the multitude sat about him, and they said unto him, Behold, thy mother and thy brethren without seek for thee. **33** And he answered them, saying, Who is my mother, or my brethren? **34** And he looked round about on them which sat about him, and said, Behold my mother and my brethren! **35** For whosoever shall do the will of God, the same is my brother, and my sister, and mother.

Luke

8:19 Then came to him his mother and his brethren, and could not come at him for the press. **20** And it was told him by certain which said, Thy mother and thy brethren stand without, desiring to see thee. **21** And he answered and said unto them, My mother and my brethren are these which hear the word of God, and do it.

John

15:14 Ye are my friends, if ye do whatsoever I command you.

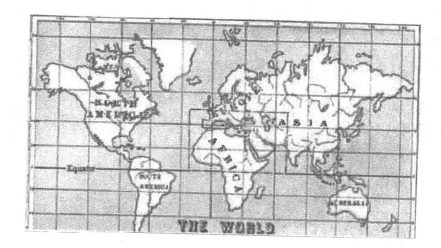

2/22/2004

TOPIC : SELF - CONTROL Don't be controlled by your lust; keep your passions in check. If you allow yourself to satisfy your every desire, you will be a joke to your enemies. Don't indulge in luxurious living; the expense of it will ruin you. Don't make yourself a beggar by borrowing for expensive banquets when you don't have enough money of your own if you do, you will never get rich; if you don't pay attention to small matters, you will gradually ruin yourself. Wine and women make sensible men do foolish things.. A man who goes to prostitutes gets more and more careless, and that carelessness will cost him his life. Worms will feed on his decaying body. It is silly to trust people too quickly. If you sin, you are hurting yourself. If wickedness makes you happy, you will be condemned.   SIRACH 18:30-33 / 19:1-5

TOPIC : Sincerity and Self - control Be certain about what you believe and consistent in what you say. Don't try to please everyone or agree with everything people say. Always be ready to listen, but take your time in answering. Answer only if you know what to say, and if you don't know what to say, keep quiet. Speaking can bring you either honor or disgrace; what you say can ruin you. Don't get a reputation for being a gossip, and don't tell tales that will hurt people. Just as robbers will suffer disgrace, so liars will suffer severe condemnation. Do nothing destructive, whether it seems insignificant or not, and not be an enemy when you should be a friend. A bad reputation brings you the disgrace that lying sinners deserve. Do not let your passions carry you away; this can tear your soul to pieces like a bull. You will be left like a dead tree without any leaves or fruit. Evil desire will destroy you and make you a joke to your enemies..   SIRACH 5:9-15 / 6:1-4

COMMANDMENT KEEPERS

WORDS Of WISDOM
AMMISHADDAI

TOPIC : FEAR יהוה' Those who fear YHWH will live, because they have put their trust in the one who can save them. Fear YHWH, and you will have nothing else to fear. If your trust is in him, you will NEVER ACT LIKE A COWARD. People who fear YHWH are fortunate, because they know where they can look for help. YHWH watches over those who love him; he is their STRONG PROTECTION and FIRM SUPPORT. HE shelters them from the heat, shades them from the noonday sun, and keeps them from stumbling and falling. HE makes them cheerful and puts a sparkle in their eyes. HE blesses them with LIFE and HEALTH..

SIRACH 34:13-17

TOPIC : DREAMS MEAN NOTHING.. Foolish people are deceived by vain hopes, and dreams get them all excited. A person who pays any attention at all to dreams is like someone who tries to catch shadows or chase the wind. What you see in a dream is no more real than the reflection of your face in a mirror. What is unreal can NO MORE PRODUCE SOMETHING REAL than what is dirty can produce something clean. DREAMS, DIVINATION, and OMENS are all NONSENSE.. You see in them only what you want to see. Unless the MOSTHIGH has sent you the DREAM, pay NO ATTENTION to it. Dreams have misled many people; they put their faith in them, only to be disappointed. The LAW is complete without such falsehood. WISDOM, as spoken by the righteous, is also complete without it..   SIRACH 34:1-8

For a DREAM COMES through much activity, for in the multitude of dreams and many words there is also vanity.. BUT FEAR YHWH..

ECCLESIASTES 5:3,6,7

And it shall come to pass afterward that I will pour out MY SPIRIT on all flesh; your sons and your daughters shall prophesy, your old men shall DREAM DREAMS, your young men shall see visions. I will pour out MY SPIRIT in those days.   JOEL 2:28-32 / ACTS 2:14-21

COMMANDMENT KEEPERS
WORDS of WISDOM
AMMISHADDAI

TOPIC : WISDOM and REVERENCE for יהוה There is NO EXCUSE for unjustified anger; it can bring about your downfall. Wait and be patient, and later you will be glad you did. Keep quiet until the right time to speak, and you will gain a reputation for good sense.. WISDOM has a treasury of wise sayings, but sinners have nothing but contempt for godliness. If you want to be WISE, Keep YHWH'S Commands, and HE will give you WISDOM in abundance. FEARING YHWH is WISDOM and an education in itself. He is pleased by loyalty and humility. Be faithful in the practice of your BELIEF; when you worship the MOSTHIGH, do it with all your heart. Be careful about what you say, and don't be a hypocrite. Don't be arrogant; you may suffer a fall and be disgraced. The MOSTHIGH will reveal your secrets and humble you in front of everyone in the synagogue, because you did not come there with REVERENCE for YHWH, but with a heart full of hypocrisy.   SIRACH 1:22-30

TOPIC : RULERS A skilled worker is admired for the things he makes, and a leader's wisdom is proved by his words. Someone who speaks rashly and recklessly is feared and hated by everyone in town. A wise ruler will educate his people and his government will be orderly. All the officials and all the citizens will be like their ruler. An uneducated king will ruin his people, but a government will grow strong if its rulers are wise. YHWH sees to the government of the world and brings the right person to power at the right time. The success of that person is in the MOSTHIGH'S hands. YHWH is the source of the honor given to any official.   SIRACH 9:17,18 / 10:1-5

COMMANDMENT KEEPERS

WORDS Of WISDOM..
AMMISHADDAI

TOPIC : RECOGNIZING REAL WISDOM; Fear YHWH and keep HIS Law; that is what WISDOM is all about. You may know everything there is to know about wickedness, but that does not make you wise. It is not sensible to follow the advice of sinners. It is possible to use cleverness for wicked purposes, but some people act like fools because they don't know any better. A devout person, even if he is not very intelligent, is better off than the cleverest of sinners. It is possible to be marvelously clever and still be dishonest, or to get what you want by being absurdly polite. Then there are those wicked people who go about looking very solemn and mournful, but who are only trying to deceive you. They will turn their faces away and pretend not to hear you, but they'll take advantage of you when you least expect it. If for some reason they are unable to sin now, they'll get around to it at the first opportunity. You can know people by their appearance. The first time you look at them, you can tell if they have good sense. Their characters shows in the way they dress, the way they laugh, and the way they walk.   SIRACH 19:20-30

TOPIC : WISDOM as a TEACHER: WISDOM takes care of those who look for her; she raises them to greatness. Loving her is loving life itself; rising early to look for her is pure joy. Anyone who obtains WISDOM will be greatly honored. Wherever he goes, YHWH will BLESS him. WISDOM'S servants are the servants of the HOLY ONE, and YHWH loves everyone who loves her. Those who obey her will give SOUND JUDGEMENTS; those who pay attention to her, have true security. Put your trust in WISDOM, and you will possess her and pass her on to your descendants. At first, WISDOM will lead you along difficult paths. She will make you so afraid that you will think you cannot go on. The discipline she demands will be tormenting, and she will put you to the test with her requirements until she trust you completely. Then she will come to you with NO DELAY, reveal her secrets to you, and make you happy. But if you go astray, she will abandon you and let you go to your own ruin.   SIRACH 4:11-19

WORDS Of WISDOM

   AMMISHADDAI

TOPIC : FREE WILL Don't blame YHWH for your sin; YHWH does not cause what HE hates. Don't claim that he has misled you; HE doesn't need the help of sinners to accomplish his purposes. <u>YHWH hates evil in all its forms</u>, and those who fear YHWH find nothing attractive in evil. When, in the beginning, YHWH created human beings, HE left them free to do as they wished. If you want to, you can keep YHWH COMMANDS. <u>You can decide whether you will be loyal to HIM or not</u>. HE has placed fire and water before you; reach out and take whichever you want. <u>You have a choice between LIFE and DEATH</u>; you will get whichever you choose. YHWH'S WISDOM and POWER are great and HE sees everything. HE is aware of everything a person does, and HE takes care of those who FEAR HIM.. HE <u>has never commanded anyone</u> to be <u>wicked or given anyone permission to sin</u>.   SIRACH 15:11-20

TOPIC : A Call to Repentance: Come to YHWH, and leave your sin behind. <u>Pray sincerely that he will help you live a better life</u>. Return to the MOSTHIGH and <u>turn away from sin</u>. Have an intense hatred for wickedness. Those who are alive can give thanks to YHWH, but can anyone in the world of the dead sing praise to the MOSTHIGH? A person who is alive and well can sing YHWH'S praises, but the dead, who no longer exist, have NO WAY TO GIVE THANKS.. <u>How great is YHWH'S merciful forgiveness of those who turn to him</u>! But this is not the nature of human beings; NOT ONE OF US IS IMMORTAL. Nothing is brighter than the sun, but even the sun's light fails during an eclipse. <u>How much easier it is for human thoughts to be eclipsed by evil</u>! YHWH can look out over all the stars in the sky. Human beings? They are dust and ashes.   SIRACH 17:25-32

COMMANDMENT KEEPERS

WORDS OF WISDOM..

AMMISHADDAI

TOPIC : SIN.. My child, have you SINNED? <u>Don't do it again</u>, and pray for Forgiveness for what you have already done. <u>Avoid SIN as if it were a snake</u>. If you get too near, it will sink its teeth into your soul like a lion, and destroy you. Every lawless act leaves an incurable wound, like one left by a double - edged sword. If a person is insolent and arrogant, he may lose everything he has. When poor people pray, YHWH hears them and quickly answers their prayers. <u>If you refuse to accept correction, you are committing a SIN</u>; and if you fear YHWH, <u>you will make a sincere change in your ways</u>. Someone may be famous as a good speaker, but when he is wrong, a sensible person will detect it. Anyone who borrows money to build a house is just collecting stones for his own tomb. A group of people who have *NO RESPECT FOR THE LAW* is like a pile of kindling; they will meet a fiery end.. The road that sinners walk is smooth and paved, but it leads to the world of the dead.

SIRACH 21:1-10

TOPIC : **WHO SHOULD BE HONORED** Who deserves honor? The human race does, <u>because people fear YHWH</u>. Who does NOT deserve honor? The human race does NOT, <u>because people break YHWH'S COMMANDS</u>.. A leader should be honored by those who follow HIM, and YHWH honors those who fear HIM. Rich people, famous people, and poor people all take pride in their fear of YHWH. It is NOT RIGHT <u>to refuse honor to a poor person who is intelligent</u>, and it is NOT RIGHT <u>to give honor to a SINNER</u>. People of influence, rulers, and judges will be HONORED, but <u>none of them is greater than a person who fears the MOSTHIGH</u>. A slave who is wise will have free citizens serving him; and if they are sensible, they will NOT RESENT it.

SIRACH 10:19-25

WORDS Of WISDOM
AMMISHADDAI

TOPIC : FALSE FRIENDS.. Anyone can claim to by your friend, but <u>some people are friends in name only</u>. The grief caused when a close friendship turns sour is as bad as death. This evil impulse we have! Why was it ever formed? How did it manage to cover the earth with deceit? <u>Some people will be your friend as long as things are going well</u>, but they will <u>turn against you when trouble comes</u>. A real friend will help you against your enemies and protect you in the fight. Never forget such companions in battle; share the results of your victory with them..

SIRACH 37:1-6

TOPIC : FRIENDSHIP with OTHERS. Never abandon old friends; you will never find a new one who can take their place. Friendship is like wine; <u>it gets better as it grows older</u>. Don't be jealous of a SINNER'S SUCCESS; <u>you don't know what kind of disaster is in store for him</u>. Don't take pleasure in the things that make ungodly people happy; remember that they will be held guilty as long as they live. If you keep away from someone who has the power to put you to death, you will not have to fear for your life; but if you must go near him, be very careful, or he may kill you. Be conscious that you are walking among hidden traps, that you are an easy target. <u>Get to know the people around you as well as you can</u>, and take advice only from those who are qualified to give it. <u>Engage in conversation with intelligent people, and let the LAW Of the MOSTHIGH be the topic of your discussions</u>. Choose righteous people for your dinner companions. Your chief pride should be your FEAR OF YHWH..

SIRACH 9:10-16

COMMANDMENT KEEPERS

WORDS Of WISDOM..
   AMMISHADDAI

TOPIC : (SPIRITUAL MOVEMENT) THE WAY.. In those days JOHN the Baptist came preaching in the wilderness of YAHUDAH, and saying, " Repent, for the KINGDOM OF HEAVEN is at hand!" For this is he who was spoken of by the prophet ISAIAH saying: " The voice of one crying in the wilderness: prepare THE WAY OF YHWH; Make His paths straight." Enter by the narrow gate; for wide is the gate and broad is the way that leads to destruction, and there are many who go in by it. " Because NARROW is the gate and DIFFICULT is THE WAY which leads to life, and there are few who find it; " For many are CALLED, but few are CHOSEN."   MATTHEW 3:1-3 / 7:13,14 / 22:14,16

He said: " I am the voice of one crying in the wilderness: MAKE STRAIGHT THE WAY OF YHWH," And where I go you know, and THE WAY you know." YAHSAVIOR said to him, " I am THE WAY, the TRUTH, and THE LIFE.. No one comes to the FATHER (ABBA) except through ME.   JOHN 1:23 / 14:4-7

" I persecuted THIS WAY to the death, binding and delivering into prisons both men and women, but this I confess to you, that according to THE WAY which they call a sect, so I worship YHWH of my fathers, believing all things which are written in the LAW and in the PROPHETS. But when Felix heard these things, having more accurate KNOWLEDGE OF THE WAY, he adjourned the proceedings and said,
                    ACTS 22:4 / 24:14,22

By a NEW and LIVING WAY which HE consecrated for us, through the veil, that is, HIS flesh, and having a HIGH PRIEST over the house of YHWH, let us draw near with a TRUE HEART in full assurance of FAITH, having our hearts sprinkled from an EVIL conscience and our bodies washed with pure water,   .   HEBREWS 10:19-25

And many will follow their destructive ways, because of whom THE WAY OF TRUTH will be blasphemed. They have FORSAKEN the RIGHT WAY and gone astray, following the way of Balaam the son of Beor, who loved the wages of unrighteousness; For it would have been better for them NOT TO HAVE KNOWN THE WAY OF Righteousness, than having known it, to turn from the HOLY COMMANDMENT delivered to them.
AMMISHADDAI   2 PETER 2:2,15,21

TOPIC : INHERITANCE and BIRTHRIGHT.. Gilead's wife bore sons; and when his wife's sons grew up, they drove YEPHTHAH out, and said to him, " You shall have NO inheritance in our father's house, for you are the SON of another woman."

JUDGES 11:1,2

Now the sons of REUBEN the FirstBorn Of YISRAEL - he was indeed the FIRSTBORN, but because he defiled his father's bed, his BirthRight was given to the sons of Yoseph, the son of YISRAEL, so that the Genealogy is not listed according to the BIRTHRIGHT;   1CHRONICLES 5:1,2

Therefore she said to ABRAHAM, cast out this bond woman and her son; for the son of this bond woman shall not be heir with my son, namely ISAAC." and ABRAHAM gave all that he had to ISAAC   GENESIS 21:10 / 25:5,6 / GALATIANS 4:28-31

" If a man has two wives, But he shall acknowledge the son of the unloved wife as the firstborn by giving him a DOUBLE PORTION of all that he has, for he is the beginning of his strength; the right of the firstborn is his. DEUTERONOMY 21:15-17

HOUSES and RICHES are an inheritance from fathers (parents) a GOOD man leaves an inheritance to his children's children, but the wealth of the sinner is stored up for the righteous. " And you shall speak to the children of YISRAEL, saying if a man dies and has no son, then you shall cause his inheritance to Pass to his Daughter, If he has no daughter, then you shall give his inheritance to his brothers.' If he has no brothers, then you shall give his inheritance to his father's brothers. ' And if his father has no brothers, then you shall give his inheritance to the relative closest to him in his family, and he shall possess it." And it shall be to the children of YISRAEL a statute of judgment, just as יהוה Commanded Moses..

PROVERBS 19:14/13:22 / NUMBERS 27:8-11

" To these the land shall be divided as an INHERITANCE, according to the number of names. To a large tribe you shall give a larger INHERITANCE, and to a small tribe you shall give a smaller INHERITANCE. Each shall be given its inheritance according to those who were numbered of them. " But the land shall be divided by lot; they shall inherit according to the names of the tribes of their fathers " According to the lot their INHERITANCE shall be divided between the larger and the smaller."

NUMBERS 26:51-56

" And it shall be that the FIRSTBORN son which she bears will succeed to the name of his dead brother, that his name may not be blotted out of YISRAEL.

DEUTERONOMY 25:6

COMMANDMENT KEEPERS..

    AMMISHADDAI

        TRUE

        BELIEVER

TOPIC : SEEKING A SIGN.. 'I am YHWH your MIGHTYONE (GOD): Walk in MY STATUTES, keep MY JUDGMENTS, and <u>DO THEM</u>; HALLOW MY SABBATHS and they will be a *SIGN* between ME and you, that you may know that I am YHWH your MIGHTYONE.'   EZEKIEL 20:19,20

" Speak also to the children of YSRAEL, saying: Surely MY SABBATHS you shall keep, for it is a *SIGN* between ME and you throughout your generations, that you may know that I am YHWH who <u>sanctifies you</u>. Therefore the children of YSRAEL shall keep the SABBATH throughout their generations as a perpetual covenant. It is a SIGN between ME and the children of YSRAEL FOREVER;   EXODUS 31:13,16-18

" <u>Therefore YHWH HIMSELF will give you a SIGN</u> : Behold the Virgin shall conceive and bear a SON, and shall call HIS NAME IMMANUEL." For there is born to you this day in the city of DAVID A SAVIOR, who is MESSIYAH IMMANUEL. And this will be <u>the SIGN to you</u>: you will find a babe wrapped in swaddling cloths, lying in a manger."   ISAIAH 7:14 / LUKE 2:11,12,34

This is an EVIL generation. It seeks a SIGN, and <u>NO SIGN will be given to it except the SIGN of JONAH the prophet</u>.. " For as JOHAN became a SIGN to the Ninevites, so also the SON OF MAN will be to this generation.
        LUKE 11:29,30 / MATTHEW 12:38-40 / 16:4 / MARK 8:11,12
    For HEBREWS *request A SIGN*, and Greeks seek after wisdom; but we preach MESSIYAH crucified, to the HEBREWS a stumbling block and to the Greeks foolishness, Therefore <u>tongues are for a SIGN</u>, not to those who believe but to unbelievers; but PROPHESYING is not for unbelievers but for those who believe. "And these *SIGNS* will follow those who believe: In MY NAME they will cast out demons; they will speak with new tongues; they will take up serpents; and if they drink anything deadly, it will by no means hurt them; they will lay hands on the sick, and they will recover."   1CORINTHIANS 1:22,23 / 14:22-25 / MARK 16:17,18

Now as YAHSAIOR sat on the Mount of Olives, the disciples came to HIM privately, saying, " Tell us, when will these things be? And what will be the *SIGNS* OF Your coming, and of the END OF THE AGE?? But of that day and hour NO ONE KNOWS, not even the angels of heaven, but MY ABBA ONLY. " But as the days of NOAH were, so also will the coming of the SON OF MAN be..
        MATTHEW 24:3-14,36,37 / MARK 13:4-13 / LUKE 21:7-19

    (A) SIGN (N) Something that indicates a fact; *YHWH IS WITH YOU*

COMMANDMENT KEEPERS
    AMMISHADDAI

TOPIC : EARRING / NOSERING / RING.. So I put the NOSERING on her nose and the BRACELETS on her wrists. " And I bowed my head and worshiped the MOSTHIGH, and blessed the MOSTHIGH Of my forefather ABRAHAM, who led me in the *WAY Of TRUTH* to take the daughter of my forefather's brother for his son..
                                                            GENESIS 24:22,30,47,48

Then all his brothers, all his sisters, and all those who had been his acquaintances before, came to him and ate food with him in his house; and they consoled him and comforted him for all the adversity that the MOSTHIGH had brought upon him. Each one gave him a piece of silver and each a RING Of gold.   JOB 42:11

They came, both men and women, as many as HAD A WILLING HEART, and brought EARRINGS and NOSE RINGS, RINGS and NECLACES, all jewelry of gold, that is, every man who made an offering of gold to the MOSTHIGH.. The children Of YSRAEL brought a FREEWILL OFFERING to the MOSTHIGH, all the men and women whose hearts were willing to bring, MATERIAL for all kinds of work which the MOSTHIGH, by the hand of MOSES, had commanded to be done.
                                                            EXODUS 35:22,29

" Therefore we have brought an offering for the MOSTHIGH, what every man found of ornaments of gold: armlets and bracelets and signet rings and earrings and necklaces, to make atonement for ourselves before the MOSTHIGH." and MOSES and ELEAZAR the priest received the gold from the captains of thousands and of hundreds, and brought it into the tabernacle of meeting as a *MEMORIAL FOR THE CHILDREN OF YSRAEL* before the MOSTHIGH..   NUMBERS 31:50,54

" Then I washed you in water; yes, I thoroughly washed off your blood, and I anointed you with oil. I adorned you with ornaments, put bracelets on your wrists, and a chain on your neck. " And I put a RING in your nose, EARRINGS in your ears, and a beautiful crown on your head. " Your fame went out among the nations because of your beauty, for it was perfect through MY SPLENDOR which I had BESTOWED on you," says the MOSTHIGH GOD..   EZEKIEL 16:9,11,12,14

** WARNING ON OPPRESSION and LUXURY **
In that day the MOSTHIGH will take away the finery: the HEADDRESSES, the LEG ORNAMENTS, and the HEADBANDS; the perfume boxes, the charms, and the RINGS; the NOSE JEWELS (Rings) the fine linen, the turbans, and the robes. And so it shall be: I will punish her for the days of the Baals to which she burned incense. She decked herself with her earrings and jewelry, and went after her lovers; but ME she forgot," says the MOSTHIGH.   ISAIAH 3:18-23 / HOSEA 2:13

COMMANDMENT KEEPERS
      AMMISHADDAI

TOPIC : DON'T BEAR FALSE WITNESS AGAINST YOUR NEIGHBOR.

But if you want to enter into life, KEEP the COMMANDMENTS." You shall not bear FALSE WITNESS against your neighbor.

MATTHEW 19:17,18 / EXODUS 20:16 /DEUTERONOMY 5:20

" You shall NOT CIRCULATE a FALSE REPORT. Do not put your hand with the wicked to be an unrighteous witness. " You shall NOT FOLLOW a crowd to do evil; nor shall you testify in a dispute so as to turn aside after many to pervert justice.. " Keep yourself far from a false matter;   EXODUS 23:1,2,7

" Your eye shall NOT PITY him, but you shall put away the guilt of innocent blood from YSRAEL, that it may go well with you. " One witness shall not rise against a man concerning any iniquity or any sin that he commits; by the mouth of two or three witnesses the matter shall be established. If a FALSE WITNESS rises against any man to testify against him of wrongdoing, " Then both men in the controversy shall stand before YHWH, before the priests and the judges who serve in those days. " And the judges shall make careful inquiry, and indeed, if the witness is a false witness, who has testified falsely against his brother, then you shall do to him as he thought to have done to his brother; so you shall put away the evil from among you. And those who remain shall hear and fear, and hereafter they shall not again commit such evil among you. " Your eye shall not pity: life shall be for life, eye for eye, tooth for tooth, hand for hand, foot for foot..   DEUTERONOMY 19:13,15-21

These six things YHWH hates, Yes, seven are an abomination to HIM: a proud look, A LYING TONGUE, hands that shed innocent blood, a heart that devises wicked plans, feet that are swift in running to evil, A FALSE WITNESS who speaks lies, And one who sows discord among brethren. A FALSE WITNESS shall perish,
PROVERBS 6:16-19 / 21:28

ALL the PEOPLE shall HEAR and FEAR and NO LONGER ACT PRESUMPTUOUSLY..   DEUTERONOMY 17:13

** EXAMPLE Of ABRAM IN EGYPT **

Now there was a famine in the land, and ABRAM went down to Egypt to dwell there, for the famine was severe in the land. And it came to pass,   GENESIS 12:10-20

(A) PRESUMPTUOUSLY (adv) acting without permission or right; too bold;
(B) AGAINST (prep) in opposition to; contrary to:
(C) LIE (v) speak Falsely; Intentional Untruth.

PROPHETIC MESSAGE MINISTRY
        AMMISHADDAI

TOPIC : BLESSINGS OF YAH.. " In your seed all the nations of the earth shall be BLESSED, because you have OBEYED MY VOICE."

GENESIS 22:18

" For You have made Your people YSRAEL Your very own people FOREVER; and You, YHWH, have become their GOD (MIGHTY ONE). Now, O YHWH GOD, the word which You have spoken concerning Your servant and concerning his house, establish it forever and do as You have said. " So let Your name be magnified forever, saying, ' YHWH of hosts is the GOD over YSRAEL.' And let the house of Your servant DAVID be established before You. " For You, O YHWH of hosts, GOD of YSRAEL have revealed this to Your servant, saying, 'I will build you a house.' Therefore Your servant has found it in his heart to pray this prayer to You. " And now, O YHWH GOD, You are GOD, and Your words are true, and You have promised this goodness to Your servant. " Now therefore, let it please You to bless the house of Your servant, that it may continue before You forever; for You, O YHWH MIGHTYONE, have spoken it, and with Your blessing let the house of Your servant be blessed forever."

2 SAMUEL 7:24-29

SALVATION BELONGS TO YHWH, YOUR BLESSINGS IS UPON YOUR PEOPLE..

PSALM 3;8

The earth is YHWH'S, and all its fullness, the world and those who dwell therein. Who may ascend into the hill of YHWH? Or who may stand in HIS HOLY PLACE? He who has clean hands and a pure heart, Who has not lifted up his soul to an idol, Nor sworn deceitfully. He shall receive blessing from YHWH, and righteousness from the GOD of his salvation. This is YAHCOB, the generation of those who seek HIM, who seek Your face..   PSALM 24:1-6

Whoever walks BLAMELESSLY will be SAVED, But he who is perverse in his ways will suddenly fall. The BLESSING of YHWH makes one rich, And He adds no sorrow with it. A faithful man will abound with blessings,   PROVERBS 28:18 / 10:22 / 28:20

But those who rebuke the wicked will have delight, And a good blessing will come upon them.

PROVERBS 24:26

" I will make them and the places all around My hill a blessing; and I will cause showers to come down in their season; there shall be showers of blessing..   EZEKIEL 34:26

FINALLY, ALL Of you be of ONE MIND, having compassion for one another; LOVE as brothers, be tenderhearted, be courteous; not returning evil for evil or reviling for reviling, but on the contrary BLESSING, knowing that you were called to this, that you may INHERIT A BLESSING.. Let him turn away from evil and do good; Let him seek peace and pursue it. For the eyes of YHWH are on the righteous, And His ears are open to their prayers; But the face of YHWH is against those who do evil."   1 PETER 3:8-12

** BLESSING ON OBEDIENCE **
DEUTERONOMY 28:1-14

PROPHETIC MESSAGE MINISTRY
AMMISHADDAI

KINGDOM PRINCIPLES

QUESTION.. How do you know when you are in the World, but not transformed to the World ?? Answer.. Desires and Passions should be TOTALLY DIFFERENT from the World..
                                                                    (TRUE)

For this reason we also, since the day we heard it, do not cease to pray for you, and to ask that <u>you may be filled with the knowledge of HIS will in all wisdom and spiritual understanding</u>; that you may walk worthy of YHWH, fully pleasing HIM, being <u>fruitful in every good work and increasing in the knowledge of YHWH</u>;
                                                        COLOSSIANS 1:9,10

TRUST IN YHWH, and do good; Dwell in the land, and feed on HIS FAITHFULNESS. Delight yourself also in YHWH, And HE shall give you the *DESIRES OF YOUR HEART..*   PSALM 37:3,4

Brothers, *MY HEART'S DESIRE* and prayer to YHWH for YSRAEL is that they may be saved.. For I bear them witness that they have a zeal for YHWH, but not according to KNOWLEDGE. For they being IGNORANT of YHWH'S RIGHTEOUSNESS, and seeking to establish their own righteousness, <u>have not submitted to the righteousness of YHWH</u>..   ROMANS 10:1-3   For *I DESIRE MERCY and NOT SACRIFICE,* And the Knowledge of YHWH more then burnt Offerings..   HOSEA 6:6   Therefore, laying aside all malice, all deceit, hypocrisy, envy, and all evil speaking, as newborn babes, *desire the pure milk of the Word,* that you may grow thereby, if indeed you have tasted that YHWH is gracious.   1 PETER 2:1-3

" *IF ANYONE DESIRES TO BE FIRST, HE SHALL BE LAST OF ALL and SERVANT OF ALL.* "   MARK 9:35   Pursue love, and *DESIRE SPIRITUAL GIFTS,* but especially that you may prophesy. I wish you all spoke with tongues, but even more that you PROPHESIED; <u>for he who prophesies is greater than he who speaks with tongues, unless indeed he interprets</u>, that the church may receive edification..   1 CORINTHIANS 14:1   And those who are MESSIYAH'S <u>have crucified the flesh with its PASSIONS and DESIRES</u>..   GALATIANS 5:24

For those who say such things declare plainly that they seek a homeland. But now they *DESIRE A BETTER,* that is, a heavenly country. Therefore YHWH is not ashamed to be called their EL, for HE has prepared a city for them.. Therefore gird up <u>the loins of your mind</u>, be sober, and rest your hope fully upon the grace that is to be brought to you at the revelation of YAHSAVIOR MESSIYAH.. As obedient children, <u>not conforming yourselves to the former lusts, as in your ignorance</u>;
                                        HEBREWS 11:14-16 / 1 PETER 1:13-17

(1) DESIRE (N) awaiting or longing; strong wish
(2) PASSION (N) a very strong feeling or emotion

TOPIC : WEARISOME.. *ready to give up ??* Have you not known? Have you not heard? The everlasting Mighty One, YHWH, the Creator of the ends of the earth, His understanding is unseachable. He gives power to the weak, And to those who have no might He increases strength.. Even the <u>youths shall faint and be weary</u>, And the young men shall utterly fall, but those who wait on YHWH shall renew their strength; they shall mount up with wings like eagles, They shall run and not be weary, They shall walk and not faint.. YHWH has given Me The tongue of the learned, That I <u>should know how to speak A word in season to him who is</u> <u>weary</u>..   ISAIAH 40:28-31 / 50:4,5   " For I have satiated the weary soul, and I have replenished every sorrowful soul. " After this I awoke and looked around, <u>and my sleep was sweet to me</u>. Behold, is it not of YHWH of host that the peoples labor to feed the fire, And nations weary themselves in vain? For the earth will be filled with the Knowledge of the Glory of YHWH As the water cover the sea.

          JEREMIAH 31:25-28 / HABAKKUK 2:13,14

Let us not grow weary while doing good, for in due season we shall reap if we do not lose heart. Therefore, as we have opportunity, let us do good to all, especially to those who are of the *household of FAITH* But as for you, brothers, do not grow weary in doing good. And if anyone does not obey our word in this letter note that person and do not keep company with him, that he may be ashamed. Yet do not count him as an enemy, but admonish (warn) him as a brother.

          GALATIANS 6:9,10 / 2 THESSALONIANS 3:14,15

          ** *EXAMPLES Of READY TO GIVE UP WITHOUT NO HOPE* **
          JOB 7: 3-21

(1) WEARY (ADJ) Tired: fatigued exhausted of Tolerance or Patience ..
PROPHETIC MESSAGE MINISTY
          AMMISHADDAI
          TRUE
          BELIEVER

TOPIC : BUILDING CHARACTER with ENDURANCE..

" Now brother will deliver up brother to death, children will rise up against parents and cause them to be put to death. " And <u>you will be hated by all for My name's sake</u>. <u>But he who endures to the end will be saved</u>. When they persecute you in this city, flee to another. For assuredly, I say to you, you will not have gone through the cities of YSRAEL before the SON OF MAN comes.. Therefore settle it in your hearts not to meditate beforehand on what you will answer; " For I will give you a mouth and wisdom which all your adversaries will not be able to contradict or resist. " You will be betrayed even by parents and brothers, relatives and friends; and <u>they will put some of you to death</u>.. " But watch out for yourselves, for they will deliver you up to councils, and you will be beaten in the synagogues. You will be brought before rulers and kings for My sake, for a testimony to them. " And the GOSPEL MUST (FIRST) BE PREACHED TO ALL NATIONS.   But whatever is given you in that hour, speak that; for it is not you who speak, but the HOLY SPIRIT.. " And you will be hated by all for My name's sake. <u>But he who endures to the end shall be saved</u>.

MATTHEW 10:21-23 / LUKE 21:14-19 / MARK 13:9-13

But with the precious blood of MESSIYAH, as of a lamb without blemish and without spot. HE indeed was foreordained before the foundation of the world, but was manifest in these last times for you. Who through HIM BELIEVE IN YHWH, who raised HIM from the dead and gave HIM GLORY, so that your faith and hope are in YHWH. Since you have purified your souls in obeying the truth through the SPIRIT in sincere love of the brothers, love one another fervently with a pure heart, For this is commendable, if because of conscience toward YHWH one endures grief, suffering wrongfully. For what credit is it if, when you are beaten for your faults, you take it patiently? But when you do good and suffer, if you take it patiently, this is commendable before YHWH.. For to this you were called, because MESSIYAH also suffered for us, leaving us an example, that you should follow HIS STEPS; And not only that, but we also glory in tribulations, knowing that tribulation produces perseverance; and perseverance, character; and character, hope. Now hope does not disappoint, because the love of YHWH has been poured out in our hearts by the HOLY SPIRIT who was given to us. COUNT IT ALL JOY when you fall into various trials, <u>knowing that the testing of your faith produces patience</u>. But let patience have its perfect work, that you may be perfect and complete, lacking nothing.

1 PETER 1:19-22 / 2:18-22 / ROMANS 5:3-5 / JAMES 1:2-5

DO NOT BE RASH WITH YOUR MOUTH, AND LET NOT YOUR HEART UTTER ANYTHING HASTILY BEFORE YHWH .. But avoid foolish and ignorant disputes, knowing that they generate strife. And a servant of YHWH must not quarrel but be gentle to all, able to teach, patient, to the weak I became as weak, that I might win the weak. I have become all things to all men, that I might by all means save some.. Warn those who are unruly, comfort the faint hearted, uphold the weak, be patient with all..

ECCLESIASTES 5:2 / 2TIMOTHY 2:23-26 / 1CORINTHIANS 9:21,22 / 1THESSALONIANS 5:14

TOPIC : *THANKFUL IN ALL THINGS*.. It is good to give thanks to יהוה and to sing praises to your name, O MOSTHIGH; <u>in everything give THANKS</u>; for this is the will of יהוה in MESSIYAH YAHSHUAH for you..

PSALM 92:1,2 / 1THESSALONIANS 5:18

Let us come before <u>His presence with THANKSGIVING</u>; Let us shout joyfully to Him with Psalms.. Enter into His gates with THANKSGIVING, And into His courts with Praise. Be thankful to Him, and bless His name. Oh, give THANKS to יהוה for He is good! For His mercy endures forever. יהוה is merciful and gracious, Slow to anger, and abounding in mercy. He will not always strive with us, Nor will He keep His anger forever. He has not dealt with us according to our sins, Nor punished us according to our iniquities. For as the heavens are high above the earth, so great is His mercy toward those who fear Him; As far as the east is from the west, so far has he removed our transgressions form us. As a father pities his children, So יהוה <u>pities those who fear Him</u>. Those who sat in darkness and the shadow of death, Bound in affliction and irons- Because they rebelled against the words of יהוה And despised the counsel of the MOSTHIGH, therefore He brought down their heart with labor; they fell down, and there was none to help. Then they cried out to יהוה in their trouble, And He saved them out of their distresses. He brought them out of darkness and the shadow of death, And broke their chains in pieces. Oh, that men would give THANKS to יהוה for His goodness, And for His wonderful works to the children of men! He sent His word and healed them, And delivered them from their destructions..

PSALM 95:2 / 100:4 / 107:1 / 103:8-13 / 107:10-15,20

I thank my Mighty One, making mention of you always in my prayers, that the sharing of your faith may become effective by the acknowledgment of <u>every good thing</u> which is in you in MESSIYAH YAHSHUAH.. Yahshuah said to him, " I am the way, the truth, and the life. No one comes to the FATHER except through Me. "But the helper, the holy spirit, whom the Father will send in my name, He will teach you all things, and bring to your remembrance all things that I said to you. Peace I leave with you, My peace I give to you; not as the world gives do I give to you. Let not your heart be troubled, neither let it be afraid. <u>Every good gift and every perfect gift is from above, and comes down form the FATHER Of Lights</u>, with whom there is no variation or shadow of turning. Who shall separate us from the love of MESSIYAH? Shall tribulation, or distress, or persecution, or famine, or nakedness, or peril, or sword? Height nor depth, nor any other created thing, shall be able to separate us from the love of יהוה which is in MESSIYAH YAHSHUAH OUR IMMANUEL.

PHILEMON 1:4-6 / JOHN 14:6,26,27 / JAMES 1:17-20 / ROMANS 8:35-39

And you He made alive, who were dead in trespasses and sins..   EPHESIANS 2:1-5

(A) THANKS (VT) Gratitude or Grateful thoughts
(B) THANKFUL (ADJ) Feeling or expressing thanks; Grateful
(C) THANKSGIVING (N)A giving of thanks. Expression of thanks: AMMISHADDAI

TOPIC : PERSECUTED FOR RIGHTEOUS SAKE.. " Those who fear YOU (YHWH) will be glad when they see me, I know, O יהוה that your Judgments are right, and that in faithfulness you have afflicted me.. How many are the days of Your servant?. When You execute Judgment on those who persecute me?. The proud have dug pits for me, which is not according to YOUR LAW.. All Your Commandments are Faithful; They persecuted me wrongfully; Help me! PSALM :119: 74,75,84,85,86

" BLESSED are you when they revile and persecute you, and say all kinds of evil against you falsely for My sake. Rejoice and be exceedingly glad, for great is your reward in heaven, for so they persecuted the prophets who were before you. " But I say to you, love your enemies, bless those who curse you, do good to those who hate you, and pray for those who spitefully use you and persecute you, " that you may be sons of your FATHER in heaven; for HE makes HIS sun rise on the evil and on the good, and sends rain on the just and on the unjust.. " For if you love those who love you, what reward have you?? Therefore, indeed, I send you prophets, wise men, and scribes: some of them you will kill and crucify, and some of them you will scourge in your synagogues and persecute form city to city,
                              MATTHEW 5: 11,12,44,-46 / 23:34

Therefore the wisdom of יהוה also said, I will send them prophets and apostles, and some of them they will kill and persecute,' that the blood of all the prophets which was shed from the foundation of the world may be required of this generation.. Yes, I say to you, it shall be required of this generation.. "But before all these things, they will lay their hands on you and persecute you, delivering you up to the synagogues and prisons. You will be brought before kings and rulers for MY Name's sake..
                              LUKE 11:49-51 / 21:12,13

" Remember the word that I said to you, A servant is not greater then his master.' If they persecuted ME, they will also persecute you. If they kept MY word, they will keep yours also..   JOHN 15:20
Blessed those who persecute you; bless and do not curse. ' Also יהוה your Mighty One will put all these curses on your enemies and on those who hate you, who persecuted you. Blessed are those who are persecuted for righteousness' sake, For theirs is the KINGDOM OF HEAVEN..
                    ROMANS 12:14 / DEUTERONOMY 30:7 / MATTHEW 5:10
But we have this treasure in earthen vessels, that the excellence of the power may be of יהוה and not of us. We are hard pressed on every side, yet not crushed; we are perplexed, but not in despair; persecuted, but not forsaken; struck down, but not destroyed- Now when the dragon saw that he had been cast to the earth, he persecuted the woman who gave birth to the male Child.. Nevertheless she will be saved in childbearing if they continue in faith, love and holiness, with self - control..
          2 CORINTHIANS 4:7-9 / REVELATIONS 12:13 / 1 TIMOTHY 2:15

(A) PERSECUTE (V.T.) Cause to suffer; do harm; Oppress: Oppress because of ones principles and beliefs

- QUESTION -

How can you be a sinner having the FAITH OF YAHSAVIOUR which take away the sins of the world ???

FAITH and CULTER
 AMMISHADDAI
  TRUE
  BELIEVER

FAITH and CULTER

TOPIC : ITS BEST NOT TO KNOW, THEN TO KNOW and NOT DO..

" Blessed is that servant whom his master will find so doing when he comes.. The master of that servant will come on a day when he is not looking for him, and at an hour when he is not aware, and will cut him in two and appoint him his portion with the UNBELIEVERS. " And that servant who <u>knew his master's will, and did not prepare himself or do according to his will,</u> shall be beaten with many stripes. " But he who did not know, yet committed things deserving of stripes, shall be beaten with few. For everyone to whom much is given, from him much will be required; and to whom much has been committed, of him they will ask the more.   LUKE 12:43-48

For it is impossible for those who were once enlightened, and have tasted the heavenly gift, and have become partakers of the *HOLY SPIRIT*, and have tasted the GOOD WORD of YHWH and the powers of the Age to come, " if they fall away, to RENEW them again to REPENTANCE, since they Crucify again for themselves the SON Of YHWH, and put Him to an open shame.. For if we sin willfully after we have received the knowledge of the truth, there no longer remains a sacrifice for sins..
                              HEBREWS 6:4-6 / 10:26

<u>Therefore, to him who knows to do good and does not do it, to him it is sin</u> ..
                                        JAMES 4:17

For if, after they have escaped the pollutions of the world through the KNOWLEDGE of YHWH and YAHSHUAH MESSIYAH, they are again entangled in them and overcome, the latter end is worse for them than the beginning. <u>For it would have been better for them not to have known the way of righteousness,</u> than having known it, to turn from the HOLY COMMANDMENT delivered to them..   2 PETER 2:20-22

As a dog returns to his own vomit, so a fool repeats his folly.. Be sober, watchful; because your adversary the devil walks about like a roaring lion, seeking whom he may devour. Resist him, steadfast in the FAITH, KNOWING that the same sufferings are experienced by your brotherhood in the world..
                              PROVERBS 26:11 / 1 PETER 5:8,9

" When an unclean spirit goes out of a man, he goes through dry places, seeking rest, and finds none. " Then he says, 'I will return to my house from which I came.' And when he comes, he finds it empty, swept and put in order. " Then he goes and takes with him seven other spirits more wicked than himself, and they enter and dwell there; and <u>the last state of that man is worse than the first.</u> So shall it also be with this wicked generation."   MATTHEW 12:43-45

(A) KNOWING (V) perceive or understand as fact or truth, to be aware of;
COMMANDMENT KEEPERS
        AMMISHADDAI

FAITH and CULTURE..

TOPIC : TEMPLE WORSHIP.. Then the word of YHWH came to Solomon, saying: " Concerning this Temple which you are building, if you walk in My Statutes, execute My Judgments, Keep All My Commandments, and Walk in them, then I will Perform My WORD with you, which I Spoke to your father David. " And I will dwell among the children of Ysrael, and will Not Forsake My people Ysrael." Our fathers WORSHIPED on this mountain, and you Hebrews say that in Yahrusalem is the place where one ought to Worship." YAHSavior said to her, " Woman, Believe Me, the hour is coming when you will neither on this mountain, nor in Yahrusalem, Worship the FATHER.. You worship what you do not know; we know what we WORSHIP, for Salvation is of the Hebrews.. But the hour is coming, and NOW IS, when the TRUE WORSHIPERS will worship the FATHER in Spirit and Truth; for the FATHER is seeking such to WORSHIP HIM.. YHWH is SPIRIT, and those who Worship HIM Must Worship in Spirit and Truth."   1KINGS 6:11-14 / JOHN 4:20-24

" Yet I say to you that in this Place there is ONE GREATER than the Temple.. YHWH stands in the Congregation of the MIGHTY; HE Judges among the gods (Mighty ones)
I said, You are gods And all of you are children of the MOST HIGH.. " And it shall come to PASS afterward That I will pour out MY SPIRIT on all flesh; Your sons and your daughters shall Prophesy, Your old men shall see Visions, And also on My menservants and on My maidservants I will Pour out MY SPIRIT in those days..
                    MATTHEW 12:6 / PSALM 82:1,6 / JOEL 2:28,29
" However, the Most High does NOT Dwell in temples made with hands, as the prophet says: 'Heaven is MY Throne, And earth is MY Footstool. What house will you build for ME?? Says YHWH, Or what is the place of MY Rest?? Has MY Hand not made all these things?'
                    ACTS 7:47-50

Do you Not Know that you are the TEMPLE of YHWH and that the SPIRIT of YHWH Dwells in you? If anyone defiles the Temple of YHWH, YHWH will destroy him. For the TEMPLE of YHWH is HOLY, which temple you are.. Or do you NOT Know that your body is the TEMPLE of the HOLY SPIRIT who is in you, whom you have from YHWH, and you are NOT your Own? For you were bought at a Price; Do Not be unequally yoked together with unbelievers. For what fellowship has righteousness with lawlessness? And what communion has light with darkness? And what accord has MessiYah with Belial? Or what part has a Believer with an unbeliever? And what AGREEMENT has the TEMPLE of YHWH with idols? For you are the Temple of the Living ALLMIGHTY ONE.. As YHWH has said:
                    1CORINTHIANS 3: 16,17 / 6:19,20 / 2CORINTHIANS 6:14-18
When the Day of Pentecost had fully come, they were all with ONE ACCORD in one Place. And suddenly there came a sound from heaven, as of a rushing mighty wind, and it filled the whole house where they were sitting.. So continuing daily with ONE ACCORD in the TEMPLE, breaking bread from house to house, they ate their food with Gladness and Simplicity of Heart, Praising YHWH and having favor with all the people.. And YHWH added to the Church daily those who were being saved..   ACTS 2:1,2,46,47

(1) Temple (n) House of Prayer; Synagogue
(2) Church (n) House of YHWH, YHWH's house; Synagogue, Temple, Mosque
(3) Synagogue (n) Place of WORSHIP, House of YHWH: AMMISHADDAI

Which Day Is The Sabbath Day?

Every Sunday, millions upon millions of people all over the world attend church services without given their actions a second thought. It probably would seem blasphemous for these people to change their day of worship. After all, this is the way of the world. Nevertheless...

Revelation 12:9 And the great dragon was cast out, that old serpent, called the Devil, and Satan, WHICH DECEIVETH THE WHOLE WORLD: he was cast out into the earth...

One way that Satan has deceived the world is through the neglect (or change) of the weekly sabbath day.

Many theologians teach that Saturday is the JEWISH sabbath, and Sunday is the Christian sabbath. When Yahweh instituted the sabbath there was neither Jew nor Christian around.

Genesis 2:2-3 And on the seventh day Elohim ended his work which he had made. And Elohim BLESSED THE SEVENTH DAY, AND SANCTIFIED IT: because that in it HE rested from all his work which Elohim created and made.

The sabbath observance is so important that YAHWEH listed it in the Ten Commandments!

Exodus 20:8-11 Remember the sabbath day, to keep it holy. Six days shall thy labor and do all thy work: But the seventh day is the sabbath of Yahweh thy Elohim: in it thou shalt not do any work, thou, nor thy son, nor thy daughter, thy manservant, nor thy maidservant, nor thy cattle, nor thy stranger that is within thy gates: For in six days Yahweh made heaven and earth, the sea, and all that in them is, and rested the SEVENTH day: wherefore YAHWEH BLESSED the sabbath day, and HALLOWED it.

On the sabbath we refrain from work and we have a holy gathering.

Leviticus 23:3 Six days shall work be done: but the seventh day is the sabbath of rest, an HOLY CONVOCATION; ye shall do NO work therein: it is the sabbath of YAHWEH in all your dwellings.

Yahshua gave us some very important info here in

Matthew 15:5,7-9 3 But he answered and said unto them, Why do ye also transgress the commandment of Elohim by your tradition?......Ye hypocrites, well did Isaiah prophesy of you, saying, This people draweth nigh unto me with their mouth, and honoureth me with their lips; but their heart is far from me. But in vain they do worship me, teaching for doctrines the commandments of men.

The true Messiah taught us to do the will of the Father (YAHWEH) by keeping his commandments. Churches are not teaching people the message of REPENTENCE and HOLINESS!

Acts 13:42 And when the Jews were gone out of the synagogue, the Gentiles besought that these words might be preached to them the next SABBATH day.

The apostle Paul observed the sabbath!:

Acts 18:4 And he reasoned in the synagogue every SABBATH, and persuaded the Jews and the Greeks.

Yahshua observed the sabbath!

Luke 4:16 ...and as his (Yahshua's) custom was, he went into the synagogue on the SABBATH day to read.

All the servants of YAH observed his laws, statutes, and ordinances.

Isaiah 24:5-6 The earth also is defiled under the inhabitants thereof; because they have transgressed the laws, changed the ordinance, broken the everlasting covenant.

Therefore hath the curse devoured the earth, and they that dwell therein are desolate: therefore the inhabitants of the earth are burned, and few men left.

Colossians 2:8 Beware lest any man spoil you through philosophy and vain deceit, after the tradition of men, after the rudiments of the world, and not after Messiah.

Learn the truth of the scriptures!

Isaiah 56:6-8 Also the sons of the stranger, that join themselves to YAHWEH, to serve him, and to love the name of YAHWEH, to be his servants, EVERYONE THAT KEEPETH THE SABBATH FROM POLLUTING IT, AND TAKETH HOLD OF MY COVENANT; Even them will I bring to my holy mountain, and make them joyful in my house of prayer: their burnt offerings and their sacrifices shall be accepted upon my altar; for mine house shall called an HOUSE OF PRAYER FOR ALL PEOPLE.

www.yahshuah.com

Article courtesy of "The Gospel: Raw, Uncut & Unheard!

...What is His Name, and What is His Son's Name... Proverbs 30:4

What IS the Messiah's name?.

Yahshua is HIS name which means *"YAH is salvation"* unlike the name Jesus, who's origin is actually of PAGAN origin. "Joshua," is actually the correct English translation IF a translation was need, but it isn't. In the New Testament (KJV). One very glaring "translation" is found in Luke 4:27 where the name *"Eliseus"* is used instead of Elisha. In the Greek, "Eliseus" means "God (Elohim) is Zeus."

Luke 4:27 And many lepers were in Israel in the time of Eliseus the prophet; and none of them was cleansed, saving Naaman the Syrian.

In the original KJV, Eliseus is ACTUALLY rendered as EliZeus! Translators let the "z" that clearly represent Zeus get past them back in 1611 but they rectified the "deceit" later. The same "s" that they put in Eliseus is the SAME "s" they put in JeSus replacing the "z" that is really Zeus. Zeus and salvation are synonymous to the ancient Greeks. The tie-in brothas and sistas, is that Elizeus to the Greeks mean "God/Elohim saves, because the "sha" in Elisha (the true Hebrew name of the prophet as opposed to Elizeus) means saves just as "shua" in Joshua or Yahshua means "saves." To the Greeks, salvation is of ZEUS. So the point is that Jesus is neither transliterated NOR translated from Yahshua because Zeus saves no one!

Acts 7:45 Our fathers had the tabernacle of witness in the wilderness, as he had appointed, speaking unto Moses, that he should make it according to the fashion that he had seen.

Before the 1600's, "Jesus" was pronounced closer to *the way the LATIN-OS (LATINOS)* pronounce it today (Hey-ZEUS). Why also did they decide to change the long "u" sound as in truth, (Zeus), to the short "u" sound, as in lust, *(Jesus)??!!* Hmmmmm....

Names should not be neither translated nor transliterated!

Psalm 68:4 Sing unto Elohim, sing praises to HIS NAME: (which name?) extol him that ride upon the heavens by his name YAH, and rejoice before him.

YAHWEH is shortened to Yah there. Even Yahshua is actually a shortened form of Yahoshua.

Yah is found in many *of the prophets and* kings names like IsaiYah, ZechariYah, JeremiYah, and EliYah and the praise, Hallelujah!

YHWH is the English equivalent to the Hebrew characters "Yod-He-Waw-He." Psalms 119 is broken up by the Hebrew Aleph-Bet. "YaHWeH" is how it's pronounced.

Genesis 41:43 And Pharaoh called Joseph's name ZAPH'-NATH-PA-A-NE'-AH; and he gave him to wife Asenath the daughter of Potipherah priest of On. And Joseph went out over all the land of Egypt.

Even more examples!

Daniel 1:6-7 Now among these were of the children of Judah, Daniel, Hananiah, Mishael, and Azariah: Hananiah, Mishael, and Azariah, are three Hebrews chosen to be raised up in the king's house. Hananiah means "Yah has shown favor."

" Mishael, or Michael, means "Who is like unto Elohim." Azariah means "Yah has helped." The Babylonians changed their names to reflect their deities.

Unto whom the prince of the eunuchs gave names: for he gave unto Daniel the name of Belteshazzar; ("Bel's Prince") and to Hananiah, of Shadrach; ("Illuminated by the Sun") and to Mishael, of Meshach; ("Who is like Shach?") and to Azariah, of Abednego. (The Servant of Nego)

Acts 14:11-15 And when the people saw what Paul had done, they lifted up their voices, saying in the speech of Lycaonia, The gods are come down to us in the likeness of men. And they called Barnabas, Jupiter; and Paul, Mercurius, because he was the chief speaker. Then the priest of Jupiter, which was before their city, brought oxen and garlands unto the gates, and would have done sacrifice with the people.

Not only was the name Yahshua reduced to the Greek deity Zeus by the name Jesus, but the translators also did not want people to know or use YHWH (Yahweh). Every where you read "LORD God" in the Bible, it was actually "YAHWEH Elohim" The "LORD God" is not a name. By putting the correct name in the scriptures, the scriptures come alive. Notice:

Exodus 20: 1-2,7 I am YAHWEH thy Elohim, which have brought thee out of the land of Egypt, out of the house of bondage.
Thou shalt not take the name of YAHWEH thy Elohim in vain; for YAHWEH will not hold him guiltless that taketh his name in vain.

Do you see that?!

Jeremiah 23:1,27 Woe be unto the pastors that destroy and scatter the sheep of my pasture! saith YAHWEH.
Which think to cause my people to FORGET MY NAME by their dreams which they tell every man to his neighbour, as their fathers have forgotten my name for Baal.

What was the name that the people of forgotten? YHWH (YAHWEH) is the name.

If the name "Yahweh or Yahshua" offends you, Yahshua said "MANY shall be offended by my namesake." For more information visit

Which also our fathers that came after brought in with JESUS into the possession of the Gentiles, whom God drave out before the face of our fathers, unto the days of David; "Jesus" in this passage, was originally "Yahshua" because Joshua the son of Nun, and the successor to Moshe (Moses) was who was being referred to here as the one that brought the tabernacle of witness into the possession of the "Gentiles."	In Israel's bondage, our oppressors have always taken the *wisest amongst us* and changed our names (which contained our Father's name) to reflect their deities	*Daniel 4:8 But at the last Daniel came in before me, whose name was Belteshazzar, ACCORDING TO THE NAME OF MY GOD,...* *Even the Hebrew names of Paul and Barnabas were "paganized."*	**The Gospel: Raw, Uncut & UNHEARD! www.YAHSHUAH.com**

THE BIBLE IS REAL BLACK HISTORY

WHO ARE YOU "BLACK MAN AND WOMEN"?
WHO ARE YOUR ANCIENT FOREFATHERS?
WHY DOES EVERYBODY HATE YOU?

For over 400 years black people have suffered at the hands of wicked oppressors. How did this happen, what event in our ancient past allowed this to take place? Did you know, the majority of the people mention in the bible were black people? The scriptures says the Children of Israel look like the ancient Egyptians & Ethiopians in Physical Appearance, both the Egyptians and Ethiopians were black people.

Abraham, Isaac, Jacob, Moses, King David, all the Prophets, Apostles, Messiah and Israelites were black people. African Americans are direct descendants of the biblical Hebrew Israelites, the bible proves this. Did you know that the bible foretold of our entire history in this country thousands of years before we made it here? Prophecies such as:

THE TRANS ATLANTIC SLAVE TRADE-BROUGHT INTO SLAVERY IN SHIPS **(Deuteronomy 28:68)**
HIGH PRISON POPULATION **(Isaiah 42:22)**
A SICK AND DISEASE STRICKEN PEOPLE **(Deuteronomy 28: 59-61)**
SUFFERING FROM MENTAL ILLNESS BECAUSE OF HOW WE ARE TREATED **(Deuteronomy 28:28,34)**
CHILDREN BEING TAKEN AWAY AND GIVEN TO OTHER PEOPLE **(Deuteronomy 28:32)**
EVERY RACIAL GROUP COME IN OUR NEIGHBORHOOD AND RUN SUCCESSFUL BUSINESSES **(Deut 28:43-44)**
NOT BEING ABLE TO STAND AGAINST OUR ENEMIES **(Leviticus 26:37-38, Deuteronomy 28:25)**
OUR SONS STAND ON THE CORNERS GOING BUCK WILD **(Isaiah 51:20)**
HAVING MANY PLACES OF WORSHIP (Churches) ON EVERY STREET **(Ezekiel 16:24-25)**
LYNCHING, BEING BURNED ALIVE BY OUR ENEMIES, **(Deuteronomy 28:22)**
TEENAGE GANGS RUNNING THE NEIGHBORHOODS, & NONE EFFECTIVE LEADERS **(Isaiah 3:12)**

Have you ever wondered why, we are the only people who were forbidden to practice our original culture upon our arrival to this land?
Have you ever wondered why, they made it against the law for us to sing "Negro spiritual songs" that talked about the old testament?
Have you ever wondered why, they changed our names.
Have you ever wondered why, they didn't want us to read the bible?

Your true history, and heritage has been taken away and hidden from you.
Now is the time to reclaim your identity and return back to the Most High.
Black Men and Women you are the true Israelites spoken of in scripture.
The bible is our true history book.

Contact brother Obadiyah For More Information:
Phone:773-957-3762
Email:hebrewheritage@hebrewisraelites.org

Or Visit the Hebrew Israelite Website
http://www.hebrewisraelites.org

5/28/2006

The Book Of Revelations
Chapters 2:9 and 3:9

2:9 "I KNOW YOUR WORKS, AND TRIBULATION AND POVERTY, (BUT YOU ARE RICH) AND I KNOW THE BLASPHEMY OF THEM WHICH SAY THEY ARE Ysrayl (Israel) AND ARE NOT, BUT ARE THE SYNAGOGUE Of Satan

In the year 450 A.D. one of Europe's barbaric tribes was beginning to show signs of restlessness. This tribe was called the KHAZARS (Chazars). Within the next two hundred years, the KHAZARS would form Eastern Europe's largest and most powerful kingdom. They would rule supreme for about 200 years, ranking in power with the Muslim Caliphate and the Byzantine Empire. Their kingdom, of approximately one million square miles, bordered the Aral sea on the east; Kiev and the Ukrainian Steppes on the west: the Caucasus mountain and the Black Sea on the south: and the Ural mountain on the north.

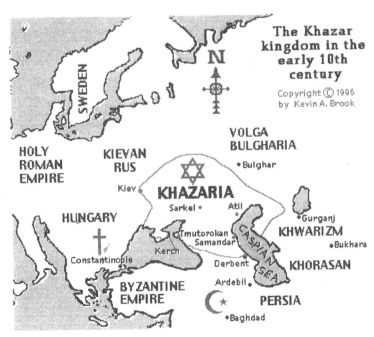

The Khazaria represented a very important period in European history, without their valor, Europe would have probably been one 100% Muslim today. Why don't we hear more about the KHAZARS and their mighty empire today?

153

KINGDOM PRINCIPLES

TOPIC : HOUSE Of WORSHIP.. Yahshuah said to her, "Women, believe ME, the hour is coming when you will neither on this mountain, nor in Yahrusalem, WORSHIP the FATHER. "But the hour is coming, and now is, when the TRUE WORSHIPERS will worship the FATHER in SPIRIT and TRUTH; for the Father is seeking such to worship HIM.. יהוה is SPIRIT, and those who worship HIM must worship in SPIRIT and TRUTH."

JOHN 4:20-24

When the DAY of PENTECOST had fully come, they were all <u>with ONE Accord in ONE Place</u>.. And suddenly there came a sound from heaven, as of a rushing mighty wind, and it filled the WHOLE HOUSE where they were sitting. So continuing Daily <u>with ONE Accord</u> in the temple, and breaking bread from HOUSE to HOUSE, they ate their food with Gladness and Simplicity of Heart, PRAISING יהוה and having FAVOR with All the people. And the MOSTHIGH added to the church Daily those who were being SAVED..   ACTS 2:1,2,46,47

The Churches of Asia greet you.. With the Church that is in their HOUSE.. Greet the Brothers who are in Laodicea, and Nymphas and the Church that is in his HOUSE.. To Philemon our beloved friend and fellow laborer, to the beloved Apphia, Archippus our fellow soldier, and to the Church in your HOUSE..

1CORINTHIANS 16:19 / COLOSSIANS 4:15 / PHILEMON 1:1,2

DO you NOT KNOW that you are the temple of יהוה *and that the* SPIRIT of יהוה dwells in you?? <u>Or do you NOT KNOW that your body is the temple of the HOLYSPIRIT who is in you</u>, whom you have from יהוה and you are NOT your own?? For you were bought at a price; therefore GLORIFY יהוה in your body and in your Spirit, which are יהוה 's

1CORINTHIANS 3:16,17 / 6:19,20

(A) Synagogue (N) Place of Worship; HOUSE Of YHWH.
(B) Temple (N) HOUSE Of Prayer; Synagogue.
(C) Church (N) HOUSE Of YHWH, YHWH's HOUSE; Synagogue, Temple
                    or Mosque..

PROPHETIC MESSAGE MINISTRY
        AMMISHADDAI

PROPHETIC MESSAGE MINISTRY
Art of Studies.. Kingdom principles..

TOPIC : The Search for Wisdom.. When I was still young, before I started out on my travels, I boldly prayed for WISDOM.. I went to the temple and asked for her, and <u>I will look for her as long as I live</u>. From my blossoming youth to my ripe old age she has been my delight. I have followed directly in her path ever since I was young. <u>*I received WISDOM as soon as I began listening for her*</u>, and I have been rewarded with great knowledge.. I have always been a learner and I'm grateful to everyone who has been my teacher, I was determined to live WISELY and was devoted to the cause of GOODNESS.. I have NO REGRETS. I fought for WISDOM and was strict in my conduct, *When I prayed*, I <u>sadly confessed how far short of WISDOM I fell</u>.. But I was determined to have her,

And I found her by keeping myself *free from sin.* I have grown in WISDOM since first I found her. And I will never be without her. Because I was driven by the disire to find her. I have been richly rewarded. YHWH <u>gave me a gift for words, and I have used it in his praise</u>.. Come to me, all you that need instruction, and learn in my school. Why do you admit that you are ignorant and do nothing about it?? Here is what I say; it costs nothing to be wise. Put on the yoke, and be willing to learn. The opportunity is always near. See for your selves! I have really not studied very hard. But I have found great contentment. No matter how much it costs you to get WISDOM, it will be well worth it. Be joyfully grateful for YHWH's mercy, and never be ashamed to praise HIM. Do your duty at the proper time, and YHWH, at the time he thinks proper, will give you your reward..

PROPHETIC MESSAGE MINISTRY   SIRACH 51:13-30
          AMMISHADDAI

TOPIC : WISOM and CONFIDENCE.. Planning and thought lie behind everything that is done. The mind concerns itself with four things; these are good and evil, life and death, They all begin in the mind, but the tonque is their absolute ruler, Someone may have the ability to teach. But still not be of much use to himself. He may be clever with words, but end up starving because people hate him. This may happen if he doesn't have good sense..

If YHWH has not given him tact.. Someone may consider himself wise and let you know that he is certain about what he knows. Anyone who really is wise will be the teacher of his people, and they can be certain that what he teaches is the truth. Everyone will praise such a person and speak of him as fortunate..

A person's life has only a limited number of days, but the life of Ysrael cannot be measured in days at all.. The *WISE* will win the *CONFIDENCE* of others, and will be remembered forever..

SIRACH 37:16-26

PROPHETIC MESSAGE MINISTRY
    AMMISHADDAI

TOPIC : LOANS and REPAYMENTS.. Be kind enough to lend to your neighbor when he needs help. You are keeping YHWH's Commands if you help him. If he needs something, lend it to him. And when you are in debt, <u>pay it back as soon as you can</u>. If you meet your obligations, you will always be able to borrow what you need. Many people treat a loan as something they found and can keep, causing embarrassment to those who helped them. Some people will speak politely, bow and scrape until they get the loan they want, but when the <u>time comes to pay it back</u>, they'll put if off, <u>say that it's inconvenient</u>, and make a lot of worthless excuses.

    <u>If the lender insists on being paid</u>, he can count himself Blessed to get back half. If he doesn't insist, the borrower has robbed him and made an unnecessary enemy. All the lender will get from him are curses, insults, and disrespect, but never any gratitude, many people refuse to lend at all, <u>not because they are stingy</u>, but because they don't want to be cheated if they can avoid it..   SIRACH 29:1-7

TOPIC : GUARANTEEING DEBTS.. A good man is willing to guarantee his neighbor's debts. Only someone who has lost all sense of decency would refuse to do so. If someone does this favor for you, don't forget it; he has risked his good name for you. There are some ungrateful sinners who abandon those who stand behind them, and they cause them loss of property. <u>Guaranteeing loans has ruined many prosperous people</u> and caused them unsettling storms of trouble. Influential people have lost their homes over it and have had to go wandering in foreign countries, A sinner who hopes to make a profit by guaranteeing a loan is going to find himself involved in lawsuits. So help your neighbor as much as you can, <u>but protect yourself against the dangers involved</u>.

SIRACH 29:14-20

(1) GUARANTEE (N) To assume responsibility for the debt, default, or
           miscarriage of. (co-signer)

PROPHETIC MESSAGE MINISTRY
AMMISHADDAI

TOPIC : PROBLEMS CAUSED BY MONEY.. Worrying about money will make you lose weight and lose sleep. Worrying about business will keep you from sleeping just as surely as a serious illness does.

Rich people work hard to make a lot of money; then they can sit back and live in luxury. Poor people work hard and have nothing to show for it, and when they rest, they are still poor..

No ONE who LOVES money can be judged innocent; his efforts to get rich have led him into sin. Many people have been ruined because of money, brought face-to-face with disaster. Money is a trap for those who are fascinated by it, a trap that every fool falls into.

A person who gets rich without sinfully chasing after money is fortunate. Do you know anyone like that?? If so, we will congratulate him for performing a miracle that no one else has ever been able to do. If anyone has ever passed this test, he can well be Happy. Has anyone ever known that he could get away with cheating someone, and not taken advantage of it?? If so, he deserves his wealth, and everyone will praise him for his generosity..

SIRACH 31:1-11

PROPHETIC MESSAGE MINISTRY
      AMMISHADDAI

JEWISH VIRTUAL LIBRARY
A Division of The American-Israeli Cooperative Enterprise

The Return to Zion

(538-142 BCE)

Following a decree by the Persian King Cyrus, conqueror of the Babylonian empire (538 BCE), some 50,000 Jews set out on the First Return to the Land of Israel, led by Zerubabel, a descendant of the House of David. Less than a century later, the Second Return was led by Ezra the Scribe. Over the next four centuries, the Jews knew varying degrees of self-rule under Persian (538-333 BCE) and later Hellenistic (Ptolemaic and Seleucid) overlordship (332-142 BCE).

The repatriation of the Jews under Ezra's inspired leadership, construction of the Second Temple on the site of the First Temple, refortification of Jerusalem's walls and establishment of the *Knesset Hagedolah* (Great Assembly) as the supreme religious and judicial body of the Jewish people marked the beginning of the Second Jewish Commonwealth (Second Temple period). Within the confines of the Persian Empire, Judah was a nation centered in Jerusalem whose leadership was entrusted to the high priest and council of elders.

As part of the ancient world conquered by Alexander the Great of Greece (332 BCE), the Land remained a Jewish theocracy under Syrian-based Seleucid rulers. When the Jews were prohibited from practicing Judaism and their Temple was desecrated as part of an effort to impose Greek-oriented culture and customs on the entire population, the Jews rose in revolt (166 BCE). First led by Mattathias of the priestly Hasmonean family and then by his son Judah the Maccabee, the Jews subsequently entered Jerusalem and purified the Temple (164 BCE), events commemorated each year by the festival of *Hanukkah*.

Source: Israeli Foreign Ministry

TOPIC : The NATURE Of WISDOM.. The SPIRIT Of WISDOM is intelligent and HOLY. It is of ONE NATURE but reveals itself in many ways. It is not made of any material substance, and it moves about freely, it is clear, clean, and confident; it cannot be harmed.. It loves what is good. It is sharp and unconquerable, kind, and a friend of humanity. It is dependable and sure, and has no worries. It has POWER over everything, and sees everything. It penetrates every spirit that is intelligent and pure, no matter how delicate its substance may be.

WISDOM Moves More Easily then MOTION itself; she is so pure that she penetrates everything. She is a breath of יהוה POWER – a pure and radiant stream of GLORY from the ALMIGHTY (ELSHADDAI) Nothing that is defiled can ever steal its way into WISDOM, SHE is a reflection of eternal light, a perfect mirror of יהוה activity and goodness. Even though WISDOM acts alone, she can do anything she makes everything new, although she herself never changes. From generation to generation she enters the souls of HOLY people, and makes them יהוה friends and prophets.

There is nothing that יהוה loves more than people who are at home with WISDOM. WISDOM is more beautiful than the sun and all the constellations. She is better than light itself. Because night always follows day, but evil never overcomes WISDOM, her great POWER reaches into every part of the world, and she sets everything in useful order..

WISDOM 7:22-30/8:1

TOPIC : The VALUE Of WISDOM.. WISDOM shines bright and never grows dim; those who love her and look for her can easily find her. She is quick to make herself known to anyone who desires her. Get up early in the morning to find her, and you will have no problem; you will find her sitting at your door. To fasten you attention on WISDOM is to gain perfect understanding. If you look for her. You will soon find PEACE of MIND, because she wil be looking for those who are worthy of her.. And she will find you wherever you are. She is kind and will be with you in your every thought. WISDOM begins when you sincerely want to learn. To desire WISDOM is to love her; to love her is to keep her laws; to keep her laws is to be certain of immortality; immortality will bring you close to יהוה this desire for Wisdom can prepare you to rule a kingdom. So then, you that rule the nations, if you value your thrones and symbols of authority, honor Wisdom so that you may rule forever..

WISDOM 6:12-21

TOPIC : *Be Careful in Choosing Friends / Distrust the wicked.*
Be careful about the kind of person you invite into your home, because <u>clever people</u> can fool you in <u>many ways</u>. A proud person is a decoy to lure you into danger; like a spy, he will look for your weaknesses. He will make good appear evil and find fault with the noblest actions..

A single spark can set a pile of coals ablaze, and a sinner is just waiting for a chance to do violence. Watch out for such people and their evil plans; they will ruin you permanently. If you bring a stranger home with you, it will only cause trouble, even <u>between you and your own family</u>..   SIRACH 11:29-36

TOPIC : *RULES for DOING GOOD..* When you do good deed, make sure you know who is benefiting from it; then what you do will not be wasted.. <u>You will be repaid for any kindness you show</u> to a devout person. If he doesn't repay you, the MOSTHIGH will, No good ever comes to a person who gives comfort to the wicked; it is not a righteous act.

Give to SPIRITUAL people, but don't help sinners. Do good to humble people, but don't give anything to those who are not devout. Don't give them food, or they will use your kindness against you. <u>Every good thing you do for such people</u> will bring you <u>twice as much trouble in return</u>. The MOSTHIGH hates sinners and HE will Punish them. Give to good people, but do not help sinners..   SIRACH 12:1-7

PROPHETIC MESSAGE MINISTRY
          AMMISHADDAI

TOPIC : The Search for Justice.. Love Justice, you rulers of the world. Set your minds sincerely on יהוה and look for him with all honesty. Those who do not try to test him will find him; he will show himself to those who trust him, dishonest thoughts *separate people from* יהוה *and if we are foolish enough to test* him, his POWER will put us to shame. WISDOM will never be at home with anyone who is deceitful or a slave of sin. Everyone who is HOLY has <u>learned to stay away from deceitful people</u>. He will <u>not stay around when foolish thoughts</u> are being expressed; he will not feel comfortable when injustice is done..   WISDOM 1:1-6

TOPIC : The Destiny of the WICKED.. The ungodly, however, will get the punishment their wicked thoughts deserve, because *they rebelled against* יהוה *and ignored what was right. A man* who has no use for Wisdom or education has a miserable life in store for him. He has nothing to hope for. His labors are useless, and <u>he will never accomplish anything worthwhile</u>. The woman he marries will turn out to be irresponsible, and his children will go wrong. All his descendants will be under a curse..

WISDOM 3:10-13

TOPIC : יהוה *is aware of what we say..* Wisdom is a SPIRIT that *is friendly to people, but she will not forgive anyone who speaks against* יהוה for יהוה knows our feelings and thoughts, and hears our every word. Since יהוה Spirit fills the entire world, and holds everything in it together, *she knows every word that people say. No one who speaks wickedly will* escape notice; <u>sooner or later he will receive just punishment</u>. The intentions of ungodly people will be closely examined; their words will be reported to יהוה *and then they will get the punishment that their wickedness deserves.* יהוה will tolerate no challenge, and since he hears everything, you cannot hide your complaining from him. <u>So be sure that you do not go around</u> *complaining – it does no good – and don't engage in bitter talk. The most* secret things you say will have their consequences, and lying will destroy your soul..   WISDOM 1:6-11

PROPHETIC MESSAGE MINISTRY   AMMISHADDAI

TOPIC : DESPAIRED or DEPRESSED?? And David said in his heart. "Now I shall perish someday by the hand of Saul. There is nothing better for me than that I should speedily escape to the land of the Philistines; and Saul will despair of me, to seek me anymore in any part of Ysrael. So I shall escape out of his hand." And it was told Saul that David had fled to Gath; so he sought him no more..   1SAMUEL 27:1-4

Then I hated all my labor in which I had toiled under the sun, because I must leave it to the man who will come after me. Therefore I turned my heart and despaired of all the labor in which I had toiled under the sun. For there is a man whose labor is with Wisdom, Knowledge, and Skill; yet he must leave his Heritage to a man who has not labored for it. This also is vanity and a great evil.   ECCLESIASTES 2:18-21

Because you have forgotten the GOD of your salvation. And have not been mindful of the ROCK of your stronghold, Therefore you will plant pleasant plants and set out foreign seedlings; in the day you will make your plant to grow, And in the morning you will make your seed to flourish; But the harvest will be a heap of ruins in the day of grief and desperate sorrow. " The heart is deceitful above all things, And desperately wicked; Who can know it??   ISAIAH 17:10,11 / JEREMIAH 17:9

For we do not want you to be ignorant, brethren, of our trouble which came to us in Asia; that we were burdened beyond measure, above strength, so that we despaired even of life. Yes, we had the sentence of death in ourselves, that we should not trust in ourselves but in יהוה who raises the dead, who delivered us from so great a death, and does deliver us; in whom we trust that HE will still deliver us, We are hard pressed on every side, yet not crushed; we are perplexed, but not in *despair*, persecuted, but not forsaken; struck down, but not destroyed - Let your conduct be without covetousness; be content with such things as you have. For HE HIMSELF has said, "I will never leave you nor forsake you." So we may boldly say; יהוה is my helper; I will not fear. What can man do to me?"
                    2CORINTHIANS 1:8-11 / 4:8,9 / HEBREWS 13:5,6

(A) Despair (VI) utter lack of hope; something destroying all hope.
(B) Depress (VT) made sad or gloomy; causes to have low Spirits.
AMMISHADDAI   PROPHETIC MESSAGE MINISTRY

TOPIC : LOVE FULFILLS the LAW.. Brethren, if a man is overtaken in any trespass, you who are spiritual restore such a one in a spirit of gentleness, <u>considering yourself lest you also be tempted</u>. Bear one another's burdens, and so fulfill the LAW of MessiYah. I say then; WALK in the SPIRIT, and you shall not fulfill the lust of the flesh. <u>But if you are led by the Spirit</u>, you are not under the LAW. And those who are MessiYah's have crucified the flesh with its passions and desires. If we live in the Spirit, let us also walk in the Spirit.

GALATIANS 6:1,2,4,5 / 5:14-26

Now I myself am confident concerning you, my brethren, that you also are full of goodness, filled with all knowledge, <u>able also to admonish one another</u>. Can two walk together, unless they are agreed? ROMANS 15:14 / AMOS 3:3

"As the FATHER love ME, I also have loved you; abide in MY LOVE. "If you keep MY commandments, you will abide in MY LOVE, just as I have kept MY FATHERS commandments and abide in HIS LOVE. "These things I have spoken to you, that MY joy may remain in you, and that your joy may be full. "This is MY commandment, that you love one another as I have loved you. JOHN 15:9-12

And now, Ysrael, what does YHWH your GOD require of you, but to fear YHWH your GOD, to walk in all HIS ways and to LOVE HIM, to serve YHWH your GOD with all your heart and with all your soul, "and to keep the commandments of YHWH and HIS statutes *which I command you today for your good?* DEUTERONOMY 10:12-15

Therefore if there is any consolation in MessiYah, if any comfort of LOVE, if any fellowship of the Spirit if any affection and mercy, fulfill my joy by being like-minded, having the same LOVE, being of ONE Accord, of ONE Mind. <u>Let each of you look out not only for his own interests, but also for the interests of others</u>. Let this mind be in you which was also in MessiYah Yahshuah.. PHILIPPIANS 2:1-4

That their hearts may be encouraged, being knit together in LOVE, and attaining to all riches of the full assurance of understanding, to the KNOWLEDGE of the mystery of YHWH, both of the FATHER and of MessiYah, in whom are hidden all the treasures of WISDOM and KOWLEDGE. As you therefore have received MessiYah Yahshuah so walk in HIM, rooted and built up in HIM and established in the faith, as you have been taught, abounding in it with thanksgiving. COLOSSIANS 2:2,3,6,7

LOVE (n) YHWH mercy and benevolence toward creation.

PROPHETIC MESSAGE MINISTRY
    AMMISHADDAI

(A) Church Governing the State of Community..

TOPIC : *TABERNACLE Of MEETINGS* :

(1) <u>First time mentioned</u>; "And they shall make an ark of acacia wood; two and a half cubits shall be its length, a cubit and a half its width, and a cubit and a half is height. "You shall put the poles into the rings on the sides of the ark, that the ark may be carried by them. "And you shall put into the ark *the Testimony which I will give you*..   EXODUS 25:10-16

Then he said to the Levites who taught all Ysrael, who were HOLY to YHWH; Put the Holy Ark in the house which Solomon the son of David, King of Ysrael, built. *It shall no longer be a burden on your shoulders*. Now serve YHWH your GOD and HIS people Ysrael..   2CHRONICLES 35:3,4

"Then it shall come to pass, when you are multiplied and increased in the land in those days." Says YHWH, that they will say no more, 'The Ark of the Covenant of YHWH.' It shall not come to mind, *nor shall they remember it*, nor shall they visit it, nor shall it be made anymore. "*At that time Yahrusalem shall be called the Throne of YHWH*, and all the nations shall be gathered to it, to the name of YHWH, to Yahrusalem, No more shall they follow the dictates of their evil hearts.. "In those days the house of Yahudah shall walk with the house of Ysrael, and *they shall come together out of the land of the north* to the land that I have given as and inheritance to your fathers.   JEREMIAH 3:16-18

(2) <u>Last time mentioned</u>; So they brought the ark of YHWH, and set it in the midst of the Tabernacle that David had erected for it. Then they offered burnt offerings and peace offerings before YHWH. "*And there I have made a place for the ark*, in which is the covenant of YHWH which HE made with our fathers, when HE brought them out of the land of Egypt."
                    1CHRONICLES 16:1-3 / 1KINGS 8:21

DESTRUCTION of YSRAEL (721 BCE)

DESTRUCTION of YAHUDAH (586 BCE)

In that HE says, "A new covenant," HE has made the first obsolete. Now *what is becoming obsolete and growing old is ready to vanish away*. Therefore, if anyone is in MessiYah, he is a new creation; old things have passed away; behold, all things have become new..

AMMISHADDAI   HEBREWS 8:13 / 2CORINTHIANS 5:17

TOPIC : SIN and the CHILD Of YHWH.. And now, little children, abide in HIM, that when HE appears, we may have confidence and not be ashamed before HIM at HIS coming. If you know that HE is righteous, you know that everyone who practices righteousness is born of HIM. Behold what manner of love the FATHER has bestowed on us, that we should be called children of YHWH! Therefore the world does not know us, because it did not know HIM. *Whoever has been born of YHWH does NOT SIN,* for HIS seed remains in him; and he cannot SIN, because he has been born of YHWH..

1JOHN 2:28,29 / 3:1,4-10

The next day JOHN saw YAHsavior coming toward him, and said, *BEHOLD!* The *LAMB of YHWH* who takes away the SIN of the world! Therefore, if anyone is in MessiYah, he is a new creation; old things have passed away; behold, all things have become NEW. Now all things are of YHWH, who has reconciled us to HIMSELF through YAHSavior MessiYah, and has given us the ministry of reconciliation. *Now then we are ambassadors for MessiYah,* as though YHWH were pleading through us; we implore you on MessiYah behalf, be reconciled to YHWH. For HE made HIM who knew NO SIN to be SIN for us, that we might become the righteousness of YHWH in HIM..

JOHN 1:29 / 2CORINTHIANS 5:17-21

But HE was wounded for our transgressions, HE was bruised for our iniquities; the chastisement for our peace was upon HIM, And by HIS stripes *we are healed.* We are all like sheep have gone astray; We have turned, every one, to his own way; And YHWH has laid on HIM the iniquity of us all. And they made HIS grave with the wicked; But with the rich at HIS death, *because HE had done NO Violence,* nor was any deceit in HIS mouth.

ISAIAH 53:5,6,9

If anyone sees his brother SINNING a SIN which does not lead to death, he will ask, and HE will give him life for those who commit SIN not leading to death. There is SIN leading to death. I do not say that he should pray about that. All unrighteousness is SIN, and there is SIN not leading to death. Therefore, to him *who knows to do good and does not do it,* to him it is SIN. What shall we say then?? Shall we continue in SIN that GRACE may abound??

1JOHN 5: 16-20 / JAMES 4:17 / ROMAN 6:1

PROPHETIC MESSAGE MINISTRY
    AMMISHADDAI

TOPIC : RESTORATION.. YAHSavior answered and said to them, "Indeed, EliYah is coming first and will *RESTORE ALL THINGS..* Behold, I will send you EliYah the prophet before the coming of the great and dreadful day of YHWH. And He will turn the hearts of the fathers to the children, And the hearts of the children to their fathers, lest I come and strike the earth with a curse."

MATTHEW 17:11 / MALACHI 4:4-6

Then you shall call, and YHWH will answer; you shall cry and HE will say 'Here I am.' *Those from among you Shall build the old waste places*; you shall raise up the foundations of many generations; And you shall be called the Repairer of the Breach, The Restorer of Streets to Dwell in.. Then you shall delight yourself in YHWH; And I will cause you to ride on the high hills of the earth, And feed you with the heritage of Yahcob your father, The mouth of YHWH has spoken." HE restores my soul; HE leads me in the paths of righteousness For HIS NAME'S sake.

ISAIAH 58:9-14 / PSALM 23:3-6

Create in me a clean heart, O YHWH, *And renew a steadfast spirit within me.* Do not cast me away from YOUR presence, And do not take YOUR HOLY SPIRIT from me.. *Restore to me the JOY of YOUR Salvation*, And uphold me by Your generous Spirit. Then I will teach transgressors Your ways, And sinners shall be converted to YOU.   PSALM 51:11,12,13

"Repent therefore and *be converted*, that your sins may be blotted out, *so that times of refreshing may come from the presence of YHWH,* "and that HE may send Yahshuah (YAHSavior) MessiYah, who was preached to you before, whom heaven must receive until the times of restoration of all things, which YHWH has spoken by the mouth of all HIS Holy prophets since the world began. Then HE said to Abram; *"Know certainly* that your descendants will be strangers in a land that is not theirs, and will serve them, and they will afflict them four hundred years. "And also the nation whom they serve I will judge; afterward they shall come out with great possessions. Now the sojourn of the children of Ysrael who lived in Egypt was four hundred and thirty years. And it came to pass at the end of the four hundred and thirty years – on that very same day – it came to pass that all the armies of YHWH went out from the land of Egypt.

ACTS 3:19-21 / GENESIS 15:12-14 / EXODUS 12:37-42

(A) RESTORE (vb) Give back
(B) RESTORATION (n) put back into use; or into a former state.

PROPHETIC MESSAGE MINISTRY
AMMISHADDAI

TOPIC : ABOMINATION of DESOLATION.. "Therefore prophesy and say to them. 'Thus says YHWH GOD; "Behold, "O My people, *I will open your graves* and cause you to come up from your graves, and *bring you into the land of Ysrael.* "Then you shall know that I am YHWH, when I have opened your graves, O My people, and brought you up from your graves. "I will put My Spirit in you, and you shall live, and *I will place you in your own land.* Then you shall know that I, YHWH; have spoken it and performed it," says YHWH   EZEKIEL 37:1-14

He shall speak pompous words against the MOSTHIGH, Shall persecute the saints of the MOSTHIGH, And shall intend to change times and law, Then the *saints shall be given into his hand* for a time and times and half a time. Then he shall confirm a covenant with many for one week; But in the middle of the week He shall bring an end to sacrifice and offering. And on the wing of abomination shall be one who makes desolate, Even until the consummation, which is determined, Is poured out on the desolate."   DANIEL 7:25 / 9:27

Those who do wickedly against the covenant he shall corrupt with flattery; but the people who know their GOD (YHWH) shall be strong, and carry out great exploits. "*And those of the people who understand shall instruct many; yet for many days they shall fall* by sword and flame, by captivity and plundering. Now when they fall, they shall be aided with a little help; but many shall join with them by intrigue. "And *some of those of understanding shall fall,* to refine them, purify them, and make them white, until the time of the end; because it is still for the appointed time. Many shall be purified, made white, and refined, but the wicked shall do wickedly; and none of the wicked shall understand, *but the wise shall understand.*   DANIEL 11:31-35 / 12:10-12

"And *this gospel of the kingdom will be preached in all the world* as a witness to all the nations. And then the end will come. "Therefore when you see the abomination of desolation, spoken of by DANIEL the prophet, standing in the holy place." *Who ever reads, let him understand,* "*When an unclean spirit goes out of a man,* he goes through dry places, seeking rest; and finding none, he says, I will return to my house from which I come.' And when he comes, he finds it swept and put in order. "Then he goes and takes with him seven other spirits more wicked than himself, and they enter and dwell there; and the last state of that man is worse than the first." MATTHEW 24:14,15 / 12:43-45 / LUKE 11:24-26

Here is the patience of the saints; here are those who keep the commandments of YHWH and the faith of Yahshuah. Then I heard a loud voice from the temple saying to the seven angels Go and pour out the bowls of the Wrath of YHWH on the earth."
                                        REVELATION 14:7-13 / 16:1-7

(A) Desolate (adj) Life less; Disconsolate, lay waste
(B) Abomination (adj) thoroughly unpleasant of revolting; hate

PROPHETIC MESSAGE MINISTRY
        AMMISHADDAI

COMMANDMENT KEEPERS

TOPIC : The (BELIEVERS) WAY or Christian.. "All authority has been given to ME in heaven and on earth. "Go therefore and make disciples of all the nations, baptizing them in the name of the ABBA and of the SON and of the HOLY SPIRIT, "*teaching them to observe all things that I have commanded you*; and lo, I am with you always, even to the end of the age." Amen..   MATTHEW 28:18-20

And he went into the synagogue and spoke boldly for three months, reasoning and persuading concerning the things of the kingdom of יהוה. But when some were hardened and did not believe, but spoke evil of *the WAY* before the multitude, he departed from them and withdrew the disciples, reasoning daily in the school of Tyran'nus.   ACTS 19:8,9

And about that time there arose a great commotion about *the WAY*. "I persecuted this WAY to the death, binding and delivering into prisons both men and women,   ACTS 19:23 / 22:4

"But this I confess to you, that according to *the WAY* which they call a sect, so I worship יהוה of my fathers, believing all things which are written in the LAW and in the PROPHETS.
                                                        ACTS 24:14
But when Felix heard these things, having more accurate knowledge of *the WAY*, he adjourned the proceedings and said,   ACTS 24:22

And when he had found him, he brought him to Antioch. So it was that for a whole year they assembled with the church and taught a great many people. *And the disciples were first called Christians in Antioch*. And in these days prophets came from Yahrusalem to Antioch. Then Agrip'pa said to Paul, "You almost persuade me to become a Christian." Yet if anyone suffers as a Christian, let him not be ashamed, but let him glorify יהוה in this matter..   ACTS 11:26 / 26:28 / 1PETER 4:16

(THE WAY)	(HERESY)
PASSOVER (LEVITICUS 23:4,5)	EASTER
FEAST OF WEEKS (LEVITICUS 23:15-22)	GOOD FRIDAY
DAY OF ATONEMENT (LEVITICUS 23:26,27)	PALM SUNDAY
HANUKKAH (JOHN 10:22)	CHRISTMAS
FEAST OF PURIM (ESTHER 9:18-32)	THANKSGIVING

(A) Christian (adj) relating to or characteristic of Christianity or its adherents.
(B) Disciple (N) One who embraces and assists in spreading the teachings of MessiYah..

PROPHETIC MESSAGE MINISTRY
   AMMISHADDAI

Devotional # 1

TOPIC : SATAN IS A THIEF..

Behold, יהוה shall come with a strong hand, And HIS arm shall rule for HIM; Behold, HIS reward is with HIM, And HIS work before HIM, HE will feed HIS flock like a shepherd; HE will gather the lambs with HIS arm, And carry them in HIS bosom, And gently lead those who are with young.　　ISAIAH 40:10,11

"I am the door, if anyone enters by ME, he will be SAVED, and will go in and out and find pasture, "The thief does not come except to steal, and to kill, and to destroy. I have come that they may HAVE LIFE, and that they may have it more abundantly.. "I am the good shepherd. The good shepherd gives HIS LIFE for the sheep.　　JOHN 10:9-11

Therefore *humble yourselves* under the mighty hand of יהוה that HE may exalt you *in due time*. Casting all your care upon HIM, for HE cares for you. Be sober, be vigilant; because your adversary the devil walks about like a roaring lion, seeking whom he may devour, Resist him, steadfast in the FAITH, knowing that the same sufferings are experienced by your brotherhood in the world. But may יהוה of all grace, who called us to HIS eternal glory by MessiYah YAHSavior, after you have suffered a while, perfect, establish, strengthen, and settle you. To HIM be the glory and the dominion forever and ever AMEN..　　1PETER 5:6-11

THOUGHTS to Grow On:　The BIBLE describes the Devil as a "roaring lion looking for someone to eat" – something you definitely want to try to avoid. YAHSavior gives you three clues to determine if something is from the Devil.

(1) if it will "steal" anything of yours, such as your honesty or your innocence,
　　　it is of the devil.

(2) if it will "kill" anything of yours, such as your hope or your desire to do good,
　　　it is of the devil.

(3) if it will "destroy" anything of yours, such as your good reputation or your faith,
　　　it is of the devil.

Satan wants to ruin your life, YAHSavior wants to BLESS your life, When you choose YAHS Way, you win a great VICTORY over the devil..

TODAY:

Seek a Blessed Life in YAHSavior

Devotional # 2

TOPIC : You are יהוה special project..

For you formed my inward parts; You covered me in my mother's womb. I will praise You, for I am fearfully and wonderfully made; Marvelous are Your works, And that my soul knows very well.   PSALM 139:13,14

For your fellowship in the gospel from the first day until now, Being confident of this very thing, that *HE who has begun a good work in you* will complete it until the day of Yahshuah MessiYah;   PHILIPPIANS 1:5,6

But in a great house there are not only vessels of gold and silver, but also of wood and clay, some for honor and some for dishonor. Therefore if anyone cleanses himself from the latter, he will be a vessel for honor, sanctified and useful for the Master, *prepared for every good work.* That the man of יהוה may be complete, thoroughly equipped for every good work..

2TIMOTHY 2:20,21 / 3:17

THOUGHTS to Grow On: Have you ever made something you really liked? A drawing, an invention, or a special project? You probably kept it in a place where everyone could see it and where it would be safe. Can you remember how pleased you felt? Guess what? יהוה feels the same way about you – only a zillion times stronger! HE knows that no two of HIS children are a like. יהוה not only loves you; יהוה is happy with you and wants to present you to the whole world.

Todays action of the day: look in your mirror and say "Hello, child of the KING of Ysrael!" say if five times, and believe it because you are a child of the KING of Ysrael.

PROPHETIC MESSAGE MINISTRY
        AMMISHADDAI

Devotional # 3

    TOPIC : From a caterpillar to a butterfly..

Therefore, if <u>*anyone is in MessiYah, he is a New Creation*</u>; old things have passed away; behold, all things have become New.   2CORINTHIANS 5:17

Therefore we were buried with HIM through baptism into death, that just as MessiYah was raised from the dead by the glory of the ABBA, even so we also should <u>*walk in newness of life*</u>. Therefore do not let sin reign in your mortal body, that you should obey it in its lusts..   ROMANS 6:4,12

Do not lie to one another, since you have put off <u>*the old man with his deeds*</u>, and have <u>*put on the New man who is renewed in KNOWLEDGE*</u> according to the image of HIM who created HIM,   COLOSSIANS 3:9,10

THOUGHTS to Grow On: have you ever seen a caterpillar spin itself into a cocoon? An amazing thing is quietly happening inside the silky womb: the caterpillar is being transformed into a butterfly. יהוה is working an even more amazing transformation in you!! And you don't have to curl up inside a cocoon to experience it. יהוה is transforming the "regular you" into the "New creation you" that "New creation you" can do something the "regular you" could never do – it can be like Yahshuah!

Todays action of the day; Find or draw a mental picture of a butterfly. Let it remind you of the wonderful changes יהוה is working in you..

PROPHETIC MESSAGE MINISTRY
    AMMISHADDAI

TOPIC : *Witchcraft, Spiritualist, Psychic / Soothsayer* "You *shall not permit a sorceress to live*.. "There shall not be *found among you anyone* who makes his son or his daughter pass through the fire. Or one *who practices WICHCRAFT, or a SOOTHSAYER, or one who interprets omens, or a sorcerer, or one who conjures spells, or a MEDIUM, or a SPIRITIST*, or one who calls up the dead..

EXODUS 22:18 / DEUTERONOMY 18:10,11

Also he caused his sons to pass through the fire in the Valley of the Son of Hin'nom; *he practiced soothsaying, used witchcraft and sorcery, and consulted mediums and spiritists*. He did much evil in the sight of יהוה to provoke HIM to anger. Now the works of the flesh are evident, which are; adultery, fornication, uncleanness, lewdness, idolatry, *SORCERY*, hatred, contentions, jealousies, outbursts of which I tell you beforehand, just as I also told you in time past, that those who practice such things will not inherit the Kingdom of יהוה

2CHRONICLES 33:6 / GALATIANS 5:20

I will cut off *SORCERIES* from your hand And you shall have NO *SOOTHSAYERS*. But there was a certain man called Simon, who previously practiced *SORCERY* in the city and astonished the people of Samaria, claiming that he was someone great. And they heeded him because he had astonished them with his *SORCERIES* for a long time.. Now it happened, as we went to prayer, that a certain slave girl *possessed with a spirit of divination* met us, who brought her masters *much profit by fortune-telling*.   MICAH 5:12 / ACTS 8:9-11 / 16:16

And *they did not repent* of their murders or their *SORCERIES* or their sexual immorality or their thefts. "The light of a lamp shall not shine in you anymore, and the voice of bridegroom and bride shall not be heard in you anymore, For your merchants were the great men of the earth, for by your *SORCERY* all the nations were deceived. Blessed are those who do HIS Commandments, that they may have the right to the tree of life, and may enter through the gates into the city. But outside are dogs and *SORCERERS* and sexually immoral and murderers and idolaters, and whoever loves and practices a lie.   REVELATION 9:21 / 18:23 / 22:14,15

(A) Mediums (n) means of communication.
(B) Spiritists (n) Belief that spirit communicate with the living.
(C) Witch (n) person believed to have magic Power.
(D) Soothsayer (n) False Prophet.
(E) Psychic (adj) MEDIUM.
(F) Sorcery (n) WITCHCRAFT.
(G) Witchcraft (n) Power or practices of a WITCH.

PROPHETIC MESSAGE MINISTRY
AMMISHADDAI

TOPIC : The Pursuit to JOY or Happiness.. A merry heart makes a cheerful countenance, But by sorrow of the heart the spirit is broken. All the days of the afflicted are evil, But he *who is of a merry heart has a continual feast.. A merry heart does good like medicine, But a* broken spirit dries the bones..   PROVERBS 15:13 / 15:15 / 17:22

Happy is the man who finds wisdom, And the man who gains understanding; she is more precious than rubies, And *all the things you may desire* cannot compare with her. Her ways are ways of pleasantness, And *all her paths are PEACE..* She is a tree of life to those who take hold of her, And *Happy are all who retain her.*   PROVERBS 3:13,15,17,18

I said in my heart, "Come now, I will test you with mirth; therefore enjoy pleasure" but surely, this also was vanity. I said of laughter – "Madness!" and of mirth, *what does it accomplish?*" whatever my eyes desired I did not keep from them. I did not withhold my heart from any pleasure, For my heart rejoiced in all my labor; And this was my reward from all my labor. Then I looked on all the works that my hands had done And on the labor in which I had toiled; And indeed all was vanity and grasping for the wind. There *was NO Profit* under the sun.   ECCLESIASTES 2:1,2,10,11

Better to go to the house of mourning, Than to go to the house of feasting, For that is the end of all men; And the living will take it to heart. *Sorrow is better than laughter,* For by a *sad countenance the heart is made better.* The heart of the wise is in the house of mourning, *But the heart of fools is in the house of mirth.* For like the crackling of thorns under a pot, So is the laughter of the fool. This also is vanity..   ECCLESIASTES 7:2-6

My brethren, *Count it all JOY* when you fall into various trials, knowing that the testing of your faith produces patience. But let patience have its perfect work, that you may be perfect and complete, lacking nothing. *Even in laughter the heart may sorrow,* And the end of mirth may be grief. The backslider in heart will be *filled with his own ways,* But a good man will be SATISFIED from ABOVE.. But I rejoiced in יהוה greatly that now at last your care for me has flourished again; though you surely did care, but you lacked opportunity. Not that I speak in regard to need, for *I have learned in whatever state I am, to be CONTENT:* I *know how to be abased, and I know how to abound. Everywhere and in all things I have learned both to be full and to be hungry,* both to abound and to suffer need. I can do all things through MessiYah who strengthens me.
                    JAMES 1:2-4 / PROVERBS 14:13,14 / PHILIPPIANS 4:10-13

(1) JOY (n) A source of Object or Pleasure or Satisfaction.
(2) Mirth (n) Gaiety and Gladness, esp when expressed by Laughter.
(3) Happy (adj) Marked by good luck (Blessings) fortunate; Cheerful.
(4) Gaiety (n) Festive or joyful activity.
(5) Merry (adj) Characterized by offering Fun and Festivity.
(6) PEACE (n) Freedom from Quarrels and disagreement; Harmonious Relations (ONE)
                    PROPHETIC MESSAGE MINISTRY
                    AMMISHADDAI

KINGDOM PRINCIPLES

TOPIC : JUDGEMENT ON MATTERS OF TODAY!! Truly, these times of ignorance YHWH overlooked, but now commands all men everywhere to repent, "because HE has appointed a day on which HE will judge the world in righteousness by the Man whom HE has ordained, *HE has given assurance of this to all by raising Him from the dead."* "After that HE gave them judges for about four hundred and fifty years, until Samuel the prophet. Afterward they asked for a King; so YHWH gave them Saul the son of Kish, a man of the tribe of BenYahmin, for forty years. "And when HE had removed him, HE raised up for them David as King, to whom also HE gave testimony and said, 'I have found David the son of Yesse. A man after MY own heart, who will do all MY will.' "From this man's seed according to the promise, *YHWH raised up for Ysrael a Savior-Yahshuah-* So then *each of us shall give account of himself* to YHWH. Therefore let us not Judge one another anymore, but rather resolve this, not to put a stumbling block or a cause to fall in our brothers way..

ACTS 17:30,31 / 13:20-23 / ROMANS 14:12,13

Let us hear the conclusion of the whole matter: Fear YHWH and Keep HIS Commandments, For YHWH will bring every work into Judgment, Including every secret thing, Whether good or evil.   *ECCLESIASTES 12:13,14*

These things we also speak, not in words which mans wisdom teaches but which the HOLY SPIRIT teaches, comparing spiritual things with spiritual. But the natural man does not receive the things of the Spirit of YHWH, for they are foolishness to him; nor can he know them, because they are spiritually discerned. But *he who is Spiritual Judges all things*, yet he himself is rightly Judged by NO one. But we have the mind of MessiYah. For what have I to do with judging those also who are outside? Do you not judge those who are inside? But *those who are outside YHWH JUDGES.* Therefore put away from yourselves the evil person." Dare any of you, having a matter against another, go to law before the unrighteous, and not before the saints? Do you not know that we shall judge angels? How much more, things that pertain to this life? Do you appoint those who are least esteemed by the church to judge? I speak as to wise men; JUDGE for yourselves what I say. For this reason many are weak and sick among you, and many sleep. For if we would JUDGE ourselves, we would not be JUDGED, But when we are JUDGED, we are chastened by YHWH, that we may not be condemned with the world.

1CORINTHIANS 2:13-16 / 5:12,13 / 6:1-5 / 10:15 / 11:30-32

(A) Judge (v) to declare after determination; to form an Opinion About.
(B) Matters (n) the actual substance of thought or expression as opposed to the way in
        Which it is stated or conveyed
(C) Judgement (n) the ability to make a decision by discerning and evaluating.

TOPIC : CONSIDER THE MATTER, and UNDERSTAND the VISON; יהוה is Spirit, and those who worship HIM must worship in spirit and truth." Then HE said to Abram: "Know certainly that your descendants will be strangers in a land that is not theirs, and will serve them, and they will afflict them four hundred years. "And also the nation whom they serve I will judge; afterward they shall come out with great possessions..   JOHN 4:23,24 / GENESIS 15:12-14

"Up, up! Flee from the land of the north," says יהוה "for I have spread you abroad like the four winds of heaven." Says יהוה "Up, Zion! Escape, you who dwell with the daughter of Babylon." "Sing and rejoice, O daughter of Zion! For behold, I am coming and I will dwell in your midst," says יהוה many nations shall be joined to יהוה in that day, and they shall become My people. And I will dwell in your midst. Then you will know that יהוה of host has sent me to you. And יהוה will take possession of Yahudah as HIS inheritance in the HOLY LAND, and will again choose Yahrusalem. "Be silent, all flesh before יהוה for HE is aroused from HIS holy habitation!" The sons of foreigners shall build up your walls, And their kings shall minister to you: For in My wrath I struck you, But in My favor I have had mercy on you. You shall drink the milk of the Gentiles, And milk the breast of kings; You shall know that I, יהוה am your SAVIOR and your Redeemer, the Mighty One of Yahcob. Violence shall no longer be heard in your land, Neither wasting nor destruction within your borders; But you shall call your walls Salvation. And your gates Praise. The GLORY of this latter TEMPLE shall be GREATER then the former.   ZECHARIAH 2:1-13 / ISAIAH 60:10-18 / HAGGAI 2:1-9

"And in the days of these kings the God of heaven will set up a kingdom which shall never be destroyed; and the kingdom shall not be left to other people; it shall break in pieces and consume all these kingdoms, and it shall stand forever.. Until the ANCIENT of Days came, and a judgment was made in favor of the saints of the MOSTHIGH, and the time came for the saints to possess the kingdom. Then the kingdom and dominion And the greatness of the kingdoms under the whole heaven, Shall be given to the people, the saints of the MOSTHIGH. HIS kingdom is an everlasting kingdom, And all dominions shall serve and obey HIM.'
                                          DANIEL 2:44,45 / 7:21,22,25-28
"And those of the people who understand shall instruct many; yet for many days they shall fall by sword and flame, by captivity and plundering. "And some of those of understanding shall fall, to refine them, purify them, and make them white, until the time of the end; because it is still for the appointed time. Then the women fled into the wilderness, where she has a place prepared by יהוה that they should feed her there one thousand two hundred and sixty days. (3.5)   DANIEL 11:32-35 / REVELATION 12:6,13-17

AMMISHADDAI

TOPIC : PRAYER – PUBLIC OR PRIVATE.. Be anxious for nothing, but in everything by PRAYER and supplication, with thanksgiving, let your requests be made known to YHWH; and the Peace of YHWH, which surpasses all understanding, will guard your hearts and minds through MessiYah Yahshauh..

PHILIPPIANS 4:6,7

Pray without ceasing, " And whatever you ask in MY NAME, that I will do, that the FATHER may be glorified in the SON.. If you ask anything in MY NAME, I will do it..

1THESSALONIANS 5:17 / JOHN 14:13,14

You ask and do not receive, *because you ask amiss*, that you may spend it on your pleasures. When you spread out your hands, I will hide MY eyes from you; Even though you make many prayers, I will not hear. Your hands are full of blood..

JAMES 4:3 / ISAIAH 1:15

*** Public Prayer and Worship Acceptable!! ***

And the *whole multitude of the people was praying outside* at the hour of incense..

LUKE 1:10

Now **all the people gathered together as ONE MAN in the open square** that was in front of the Water Gate; and they told Ezra the scribe to bring the Book of the LAW of Moses, which YHWH had commanded Ysrael.. And Ezra Blessed YHWH, the great GOD.. (EL) then all the people answered, " Amen, Amen!" while lifting up their hands. And they bowed their heads and worshiped YHWH with their faces to the ground..

NEHEMIAH 8:1-6

And when you pray, *you shall not be like the hypocrites*, For they love to PRAY standing in the synagogues and on the corners of the streets, that they may be seen by men.. Assuredly, I say to you they have their reward.. But you when you PRAY, *go into your room*, and when you *have shut your door PRAY to your FATHER who is in the secret place*; and your FATHER who sees in secret will reward you openly, " And when you PRAY, do not use vain repetitions as the heathen do, for they think that they will be heard for their many words..

MATTHEW 6:5-7

(1) Supplicate (vt) To make a humble Request of; Petition earnestly..

(2) Amiss (adv) In a wrong way; Astray, wrongly, faultily, Improperly, ect..

PROPHETIC MESSAGE MINISTRY
    AMMISHADDAI

Head Of Household!!

TOPIC : Family (Bibically) Defined.. But HE answered them, saying, "Who is My mother, or My brothers?" And *HE looked around in a circle* at *those who sat about HIM*, and said, "<u>Here are My mother and My brothers!</u> "For <u>*whoever does the will of YHWH is* My brother</u> and <u>My sister</u> and <u>mother.</u>"   MARK 3:33-35

"And <u>*whoever will not receive you nor hear your words*</u>, when you depart from that house or city, shake off the dust from your feet.   MATTHEW 10:14

Can two walk together unless they are agreed??   AMOS 3:3

"And when HE brings out his own sheep, HE goes before them; and the sheep follow HIM, <u>*for they know HIS voice*</u>. "Yet they will by no means follow a stranger, but will flee from him, for they do not know the voice of strangers,"   JOHN 10:4,5

I, the Master, search the heart, I test the mind, Even to give every man according to his ways, *According to the fruit of his doings.*   JEREMIAH 17:10

'For I was hungry and you gave ME food; I was thirsty and you gave ME drink; I was a stranger and you took ME in; 'I was naked and you clothed ME; I was sick and you visited ME; I was in prison and you came to ME.' "Then the righteous will answer HIM, saying, 'Master, when did we see You hungry and feed You, or thirsty and give You drink?? 'Or when did we see You sick, or in prison, and come to You?? "And the KING will answer and say to them, 'Assuredly, I say to you, <u>*inasmuch as you did it to one*</u> of the least of <u>*these My brethren, you did it to ME*</u>..

                                        MATTHEW 25:34-40

But the Fruit of the Spirit is LOVE, Joy, Peace, Longsuffering, Kindness, Goodness, Faithfulness.. If we LIVE in the Spirit, let us also walk in the Spirit.

                                        GALATIANS 5:22-26

With all lowliness and gentleness, with longsuffering, bearing with one another in LOVE. *<u>Endeavoring to keep the unity of the Spirit</u>*, in the bond of peace. And <u>let us not grow weary</u> while doing good, *for in due season* we shall reap if we do not lose heart. Therefore, <u>as we have opportunity</u>, let us do good to all. ***Especially to those who are of the household of FAITH..***

                                        EPHESIANS 4:2-6 / GALATIONS 6:9,10

Family (N) household; group of related things..

PROPHETIC MESSAGE MINISTRY

        AMMISHADDAI

COMMANDMENT KEEPERS

TOPIC : Dealing with UnBelievers / Unbelief.. although I was formerly a Blasphemer, a persecutor, and an insolent man; but I obtained MERCY because *I did it ignorantly in unbelief*..   1TIMOTHY 1:12,13

Beware, brethren, lest there be in any of you an evil heart of unbelief in departing from the living Mighty One (YHWH)   HEBREWS 3:12-14

To the pure all things are pure, but to those who are defiled and unbelieving nothing is pure; but even their mind and conscience are defiled. They profess to know YHWH, but in works they deny HIM, being abominable, disobedient, and *disqualified for every good work*..   TITUS 1:15,16

Now HE did not do many mighty works there because of their unbelief. Later *HE appeared to the eleven as they sat at the table; and HE rebuked their* unbelief and hardness of heart, because *they did not believe* those who had seen HIM after HE had risen.   MATTHEW 13:55-58 / MARK 16:14

Therefore *tongues are for a sign*, not to those *who believe* but to *unbelievers;* but prophesying is not for unbelievers but for those who believe.. But if all prophesy, and an unbeliever or an uninformed person comes in, he is convinced by all, he is convicted by all. And thus the secrets of his heart are revealed; and so, falling down on his face, he will worship YHWH and *report that YHWH is truly among you*..   1CORINTHIANS 14:22-25

Do not be unequally yoked together with unbelievers.. For what fellowship has righteousness with lawlessness? And what communion has light with darkness? *Therefore "Come out from among them And be separate*, says the Master, do not touch what is unclean, And I will receive you. But to the rest, I not the Master, say; if any brother has a wife who does not believe, and she is willing to live with him, let him not divorce her. For the *unbelieving husband is sanctified by the wife*, and the *unbelieving wife is sanctified by the husband;* 2CORINTHIANS 6:14-18 / 1CORINTHIANS 7:12-16

PROPHETIC MESSAGE MINISTRY
AMMISHADDAI

179

TOPIC : If you are OFFENDED?? Then HE said to the disciples, It is *impossible that no offenses should come*, but woe to him through whom they do come!! "Moreover if your brother sins against you, *go and tell him* his *fault between you and him alone*.. If he hears you, you have gained your brother..   LUKE 17:1 / MATTHEW 18:15-17

I have hope in YHWH, which they themselves also accept, that there will be a resurrection of the dead, both of the just and the unjust. "This being so, I myself always *strive to have a conscience without offense* toward *YHWH and men*.   ACTS 24:15,16

Therefore, if food makes my brother stumble, I will never again eat meat, lest I make my brother stumble..   1CORINTHIANS 8:13

For we all stumble in many things. If anyone does not stumble in word, he is a perfect man, able also to bridle the whole body.   JAMES 3:2

A brother OFFENDED is harder to win than a strong city, And contentions are like the bars of a castle..   PROVERBS 18:19

"Therefore if you bring your gift to the altar, <u>and there remember</u> that your *brother has something against you*, "leave your gift there before the altar, and go your way. *First be reconciled to your brother*, and then come and offer your gift. "*Agree with your adversary quickly*, while you are on the way with him, lest your adversary deliver you to the Judge, the Judge hand you over to the officer, and you be thrown into prison..   MATTHEW 5:23-25

(A) OFFEND (vb) hurt, annoy, or Insult..

(B) RECONCILE (vb) cause to be friendly again; bring to acceptance..

PROPHETIC MESSAGE MINISTRY
        AMMISHADDAI

TOPIC : *Hosting the Household of FAITH..*

(1) *Establish the House..*
(2) *Who these people are..*
(3) *How YHWH knows who they are..*
(4) *Can you live together and Not Agree..*
(5) *If you can agree to live together, this is reasonable service..*
(6) *Should there be any Disagreement Not Agreeing??*

But HE answered them saying, "Who is My mother, or My brothers.?" And HE looked around in a circle at those who sat about HIM, and said, "Here are My mother and My brothers! *"For whoever does the will of YHWH is My brother and My sister and mother."*
                                                    MARK 3:33-35

"And when HE brings out HIS own sheep HE goes before them; and the sheep follow HIM *for they know HIS voice..* "Yet they will by NO means follow a stranger, but will flee from him for they do NOT know the voice of strangers." *Can two walk together, unless they are AGREED?* "And whoever will not receive you *nor hear your words*, when you depart from that house or city, shake off the dust from your feet.
                                    JOHN 10:4,5 / AMOS 3:3 / MATTHEW 10:14

"For I was hungry and you gave Me food; I was thirsty and you gave Me drink; I *was a stranger and you took Me in;* 'I was naked and you clothed Me; *I was sick and you visited Me;* I was in prison and you came to Me.' "Then the righteous will answer HIM saying MASTER, when did we see You hungry and feed You, or thirsty and give You drink? 'Or when did we see You sick, or in prison and come to You?' "And the KING will answer and say to them *'Assuredly, I say to you, inasmuch as you did it to one of the least of these My brethren, you did it to Me.'*
                                                    MATTHEW 25:34-40

Is it not to share your bread with the hungry, And that *you bring to your house the poor who are cast out*; When you see the naked, that you cover him. And not hide yourself from your own flesh? Then your light shall break forth like the morning Your healing shall spring forth speedily, *And your righteousness shall go before you: Do NOT be unequally yoked together with unbelievers.* For what fellowship has righteousness with lawlessness? And what communion has light with darkness? And what accord has MessiYah with Belial?? Or what part has a believer with an unbeliever? And what agreement has the temple of YHWH with idols? For you are the temple of the living YHWH. As YHWH has said: Therefore, having these promises, beloved, let us cleanse ourselves from all filthiness of the flesh and spirit, perfecting holiness in the fear of YHWH..
                            ISAIAH 58:6-14 / 2CORINTHIANS 6:14-18 / 7:1
(A) Host (n) One who receives or entertains quest..   AMMISHADDAI

TOPIC : Remind them of these things, charging them before יהוה

not to strive about words to no profit, to the ruin of the hearers.. But *avoid foolish and ignorant disputes, knowing that they generate strife*. And a servant of יהוה must not quarrel but be gentle to all, able to teach, patient, in humility correcting those who are in opposition, if יהוה perhaps will grant them repentance, so that they may know the truth, and that they may come to their senses and *escape the snare of the devil*, having been taken *captive by him to do his will*.   2TIMOTHY 2:14 / 23-26

Casting down arguments and every high thing that exalts itself against the knowledge of יהוה *bringing every thought* into captivity to the obedience of MessiYah..   2CORINTHIANS 10:5

Now therefore, listen to ME, My children; *Pay attention to the WORDS* of My mouth: PROVERBS 7:24,25

Charge some that they teach no other doctrine. Nor give heed to fables and endless genealogies, *which cause disputes rather then godly edification* which is in faith.   1TIMOTHY 1:4

But *avoid foolish disputes*, genealogies, contentions, and strivings about the law; for they are *unprofitable and useless*. Reject *a divisive man* after the *first and second admonition*, knowing that such a person is warped and sinning, being self-condemned.   TITUS 3:9-11

He is proud, knowing nothing, but is *obsessed with disputes, and arguments over words*, from which come envy, strife, reviling, evil suspicions, useless wranglings of men of corrupt minds and destitute of the truth, who suppose that godliness is a means of gain. *From such withdraw yourself*.   1TIMOTHY 6:3-5

(A) Fable (n) a story that is not true.

(B) Strive (vb) to carry on a conflict of effort: contend

(C) Contentions (n) An idea or point for which a person argues (as in a debate or argument)

TOPIC : WHO'S the Teacher?? "It is written in the Prophets. 'And they *shall all be taught by YHWH*." Therefore everyone who has heard and learned from the Father comes to Me..   JOHN 6:45

All your children shall be taught by YHWH, And great shall be the peace of your children. Show me your ways, O YHWH; *Teach me Your paths*. Lead me in Your truth and Teach me, For Your are the *Mighty One of my salvation*;

ISAIAH 54:13 / PSALM 25:4,5

These things we also speak, not in words which man's wisdom teaches but which *the Holy Spirit teaches*, comparing spiritual things with spiritual.. But the natural man does not receive the things of the Spirit of YHWH, for they are foolishness to him; nor can he know them, because they are spiritually discerned. But he *who is spiritual judges all things* yet he himself is rightly judged by no one.   1CORINTHIANS 2:13-15

"Go therefore and make disciples of all the nations. Baptizing them to the name of the Father and of the Son and of the Holy Spirit. "*Teaching them to observe all things that I have commanded you*, and lo, I am with you always even to the end of the age." Amen. "But the Helper, *the HOLY SPIRIT*, whom the Father will send in My name, He *will teach you all things*, and *bring to your remembrance all things* that I said to you.

MATTHEW 28:19,20 / JOHN 14:26

My brethren, *let not many of you become teachers*, knowing that we shall receive *a stricter judgment*. For *we all stumble in many things*. If anyone does not stumble in word. He is a perfect man, able also to bridle the whole body. *But no man can tame the tongue*. It is an unruly evil, full of deadly poison.. Now the *purpose of the commandment is LOVE from a pure heart*, from a good conscience, and from *sincere faith*, from which some, having strayed *have turned aside to idle talk*. Desiring to be teachers of the law, *understanding neither what they say* nor the *things which they affirm*.   JAMES 3:1,2,8 / 1TIMOTHY 1:5-10

(1) Teacher (n) To show how, to guide the studies of..

(2) Shepherd (n) a person who takes care of a flock of sheep.

(3) Disciple (n) one who helps spread another's teachings..

PROPHETIC MESSAGE MINISTRY
AMMISHADDAI

TOPIC : QUESTION ?? "But in every nation whoever fears Him and works righteousness is accepted by HIM.. "For YHWH your Mighty One is Mighty One of gods and Master of masters, the Great Mighty One Mighty and awesome, who shows no partiality nor takes a bribe.
                                            ACTS 10:34,35 / DEUTERONOMY 10:17

Knowing this first, that *NO Prophecy of Scriptures* is *of any private interpretation.* For prophecy never came by the will of man, but holy men of YHWH spoke as they were *moved by the Holy Spirit.* These things we also speak, not in words which man's wisdom teaches but which the Holy Spirit teaches, *comparing spiritual things with spiritual.* But the *natural man does not receive the things* of the Spirit of YHWH, for they are foolishness to him; nor can he know them, because *they are spiritually discerned.*
                                            2PETER 1:20,21 / 1CORINTHIANS 2:13-15

What *advantage then has the Hebrew* or *what is the profit of circumcision?* Much in every way! Chiefly because to them were committed the oracles of YHWH. For what if some did not believe? Will their unbelief make the faithfulness of YHWH without effect? Certainly not! Indeed, *let YHWH be true but every man a liar.* As it is written: He who did not spare His own Son, but delivered Him up for us all, how shall He not with Him also freely give us all things?
                                            ROMANS 3:1-4 / 9:32

For *circumcision is indeed profitable* if you keep the law; but if you are a breaker of The law, your *circumcision has become uncircumcision.* Therefore, if an *uncircumcised man keeps the righteous requirements of the law,* will not his *uncircumcision be counted as circumcision?* And will not the physically uncircumcised, if he fulfills the law, judge you who, even with your written code and circumcision, are a transgressor of the law? For he is not a Hebrew who is one outwardly, *nor is circumcision that which is outward in the flesh;* but he is *a Hebrew who is one inwardly;* and *circumcision is that of the heart, in the Spirit, not in the letter;* whose praise is not from men but from YHWH..
                                            ROMANS 2:25-29

** EXAMPLES of BREAKING the LAW **

YHWH's Holy people *had become contaminated because* Hebrew men were marrying foreign women. Even the leaders and the officials had taken part in *this breaking of the Law* from the very beginning. We have *trespassed against our Mighty One,* and have taken pagan wives from the peoples of the land; *yet there is hope in Ysrael in spite of this..* "For they have taken some of their daughters as wives for themselves and their sons, so that the holy seed is mixed with the peoples of those lands. Indeed, *the hand of the leaders and rulers has been foremost in this trepass."*   1ESDRAS 8:68-71 / EZRA 10:2 / 9:2

Was anyone called while circumcised? Let him not become uncircumcised. *Was anyone called while uncircumcised?* Let him not be circumcised. *Circumcision is nothing and uncircumcision is nothing,* but keeping the commandments of YHWH is what matters..
                                            1CORINTHIANS 7:18,19

PROPHETIC MESSAGE MINISTRY
        AMMISHADDAI

TOPIC : What can I do to inherit eternal LIFE??   For the *commandment is a lamp*, And *the law a light*; Reproofs of instruction are the way of life.. *Knowing this first*, that no prophecy of Scripture is of *any private interpretation*. For prophecy never came by the will of man, but holy men of יהוה spoke as they were moved by the Holy Spirit..

PROVERBS 6:23 / 2PETER 1:20,21

All Scripture is given by inspiration of יהוה and is profitable for doctrine, for reproof, for correction, *for instruction in righteousness*, that the man of יהוה may be complete, *thoroughly equipped for every good work*. For whatever things were written before were *written for our learning*, that we through the patience and comfort of the Scriptures might have hope..

1TIMOTHY 3:16 / ROMANS 15:4

Then Peter opened his mouth and said: "In truth I perceive that יהוה *shows no partiality* "But in *every nation whoever fears HIM and works righteousness is accepted* by HIM. "For יהוה your MIGHTYONE is MIGHTYONE of Mighty Ones and MASTER of Masters, the GREAT MIGHTYONE, mighty and awesome, *who shows no partiality* nor takes a bribe.

ACTS 10:34,35 / DEUTERONOMY 10:17

For *you can all prophesy* one by one, *that all may learn and all may be encouraged*. "Today you have proclaimed יהוה to be your MightyOne, and that you will walk in HIS ways and keep HIS statutes. HIS commandments, and HIS judgments, *and that you will obey HIS voice*. "Behold, I stand at the door and knock. *If anyone hears MY voice* and opens the door, I will come in to him and dine with him, and he with ME..

1CORINTHIANS 14:31 / DEUTERONOMY 26:17 / REVELATION 3:20

** EXAMPLES of Hearkening unto the VOICE of יהוה **

Abraham hearkened unto the VOICE.. / Yahshuah counsels the rich young ruler..

(A) Now it came to pass after these things that יהוה tested Abraham and said to him, "Abraham!" And he said, "Here I am."   GENESIS 22:1-13

(B) Now behold, one came and said to HIM, "Good Teacher, what good thing shall I do that I may have eternal life?"   MATTHEW 19:16-22

(1) Prophecy (N) prediction.

(2) Prediction (N) declare in advance..

PROPHETIC MESSAGE MINISTRY
     AMMISHADDAI

TOPIC : PEACE OFFERING.. *This is the LAW of the sacrifice of PEACE offerings* which he shall offer to YHWH: The flesh of the sacrifice of his PEACE Offering for thanksgiving shall be *eaten the same day it is offered*. He shall not leave any of it until morning.. *But if the sacrifice of his offering is a vow or a voluntary offering*, it shall be eaten the same day that he offers his sacrifice; *but on the next day the remainder of it also may be eaten*; the remainder of the flesh of the sacrifice on the third day must be burned with fire. 'And if any of the flesh of the sacrifice of his peace offering is *eaten at all on the third day*. It *shall not be accepted*, nor shall it be imputed to him; it shall be an *abomination to him who offers it*, and the *person who eats of it shall bear* guilt.   LEVITICUS 7:11,15-18

*** Spirit of the LAW ***

Great peace have those who love Your LAW, And nothing causes them to stumble.. Depart from evil and do good; seek peace and pursue it..
                                        PSALM 119:165 / 34:14

A time to love, And a time to hate; A time of war, And a time of PEACE. "There is no peace, "says YHWH, for the wicked."   ECCLESIASTES 3:8 / ISAIAH 48:22

You will keep him in perfect peace, *whose mind is stayed on You*, Because he trusts in You.. Therefore *let us pursue the things which make for peace* and the things by which one may edify another.   ISAIAH 26:3 / ROMANS 14:19

I, beseech you to walk worthy of the calling with which you were called, with all lowliness and gentleness, with longsuffering, bearing with one another in love. Endeavoring to *keep the unity of the Spirit in the bond of PEACE*..   EPHESIANS 4:1-3

And *let the peace of YHWH rule in your hearts*, to which also you were called in one body; and be thankful. Be anxious for nothing, but in everything by prayer and supplication, with thanksgiving, let you requests be made known to YHWH; and the peace of YHWH, which *surpasses all understanding*, will guard your hearts and minds through MessiYah Yahshuah..   COLOSSIANS 3:15 / PHILIPPIANS 4:6,7

(A) PEACE (n) State of calm and quiet; Absence of war or strife..
(B) IMPUTE (vb) Putting: credit to or blame on a person or cause.

PROPHETIC MESSAGE MINISTRY
    AMMISHADDAI

- First Off I thank YAH!! -

Learn about about the ranks!! A spiritual cat (is) from with in (spokenword) maybe manifested (thru) the physical (thangs) (we) see spoken (into) (existence) what will (be) whether U know or not.. don't walk around claim to be a teacher.. (preacher) proclaim to be (her) LOAMMI the ONE to show (me) MIGHTYONE led me into all (true) teach (me) all thangs (swang) in my soul Joy to keep (me) separate myself from such (kind) circumcised from the heart inspiration from (in) the Light that lead (me) (its that deep).. I go were the master (go) follow the LAMB wherever HE may (be) Blessed ONE day Open up my eyes to (see) it's the LAMB (Father) and (me) were WE (go) U cant (go).. in (Due) time Appointed we gone (holla) call to get the (fam) coming home back to Ur own!! (reality) U thought was (Fantasy) reminsion of the (activity) buster had the nerve to say.. *I had to sit among a man.* Taught to get my *FATHERS WORD..* (cat) U don't know (me) don't know what I'm going thru.. don't know were I been.. SAINTS Off the MOSTHIGH!! Friends with YAHSavior. Blessed and (Highly Favored) before I fall victim to the man. (In) trapped with traditions of a man. Slave to the sin Legalistic self - righteous (ways) folly in the land here and abroad.. I got to say.. Nigga (Please)

SUPERNATUAL.. SUPERNATUAL YSRAEL..

The Spirit that's (in) (me) FAR Greater then the Spirit that's in the world!! So don't let me catch U (lying) if it don't make dollars it don't make sense Cuz that's a (lie) - *we know* my real Nigga's (do) *we know* the WORD Freely give.. WORD Freely (Received) which makes plenty (sense) Proclaim Teacher (to) the People the soul that's not gone die. The second Death!! Real talk Achki (get) Ur (walk) in order before U step to (me) remove the Blank that's in Ur own I And (then) U could step to (me) (help) me get the spick that in my own eye.. Feel (me) Forgive (me) if U don't!! FRESHER then many (men) U know I Love U with many (men) show NO Partiality with Plenty of (men) cuz many (men) has testified to the (true) SPIRIT override the Flesh. Didn't take the Covenant (in) the Flesh so lets step with the (Best) Sacrifice from with (in) Cuz many (men) *forgot about the WAY* Building the KINGDOM Of YHWH.. YHAYH brought to another LEVEL. (Explain) to many (men) to rightly DIVIDE the WORD Of TRUE.. if it wasn't MessiYah SPIRIT from with (in) I would Believe many (men) cuz at the end if U anit right from with (in) how U gone win?? Show that love to the daughters!! And the Sons children left to society mental (ill) getting Ur D—K sucked in the Presents of the Kids.. Everything U say its Negative "Grand Ma" Grand "Pa" I got Love for my Fam lets start to forgive cuz two wrongs don't make a right. Who gone be the better (man) among many (men) spending time trying to make (mad) money in the land of Captivity forgot about Ur FIRST LOVE: Fishing for many (men) with the LOVE Of MessiYah.. *TOWARDS many (men)*

SUPERNATUAL.. Study Ur - Self's APPROVED.. AMEN

PROPHETIC MESSAGE MINSTRY
AMMISHADDAI

TOPIC : PEACE MAKER.. Blessed are the peacemakers, for they shall be called sons of יהוה'.. *These are the things you shall do*.. Speak each man the truth to his neighbor; Give judgment in your gates for truth, justice and *PEACE*..   MATTHEW 5:9 / ZECHARIAH 8:16

For to be carnally minded is death, but to *be spiritually minded* is life and peace. Therefore I exhort first of all that supplications, prayers, intercessions, and giving of thanks be made for all men, for kings and all who are in authority, *that we may lead a quiet and peaceable life* in all godliness and reverence..   ROMANS 8:6 / 1TIMOTHY 2:1,2

But the wisdom that is from above is first pure, *then peaceable*, gentle, *willing to yield*, full of mercy and good fruits, without partiality and without hypocrisy.. If it is possible, as much as depends on you, *live peaceably with all men*.   JAMES 3:17,18 / ROMANS 12:18

Therefore, since *a promise remains of entering HIS rest*, let us fear lest any of *you seem to have come short of it*. Pursue *peace with all people*, and holiness, without which no one will see יהוה'; looking carefully lest anyone fall short of the grace of יהוה'; lest any root of bitterness springing up cause trouble, and by this many become defiled;   HEBREWS 4:1 / 12:14,15

יהוה' will give strength to HIS people; יהוה' will *BLESS HIS* people with PEACE.. "The *glory of this latter temple shall be greater than the former*,' says יהוה' of hosts. 'And *in this place I will give peace*,' says יהוה' of hosts."   PSALM 29:11 / HAGGAI 2:9

Therefore, beloved, *looking forward to these things*, be diligent to be found by HIM *in PEACE*, without spot and blameless;   2PETER 3:14

(A) Yield (vt) to submit; to comply; to grant; to give up. To produce.
(B) Peace (n) Freedom from upsetting thoughts or feelings; agreement and harmony among persons..

PROPHETIC MESSAGE MINISTRY
AMMISHADDAI

TOPIC : TIME and CHANCE!! I returned and saw under the sun that – the race is not to the swift, nor the battle to the strong, nor bread to the wise, nor riches to men of understanding, nor favor to men of skill; but *time and chance happen to them all*, for man also does not know his time; like fish taken in a cruel net, so the sons of men are snared in an evil time. *When it falls suddenly upon them*.

ECCLESIASTES 9:11,12

"And watch: *if it goes up the road to its own territory*, to Beth Shem'esh, then He has done us this great evil. But if not, then we shall know that it is not His hand that struck us – it happened to us by chance."   1SAMUEL 6:9

Therefore flight shall perish from the swift, the strong shall not strengthen his power, *nor shall the mighty deliver himself*; he shall not stand who handles the bow the swift of foot shall not escape, nor shall he who rides a horse deliver himself. The most courageous men of might shall flee naked in that day." Says יהוה

AMOS 2:14-16

He who *KEEPS HIS COMMAND* will experience nothing harmful; And a *wise man's heart discerns both time and judgment*, because for every matter there is a *time and judgment* though the misery of man increases greatly.. For he does not know what will happen; so who can tell him when it will occur?? For יהוה gives wisdom and knowledge and joy to a man who is good in HIS sight; but to the sinner HE gives the work of gathering and collecting, that he may give to him who is good before יהוה that also is vanity and grasping for the wind.. *To everything there is a season, A TIME for EVERY PURPOSE under heaven:* A time to gain, And a time to lose; A time of war And a time of peace.. etc.   ECCLESIASTES 8:5-7 / 2:26 / 3:1-8

But יהוה has chosen the foolish things of the world to put to shame the wise, and *יהוה has chosen the weak things of the world to put to shame the things which* are mighty; that NO Flesh should glory in HIS presence. But of HIM you are in MessiYah Yahshuah, who became for us wisdom from יהוה – and righteousness *and sanctification and redemption – that, as it is written, " He who glories, let him* glory in the Master."   1CORINTHIANS 1:27-31

SHABBAT = is to Receive Sanctification or power for the week!!
In Healing (Health) Wealth etc.
WEEKLY SERVICE = 1ST DAY thru 6th DAY serve יהוה give HIM your all..   (100 %)

_____ School / work
_____ Entertainment
Worship@service towards YAH

AMMISHADDAI   PROPHETIC MESSAGE MINISTRY

TOPIC : CUTTINGS in the Flesh or TATTOO'S.. My people are destroyed for lack of KNOWLEDGE. *Because you have rejected KNOWLEDGE,* I also will reject you from being priest for ME; because you have *forgotten the LAW of your GOD.* I also will forget your children..   HOSEA 4:6

Therefore *my people have gone into captivity,* Because they have **NO KOWLEDGE;** their honorable men are famished, And their multitude dried up with thirst..   ISAIAH 5:13

Therefore you shall keep MY ordinance, so that you *do not commit* any of these *abominable customs* which were committed before you, and that you do not defile yourselves by them: I am יהוה your GOD."   LEVITICUS 18:30

For the *customs of the peoples* are futile; (vain) You shall not make any cuttings in your flesh for the dead, nor **tattoo any marks** on you; I am יהוה "They shall not make any bald place on their heads, nor shall they shave the edges of their beards nor *make any cuttings in their flesh..*
                    JEREMIAH 10:3 / LEVITICUS 19:28 / 21:5

" You are the children of יהוה your GOD; *you shall not cut yourselves* nor shave the front of your head for the dead. "For you are a holy people to יהוה your GOD, and יהוה has chosen you to be a people for HIMSELF, a *special treasure above all the peoples who are on the face of the earth..*
                              DEUTERONOMY 14:1,2

*** EXAMPLES OF DEMONS: THEIR CUSTOMS and POWERS ***
And always, night and day, he was in the mountains and in the tombs, crying out and cutting himself with stones..   MARK 5:5

CUSTOM (n) habitual course of action.
CUT (vb) penetrate or divide with a sharp edge.
TATTOO (vb) mark the skin with indelible designs or figures – tattoo
INDELIBLE (adj) not capable of being removed or erased..

PROPHETIC MESSAGE MINISTRY
        AMMISHADDAI

PEACE שלום SHALOM

soundness   tranquillity

peace   safety

completeness   contentment

"The Lord bless you and keep you; The Lord make His face
shine upon you, and be gracious to you;
The Lord lift up His countenance upon you,
and give you peace."

Numbers 6:24-26

SHOSHANA
2002

191

194

CAUTION!!

COLORED PEOPLE

OF BOSTON, ONE & ALL,

You are hereby respectfully CAUTIONED and advised, to avoid conversing with the

Watchmen and Police Officers of Boston,

For since the recent ORDER OF THE MAYOR & ALDERMEN, they are empowered to act as

KIDNAPPERS
AND
Slave Catchers,

And they have already been actually employed in KIDNAPPING, CATCHING, AND KEEPING SLAVES. Therefore, if you value your LIBERTY, and the *Welfare of the Fugitives* among you, *Shun* them in every possible manner, as so many *HOUNDS* on the track of the most unfortunate of your race.

Keep a Sharp Look Out for KIDNAPPERS, and have TOP EYE open.

APRIL 24, 1851.

TRANS ATLANTIC EUROPEAN SLAVE TRADE
FOR COMMERCE and PROFIT..

" Are you not like the people of ETHIOPIA to Me, O children of YISRAEL? " says YHWH..
" Behold, the eyes of YHWH ELOHIM are on the sinful kingdom, And I will destroy it from the face of the earth; Yet I will not utterly destroy the house of YAHCOB (YISRAEL) says the MOST HIGH. " For surely I will command, And will sift the house of YISRAEL among all nations,
AMOS 9:7-10

" But when you see YAHRUSALEM surrounded by armies, then know that its desolation is near. " For these are the days of vengeance, that all things which are written may be fulfilled. " And they will fall by the edge of the sword, and be led away captive into all nations. And YAHRUSALEM will be trampled by GENTILES until the times of the GENTILES are fulfilled.
LUKE 21: 20-24

EDOMITES / ESAU DESCRIBE..

" Behold, your dwelling shall be of the fatness of the earth, and the dew of heaven from above. By your sword you shall live, and you shall serve your brother; and it shall come to pass, when you become restless, that you shall break his yoke from your neck."
GENESIS 27: 38,39,40

CONSPIRACY AGAINST YISRAEL

They have taken crafty counsel against your people, and consulted together against your sheltered ones. They have said, " Come, and let us cut them off from being a Nation, that the name of YISRAEL may be remembered NO MORE." For they have consulted together with one consent; they form a confederacy against You:
PSALM 83 :1-18

70 CE. YISRAELITES Flee from the land of YISRAEL..

700 CE. ARABS / ISHMAELITES
1400 - 1441 CE. PORTUGAL / DUCTH
1490's CE.   SPAIN
1562 CE. ENGLAND
1597 CE. HOLLAND
1640 CE. FRANCE
1649 CE. SWEDAN
1651 CE. DEMARK / NORWAY
1685 CE. GERMANY
1700 - 1776 CE. (Legally) AMERICA
1822 CE. BRAZIL

PROPHETIC MESSAGE MINISTRY
AMMISHADDAI

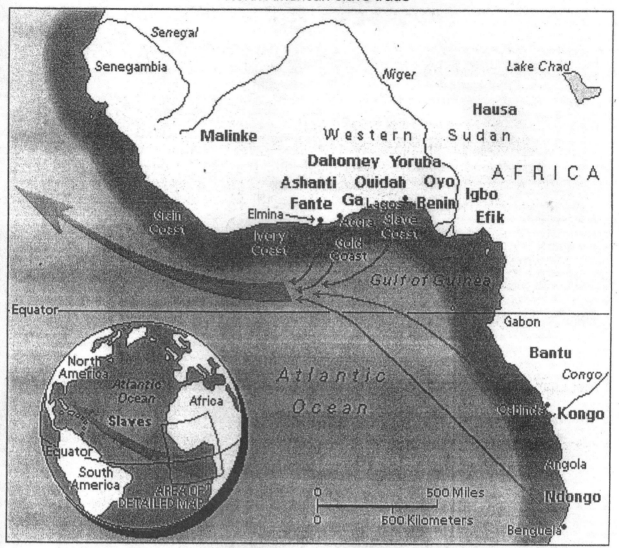

The red type on this map indicates the groups from which most slaves were taken. The groups that captured the most Africans for European and American slave traders are shown in black bold type.

World Book map

crowded conditions led to the chief horrors of the Middle Passage-filth, stench, disease, and death.

The Atlantic slave trade operated from the 1500's to the mid-1800's. No one knows how many Africans were enslaved during this period. The most reliable estimates suggest about 10 million blacks. Of this total, what is now the United States received about 5 percent.

The years of slavery

" And יהוה‎ will take you back to Egypt in ships, by the way of which I said to you, ' You shall never see it again.' And there you shall be offered for sale to your enemies as male and female slaves, but no one will buy you."

                                        DEUTERONOMY 28:68

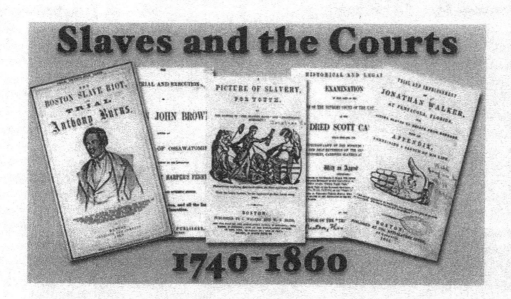

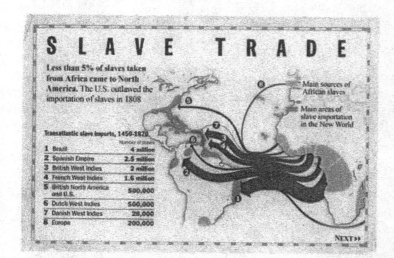

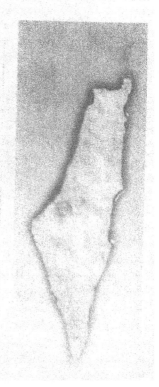

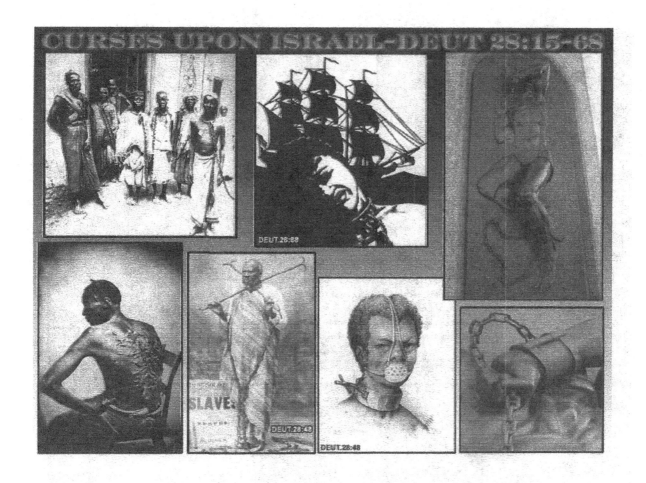

ALL YOUR WORDS ARE TRUE; ALL YOUR RIGHTEOUS LAWS ARE ETERNAL. PSALM 119:160

The Tanakh - Cross Reference Hebrew to English Book Names and Order

English Book	Hebrew	Transiteration	Translation
Group 1	תּוֹרָה	torah	instructions
Genesis	בְּרֵאשִׁית	b're-sheet	beginning
Exodus	שְׁמוֹת	sh'mot	names
Leviticus	וַיִּקְרָא	vayikra	He called
Numbers	בְּמִדְבַּר	b'midbar	wilderness
Deuteronomy	דְּבָרִים	d'varim	words
Group 2a	נְבִיאִים	n'vi-im	prophets (earlier)
Joshua	יְהוֹשֻׁעַ	Y'hoshua	salvation
Judges	שׁוֹפְטִים	shofetim	judges
I/II Samuel	שְׁמוּאֵל	sh'muel	heard of God
I/II Kings	מְלָכִים	mal-khim	kings
Group 2b	נְבִיאִים	n'vi-im	prophets (later)
Isaiah	יְשַׁעְיָה(וּ)	y'sha'yah(u)	God has saved
Jeremiah	יִרְמְיָה(וּ)	yirmyah(u)	God will rise/be exalted
Ezekiel	יְחֶזְקֵאל	y'chez'kiel	God will strengthen
Hosea	הוֹשֵׁעַ	hoshea	deliverer
Joel	יוֹאֵל	yoel	God (is his) God
Amos	עָמוֹס	amos	burdensome
Obadiah	עֹבַדְיָה	ovad'ya	serving God
Jonah	יוֹנָה	yonah	dove, wine?
Micah	מִיכָה	michah	who is like God
Nahum	נַחוּם	nachum	sigh, to be sorry, pity, rue, repent, comfort
Habakuk	חֲבַקּוּק	chavakuk	embrace, clasp hands
Zephaniah	צְפַנְיָה	ts'fanyah	God has secreted (hidden, denied)
Haggai	חַגַּי	chagai	festive
Zachariah	זְכַרְיָה	z'char'ya	God has remembered
Malachi	מַלְאָכִי	malachi	ministrative, messenger

5/3/2002

The Western Wall in Jerusalem's Old City is the holiest site in Judaism. The wall was part of the Second Temple built by Herod and destroyed by the Romans in A.D. 70. Jews from throughout the world come to pray at the wall and insert messages and prayers in its crevices.

Jerusalem is the capital of Israel and the country's largest city. This view shows Jerusalem from the east as seen from the Mount of Olives. A Muslim cemetery appears in the foreground. The golden Dome of the Rock, a Muslim shrine, rises above the walls of the Old City, Jerusalem's oldest district.

ANCIENT EGYPTIANS

AS YOU HAVE JUST READ FROM SCRIPTURES THERE WAS NO PHYSICAL DIFFERENCE BETWEEN ISRAEL AND THE EGYPTIANS THEY HAD THE SAME PHYSICAL APPEARANCE

Temple drawing of Pharaoh Seti I, Scholars identify Seti as being on the throne of Egypt during the time of Moses birth.

Ancient Egyptian Pharaoh

Amenhotep III the Father of Pharaoh Akhenaten, the husband of Queen Tiye and the Grandfathr of King Tut.

Pharaoh Mentuhotep II

Princess Aushead, the Daughter of Pharaoh Mentuhotep II

Ancient Egyptian Princess

5/26/2006

Ancient and Modern Images of Israelites

Ancient Israelites going into captivity by the Assrayians

Modern Israelites in Iraq

Modern Israelites

Israelites from an Egyptian Wall Painting

Israelites in ancient Babylon from a wall painting

Accurate image of what the Hebrew Prophet Moses would have looked like.

Nevertheless, there will be *those who look upon this* author, Ben Ammi Ben-Israel, Messianic Leader of *the Kingdom of God, and* wonder, "how dare this man proclaim this community to *be that spoken of by the* inspired prophets of Israel? And on what authority does he receive this mantle of messianic leadership?

Any sincere review of his works will certainly lead one to the obvious conclusions.

- In 1966, he received a *vision in which the angel* Gabriel revealed that the time had come for the *descendants of the Biblical* Israelites among African Americans, to return to the Promised Land and establish the Kingdom of God! A year later, despite his own anxiety, and the skepticism of many, he led 350 African Americans from inner-city Chicago an a journey to the bush of Liberia, West Africa.

- The challenges of the sojourn in this West African wilderness would be many, as the pioneers would face

6/1/2007

the searing heat, poisonous *snakes, driver ants by the* millions and a rainy season of monsoon proportions… all while living in tents and thatched-roofed dwellings, and forced to learn to feed themselves.

- In 1969, the first *members of that community* entered the Promised Land and laid the foundation for *God's Kingdom on earth*- simply a government of men and women governed by the laws of God. After initially being received as new immigrants, by 1971 they saw their status revoked. There without legal protection, the African Hebrews, as they came to be known, endured cyclical attempts at deportation, banishment from national educational and health care systems and repeated attacks on their character. Instead of retreating, the *Hebrews used the adversity* as motivation, building their own schools, health care *and economic* infrastructures to provide for themselves.

- By 1990, their

courageous efforts were *rewarded as legal obstacles* were removed and the community became *renowned as an oasis of* social harmony, free of crime, drug abuse and immorality. Israeli media declared the community "an island of sanity," and extolled the inspired leadership of Ben Ammi. Even the American Congress took notice, labeling the accomplishments, "the miracle in the desert."

For the last 14 years, the *general public has been* exposed to the intellect of Ben Ammi through his writings, collectively and appropriately called "The Resurrection Series." This includes the books **God the Black Man and Truth**; **God and the Law of Relativity**; **The Messiah and the End of This World**; **Everlasting Life... from thought to reality**, **Jesus the Christian Christ or Yeshua the Hebrew Messiah** and **An Imitation of Life**. Yet viewed through the prism of his achievements, we are

6/1/2007

6/1/2007

prophetic Kingdom of God... and we are here as a witness to the accomplishments of Ben Ammi. We can just as assuredly announce that God is with him and this is the Kingdom of God!"

For those who have been watchers of time, searching for the messenger sent from God, we implore you... take heart, be of good courage...

Behold the man of God...

THE **AFRICAN HEBREW ISRAELITES** OF JERUSALEM

Home

Contact Us

Our Culture

Our Projects

Our Health

Holy Calendar & Events

6/1/2007

compelled to know that he is
much more than an author.

So when on asks, "by what
authority?" I am reminded of
the words of Prince Asiel
Ben Israel, the International
Ambassador of the Kingdom
of God. Observing the
unsettled expressions of an
audience, confronted with
the realization of Ben
Ammi's work and the
accomplishments of the
community, he remarked:

*" When a man stands up and
says God inspired him to
build a church, and he
accomplishes that in spite of
obstacles like economic
shortfalls, construction
mishaps or architectural
problems, no one is angry
and they proclaim that
certainly God was with him.
Likewise, if a man declares
that God instructed him to
found a choir to proclaim
the word of truth in song,
immediately after the first
concert we are satisfied that
truly God was with him.
Well, today we have the man
who was inspired by God to
return the descendants of the
Biblical Israelites to the
Holy Land and establish the*

6/1/2007

Home

Contact Us

Our Culture

Our Projects

Our Health

Holy Calendar

Our Story

Multimedia

Our Leadership

Books, CD's, DVD's

Online Community

Photo Gallery

In the News

Ben Ammi

Anointed Spiritual Leader of the African Hebrew Israelites of Jerusalem

A review of the Biblical history shows us that it is not unusual for the Omnipotent God to anoint a personal representative on earth and to invest His authority in that representative.

Abraham was called the "friend of God." (II Chr, 20:7) Moses was told that while Aaron would speak on his behalf, Moses himself, would stand in the stead of God. (Exodus 4: 16) Jeremiah was chosen of God before he was formed in the womb. (Jeremiah 1:5) And remember, Yeshua told his disciples that "whatever ye shall ask the Father in my name, He shall give it to you." (John 16:23)

IMAGES OF ISRAELITES
& LEPROSY

Jamaican Israelite with Locks, Scripture says the Israelite Samson had seven locks, just as this Israelite from Jamaica has.

Another Jamaican Israelite with Lock Hair

False image of Samson from the Movie Called Samson. Question if Samson look like the man in this image, how was it possible for his hair to lock? where is this man locks?

Ancient Elamite Warrior from the walls of Babylon. Elam was a son of Shem, just as the Israelites are.

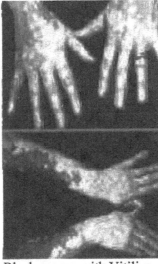

Black person with Vitiligo, a Disease that is similar to biblical Leprosy. Vitiligo turns the skin of a black person white.

Black man Skin turns white from the side effect of Liver medication. In his homeland he is shunned as a leper or a person with leprosy, because his skin has turned white.

5/26/2006

Consider Christmas

Have you ever wondered what a tree, or the hanging of bulbs and lights, has to do with the birth of Jesus? What about mistletoes, yule tides and the legend of Santa Claus, filling stockings with gifts by an improbable route, the chimney? Not to mention flying reindeers! Do all these customs surrounding Christmas really honor the birth of Jesus or do they actually stand for something else? Was Jesus really born on December 25th? Stop! The answer to these questions is as close as your nearest encyclopedia, under Christmas.

You might think that it doesn't matter where Christmas has it's origin and that the important thing is "the spirit it symbolizes." Well, it does matter and in this article we will show what Christmas truly symbolizes. Many will talk of the splendor and wonder of Christmas but Jesus himself warned us about doing wonderful works that are contrary to the will of God. On judgment day Jesus will cast away many people, who recite these wonderful works **(Read Matthew 7:21-23).** Consider this!

History tells us that no one knew the exact date of Jesus' birth. The Bible clarifies this because Herod (the King of Jerusalem at that time) didn't know when Jesus was born and therefore killed all the boys two years old and under, trying to kill Jesus **(Read Matthew 2:13-16).** None of the apostles of Jesus or his other followers attempted to celebrate his birth but instead kept his commandment in eating bread and drinking wine every Passover, in remembrance of his death. When and who started this celebration of December 25th as the birthday of Jesus? The New Standard Encyclopedia, Volume 2, states ***"The ADOPTION of December 25th was decreed by Bishop Liberius of Rome in 354."*** You mean to tell me this Bishop Liberius figured out the birth of Jesus over 300 years later, when Herod didn't know? Maybe this date was chosen for another reason. The New Standard continues, ***"This date was probably chosen because it coincided with the Pagan festival of the winter solstice" (Read you history book).***

Many nations already had festivals (feasts) surrounding the winter solstice, which honors the sun. These customs were merely grafted into Christianity and called Christmas. The Romans honored Saturn, the Germans, Brumalia and the Norsemen held a Yule feast at this time every year, without a thought of Jesus. This is why they have twelve days of Christmas, to squeeze in the customs of all the different nations. Most of these customs started before Jesus was born. Again, I ask you what is a yule tide or yule log?

These customs are not honoring Jesus but instead honoring the SUN. The winter solstice represents the shortest day of the year, after which the days get longer and longer because the SUN stays up longer and longer. Yes, the SUN is born or reborn if you will. This was a joyous occasion because the pagans (nations) were afraid of the dark. Maybe now you can understand why houses and trees are draped with lights.

The Lord warned us about following the customs of the nations saying, ***"...Learn not the way of the heathen (nations), and be not dismayed at the signs of heaven; for the heathen are dismayed at them. FOR THE CUSTOMS OF THE PEOPLE ARE VAIN: FOR ONE CUTTETH A TREE OUT OF***

11/7/2004

THE FOREST. the work of the hands of the workman, with the axe. THEY DECK IT WITH SILVER AND WITH GOLD; THEY FASTEN IT WITH NAILS AND WITH HAMMERS, THAT IT MOVE NOT" (Jeremiah 10:2-4). Many people have not took heed to the Lord's warning and have learned this custom very well. Although this worshiping of trees is also a very old tradition it was not applied to Christmas until the sixteenth century, in Germany. Many will protest and say that they are not actually worshiping a tree but I ask you again, what does the decorating of a tree have to do with the birth of Jesus? Remember, God said, *"Learn not the way of the heathen..."* And again, *"Shall I fall down to the stock of a tree" (Isaiah 44:19).* OH CHRISTMAS TREE! Yes, they even sing songs to the tree.

Many should know that Santa Claus comes from "Saint Nicholas" the Roman patron saint of children. I still have not found where Jesus fits in any of this. Even the gift giving derived from the Romans worship of Saturnalia (Saturn) and not because the wise men brought Jesus gifts. Furthermore, the Bible never mentions three wise men, only wise men. Nevertheless, if Jesus wanted us to give gifts to each other commemorating his birthday, wouldn't he have told us? Remember, he told us how to commemorate his death *(Read Luke 22:19-20).*

This article is not intended to condemn anyone but only something to consider. We know that most people celebrate Christmas without giving a second thought to it's validity. It's a tradition passed down from our fathers, so we observe it instinctively, until the truth comes. The Pharisees (religious leaders) had many traditions during the time of Jesus and even questioned him for not observing them. Jesus replied, *"Why do ye also transgress the commandment of God by your traditions?" (Matthew 15:3).* As you have seen from this article Christmas is a tradition of man (Bishop Liberius) and not a commandment of God. *"But in vain they do worship me, teaching for doctrines the commandments of men" (Matthew 15:9).*

Many will still disagree and claim that Christmas is OK, especially, those who get richer and richer every year, selling everything from evergreen trees to toys and other gifts. The Apostle Paul faced similar opposition when he spoke out against pagan worship. In Acts 19:26, the beneficiaries of pagan worship spoke, saying, "moreover ye see and hear, that not alone at Ephesus, but almost throughout all Asia, this Paul hath persuaded and turned away much people, saying that they be no Gods, which are made with hands." These people were not concerned about serving God correctly but only their wealth. The same is true today because most merchants make 50% of their income at Christmas and mostly from people who can't afford it.

I too, grew up celebrating Christmas but when I learned the truth I turned from it, just as the people turned from pagan worship in Paul's day. If people would only consider and investigate Christmas they too would know the truth. Most people don't even know that CHRISTMAS means "MASS OF CHRIST." Now, I ask you, when did Jesus have a mass? NEVER! CONSIDER THIS!

Click Wheel Back To Text Lessons

11/7/2004

THE TRUTH ABOUT KING JAMES VI:

In our world and in society, it is extremely important and urgent for us to get the facts for ourselves. We must stop taking things for face value and believing things based upon what others have told us and empower our own minds through constant search and research. We have written this literature with that in mind. So we can finally get the true facts on who this man King James VI was, and the importance of his nationality.

The first point that must be established out the gate is that King James was not what most would consider today to be a white man. In fact he was an Israelite. He was a man of color, and one of the last true Israelites to rule in Europe during the period of the Dark Ages.

Let us examine the evidence of this little known historical fact:

In approximately 193ad, Septimus Severus, a Black Hebrew Israelite Gladiator, crushed Rome and the Greco-Roman rule throughout the known world and ushered in an era called the Dark Ages, or the Holy Roman Empire. At this time Black people ruled all of England, Europe and Asia for about 1000 years. This goes back to the prophecy in **Genesis 18:19**. It also set the stage for an Israelite King, not a so-called white man to be ruling in Scotland and England during the time of the translation of the King James 1611 version of the Bible.

Author Don Luke has this to say about most researchers of Early Europe:

"The presence of blacks in the British Isles is either acknowledged or totally avoided by those scholars who do research in that area."

In a book by Scottish author David Mac Ritchie called, *Ancient and Modern Day Britons*, it is also noted of the expansion of Israelites by name and culture in such places and things as the *Black Huns, Black Topography, Moorish Marauders, Black Douglases, Black Families in Early Scotland, The Sons of the Black, Black Danes, and Black Oppressors.*

Mac Ritchie had this to write about the people inhabiting the European lands:

"We know...that the first inhabitants of Britain and more especially those of the northern parts were craniologically of a type approaching to the Negro..."

The knowledge of the Bible is fundamental in understanding any portion of history, and digging out these truths. With a basic knowledge of our past, we can lay the foundation in our minds of what is and what could not be.

King James believed in the Divine Right of Kings and the monarch's duty to reign according to God's law and the public good. In order to pass on his Kingly instruction to his eldest son, Prince Henry, King James wrote *Basilicon Doron* which means, "The Kingly Gift". It consists of three short volumes, the first of which is "A King's Christian Dutie Towards God." James D'israeli said,
"James had formed the most elevated conception of the virtues and duties of a monarch."

In Basilicon Doron, King James' offers his son this important advice on knowing God:

"Diligently read his word, & earnestly...pray for the right understanding thereof. Search the scriptures saith Christ for they will bear testimony of me. The whole Scriptures saith Paul are profitable to teach, to improve, to correct, and to instruct in righteousness, that the man of God may be perfect unto all good works."..."The whole Scripture contayneth but two things: a command and a prohibition. Obey in both... The worship of God is wholly grounded upon the Scripture, quickened by faith."

When King James Charles Stuart ascended to the English throne he became King James VI of Scotland and King James I of England--hence, King James VI & I. King James was now the first King of what he liked to call Great Britain. His ascension to the English throne forever joined the crowns of England and Scotland. He Formed the foundation for what is now known as the British Empire by uniting warring tribes of Scotland and then enjoining the crowns of Scotland and England in 1603, and was the first to call it Great Britain. The line of Scottish kings, and for that matter, Israelites ruling in Europe, ended with King James VI.

The arts flourished in Europe under the reign of this intelligent king. This lets us know that there is no possible way that the term the "Dark Ages", representing the time period that he stemmed from, could not have meant a lack of mental creativity. This title is a ploy to cover the names and faces of the true Israelite rulers, who were *dark-skinned people*, in power at this time. Learning and writing thrived under the King's reign

Not only was King James the first monarch to unite Scotland, England, and Ireland into Great Britain, but he commissioned the translation of the greatest piece of religious and literary work in the world--the Authorized King James Version of the Bible.

ECCLESIASTICUS 10:8 (Apocrypha) - BECAUSE OF UNRIGHTEOUS DEALINGS, INJURIES, AND RICHES GOT BY DECEIT, THE KINGDOM(in this case meaning the knowledge of the kingdom, found in the scriptures) **IS TRANSLATED FROM ONE PEOPLE TO ANOTHER.**

The original Holy Scriptures were written in Hebrew, on scrolls. According to the scriptures, there was need for the Bible to be translated into other tongues, because of the fact that the Israelites, due to unrighteousness, would be taken into captivities, in which our language would change.

IS.28:11 – FOR WITH STAMMERING LIPS AND ANOTHER TONGUE WILL HE SPEAK TO THE PEOPLE (when Isaiah the prophet wrote this prophecy, he was seeing a vision of Israelites getting the knowledge of this Bible in other languages, as he refers to another tongue, and seeing their lips forming words he couldn't understand is why he referred to stammering lips.)

Just the fact alone of the Bible containing such prophecies that fulfill themselves exactly how they are written, proves that the scrolls of ancient times, and the original translation we have today were by no means through the will or the writing of man, nor has it been tampered with. But from the Most High, using people that he chose to bring his word unto us, **[read II Peter 1:20-21].**

1

THE TRUTH ABOUT KING JAMES VI:

In January of 1604, the King called the Hampton Court Conference in order to hear of things "pretended to be amiss" in the church. At this conference, Dr. John Reynolds, requested of the King a new translation of the Bible because those that were allowed during the reigns of Henry the VIII and Edward the VI were corrupt. King James did not write the Bible. In July of this same year, 54 scholars in the language of Hebrew and Greek were chosen of the available tribes of Israel. These men were not only the best linguists and scholars in the kingdom, but in the world. Much of their work on the King James Bible formed the basis for our linguistic studies of today.

The translators were organized into six groups and met at Westminster, Cambridge, and Oxford. This group of great scholars had qualifications such as have not been known before or after them. They spent most of their lifetimes in the pursuit of God and knowledge. One translator, Dr. Lancelot Andrews, mastered at least 15 languages and by the time he was 6 years old, he had read the entire Bible in Hebrew. Others on the translation committee were just as qualified. Some wrote foreign language dictionaries and thesauruses, they debated in Greek, they translated and edited great works and wrote their own. These are but a few of their accomplishments. They not only knew the Hebrew, Aramaic, and Greek biblical languages but also the related languages that shed light on them such as Arabic, Persian, Coptic, Syriac, Latin, Chaldee, Spanish, French, Italian, and Dutch. These men were not only world class scholars, they were Israelites who lived holy lives as Deans and Presidents of major universities such as Oxford, Cambridge, and Westminster.

This translation of the Bible was completed in the year 1611. In the version we have today, you can read, _"THE HOLY BIBLE, Old and New Testaments, In the King James Version, TRANSLATED OUT OF THE ORIGINAL TONGUES AND WITH PREVIOUS TRANSLATIONS DILIGENTLY COMPARED AND REVISED"_. The final revision being in 1614, and made public and was the first of it's kind to be translated to English, directly from the original scrolls. Upon completion of the translation, King James then put on it his seal of approval for it to be made official and lawful, to be distributed throughout the kingdom. We must remember that without this seal, it would not have been distributed throughout the land, **[read Eccl. 8:4; Prov.21:1].** No other revision to this version of the Bible has the expertise or understanding that was put into this original translation by the Israelite king, and scholars. Nor are these different translations ordained by the Most High, because these revisions are not being put together by true men of the Most High according to the scriptures, **[read Jer.23:21-22].** Just like a cassette tape, when you take the original and copy it, then you take that copy and copy it, and so on, the duplicates lose their quality. The same goes with the constant manipulating of the word of the Most High, which is the original. These modern day translations have lost their quality and also taken away from the understanding of the truth of the Bible through their misinterpretation of words, and wordplay, **[read Rev.22:18-19].**

One last key point in understanding the truth of the Bible. Not only does it contain real and true prophecies, and curses to show the Israelites who they are in these last days, but they also contain judgments of death for laws, statutes, and commandments that have been broken. Judgments such as death to those who blaspheme the Most High, Christ, the Holy Spirit, and his children by not telling the truth of who we are, and not revealing the true image of Christ. Promoting homosexuality,

those who defile their bodies with abominable foods, kidnappers, enslavers, murderers, robbers of lands, peoples, and heritage etc. All of these things, and much more, the so-called white man, as a whole, as well as the nations are guilty of. Now if a 'man' had his hand in writing this book and giving it to us, much less a so-called white man, don't you think he would remove these laws and judgments, seeing he is guilty of them all, and as a nation condones the breaking of them? But you see, he could not, because it was not of him to bring this book to us. The one thing he could do, since we are in his hands for a time, is pervert the understanding of it through little tricks called _religion_, _philosophy_, and _revised translations_. But now it is up to us to seek out and know the truth. **[read Rev.1:3; John 8:32]**

King James loved literature and wrote extensively including the Basilicon Doron which contains instructions to his son on how to live and be a just king. King James' advice to his son concerning chastity:

"Keep your body clean and unpolluted while you give it to your wife whom to only it belongs for how can you justly crave to be joined with a Virgin if your body be polluted? Why should the one half be clean, and other defiled? And suppose I know, fornication is thought but a veniall, (meaning small, or insignificant) sin by the most part of the world, yet remember well what I said to you in my first book regarding conscience, and count every sin an breach of God's law, not according as the vain world esteems of it, but as God judge and maker of the law accounts of the same: hear God commanding by the mouth of Paul to abstain from fornication, declaring that the fornicator shall not inherit the kingdom of heaven, and by the mouth of John reckoning out fornication among other grievous sins that declares the commiters among dogs and swine."

The King also lent advice to his son on how to treat his wife:

"And for your behavior to your wife, the Scripture can best give you counsel therein. Treat her as your own flesh, command her as her lord, cherish her as your helper, rule her as your pupil, please her in all things reasonable, but teach her not to be curious in things that belong not to her. You are the head, she is your body, it is your office to command and hers to obey, but yet with such a sweet harmony as she should be as ready to obey as you to command, as willing to follow as you to go before, your love being wholly knit unto her, and all her affections lovingly bent to follow your will."

James wrote in his work _Basilicon Doron_ that:

"There are some horrible crimes that ye are bound in conscience never to forgive: such as witchcraft, willful murder, incest, and sodomy."

The Bottom Line:

There is no recorded objective documentation that King James ever practiced or promoted sodomy, the historical record only knows of King James' heterosexuality and condemnation of sodomy.

For more information call or write:

THE SONS OF JACOB
PO Box 61457
Los Angeles, CA 90061-0457
(323) 290-1745
(323) 960-2007
e-mail: sonsofjacob@hotmail.com
visit our website: www.sonsofjacob12.com
fax: 323-290-1521

Class Schedule

Tues. – Bible Study 7:30pm-10:00 pm
Fri. – Sabbath Service 7:30pm-10:00pm
Sat. – Street Teaching-Leimert Park 1pm-until
also various other locations throughout
the Los Angeles area.

2

Ancient & Modern Images of Israelites

Ancient Israelite from
the Roman Empire

Ethiopian Hebrew

Ethiopian Hebrew Women

Ethiopian Hebrew
Girl

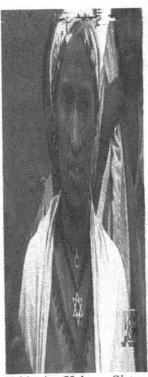

Ethiopian Hebrew Sister

Israelite from The United
States

5/26/2006

LIGHT & BODY of
Christ Church

THE MIDDLE PASSAGE WAS PROPHESIED IN THE BIBLE

DEUTERONOMY 28:15,47-48,68 · JOEL 3:6 · AMOS 7:17 ·

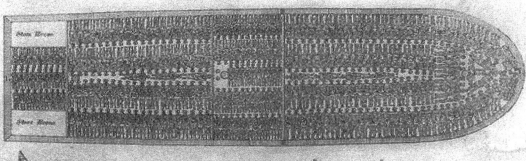

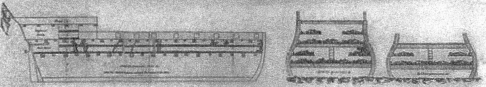

ILLUSTRATION SHOWING DECK PLANS AND CROSS SECTIONS OF BRITISH SLAVE SHIP BROOKES
UNDER THE REGULATED SLAVE TRADE ACT OF 1788 ~ LIBRARY OF CONGRESS

A Meal That Tells a Story

The Seder is a meal Jews eat during the springtime holiday of Passover. Every item on the table symbolizes part of the Passover story.

A roasted egg stands for spring as well as ancient holiday offerings.

Flat matza-bread reminds Jews how quickly their ancestors left Egypt: they had no time to let bread dough rise.

A special bowl and pitcher are often part of the opening ceremonies of the Seder. The pitcher holds water used for a ritual washing of the hands.

Four cups of wine remind the drinker of the four promises God made to the Israelites.

Like salty tears of slavery, a green vegetable dipped in salt water symbolizes the captivity and renewal of the Jewish people.

When the temple stood in Jerusalem, priests sacrificed a lamb at Passover. The roasted bone symbolizes that ancient rite.

The sharp taste of bitter herbs (horseradish) recalls the bitterness of slavery.

A mixture of apples, honey, nuts, wine, and spices, Charoset stands for the mortar binding the bricks that the enslaved Jews baked for the Egyptians.

An Agreement with God

The Torah teaches that during the Exodus Moses climbed to the top of Mount Sinai, where God spoke to him and gave him a message to pass on to his people. This message was about a **covenant,** or special agreement, that would bind the Israelites to God. According to the covenant, God promised to love and protect the Israelites. In return, the Israelites agreed to love God and follow God's laws: "And now, O Israel, what does the Lord your God demand of you? Only this: to revere the Lord your God, to walk only in His paths, to love Him, and to serve the Lord your God with all your heart and soul." (Deuteronomy 10:12)

302

Chapter 10

ISRAEL

THE CHOSEN PEOPLE

Black,
Oppressed & Cursed by God
...but WHY?

WATCH THE BIBLE WAY

5 PART SERIES:

- The Importance of Israel
  March 3rd

- The Color of Israel
  March 10th

- The Curse of Israel
  March 17th

- The King of Israel
  March 24th

- The Deliverance of Israel
  March 31st

5:00 P.M.
EVERY MONDAY IN MARCH

CHANNEL 21
GARY CABLE ACCESS

ISRAEL
The Church of Jesus

3813 S. Broadway
Gary, Indiana 46409
Bible Classes
Every Wednesday at 7:30 P.M.
and Saturday at 1:00 P.M.

BLACK? "Their visage is blacker than coal..."
LAMANTATIONS 4: 8

• A wall painting from the tomb of Nakht, an Egyptian dignitary of the 15th century B.C.

OPRESSED & CURSED?
...For it is written, cursed is everyone that hangeth on a tree" GALATIANS 3: 13

BUT WHY?

225

SOME TIMES I feel like IM (CROSSED) *CROSSED OVER* CUZ I don't floss..

Blessed to GIVE, Then RECEIVE..   YOU cant pay to be BOSS..
WHAT YOU KNOW..
   WHO YOU KNOW..
      WHERE YOU GO..
         HOW YOU FLOW..

REGARDLESS BUILD ON THE TEMPLE..   KEEP IT SIMPLE..

Maintain the WORDS OF TRUE LIGHT..
                    Which is given LIGHT to every man coming to the WORLD..

FORGET THE PHONE CALL.. Scared I might BALL.. Awaiting on your FALL.. (STALL)
                    PROLONG SUPERIORITY.. SPEAKING (ADVERSARY)
   The MOST HIGH peeps be MINORITY in the (game)   Bigger then the HIP HOP (fame)

(PLOT) that the ADVERSARY try to (STOP) Principality SPIRIT over GOVERNMENT

Conciseness out in ZION, WE anent LYING, **blow the trump** of the MOST HIGH..
                    CALLING ALL PEOPLE.. ITS TIME TO GO..

PROPHESY (LACED) THE RHYME..   Maintain the WORDS OF TRUE LIGHT..
                    Which is given LIGHT to every man coming to the WORLD..

EXPLAIN the RIGHTEOUSNESS to your GIRL..   So the Meek shall INHERIT earth..

If you wanna Sit down.. Dip down.. Flip down.. WORDS TO (RECEIVE)
                    SCIENCE that I KICK..   (SPIT)

WORDS OF TRUE LIGHT..
   WHICH IS GIVEN LIGHT TO EVERY MAN COMING TO THE WORLD..

Instill to my GIRL.. WORDS from on high.. KNOWLEDGE from with in.. why stand and LIE..

BE A MAN OF YOUR WORD.. LET YOUR (YES) BE (YES) LET YOUR (NO) BE A (NO)

WHY EVEN GO.. IM to OLD, to blunder down.. In PAGAN city.. LOOKING FOR A IDLE..
   LOOKING AT ITS (TRIFF) " YO "   *WICKED and its FOUL*   " YO "

MAINTAIN THE WORDS OF TRUE LIGHT WHICH IS GIVING LIGHT TO EVERY
                    MAN COMING TO THE WORLD..
                                        AMEN

PROPHETIC MESSAGE MINISTRY
   AMMISHADDAI

PSALM : TALKING ABOUT IMMANUEL

10/4/02

YAH is with US, I don't NEED the WORLD.. FORTUNE or FAME, *NO RELIGION TO*

CLAIM.. above YAH (YAH) **REAL** (IS) above (all) RICHES.. That the Man Claim, NO

SHAME, TO MY GAME..
TALKING ABOUT IMMANUEL..

MY (EL) MY (EL) FOLLOW IMMANUEL, I Couldn't FELL.

When its COLD out, OUT in the DARK, bring LIGHT and SPARK

FIRE, SPIRIT OF THE WORD..

SWERVE, CURVE, Any Event *THE SPIRIT IS ON THE LIPS* (SLIPS) (FLIPS)

BUT KEEP IT REAL..

So in still the MOST HIGH WAY.. People PRAY, I guest U (say) what make me feel this
(WAY)..

I don't NEED the WORLD.. FORTUNE or FAME, *NO RELIGION TO CLAIM..*

above YAH (YAH) **REAL** (IS) above (all) RICHES.. That the Man (Claim)

TALKING ABOUT IMMANUEL..
(don't) Ever let another, TAKE THE (LOVE) OF THE MOST HIGH Away,
WORSHIP Another GOD.
WOOD AND STONE.

I WILL SURELY DIE.
TALKING ABOUT IMMANUEL..
MY (EL) MY (EL) FOLLOW IMMANUEL, I couldn't FELL.. When its COLD out, OUT in the

DARK, bring LIGHT AND SPARK (FIRE) *SPIRIT of the WORD..*

I don't NEED the WORLD.. FORTUNE or FAME, *NO RELIGION TO CLAIM..*

When U *TALKING ABOUT IMMANUEL..*
YAH IS REAL.. YAH is with US.. AMEN

PROPHETIC MESSAGE MINISTRY
אממסהאדדא
תר
בלשׁ

227

PSALM: *ONCE UPON A TIME..*   9/22/02

See Nigga's like my self, BACK IN THE DAY.. And Nigga's of TODAY

EMPTY HEADED, HEADED STRAIGHT TO HELL.. then messed it up (so) BAD

ALLOW the System of a BEAST, *RED, WHITE and BLUE..*

(MENTAL MARK)

DISCRIMINATE, OPPRESS, (FORCED) TO DEMO STRAIT

The Righteous ach, to get the (say) (PRAY), (PRAY) FOR EVERY BODY EVERY (DAY)

Let the crowd step up, ANOINT TO **YAH**, *REPENT FORGIVE* your SINS..

ONCE UPON A TIME..

And get the DEMON ISH OFF YOUR MIND, AND the OPPOSITIONAL (ISH) FROM

YOUR MOUTH..

GOLD GLEAMING, BALDHEAD SCHEMING, NEVER BE AMERICAN DREAMING.

STOP Raising, " YO " Women like A HOE.. Woman on Woman turn em out to SODOMIE..

HOLLER ME, FOLLOW ME, **FEAR the MOST HIGH REGARDLESS..**

And the **HEBREW BLUNT BROWN SISTERS..**   *STOP* with the MADNESS.

GLADNESS, seek YaHWeH (FIRST) And all things like a man, could be added on..

In the LIFE LONG.. For ever STRONG..   **HEBREW BLUNT BROWN**, I love my lady..

See Nigga's like my self, BACK IN THE DAY.. And Nigga's of TODAY..

EMPTY HEADED, HEADED STRAIGHT TO HELL..

Then messed it up, (SO) BAD.. ALLOW the System of the BEAST,

RED, WHITE and BLUE

(MENTAL MARK) DISCRIMINATE, OPPRESS, (FORCED) TO DEMO STRAIGHT

ONCE UPON A TIME.. IM HIGH AS HELL, BUT TODAY IM ONLY SOBER IN THE MIND

TODAY im looking for the (SIGN)   YAH BLESS *ONCE UPON A TIME..*

AMEN

PROPHETIC MESSAGE MINISTRY
AMMISHADDAI

(COMMON GOAL)

Wonder thru my Maze, Let ME FIGURE out, words of PRAISE..

יהוה KEPT ME out the Daze.. Open up the DOORS TO THE MAZE..
                                                           CHOOSE LIFE..

                                                           CHOOSE DEATH..
MAKE A (CHOICE) right or wrong UNDERSTAND, NIGGA'S WILL BE JUDGED.

For every IDLE ish, that Proceed from his Mouth..

                    IT WILL ALL ENTER TWINE, IF ITS TRUE

GOLD GLEAMING, BALD HEAD SCHEMING, NEVER BE AMERICAN DREAMING..

U TOO BLACK, LOST SOUL, HOMELESS NATION.. Terrors in the land, bomb on the W.T.C.

Quakes in the various (places) changing the (faces) to the many (races) LOOKING AT the

(desolences) and the (pestilence) of the (providence)   *NILE VIRUS GROWING RAPID*

LOVE of many COLD.. HATED (BIRD) IN THE (AIR). (Scare)

                    IT WILL ALL ENTER TWINE, IF ITS TRUTH..

                    (COMMON GOAL)

        ONE " MO " (TIME) *SCIENCE FOR THE MIND..* PROPHECY, lace the Track,
                                                           all thru the (RHYME)

Wander thru my Maze, LET U FIGURE out..

                    WANDER THRU MY MAZE, let U figure OUT..

                    (COMMON GOAL)

                    IT WILL ALL ENTER TWINE, IF ITS TRUE   AMEN.
PROPHETIC MESSAGE MINISTRY
        אממסהאדדא.
            תר.
          בלשר

I THANK IMMANUEL for looking (out) for losing (life)

For giving up HIS SOUL for the SINS of the (world)

REGARDLESS OF THE IGNORANT, GROWING BLISS..

RESTRAIN MY MIND.. WORDS TO THOUGHT..   Before Im Pist.. Looking at my Wrist..

ITS TIME TO (GO) (SLOW) Moving OUT..
                    Time is of the ESSENCES..   Spitting PLEAS ANTS..

WORDS OF A HONEY COMB, SWEETNESS TO THE SOUL..   HEALTH TO THE BONE..

STRONG Standing LONG in the game.. (GAME) of LIFE on earth, BLESSED FROM BIRTH..

TO NEW BIRTH.. *FOREVER LIFE.. NEVER DIE A 2 DEATH..*

(F) (A) (I) (T) (H) from the TEMPTATIONS to the INSPIRATIONS..

MANIFESTATIONS of the KINGDOM OF THE MOST HIGH..

I THANK IMMANUEL for looking out.. For losing LIFE..

FOR GIVING UP HIS SOUL, FOR THE SINS OF THE WORLD..

HEAR ON EARTH (SPIRIT) of the **RIGHTEOUS..**

(STEP) TO THE QUAD..   BOW to YaHWeH..

BUILD THE TEMPLE (SIMPLE) WORDS TO THE WISE..
            (SURPRISE) (ADVISE) (REALIZE) *YaHWeH IS KING..*

(SANG) A NEW SONG..   Resistance FOOLISH (ish) in the NORM..
                                    SECULAR SOCIETY

NOTE: THE BAYN THAT WILL LIE TO (ME) CRY TO (ME) in the DARK..

SPARK (REPENT) THE FIRE IN HEART..

I THANK IMMANUEL for looking out.. For losing LIFE..

FOR GIVING UP HIS SOUL, FOR THE SINS OF THE WORLD..
PROPHETIC MESSAGE MINISTRY   AMEN
        AMMISHADDAI

230

Psalm : *Listen for the Clue*   9/14/02

INSTRUCT many in the GAME.. for many days to OVER STAND by many WAYS..

I see my nigga's (fall) by the SWORD and the FLAME

By CAPTIVITY and the PLUNDER of ACTIVITY when they (fall)

                              LISTEN FOR THE CLUE..

It shall be for a TIME, and a TIMES, an HALF a TIMES;

                    When the power of the *HOLY PEOPLE COMPLETELY SHATTER..*

(SCATTER) many run TO and FRO **KNOWLEDGE HAS INCREASED,** at the (TIME)

EVERYDAY SACRIFICE swipe away..   ABOMINATION OF DESOLATION SET UP..

              Shut up.. Put up..   *LISTEN FOR THE CLUE..*

(CUZ) IT (AREN'T T) IN THE BLUES..

ONE THOUSAND, TWO HUNDRED and NINETY DAYS..

                    BLESSED BE THE ONE WHO (WAIT)

Arise to INHERITANCE at the END OF (DAYS)

SCATTERED people (disobedience) result to CAPTIVITY (whack) ACTIVITY..

That you KEEP, advocate the EVIL (SPEAK) (PREACH) and (TEACH) the people..

                    LISTEN FOR THE CLUE..

                                        AMEN

PROPHETIC MESSAGE MINISTRY
          AMMISHADDAI
               TRUE
          BELIEVER

231

SHUT UP THE WORDS, and SEAL THE BOOK, until the END TIME..
MANY RUN TO and FRO, KNOWLEDGE SHALL INCREASE

Setting STRONG alone on SABBATH, THINK of another PLOT (HOT)

VIOLENT men of my people EXALT themselves in Fulfillment of another (VISION)

(COLLISION) according to His own will.. (VILE) person to whom you (give) the HONOR
And the ROYALTY..

SPOIL (TEE)
 enter in Peace(ably) seize the Kingdom with (INTRIGUE) HE enters IN Peace (ably)

HE acts (Deceitfully)

Both Kings heart (BE) bent on evil, Speaking (Lies) at the same (Table) *NEW WAVE FLOW*

It wont Prosper the end is coming soon REAL SOON at its own time PROPHETIC RYME..

Appointed (time) PROPHESY for a (time) and (times) an half a (times)

SHUT UP THE WORDS, and SEAL THE BOOK, UNTIL the END TIME
MANY RUN TO and FRO KNOWLEDGE SHALL INCREASE..

The good news of YaHWeH (hear) (here) to (stay) and now the END has come..

Believe that Receive that..   The people that would know there *MIGHTY ONE*

STAND STRONG, carry out great EXPLOITS.. Promote YAHS NAME
Instruct MANY in the GAME

SHUT UP THE WORDS, and SEAL THE BOOK, UNTIL the END TIME
MANY RUN TO and FRO, KNOWLEDGE SHALL INCREASE

AMEN

PROPHETIC MESSAGE MINISTRY
AMMISHADDAI
TRUE
BELIEVER

PSALM : FORGIVE ME, I KNOW HOW I USED TO BE   9/12/02

I couldn't (SEE) STROLLING thru this life..   HYPED wasn't RIGHT

STALKING IN DARKNESS..   FLOSS THIS..

Out for (anything) NEVER (cling) (SING) IDLE LIES..
Big honey Big Hoecy.. Plenty coochie..

Bling (Bling) focus on the (ring) MO MONEY HOE..   (SING) SING AMERICAN DREAM..

BIG MONEY HOE.. SIT ON MANY WATERS.
WORSHIP (RELIGION) IMAGE OF THE HARLOT (SCARLET)

DECEASED (FLEES) Nile Virus HIT THE LAND..   CURSED the hand (Mourns) Bloodshed
TEARS OF THE DEAD..

But instead I LOVE MY LADY..

FORGIVE ME, I KNOW HOW I USED TO BE..

But Now I SEE.. TEACH AND BESEECH (SPEAK) REVELATION.. SALVATION (Slash)

REVOLUTION increase the KNOWLEDGE, CONVERSATION..

BRING IT HIGHER..   A LITTLE HIGHER..   JUST A LITTLE HIGHER..

ADMIRE MOST HIGH MESSIYAH and KEEP IT REAL.

TO INSTILL THE MOST HIGH WAY..   *HONOR TRUE WAY..*

Step in the TEMPLE, KEEP IT SIMPLE..

FORGIVE ME, I KNOW HOW I USED TO BE..

AMEN

PROPHETIC MESSAGE MINISTRY
אממסהאדדא.
תר.
בלשׁרּ

233

PSALM : ART, IMITATIONS of LIFE

Fight for the Right, KEEP it REAL to Instill, the MOSTHIGH WORD..

(SWERVE) CURVE in Reality,

LOVE all your peeps, As we love OUR SELF 'S

ART , IMITATIONS of LIFE ART is the IMITATIONS of LIFE

Is YaHWeH our (GOD)   Is YaHWeH our (KING)

HIS AUTHORITY OVER ALL THE EARTH !! REMEMBER HIS COVENANT

FOREVER.. HIS WORDS of COMMAND its cleaver.. For thousand of generations

HE made the pact with Abraham , HIS oath to Yisaac , Establishing HIS LIKE - Ness for

YAHCOB.. Everlasting COVENANT for YISRAEL.. I GIVE YOU LAND.

I GIVE YOU HERITAGE..

ART , IMITATIONS of LIFE   ART is the IMITATIONS of LIFE

GIVE THANKS, to YaHWeH, call HIS NAME (aloud) Proclaim HIS deeds to the peoples

In the (crowd) SING to HIM Speak (aloud)

Play to HIS Marvels through out the (crowd)

GLORY HIS NAME, HOLY IN the GAME..

Let the Heart of those who THIRST, SEEK YaHWeH and REJOICE...

ART , IMITATIONS of LIFE   ART is the IMITATIONS of LIFE..

PROPHETIC MESSAGE MINISTRY
אבבטמהאריא .
הד ֻ
בלמשי֒

AMEN

PSALM : Just My Imagination

(cool) YaHWeH is in the (house)

YaHWeH, keep me close to U
YaHWeH save my (soul) YaHWeH YaHWeH is the KING!!
Blessed be the man, to have a (EL) like YAH its Glory unto YAH
Its Glory to (love) showing Praise unto YAH

Unto YAH unto YAH unto YAH

It was just my Imagination.. Once again, running away with me.

Out of all religion of the world, I chose (watch) over elderly and the (sick)
But Soon , soon , we will be in the land, (early) on Pass Over Day..
Save me from the world (tribulations) on the earth !!   HOUR of TRAIL
YaHWeH YaHWeH YaHWeH its clear to see
This couldn't (be) a dream YaHWeH is KING!! YaHWeH of HOST..
YaHWeH will (reign) forever MOST..

It was just my Imagination.. Running away with me...

YaHWeH is the KING that I love to (Praise)
Every night, on my knees, I pray dear YAH
Dear YAH hear my pleas, heal my dream, feel my scream,
YaHWeH will (save) in reality Married to the WORD, the MOSTHIGH
WAY
YaHWeH love is Heavily, knowing what to say, YaHWeH is KING!!
KING over land that I (love) sincerely we praise YaHWeH EL of HOST

It was just my Imagination.. Running away with me...

PROPHETIC MESSAGE MINISTRY
AMMISHADDAI
TRUE
BELIEVER   AMEN.

Understand the Wicked File nigga couldn't (comprehend) (understand) what Im saying..
In the *SPIRIT AND TRUE (Sue) Mobbing with the crew.. Striving minus CLUE.. To what to
do (Flew) off the handle cuz you NO understand " YO "..*

MIDWEST COALITION IN REDUCTION TO IMMIGRATION..

REGARDLESS IT'S A GOOD YEAR..

FEAR in the Father manifest in the LIGHT WISDOM is Beginning of KNOWLEDGE.. IN
YAH.. Hyped for right (light) shine in the dark, (spark) the *FIRE..*   (across) the world..
Upon up the Spirit to my girl.. **PLEASANT WORDS OR LIKE A HONEY COMB..**

SWEETNESS TO THE SOUL HEALTH TO THE BONE..

Standing Strong, Long Gone of the Time Past Away in my Old Way, it's a Better Way
understand by the Day, we All Pray.. **POINT OF DAY** led in the Spirit to the Way..
The TRUE WAY (PRAY) for everybody everyday so any way.. Back to the Point of the story.

THE WAY, THE TRUTH AND THE LIGHT..

Pharisees, Sadducees.. Up to date Religion Bore (me) **TRUE BELIEVERS ADORE** (me)
Listen up when U hear Christ is here.. Christ is there.. Its like a Scare.. When I see..
We Practice *ABOMINATIONS OF THE EARTH..* **IN THE TEMPLE..**

Something's (Wrong) FAKE RELIGION Sacrifice (pagan feast)
Worship to the (Beast) Look (around) when it fall and it all (seas)
In return of the LAMB.. Sheep to YEMINA Goat to SMOLA.. Kept from ETERNAL FIRE..
(Keep) it Real (Keep) it Higher to Admirer MOST HIGH MESSIYAH..

THE WAY, THE TRUTH AND THE LIGHT..

AS THE LIGHTING FLASHES FROM THE EAST, FLASHING TO THE WEST, SO SHALL
The coming of the SON OF MAN (be) **TRUE BELIEVER, RECEIVER HER,**

(AT) THE PENTECOST.. Took Belief in Her.. Taken Heed in Her..
(be) the Seed in Her.. (be) the TRUE LIGHT, which is given LIGHT, to every man come
into the world..   **SPOKEN ETERNAL WORD..**   Swerve (Curve) in HIM WAS a (life)
TO THE (LIFE) was the (light) of a man.. UNDERSTAND.. The Voice in the LAND..
Pray to Comprehend.. What the SEER (BE) SAYING..

(EXPLOIT) the Prophecy, Spit it plain, FOLLOW THE TRUE WAY..
And let TRADITION DIE ALONE.. Come into the NEW WAY, the TRUE WAY, the MOST

HIGH WAY..

YAHWEH..

יהוה

AMEN
PROPHETIC MESSAGE MINISTRY
    AMMISHADDAI
        TRUE
        BELIEVER

Re Direct " YO " (mind) so journey thru the (time) if the words that I speak or not (plain)
Or (sound) **FORGIVE ME.. READ..** wake your self (up) to be (found) so look (around)
    KORAN (BIBLE) TEX..   see me FLEX.. Was it all the (same) SIMPLE maybe (PLAIN)
To be found in the **MOST HIGH (NAME)** set back articulate (game) the HISTORY (bout)
The ISRAELITE POINT OF VIEW.. *STORY THAT I KNEW..*

                       STORY THAT I KNEW..

At the time.. All-round giving CLUE (BOO) WHO didn't leave Co - Co **BLUNT BROWN..**
SPICE (TEE) took her to the land of my Journey with me.. At the TIME set Out West..
C. H. I. Was the (bet) (set) up North.. 5th and Madison was the (STOP) BRAND NEW
(HOP) heard about Robert X (speak) about the *COVENANT OF MOST HIGH..*

                  Why (lie) simple and its (plain) patiently (maintain)
         THE KING IN YOUR LAND..

Munching on the bake (beans) coming up with the (means) to Manifest **POWER..**
Prepared FOREVER.. Now im down with the (RING) DING (DONG) up against the BELL..
Making me want to TELL.. Never FELL.. Baby (TEE) shipped out (KAT) to County JAIL..
TESTIMONY a little History..   About the ISRAELITE that I (be)   At One Time..
Smoking on the HAY..   Day to Day..   LOST AND IM FOUND..   Changed and (bound)
STUCK IN THE BELLY OF DECAY.. down in the BEAST OF AMERICA.. that's the biggest
MYSTERY in HISTORY..   *THE KING IN YOUR LAND.. THE KING IS IN THE LAND..*

WE ARE THE CHURCH.. YAHWEH IS KING.. Setting into JUDAH (Abraham) Covenant..
SIMPLE and its PLAIN. (patiently) MAINTAIN (salvation) strictly coming at U (snatch) U
Catch U.. since the (DAY) Sister SARAH HAD TO (SAY) given Birth (in) the (DAY)
         CHOICE NATION ON THE EARTH..   JUDAH Begot the NAME..
ISRAELITES STAYED THE SAME.. since My GENEALOGY.. Not BIOLOGY.. Could (not)
                       (be) the problem U (see)..

     THE KING IN YOUR LAND..

Abraham (Yisaac) Israel received the BEST.. SET APART FROM THE REST.. Manifest the
(CALL) *ANOINTED IN THE WAY..*   IMMANUEL..   IMMANUEL..
Hero for (Hire) while (Admire) YAHSavior LIKE.. MESSIYAH (CHRIST) my (inspirer)
     BELIEF.. ISRAELITE was the (case) that I (base) like the Stupid Cincinnati (Bengal)
Looking at me (mangle) Unconscious (tangle) that I had in the Mind.. For decline..
(Social) Economic Bind (decline) NO SPIRITUAL THOUGHT TO THE (MIND)
WE ARE THE CHURCH.. YAHWEH IS KING..   THE KING IS IN THE LAND..

Sit back looking at the COUNTY BOUNTY, Red Coats coming (humping) bumping (stumping)
Sometimes caught your - self slippen.. Dippen.. Down the EASTSIDE..
LOOKING FOR THE *CROSSROADS TO THE UNDERGROUND..*   stepping to the stylistic
(sound) BLESSED AND U FOUND.. The Holy Book coming with a (whole) NEW HOOK..
   KING OF KINGS.. LORD OF LORDS.. GOD OF GODS.. YAHWEH OF HOST..
Mirror (Mirror) on the wall, found out YAH BE TOP CHOICE OF EM ALL.. Set apart to be
the BEST..   THE KING IN YOUR LAND..   THE KING IS IN THE LAND..
                                        AMEN

PROPHETIC MESSAGE MINISTRY
     AMMISHADDAI

Massing thru the VALLEY of the dry BONE.. Belly of the BEAST 666

What most of the people SAY.. DAY to DAY.. Land of the (lost) pay the (cost) to (be)
                                                                            The (boss)
In the city of a FALLEN ANGEL.. Spit it plain (yo) it all started right here.. HOPING ON

The A TRACK.. Belief in the FACT. We had to maintain the *WATCH TOWER IN THE DARK*

BLESSED (LIGHT) like the (SPARK) in the (world) blessed spirit to my (girl)

WHO AM I

WE GUARD THE WAY.. it's a good (day) to PLOT AND PLAIN. The better (way)

I heard em say.. How can the DEAD RAISE.. FOOLISH ONE what U (sow) its NOT

(made) ALIVE UNLESS IT DIE. As the man of (dust) LIKEWISE those who were (made)

Of (dust) **RECEIVE THAT.. BELIEVE THAT..** truth and fact   Supernatural its NOT

(first) but the Natural and after ward the Supernatural.. The FIRST MAN of the earth.

Made of (dust) the SECOND MAN Supernatural from ABOVE. WE ALL BORN THE IMAGE.

Of the man of (dust) WE ALL BEAR THE IMAGE of the Supernatural HEAVENLY MAN..

FROM ABOVE.. Its OK (confess) from WITHIN, **GLORIFIED TESTIFIED** before your
                                                                            FRIENDS..

   WHO AM I, The RU - ACH OF THE MOSTHIGH..
                          ABBA ELOHIM YAHWEH ELOHIM OF HOST.

SO looking at the RESURRECTION OF THE DEAD.. But Instead.. The soul is SOWN

In CORRUTION.. But its RAISED in NON CORRUTION. **DESTRUCTIONS IN THE**
                                                                            (LAND)
 WHO AM I.. The RU - ACH OF THE MOSTHIGH.. WHO AM I,   I AM WHO I AM..

PROHETIC MESSAGE MINSTRY   AMEN
  COMMANDMENT KEEPERS   AMMISHADDAI
                                                    TRUE
                                                    BELIEVER

PSALM : IN THE WILDERNESS

8/14/97

Don't Blasphemy FATHERS (NAME) Don't (be) little FATHERS (GAME) **SCRIP(TRUTH)**

And FACT.. So now it come to PASS.. When MESSIYAH, finished COMMANDING. All HIS

(12) He would (preach) and (teach) in the city so now, the PROPHET JOHN laying LO IN

The (PIN) Heard about *WORKS OF ANOINTED.*. He sent TWO OF HIS CREW..

DISCIPLES EVERY.. Coming UP asking HIM.

Are U the ONE are DO we look for ANOTHER. So then YAHSAVIOR ANSWERED him
SAYING.. GO to PROPHET JOHN and (tell) about the THINGS U (see) and (hear)

ANOINTED MESSAGE (TO) PROPHET JOHN..

From YAHSavior (ANOINTED) AS HE (BE) (see)

LIVING IN THE WILDERNESS.. I was waken (up)

Early in the (morning) (yarning) at 4 in the (morning) while the MOSTHIGH kept my course.

Massing out eye 60 (110) south, got OFF ON THE GAGE, looking for another WAGE..

Staying TRUE to the CREW.. **CROSSROADS TO THE UNDERGROUND..**

Heaven (found) Now I'm (bound) living in the WILDERNESS. Looking at the LIFE AFTER

DEATH OF THE B. I. G. (learned) we (all) had to GO Know U (know) (sip) on YAH
(HONEY) TEE and the V. S. O. P. (C G) and (ME)
Chilling in the EAST.. OF THE WOOD.. DAMU (BLUE) and the CREW.. Smoking on the HAY

IN THE WILDERNESS.. LIVING IN THE WILDERNESS

STAYING ROOTED TO THE MOSTHIGH.. Knowing what to (say) BOOK of INSTRUCTION

(to) LIVING ETERNALLY.. WAKE (up) (to) SEE.. ANOINTED SEAL.. Can U feel..

The Mighty SKILL.. O its REAL..

Blessed in the time. NO nigga (man) could make me (bang) intellectual, urban (SIN)
IN THE WILDERNESS.. mirror (mirror) on the wall, YAH BE TOP CHOICE OF EM ALL..

Set apart (for) the BEST (MIDWEST) Crossroads to the Underground. *SPIRIT and the
(SOUL)* STEPPING BOLD. Story to be TOLD. I'm Black and I'm Comely.. NEVER CAN
DEBATE (me) My KNOWLEDGE OUT SHINE (all) program style of College..

LIVING RIGHTEOUS IN THE WILDERNESS..
AMEN

PROPHETIC MESSAGE MINISTRY
COMMANDMENT KEEPERS

אכמלאירדא.

PSALM : 4 POINTS OF REFERENCE 12/15/00

Point of REFERENCE.. would be my Preference.. **BELIEF IN DELIVERANCE..**

Of my people.. CREATOR LOVED HOLY ONE.. THE MOST HIGH SO LOVE THE WORLD HE

GAVE HIS HOLY (SON) *DELIVER ALL..* WAKE UP OVER STAND to your CALL..

Any other THOUGHT put a FORK IN IT.. Cuz its DONE.. HEAVEN SENT, the HOLY(ONE)

BELIEVE (RECEIVE) EVER LIFE.. The MOST HIGH destroyed His Place of (Assembly)

Appointed (feasts) and SABBATH (Day) become forgotten in the CITY CALLED (ZION)

We anent LYING.. The KING and the PRINCE (among) the NORTH AMERICAN GENTILE

COMMON WEALTH..

The Law is NO MORE.. Her Prophet (find) No Vision from YAHWEH of HOST..

The Elders, of the Daughter of ZION, sit on the ground.. Keeping Silence.. (RELIGION)

Got U like the Pharisees.. Were U cant even See.. Your IDLE Prophet (seek) and He

(speak) false and deceptive (Vision) keeping purpose in (division) Speaking (Vision)

Of the FALSE PROPHECY.. And Delusion to conclusion..

4 POINTS OF REFERENCE.. WOULD BE MY PREFERENCE..

BELIEF IN DELIVERANCE.. Of my people.. ALL WHO PASS BY CLAP THEIR HANDS..

Now we hear (some) who hiss and shake their head.. At the BAHT OF YAHRUSALEM..

(SPEAKING) CLUES TO THEM.. THIS IS THE CITY THAT IS CALLED BY THE NAME..

PERFECT AND BEAUTY.. THE JOY TO THE WORLD..

4 POINTS OF REFERENCE..

Would be my Preference.. BELIEF in Deliverance.. Of my people..
AMEN

PROPHETIC MESSAGE MINISTRY
COMMANDMENT KEEPERS

AMMISHADDAI
TRUE
BELIEVER

240

PSALM : NEIGHBOR HOOD WATCH

ABIB /18 / 99

Im Black and Comely, I can (No) longer (BE) Beneath the SHADOW that keep me

wrong.. Yet for So long.. To get the SPIRIT that keep me STRONG.. (plus) NIGGA'S (was)

NIGGA'S (bust) NIGGA'S.. (lust) NIGGA'S (idle) time was the crime..   (Unconciseness)

imparted to the mind.. Unrighteous for the time.. SUNSHINE.. over stand in the (bind)

(blind) was the (kind) So Nick (Nick) make a fist.. Wave it in the (air) wave it to your

Worries and your (care) yeah.. Had to keep it (fair) *GLORY BE TO THE MOST HIGH..*

IMMANUEL,   IMMANUEL,   IMMANUEL..

IN ALL THINGS THAT I DO.. I send out my shoots to U.. this would be the Clue..

That keep me close to U.. **FOREVER SERVING U..** LOOK I see U too.. SON OF SHADDAI..

UNDERSTAND scratch and scare was a FACT.. Truth going back.. STOP GETTING HIGH..

STOP DRINKING 40 ' S.. STOP ATTENDING WORTHLESS FUNCTIONS and PARTIES..

Understand (BLACK) Stop to look (BACK) HULK FEET could of put U out like a Foe..

Now U Know.. Cuz U got to GO..

"MO" POWER TO THE PEOPLE.. If U want to STAND in my NEIGHBOR (HOOD) WATCH..

Like they used to say back in the day.. Cuz U better watch the Fuzz..

BELIEVE THAT, TAKE HEED TO THAT..

STANDING NEIGHBOR (HOOD) WATCH.. **YAHWEH IS WHO WE BOAST IN..**

NEIGHBOR (HOOD) WATCH.. NEIGHBOR (HOOD) WATCH..

AMEN.

PROPHETIC MESSAGE MINISTRY
COMMANDMENT KEEPERS
AMMISHADDAI
TRUE
BELIEVER

PSALM : TRUE.. 8/13/97

TRUTH.. SPIRITUAL EAR.. LET HIM HEAR..
U set back looking at the REDCOATS (coming) (humming) (bumming) caught your self.

(slipping) (dipping) down the EASTSIDE.. Looking for the CROSSROADS TO THE
                                                    UNDERGROUND..
Coming out on a STYLISTIC type of (sound) **YAH BLESS, HEAVEN BOUND.. HOLY BOOK..**

COMING WITH THE HOOK.. **KING OF KINGS.. ELSHADDAI KING OF HOST..**

YAHWEH our FATHER which is in heaven, Holy be your NAME.

Your KINGDOM COME.. Your WILL be done.. On earth as it is in HEAVEN..

GIVE US THIS DAY.. Our daily Bread.. **FORGIVE US OUR DEBT..** we forgive our debtor..

LEAD us NOT into Temptation, but DELIVER us form EVIL, for Yours is the KINGDOM
                                                    (POWER)
And the GLORY FOREVER.. AMEN EVER MORE..
                              YAHWEH IS THE KING..

U cant (lose) for (winning) with the MOSTHIGH. So the GOODNEWS, TRULY been

(pass) with the GOODNEWS FLASH.. (dash) (splash) hit U like a world wind..

Got your head to spin.. Kicking back, we was kin.. *SOLD INTO CAPTIVITY.. IN ACTUALITY..*

                              KING OF KINGS, LORD OVER JUDAH..

STEPPING INTO JUDAH.. Waking up early in the (morning) (yarning) (4) in the

(morning) Blessed to (know) the MOSTHIGH kept me on my COURSE.. While we (mass)

Bogie (down) eye 60 (110) South got off on the GAGE.. Looking for a WAGE.. PONDER

What to say.. Looking at the LIFE AFTER DEATH of the B. I. G. **DEATH WAS THE
                                                    SENTENCE..**
Repent, Repent breaking COVENANTS.. (EVER WHERE) FEAR (is) in the AIR.. (scare)

PREPARE, PREPARE FOR THE END IS NEAR..
                    TRUE TO U, COMING WITH THE CLUE.. TRUE TO U..
                                                    AMEN
PROPHETIC MESSAGE MINISTRY
  COMMANDMENT KEEPERS

                                        AMMISHADDAI

242

3685 I step out on a snowy day.. I thanked the MOSTHIGH super STRUCTURED FORCE..

That kept me on my Course.. BLESSED with the WORDS of ARTICULATION.. I (pray) I
                              LEAD ALL TO EMANCIPATION..
So when U sitting back, want to DIE.. (broke) and (depressed) from the (stress) looking at

The (rest) of the (flesh) how (divided) crying out to the CROSS ROADS TO
                                                    UNDERGOUND..
MIND (SPIRIT) SOUL
              BLESSING BOLD, STORY TO BE TOLD, PROPHECY TO UNFOLD..

            THESE ARE THE DAYS OF VENGEANCE..

Cursed for everyone who would (hang) from the (tree) U black as the SOOT. Got the

Bread at the (risk) of your (life) your forefather (SIN) but now is NO MORE..

REMEMBER ABBA YAH SHALOM.. For what has come upon US (all) for SO LONG.

 THESE ARE THE DAYS OF VENGEANCE.. SO ITS WRITTEN UP TILL COMPLETION

(13) Teen triple (one) Go Ham I lay my head to (bed) to go to sleep but (instead)

I think about, what I (face) hostility (strife) and (confusion) was the (case) Biblically
                                          Ignorant (nigga) (base)
Out in Calley, south (in) Moreno valley.. Living in the WILDERNESS.. Was the place that lead
to the silly ish. That I face.. Day to Day.. All -round me gave way.. To the House Nigga play..

STRIVING WITH YOUR BROTHER (MAN) NO RESPECT FOR YOUR MOTHER (MAN)

JUDGE THE BOOK BY THE COVER (MAN) WE IN THE WILDERNESS TO GATHER
(MAN) Leaving Me ONE CHOICE. But to step back (dazed) yet (amazed) watching (sally)

And little Joe (do) what they could, BO WHO U never had my back from the start. So let

Me step back on a different (part) (smart) for my baby TEE and ME to RECEIVE HOLY

(START) to receive (part) of Inheritance from the (curse) *SPIRITUAL EAR LET HIM*
                              HEAR, WHAT THE SPIRIT SAY TO THE CHURCH..
                                                    AMEN
          DAYS OF THE VENGEANCE.. LIVING IN THE DAYS OF VENGEANCE..

PROPHETIC MESSAGE MINISTRY
  COMMANDMENT KEEPERS
    AMMISHADDAI

I'm just a (carrier) (invisible) tight with the (flow) promote the (word) (invisible)

KINGDOM OF THE MOST HIGH..   **SUPERNATURAL..**   I DON'T LIE.. (invisible) down

(low) keep it (slow) on the (row) death had to GO..

        I DON'T KNOW, I DON'T BLOW I stopped a couple of years AGO..

YAH, BLESSED me with the (flow) (slow) to GO..   Ain't No time, looking for No party.

Time is SHORT..   Buck a vote..   It ain't   (solution) to (pollution) that I see..

You know I WOUNDNT RIDE..   (hide) (tag) a long.. With the (wrong) (in) need of time

(out) for my (mind) pleading thru the (rhyme) *OFFENCE IN YOUR KIND..* STAIRING
ME DOWN.. LOOKING AT ME CRAZY.. CUZ U LAZY.. Cant hear the (book) ain't NO fancy
(HOOK) real U in devils (advocate) (tolerate) the SIN. Regardless U wont make me

                                         (bend)

point and position that I (send)   **YAHWEH IS MY KIN.. AND THE PEOPLES STRONG..**

White lips and all.. (do) what I (do) to creep (thru) the strength from (soul) keep me

(bold) prophecy (unfold) YHWH NEVER COLD.. Consuming FIRE.. Forgiving In HIS angle.

Speak it plain YO.. (behavior) (beware) citywide (scare) curfew SET, Torrence to

Inglewood, to Culver city from West Hollywood..   FIRES (FLARES) with the (evil) mental..
They (breed) the heathens (seed)   *REBERATIONS IS WHAT U OWE..*   IM NOT
broke (dick) (complacent) finding out later on, that I'm real.. Mad skill..   Who am I ?

                                  Cover (brother) love your (mother)

        YAHWEH IS MY KIN.. AND THE PEOPLES STRONG..

I'm (felling) (belling) thru the (hood)   ALL THE BLAME.. FAME.. (sins) on (me) she

all on (me) felonies (capers) threaten me with the (vapors) (understanding) I was wrong..

By the (bicth) that I called U.. your moms (yapping) I was dead (broke) everything I say is a
(Joke) when I (spoke) the WORD (WRITTEN) in its WAY..   Now U say I'm (wrong)
HEART(LESS) for lack of (tolerance) that I (show) for the (ignorance) (foolishness) that
was (bliss)

*YAHWEH IS MY KIN.. AND THE PEOPLES STRONG..   CHANGE THE COURSE THAT
WAS WRONG..*   AMEN.

               YAHWEH IS MY KIN..

PROPHETIC MESSAGE MINISTRY
      AMMISHADDAI
        TRUE
          BELIEVER

I sit (alone) AMONG the (dark) (foul) CONVERSATIONS in the (air) (Scare) I Plot , I thought TO

(THINK) **HOW TO PLANT SEEDS of YAHWEH** (bring) SALT to the earth.. FLAVOR TO THE

WORLD.. Pleasant SPIRITS (to) my girl.. Maintain the WORD OF LIGHT.. Living (right) sometimes

prepared to (fight) ASSALT verbal not (provoke) (insight) my (folk) ain't NO JOKE.. Rejoice while I'm

(BROKE) **I KNOW YOUR WORK..** YAHWEH KNOW YOUR TRAIL (tribulation) and poverty..

Situation that would (be) U (rich) don't (bitch) complain (keep) your head (Up) I (Know)

The blasphemy of those (who) CLAIM (say) they HEBREW, but ARE NOT.. Slipping (in) from

Synagogue of the (advisory) (Satan) Congregation of the Edomite.. When U over (COME)
U wont be hurt by NO (ONE)

D' NELL walk around Half (dead) Half (scared) in big city of the (dead) *MURDER CAPITAL..*

POLICE BRUTALITY.. FALL OF A LARGE COMPANY..

WEIRD TO THE WORLD..

WEIRD TO THE WORLD.. Rolling thru the (hood) rolling down the (window) caught the (thought) **HAD**

A VISION.. (tolk) a Blunt.. Collision with the (true) Divisions with Provisions of the (CLUE)

WEIRD TO THE WORLD..

POLICE BRUTALITY.. OPPRESSING (IS) ACTUALITY.. (JUGEMENT) (FALL)
OF A LARGE COMPANY..

Little man (been) stumped (again) when (will) it (end) **YAHWEH** a foolish people (blasphemy) your
(NAME)

BLESSED TO (GIVE) THEN (RECEIVE) build on the SIMPLE.. Words to ADVIZE.. (realize)

(surprise) don't (despise) when I tell U (true) sending shots out to U.. don't take my KIND (NESS)

For the WEEK (NESS) of a (punk) (chump) get BEHIND (ME)

TRY TO FIND (ME) YAHWEH OF HOST..

WEIRD TO THE WORLD..

AMEN

COMMANDMENT KEEPERS
PROPHETIC MESSAGE MINISTRY
AMMISHADDAI
TRUE
BELIEVER

PSALM : OLDER HEAD

CHECK IT OUT, ANCEINT of DAYS.. YAHWEH our FATHER which is in Heaven..

HOLY be HIS NAME.. HIS Kingdom (Come) HIS will be (Done) in Earth as in Heaven..

Give US this day.. Or daily Bread.. FORGIVE US our debts (we) FORGAVE our debtors..

Lead US into NO Temptations (delivered) US from the EVIL ONE.. So **YHWH** So LOVE

THE WORLD GAVE HIS **HOLY SON**.. *WHO BELIEVE (IN) WOULD NOT PARISH..* (But)

(Acquirer) EVER LASTING (life) **YHWH IS THE KINGDOM**.. Having (power) giving

GLORY (FOREVER)

Evermore **OLDER HEAD** it's a REASON why, U Blessed to (be) try to (see) (today)

(speak) to the YOUNGER HEAD another (day) PROCLAIM to YAHWEH (today) SPEAK

About the CHANGE in your LIFE (today) what POSITIVE did U have to (say) what

CONVERSATION did U give ear (today) was it RIGHTOUESS by the END of the (day)

SPIRITUAL in what U (say) PRAY everyday (all) day meditate in YAHWEH..

(tolk) a (blunt) the other (day) leave alone (today) Knowing what to (say) walking (in)

My (sway) time is (to) SHORT, *(STOP) TRYING TO (PLAY)* NIGGA'S in the PIN.. don't

KNOW what to (say) Living Life in ODDS, NIGGA'S need to (pray) every day to make a

Better (way) Over stand in your (way) my NIGGA'S (parish) for Lack of what to (say)

LEARNING (TRUE) WAY the MOST HIGH (WAY) **OLDER HEAD REPENT**..

TO KEEP THE BRIGHTIER (DAY)

PROPHECY (to) what to (say) *OLDER HEAD WALK AROUND NOTE WHAT U (SAY)*

To keep it (real) while instill MOST HIGH (WAY) ARTICULATE (IDENTIFY) in what U

(say) (it) ain't NO JOKE.. STRICKLY for my FOLK.. *OLDER HEAD..*

I don't like to CAST (PEARLS) Before (swine) why sit around CAST the food of the
children to the (dog) (hog) Living Life in the (smog) sending shots out to U strictly for the
(clue) *OLDER HEADS* AMEN..

PROPHECTIC MESSAGE MINISTRY
COMMANDMENT KEEPERS
אמכלאהקמרדא .

246

TWO (Witness) coming FORTH to (SHINE) *RIGHTEOUS, in PARTED TO YOUR (KIND)*
Think (Intellectual) (Science) for the (time) I'm NOT (bought) to (compromise) in my
(rhyme)
The garbage that's (promoted) on (air) (pollute) the (rhyme) (every time) SCIENCE..

That I kick in the (rhyme) **PROPHECY / SEMITIC STYLE OF RHYME..** With the
(hooks) Coming from the (books) SHOOK the higher learning (element) TIME SPENT
TIME WAISTED.. WHILE U BENT..

THOUGHTS ON MY MIND..

REPENT (STOP) with the Mad (ness) Focus on the Glad (ness) (blast) this with the
SPIRIT of the MOST HIGH.. Why lie.. (stop) crying like U Want to (die) SCARED TO

RIDE OR DIE.. NO DOUBT Talk a good (game) SCARED to (maintain) (POSITIVE) OUT
LOOK walking in the (game)

Set aside the bull (shit) that U (spit) on your RAP INCREASE the PEACE in your walk and
your talk. I'm tired of hearing the NIGGAS FLOSS.. DEATH knocking at the WINDOW

THOUGHTS ON MY MIND..

SEED of *RIGHTEOUS (SPARK) THE FIRE..* Spirit ON
the WORLD.. Sending two by (two) pulling (two) from a city (two) become plenty..

Sparking (spirit) thru the (WORD) SWURVE (CURVE) in the hood.. On the D. L.

FOR A SEASON (split) a (EL) **HAVING THOUGHTS ON MY MIND..**
EXCELLENCE OF KNOWLEDGE.. IN the
(rhymes) WISDOM GIVEN LIFE.. To the (blind) taking (heed)

To (beware) (ones) LIFE DON'T CONSIST of (abundance) of (possession) LIFE IS
MORE then FOOD.. Keeping up the BODY its MORE then clothes..

CHOSE LIFE or DEATH.. SUFFER IN YOUR WOES..

THOUGHTS IS ON MY MIND.. " YO " THOUGHTS ON MY MIND..

AMEN..

PROPHETIC MESSAGE MINISTRY
 COMMANDMENT KEEPERS

אממסהאדרא
תר
בלשׁר

PSALM : LIFE ETERNAL..   10/19/02
             THE EXCELLENCE OF WISDOM..

NO we say to the people.. THUS SAY YHWH (behold) I set before U **THE WAY..**

LIFE or DEATH (chose) HAPPY is the man who would find the WISDOM to gain
UNDERSTANDING (Over standing) to maintain the PEACE..

         SHE's A TREE OF LIFE.. Those who (would) take hold of (her) Those (who)
RETAIN (her) HAPPY BE Yeah..

    YHWH the (wisdom) founded earth (by) UNDERSTANDING established HEAVEN.. (by)
the KNOWLEDGE broke it (up) CLOUDS drop the (dew) **BLESSED.. LIGHT SHINING** out
to U.. KEEPING U sound **WISDOM** and

         DISCRETION become (life) added on to your (soul) BOLD story (unfold)

    LIFE ETERNAL.. *THE EXCELLENCE OF WISDOM..*
Listen to (me) children, BLESSED those who KEEP MY WAYS..

                        HEAR INSTRUCTION BECOME WISE..

DON'T DISPISE IT.. Who finds ME FINDS LIFE.. Obtain FAVOR from the
                                    MOST HIGH. THE WAY OF LIFE..

(*ETERNAL*) *NEVER DIE A SECOND DEATH..* CRef (LOW) A DOLLAR I heard my
people (crying) hollering in the streets.
            STANDING IN THE LINES..   HAND OUTS..

            (feed)   (feed)   With the WORD OF YAH.
              (ME)   (ME)

EXCELLENCE IN KNOWLEDGE WISDOM'S GIVEN LIFE..
                    KNOWLEDGE OF (HIM) **GLORY TO VIRTUE..**

I LOVE MY LADY, I never want to hurt U. YHWH BLESSED ME (heritage) fruit of the
(womb) REWARD in the RIGHTEOUS..

            LIFE ETERNAL.. (THE EXCELLENCE OF WISDOM)

                                                    AMEN
PROPHETIC MESSAGE MINISTRY
      AMMISHADDAI
          TRUE
            BELIEVER

So let us PRAY EVER(DAY) to maintain in the (way) the MOSTHIGH (way) TRUE (way)
          ARTICULATE REAL (way) SATAN step behind (me) check the (point)
PROCLAMATION (PROCLAIMED) to the NATION.. OPERATION to Kingdom that
(comes) those who practice such things shall NEVER INHERIT the earth.. KINGDOM OF
THE MOSTHIGH..   Regardless if U party or go to church KEEP IT REAL TO INSTILL (in)

SPIRIT AND TRUE (sue) mobbing sinning minus (clue) to what she (do) (flue) off the handle

With NO UNDERSTAND " YO " repent fall on your (knees) and beg the *FATHER PLEASE..*
Abba (please) return me on my way return me to the TRUE (way)
                              PROPHETS (LAW)
(ITS) 8:00 pm I hit the party.. Strollen on the (seen) sitting had the VISION OF A
SCEEM.. At ONE point (these) was nothing but a (dream) on the mic.. Rock the people got em

(hyped) to do the (right) stay and maintain (proclaim) in the (name) of **CREATOR..** Cut
CREATOR become inspirator CHRIST - LIKE imitator REGARDLESS in the party educate
(her) SPIT the pleasant (words) like a honey comb sweetness to the (soul) health to the bone

STRENGHT TO THE SOUL in the (cold) (bold) but love (less) SOCIETY everyday its another
(cry) to me don't (lie) to me   **PROPHETS (LAW)** YHWH I don't (come) to appear to go the
(way) of the world.. YHWH save my (soul) help me over stand guild my (girl) SWIREL (SO)

(REAL) filled in for (earl) don't cast NO PEARL before (swine) OPEN up to understanding for
your (kind) SPIRITUAL **ISRAEL** stock and bond **BLOOD** of ABRAHAM **ISRAEL FOLLOW
IMMANUEL..** " em " U never will fell.. YHWH may we cry if ain't the end.. STOP THE RAIN

For 3 ½ yrs OPEN UP THE (EARS) to my (peers) (fears) of another plague.. YHWH truly
(save) *PROPHETS (LAW)* Vision out the window make a choice LIFE OR DEATH..

          RIGHT OR WRONG..   SAVING (FRIST) for (LAST)

          RETURN of YAHSHUAH.. LAMB of YHWH..   PROPHETS (LAW)

SHARON U scared half (baked) sometimes walk around (fake) little (cult) set apart from
Major (cult) its all a (cult) REGARDLESS Religious don't divide the folk.. It ain't no Joke..

THE WORD OF YAH.. its been so much on my mind.. TEARS dripping from my eyes.. CRYS
of another (day) responsibilities while I (pray) SPIRITUAL in what I (say) YHWH if it
wasn't for U sending your SON **BELOVED HOLY ONE** to help me on my (way) I would have
never known what to (say) so now I pray for (away)

          PROPHETS (LAW)   AMEN

PROPHETIC MESSAGE MINISTRY
    אמכּסמהּאורדא.

Dump Nigga (murder) another brother man.. *TIME TO TAKE A STAND..* Rollin with the
       FOCUS Consciences FOUND in the man.. SON of MAN mighty peeps standing strong..
At the time EVIL STATES was appalled CREATED DEVATED FALL.. the hoe that sit on

Many waters..   Dump Nigga FOLLOW (her) (claim) to (attain) EVIL STATES DREAM..
EVIL schemes of another lie.. *I SEE MY PEOPLE DIE..   I SEE MY PEOPLE CRY..*

                         SO WHY LIE.. BIBICAL Intellectual style..
PROCLAIM to MAINTAIN Profess in the NAME.. **YHWH OF HOST..** your peoples strong.
They will make (it) BLESSED with the WORD of your SON.. We can't fake (it) in the LIGHT
we make (it) GETTING GONE IN THE VALLEY OF THE DRY BONE.

       TIME IS OF THE ESSENCE.. Pleasant (words) strictly spoken like some cream..
YHWH IS GOOD.. Open up my (dream) minus the scan less (scheme) the Adversary
throwing darts HOT AS HELL, straight from HELL, looking like this NIGGA FELL..
            Dump Nigga (murder) another brother man..
                    TIME TO MAKE A STAND.. WALK Simplistically (SPOT) the
(PLOT) cuz U swell EDUCATED and (HOT) **BLESSED** if U see the Vision or the (Plot)

YHWH IS KING, MY PEOPLES STRONG.. Standing (tall) CHOSEN for the (call)
At the time EVIL STATES was Appalled looking for a (flaw) Chose *LIFE or DEATH..*
Understand **RIGHT or WRONG..** way of life everlasting life is what U seek..

            THIS IS WHY I SPEAK.. PREACH (BESIEGE) to (teach) the peep in the
SPIRIT AND THE TRUE.. DESOLATION OF ABOMINATION 3 ½ yrs Tribulation (end)
U Sin Sold to Captivity Tossed over to the younger brother (Ham) TURN OUT TO BE
PAN AMERICAN SLAVE TRADE scam on slave OBIST full of graves.. HALF OF MILLION

ISRAELITE babies (kids) laying dead in the JORDAN DEAD SOULS that was lost..
                         TIME TO MAKE A STAND..
Build on MESSIYAH ANOITED Stepping to the Quad building on the temple.. Simple minded
in the way of the word save your soul   ZECHARIYAH 14 : 16   MAKE A STAND..
                                        SCREEM..

YHWH OF HOST..   LETS MAKE A STAND..

                                        AMEN..

                    PROPHETIC MESSAGE MINISTRY
                         AMMISHADDAI
                            TRUE
                          BELIEVER

I could NEVER LOVE ANOTHER (after loving U)
                    YHWH I know you are SO GOOD TO ME..

YHWH your SPIRIT has put up on my heart to (flee) I know I left U born in SIN OF THIS WORLD.. Ain't PROUD TO BEG.. Ask forgiveness.. SAVE ME and MY GIRL..

FOR the wrongs (spoke) I got a LOVE (PITTED) DEEP in the ROOT of my heart..

For the SERVICE OF **YHWH**.. if I had to (cry) to keep U.. I can't (lie) I don't mind (WEEPING) on my knees (creeping) humble down OVERSTAND all around in the days of the

DARKNESS.. FAMAINES in the (air) people RUN TO and FRO in a (scare)   (dare)

To speak out against the wrong of (society) NIGGA'S consistently LIE TO ME..
                LORD, LORD but NIGGA we never knew U.. SENDING OUT SHOTS and CLUES to U..   LIVING (LIFE) serving **YHWH** staying TRUE to the MOSTHIGH..

REMINISION of some OLD DO'S pray for everybody (everyday) *THOUGHTS ON MY MIND.. LISTENING IS THE ART..*   YHWH I know U good to (me) YHWH SPIRIT has put on my heart to (flee)

    AMMI COME OUT OF HER, UNLESS U SHARE THE SIN..

(So) (if) it don't (LINE) UP with the WORD OF YHWH..
                    HOLLOR at (me) FORGIVE (me) FELLING IN MY ABBA'S WORD.. Misdeed (mistreat) the (GIRL) in a (world) of the sinful way..

ALL WAYS OPEN UP FOR SOME PRAISE.. Walking out the (daze) out the (maze) LEAD BY THE TRUE LIGHT.. Which is given LIGHT TO EVERYMAN COME in the WORLD..

        KINGDOM OF THE MOSTHIGH..   KINGDOM OF יהוה

REGARD(LESS) of what U (say) I spit this (way) **TRUTH and REALITY**.. REGARDLESS if U can't see.. BUILD ON **A SPIRITUAL** ear to hear what the SPIRIT of the PROPHET (say) So let US (pray) LEAD by the BRIGHTIER WAY..   IMMANUEL is who I FOLLOW every(day)
                IN THE KINGDOM OF יהוה ..

                                        AMEN

PROPHETIC MESSAGE MINISTRY
        AMMISHADDAI
            TRUE
                BELIEVER

U and I struggles in the LAND.. Bump and raise (to) UNDERSTAND.. YHWH coming BACK..
Straighten up your (act) before Satan slap U against your (back) with the RAPTURE
(Theory) False PROPHET led the way to (HELL) *DEATH* (SOEL) was the name..

CRADDLE TO THE CRAVE..   U and I Struggles in the GAME of LIFE..
Doing (right) I try to spit and PROPHECY to another if I (could) understand if U (would)

REGARDLESS of the STUPIDNESS that was (spit) (retain) maintain REALITY (man)
North country (man) couldn't (keep) Control (man) (keep) me down (man) (not) allow
my MIND..
(SET) UP TO (RECEIVE) THE (SPOT) OF THE WORLD.. Open up the SPIRIT to my Girl.

U and I Struggles in the LAND.. YHWH keep me (right) Straighten up my (path)
Show me (light) pray I'm (right) hyped ready for the (fight) *CREATED with the*
CONSCIENCE SAT AMONG the SEERS.. Erase the (FEARS) NO " MO " (tears)

I got JOY thru the Cloudy (trying) day. When the people (cold) in the LOVE LESS PLACE..
I (reside) keep it HUMBLE.. I got the MOST HIGH in the month of ABIB.. I HEAR U SAY..
What (could) make me feel this way.. Then I say.. My EL my EL ELSHADDAI EVER REIGN..

Over (fortune) or (fame) that U claim.. A NEW DAY IS DAWNING.. YAWNING..
   WAKING UP IN THE MORNING.. Birds No Longer Singing.. CONCRETE Jungles..
Let it (rain) ENDURE the (pain) EXSPLAIN the Word of the MOST HIGH.. Let the people
PRAY SUNSHINE BLUE SKY don't let it snow TAKE OFF (in) the winter (on) the HOLY DAY.

IMMANUEL WILL LEAD THE WAY.. With HIM GOES the Future Everlasting LIFE..

Take away the HURT that's INSIDE.. Wipe away TEARS from our (eyes) HEAR
BELIEVERS (Cries) EXSPOSED the (lies) PHILOSOPHIES of REALITIES
                                        the MOST HIGH IS THE TRUE WAY

REGARDLESS of what the NIGGA (say) Service to YHWH Manifest a brighter (day)
Can't (sway) with the WRONG.. PLEGDE ALLENGENCE to the WRONG..
                              LORDS and DISCIPLES
                                    BLOODS and CRIPS..
These would (be) days (long) gone UNIFIED THE STRUGGLES to UNITY for the (CALL)

UNITY U and I Struggles in the LAND..   YHWH IS COMING BACK..
                              Bump and Raise (to) UNDERSTAND.
                                          AMEN..

PROPHETIC MESSAGE MINISTRY
    AMMISHADDAI
        TRUE
        BELIEVER

The HE SAID to Me.. These are the WORDS *FAITHFUL and TRUE* YHWH OF HOST..
(Sent) the Angel to the SPIRIT of the PROPHET showing the SERVANT the things (to)
Shortly take (place) *BEHOLD IM COMING QWICKLY WITH REWARD..* According to
the work TRUTH ACCORDING to the WORD **IMMANUEL DIED FOR THE SINS..**

SOUL of the WORLD.. YHWH SO LOVE THE WORLD HE GAVE HIS HOLY ONE..
Blessed is the ONE.. Who KEEP the WORDS of the PROPHECY written in the BOOK..
BLESSED with the (hook) (shook) the world (industry) tight (ministry) ware is the
PROHET in the Land..

CREATE THE IMAGE.. CREATED IMAGE..

I'm working on my SECOND (JOINT) 4 POINTS of REVERANCE was my (point) 3 ½ YRS
I SPENT OUT (WEST) *YAH SPIRIT WAS THE (BEST)* UNIFIED STRUGGLES in the
city PREACHING (KING) is in the (land) TRUTH SOJOURNER in the (land) **RECEIVE
THE SON OF (MAN)** 3 ½ YRS (to) get thru to the (east) to THE TRUE (WAY) the
MOST HIGH (WAY) I thank the MOST HIGH (day) to (day) understand by the (way)
When can I GO.. When U see JUDAH in the streets of the HOOD SPEAKING (TEACHING)
What He should (rhymes) for EDUCATION spitting TRUE PROPHAGANDA **SPIRITUAL
SPEAKING** lyrical (teaching) with out the (slander)   U FOOL ONE..

U wouldn't FOOL US ALL.. QWEEN of the DAMED.. SLAMMED OFF the (wall)
Idle (fall) *TIME IS SHORT..* The KINGDOMS at HAND..   **CREATE THE IMAGE..**

Who is Unjust.. Let him be Unjust (still) deal who is Filthy.. Let him be Filthy (still)
Keep it (real) who is RIGHTEOUS let him be RIGHTEOUS (still) Build who is HOLY (still)
COMPASION(BLESS) bad boy (soul) caught up on death ROW Coming back for some MO
Why shed a (tear) why even (lie) why even cry UNDERSTANDING THOSE WHO PRACTICE
such things NEVER Shall inherit the EARTH.. *KINGDOM, KINGDOM OF THE MIGHTY
                                        MOST HIGH..*
(Scream) why Lie ELOHIM (EL) SHADDAI..   **CREATE THE IMAGE..**

(HATE) ENVY (JEAL'OUSY) is what I see in the game.. Could it (be) cuz I'm trying to
keep it (real) maintain to keep it (sane) in the game.. DON'T TAKE MY KINDNESS for the
WEEKNESS of the PUNK walk around with the FUNK in your (head) EVIL THOUGHTS ON
Your Mind to DO ME (WRONG) cuz I'm (strong) back in the game..   ALLOW NO (pain)
Gain My SOUL.. (To) keep it (real) (to) in (still) the MOST HIGH NAME.. (MENTEL)
RENEWING OF THE MIND.. Keep AWAY from the (STAIN) (SPOT) of the WORLD..

PLEASANT WORDS IS LIKE A HONEY COMB, SWEETNESS TO THE SOUL, HEALTH TO
THE BONE.. BREATHE (LIVE) come up (out) the VALLEY of the Dry Bone..

CREATE THE IMAGE.. CREATED IMAGE..

PROPHETIC MESSAGE MINISTRY   AMEN
     AMMISHADDAI
         TRUE
         BELIEVER

PSALM : SPEAK and PROPHESY   4/10/00

VALLEY OF A DRY BONE.. Provoke a (thought) SEERS (in) the land when I seen the
BEAST TAKE A HIT..   Mortal (wound) over time it was (healed) still it was file (hell)
FEAR (TERROR) Griped the Land.. SCRACTH the DOKATE.. And what I say.. PROVIDE
I'M WRONG.. STRONG (DEAD) or LONG GONE.. PICTURE (POSITION) PROCLAIMING

Instilling (proclamation) KEEP IT REAL.. " O " ISRAEL can U feel.. The Mad (Skill)
     When I (build) (in) the NAME.. (explain) for everyday when its real to DO THE RIGHT
(THANG) KEEP IT REAL (man) like a (sponge) socked up (man) THE WISDOM said
WORD was (fed) Knowledge (spread)

                         Understanding (comprehending) but (instead) **REPARATION
IS WHAT U OWE..** stepping to the plate.. Spiting to my foe.. BIG CITY HOE.. Sit on
many waters.. Listen to the ANGEL they will call (us) sit hear the FOUR ANGELS..

SPEAK IT PLAIN " YO " Peeping out the FOUR WINDS (WISDOM) SPEAK at every
corner (Bevakasha) Educate don't interpret thinking HATE.. Taking BATE.. FAKE..
                                        SMOKED OUT and HALF BAKED..
Say U warned (her) when really U scorned (her) set apart sanctified set yourself from
the (rest) slipping like the (best) BURN from the wicked (ways) TURN from the wicked
(ways) played my Homie like a Criminal for the (sin) he know.. REPENT did he (though)

          SPEAK and PROPHESY.. VALLEY OF A DRY BONE..

Do Him Right..   *YAH IS SAVIOR* Bailing out of jail (on) another (flavor) So let the
JUDGEMENT RULE ACCORD.. HUGE (to) MINUTE.. Fall of the IDLE Queen of the
Dammed.. To the POPE of all fake religion FALSE PROPHETS with the big money scheme
VISIONS of the HOLLYWOOD (Dream)   *I HAVE A DREAM.. I HAVE A DREAM..*

   ADVERSARY and His schemes TEMPTATIONS of a (man) (mad) thru lust of his dreams
(of) the FALSE RELIGION (PAGAN) FEAST and DIETY.. *LEGENDS and HEADLINERS..*
That I see.. On the real living LIFE out south in the Desert where the grass don't GROW..
Cries and screams of the NIGHT (speaking) BOLD story (told) PROPHECY (unfold)
(cold) (is) the thought of every man.. Let me pray for every (hand) to Understand..

          PROPHESY SON OF MAN..   SAY TO THE BREATH.. So spoke YHWH
COMING FROM THE FOUR WINDS.. " O " BREATH (BREATHE) ON the SLAIN.. That
they may LIVE in the NAME.. Of YHWH **NEVER DIE A SECOND DEATH..** Keep it (real)
Can U feel.. " O " ISRAEL (TRUTH) WE INSTILL.. Mighty YHWH (is) who we (build)
POWER TRULY KILL.. Knock the dirt (off) see him (floss) from the (locale) TALK
ABOUT MONEY IS A THANG.. DIRTY NIGGA GREEN.. (screams) of a mad man
SCANLESS dreams of the NIGHT..
     SPEAK and PROPHESY..   VALLEY OF A DRY BONE..   AWAKE AND LIVE..
                                                  AMEN

PROPHETIC MESSAGE MINISTRY
     AMMISHADDAI

PSALM : U BATTLE I BUILD.. 12/5/02

When Given Thanks we ought to GIVE THANKS to the MOSTHIGH all ways CONCERNING things of LIFE.. *RIGHT OR WRONG..* LONG GONE from the (wrong) pray every day.. GROW TREMENDUSLY thru the **FAITH.. YHWH BASE..** IMMANUEL plead my (case) lacking YAH I couldn't (do) what I (do) in the land of the LOST..

That I (do)

SALT OF THE EARTH..SEED (to) the dirt (endure) until the (end) we will all see YHWH (SAVE) U of the Kingdom of the MOSTHIGH.. Regarded WORTHY of the things (we) SUFFER don't BLUFF (her) AFFLICTING (AFFLICTION) what we (suffer) Until HE Come GLORIFY the HOLY ONE (admire) to (inspire) MOSTHIGH MessiYah BELIEVED to RECEIVE (Majure) in the SPIRIT Testimony of the MOSTHIGH Just like the days of NOAH were so shall the Coming of the SON of MAN (be) I tell U the MYSTERY of the WOMAN.. Beast which will carry her.. Having SEVEN HEADS ten HORNS (scorn) wicked ONE MYSTERY (BABYLON) present the (case) **HERE IS THE MIND HAVING WISDOM..** seven HEADS (translate) seven MOUNTAINS which the woman SIT UPON..

THESE WILL (BE) SEVEN KINGS.. FIVE have (fallen) ONE is (calling) SHOTS.. The other has yet to APPEAR ON THE SEEN.. MONEY GREEN.. When He Comes last for a little while.. (file) GOES FOURTH thru the Beast.. Become EIGHT SYSTEMS APART of the SEVEN (DESTRUCTION) in the land.. BLOOD IS THICK, HOMIE SICK, UNCLE JOE LOCK DOWN with the CLICK..

U BATTLE
I BUILD..

Who is WISE understanding (set) among U let Him (Hear) **SHOW BY THE CONDUCT..** Works that are DONE in the Meekness of (wisdom) but if U bitter SELF (SEEKING) ENVY in the heart. Don't BOAST and LIE AGAINST THE TRUTH (clue) to U the WISDOM that's NOT FOUND from ABOVE (its) earthly, sensual (demonic) cant get your HEAD OUT THE CRONIC.. Were the ENVY (self) SEEKING (exist) CONFUSION every EVIL thing (is) in the (mist) this will be the (Jist) of everything..

The PREACHER sought to FIND ACCEPTABLE WORD.. What was WRITTEN upright WORDS of TRUTH..

FEAR THE MOSTHIGH and KEEP HIS COMMANDMENTS..

Cuz this is Mans (all)

U BATTLE AND LET ME SIT AND BUILD..

AMEN

PROPHETIC MESSAGE MINISTRY
AMMISHADDAI
TRUE
BELIEVER

PSALM : YHWH OF HOST

YHWH OF HOST is who we (boast) the MOSTHIGH name, the ONLY ONE TRUE CREATOR Give HIM all the PRAISE to DAY and every DAY..

THE KINGDOM TRULY COME.. YOUR WILL BE DONE..

In Earth as it is in HEAVEN give us this day another day to make a better BRIGHTER

way..

SAVE US ALL FROM the (SIN) that truly overcome SOUL SPIRIT and MIND send your **HOLY BELOVED SON**.. BEGOTTEN TRUE ONE to overcome the SOUL in bodied in MIND drawing to SPIRIT of KIND.. In MEEKNESS (humble) U Shine. Lace a rhyme with a PROPHECY..

AS THE LIGHTING FLASHING FROM EAST FLASHING OVER TO THE WEST..

YHWH OF HOST IS WHO WE PRAISE.. A formal agreement with the

HOUSE " O " ISRAEL

6:31 the SUN Rise DAWN of the NEW DAY the MOSTHIGH 's (way) UNIFY the STRUGGLES thru out all the LAND.. From the US OF A to the EAST OF JAHRUSALEM.. Coming out to UNITE " O " YHWH EL OF HOST the KING is in the LAND.. YHWH EL OF HOST Experience the **SON OF MAN**.. COMPREHANDING RIGHT FROM WRONG..

So today even (PAIN) Misfortune or NO - FAME would make me wanna CLAIM my Life..

" O " YHWH send your SON *HOLY ONE IMMANUEL.. LION OF YAHUDAH..*

Forgiving all our SINS we FORGIVING all the DEBTS lead us NOT to Temptation..
But only lead us STAND BEFORE the ONE, before the mountain (call) to ZION the people don't BELIEVE think we LIEING so to day BELIEF in the COVERNANT ISRAELITE's truly LOVEING (it) FEARING YHWH keeping COMMANDMENTS.. Spotted from the World.. Watching on the BOX world News hazardous to the ELDERLY and the SICK. Death is in the air WAR IS EVERWHERE..   Fights over (Soil) Oil is the (Spoil) COWBOY Riders running thru the LAND ALLYBABUA thief's (fleas) from the LAND.. It will all only stand so LONG and then YHWH will then RETURN like a thief in the NIGHT..
Hyped ready to (Fight) lets do it right for the (night) SPEAKING PEACE reaching PEACE KNOWLEDGE increase the PEACE.. The meek seek the Face..

YHWH OF HOST.. ALFA OMEGA FIRST AND THE LAST..   YHWH OF HOST

EL OF THE TRIBE ISRAEL IS THE SEED THAT THE GENTLE GRAFTED TO.. Its apparent if U see.. With the SPIRITUAL eye to see.. The third eye OPEN to see.. (This) is how it be.. TIME is Short listen for (clue) stand (fast) keep it (real) then we (build) looking for (activity) *WISDOM BASED UPON THE MOSTHIGH*.. Open rebuke better then LOVE CONCEALED truthful (words) of a friend pray but don't (offend) U going to (win) IF U RIGHT.. From with (in) im sitting back watching BLOODSHED in my home (land) BUS

(blast)

TERROR couldn't (last) move your (ass) do the right (thang) to keep it REAL (man) Understand *YHWH OF HOST*..   IS who we BOAST.. (IN) Send the WORD to the TRIBES from (abroad)

YHWH OF HOST.. IS THE KING OF MOST..

PROPHETIC MESSAGE MINISTRY
    AMMISHADDAI   AMEN

PSALM : YOU HATE ME, CUZ YOU CAN'T HANDLE TRUE..

MURDER (MURDER) DEATH (BE) THE PENALTY.. Why (lie) why (cry) why shed a tear..
FEAR THE MOSTHIGH keeping **COMMANDMENTS** keep it (real) to instill the (real) *LIGHT*
SALT of the EARTH **BRINGING NEW (BIRTH)** before U face Judgment 6" feet under

(dirt) so why U (hurt) UNDER (SIN) HOW CAN U (win) if U ain't right from with (in)
Now U need to (send) SHOOTS OUT TO **THE MOSTHIGH** in the inner city.. **UNIFY
(UNITY) STRUGGLES IN THE HOOD,** struggles in the (land) so understand kicking
(sand) OPEN up the heart to receive (plan) survive wake him up to (recognize) (realize)
RUN AND RACE.. get the prize (size) of understanding its really what count.. BOUNCE
(BOUNCE) BOUNCE..

The way to (soul) if U wanna change your (ways) from the wicked (ways) turn from the
(ways) in the (days) before U burn from your wicked (ways) turn from your (ways) that U
keep (seek) SPEAK don't ever wanna change from the EVIL WAYS..

YOU HATE ME, CUZ YOU CAN'T HANDLE TRUE..

ADULTERY (ADULTERY) DEATH (BE) THE PENALTY.. HOW U (seek) to sleep around
with another (hoe) apart from your girl.. OPEN up the **SPIRIT to UNDERSTAND my
WORLD..** SPIRITUAL (insight) for the Mind.. Shine for a TIME and A TIMES half of a
TIME.. Stay away for the crime of the (world) spot the spirit of this (world) PRAYING for
my (girl) staying *TRUE to My Girl..* Sanctify the girl.. Not a squirrel trying to get a NUT..

In this (world) of Emotions (commotions) Promotions (*UNTOLD*) *STORY (UNFOLD)*
(*SOLD) My last sack of trees..*
Baby please.. Baby please.. I'm sorry for the (scare) I tell U true.. IM SITTING BACK
LISTENING TO THE DEMON.. Plotting (that) with out a (fact) BALD (HEAD) and slick
(back) EMPTY (HEAD) SMOKE a sherm stick and Get a (Gat) STUPIDNESS with all
(that) disrespect to the woman it's a (fact)

YOU HATE ME, CUZ YOU CAN'T HANDLE TRUE..

CALL ME (BLACK) I would have slapped U (back) but instead I pray for U before U
(dead) locked up or on the streets and wanna (beg)
Another (Ned) the wine " O " another (Ned) U dieing " YO "

DON'T HATE ME, CUZ YOU CAN'T HANDLE TRUE..

PROPHETIC MESSAGE MINISTRY
אממסההאדדא.
תר.
בלֵשׁרֻ   AMEN

PSALM : IT AIN'T NO LUCK   12/25/02

SOME WOULD CALL, IT A FLUKE.. But actually it's a blessing and its MEANT..
TIME is SHORT stand (fast) keep it (real) then we (build) to (instill) I'M walking
I'm (talking) I'm walking I'm (talking) *PROCLAIMING THE WORD.. AROUND THE*
WORLD.. WORD PLUS DEED GO HAND to HAND.. EXSPAND the (plan) KEEP IT PURE.
Undefiled before YHWH the good news truly been (pass) WORD deed of the day..

This is what give U the knowledge to see what U (see)

This is what give U the wisdom to be who U (be)

This is what give U understanding to comprehending to over standing how U (be)

NOW COME AND (SEE) the (mystery) remove your shoe (bow) down where U stand its
HOLY GROUND.. The fire (burns) sit at my feet and (learn) I reveal my plan.. While I tell
U who *I AM..* POETRY (POETRY) cast to the (sea) looking at the evil it had to (flee)
NEW SCHOOL SPIRITUAL is what it (be) I don't CAST PEARL before SWINE.. Looking at
me UP AND DOWN like I'm (crazy) cuz U (lazy) your lunatic couldn't faze (me) Didn't
take time to educate your (mind) to comprehend (prophecy) poetry in the (rhyme)
SIGNS OF THE TIME..

IT NO AIN'T (LUCK) *some called it a fluke..* But actually it's a blessing and its MEANT..
HEAVEN (SENT) FOLLOW *IMMANUEL FOLLOW WERE HE (WENT)* today's a good day
YAHWEH is in the (land) blessed every man (peace) to understand (peace) to receive
(peace) (to) comprehend (peace) to expand (peace) thru out the (land) But on the other
(hand) laying low in the belly of the beast triple 666 across the (mind) of the unknowing
NIGGA.. Over here NIGGA'S looking like a clown dressed up in all white call your self a pimp.
(refuse) to give *GLORY UP TO THE MOSTHIGH..*   Cry another (lie)

Claim to flip the negative to positive But the negative still out way the positive that's instill
in this X generation.. (federation) of (player hation) of the MOSTHIGH *TRUE LIGHT..*
GIVING LIGHT TO EVERY MAN COME INTO THE WORLD..

RECEIVE (ME) TAKE HEED TO (ME) BELIEVE (ME) YHWH HAS GIVE (ME)

Creativity.. U CALL IT LUCK.. SOME WOULD CALL IT A FLUKE..

But Actually it's a blessing and it's MEANT..
STAYING (BENT) with that week (weed) U smoking on HOUSE Nigga can U hear (me)

IT AIN'T LUCK.. IT'S A BLESSING and IT'S MEANT..

PROPHETIC MESSAGE MINISTRY
        AMMISHADDAI
            TRUE
        BELIEVER   AMEN..

258

The SUN IS SHINING.. YHWH is (blessing) my peoples waking up to (confession)
No more days setting up in (depression) (reminiscing) of the OLD WAY it's a NEW DAY..
YHWH IS (blessing) birds singing while the children playing all across the LAND ISRAEL is
saying.. YHWH IS OUR KING sing a NEW SONG.. Before the throne of the MOSTHIGH..

AS long as the rivers (flow) YAH LOVE me even " mo " (so) plant the SEEDS (in) the head
its time to (go) (slow) moving out (TIME) is of the (Essence) *TIME IS SHORT*..
Listen for (clue) stand fast keep it real then we (build) LOOKING FOR the (wisdom)
Based upon the MOSTHIGH open (rebuke) better then LOVE (concealed) TRUTHFUL
WORDS.. Of the (friend) pray we don't (offend) words could not explain YHWH (Reign)

Over (all) many (call) few are CHOSEN looking at the SLEEP NIGGA DOZEN.. (Posing)
Position for another VIDEO.. I was (blessed) the day U called me open up my THIRD eye
to see (blessed) the day I found U.. I build my world around U.. U took me (in) so I
wouldn't (SIN) This be the story of my people WORSHIP AT THE CHURCH (steeple) if I
die to (day) *ALL PRAISE GOING OUT TO YHWH*.. the MOSTHIGH in what I (say)

I'm at the (door) please let me (in) every night I'm on my KNEES and then I pray to
understand another (way) a BRIGHTIER (day) so to (day) *ALL IS WELL*.. Falling off the
path U get your Head to Swell.. LOCK UP with out (bail) segregation within the (jail) But
SPEAKING (EXSPLICT) SPECIFIC seeking and U (find) U would (shine) for a (time) to
OVERSTAND FOR THE MIND.. What's my (crime) cuz I tell U the TRUE..

GET " YO " MIRACLE IN IMMANUEL..

I'M TIRED OF DOING (WRONG) But see myself struggle for so (long) see I'm (gone)
Stubble TRIP while I (fall) YHWH (call) at the time I'm caught up in the (brawl) just
about to (maul) another NIGGA with the lip.. Two edge SWORD (LYRICIST) on the cord..
Helmet setting up on my head (SALVATION) with the sword of the spirit which would be
the WORD of the MOSTHIGH *(ELSHADDAI)* Everyday I wake up I couldn't (LIE) (CRIE)
I open up my mouth BOLDLY make known the MYSTERY of the MOSTHIGH..

Gospel of the MOSTHIGH become ambassador in the chains blowing up living in the belly of
the beast LAND OF THE NORTH.. Of course I look around the corner see another NIGGA
PAY THE COST dwelling in the land of the (lost) sitting to the left (imp) BE THE BOSS..
Checking out DEE MOSS..   See U too Keith closs .. *MAKE A CHOICE CHOSE LIFE OR
DEATH..*
GET THE MIRACLE.. GET " YO " MIRACLE.. IN IMMANUEL

AMEN..

PROPHETIC MESSAGE MINISTRY
    AMMISHADDAI
        TRUE
        BELIEVER

PSALM : FISHERMAN OF MEN

Ain't NO (name) ONLY (race) ONLY (nationality) I'm just the HEBREW ISRAELITE that can (see) CULTER IS WHAT IT (BE) what ever I do.. What can I give.. Wanna (praise) PROCLAIM (POSITIVE) in the NAME of YHWH.. *MAKE A CHOICE* walking in the SPIRIT (life) or (death) cliff my right hand through it in the (air) wave it to the WORRIES and (CARE) Nation Wide (SCARE) (DARE) to do the right (thang) (dare) to change (man) to KEEP it real (man)

FISHERMAN OF MAN..

FORGIVE me YHWH (for) everyday here's EVIL every where I (turn) another THUG NIGGA (BURN) walking in the SPIRIT (life) or (death) *BLOOD OF THE LAMB..* COVER U this would be the (clue) to U JOHN 3 and 16 couldn't be a (dream) REALITY blessed if U see (eternity) this is what it (be) *YHWH OWN THE LAND..*

YHWH CONTROL THE LAND.. BLESSED and PUT FORTH what was owed the (land) (expand) ABBA'S (plan) BLESSING going forth thru OUT the (land) *FISHERMAN OF MAN..* Those wit out (law) as wit the (law) NOT BEING wit the (law) toward the MOSTHIGH so under (law) *GRACE IN IMMANUEL..* I might win those who be wit out the (law) of the MOSTHIGH and to the (weak) I become (weak) understand WIN THE (WEAK) in (all) things I become (all)

FISHERMAN OF MAN..

What U going to (do) How U going to (do) BEGAN TO BE the power struggle in family (unit) bringing (confusion) to the members (for) in FACT the body is not (one) member but many (members) do U not understand that the body is the (member) of *MESSIYAH..* (keep) it higher to (admire) the MOSTHIGH MESSIYAH.. HOW SHALL I PROFIT U.. UNLESS I SPEAK TO U.. either by the (revelation) by the (knowledge) of the PROPHECY.. (teaching) and maybe (preaching) in the streets of the hood for the *KINGDOM OF THE MOSTHIGH* its (not) in word (but) in (power)

FISHERMAN OF MAN..

KNOW that the (law) of the MOSTHIGH its (all) GOOD (if) its used (lawfully) SPIRITUAL (explicitly) (speaks) Concerning LATTER TIMES.. SOME will DEPART from the FAITH.. Giving HEED to DECEIVING DOCTRINES (spirits) of the (demon) (scheming) (dreaming) SPEAKING LIES (hypocrisy) U can't fool ONE who can (read) (but) U can fool a whole NATION who can (not) ask the HEBREW man ship out into CAPTIVITY 1620 AMERICAN the (proud) and the (brave) UNDERSTAND *SALVATION IS ON THE LINE.. SALVATION BELONGS TO THE MOSTHIGH OUR EL (MIGHTY ONE)* who sits on the throne and to the LAMB (blessing) and the (glory) of the (wisdom) giving (thanks) to the (honor) and (power) of the MOSTHIGH forever and ever.. Who are (those) arrayed in white (robes) and where did they come from?"

FISHERMAN OF MEN..

The evening as the SUN was going (down) (found) a deep sleep fell upon (Abram) the (vision) (terrible) (foreboding) DARKNESS and HORROR of what YHWH was saying (to) (Abram) descendents shall be (oppressed) (stressed) enslaved in a foreign (land) (understand) 400 yrs (afterwards) I will punish the nation that enslaved your (seed) at the end (send) your (seed) away with the GREATWEALTH.. BELIEVE THAT.. RECEIVE THAT.. TAKEN HEED IN THAT.. *LET MY PEOPLE GO.. REPERATIONS IS WHAT U OWE..*

FISHERMAN OF MEN.. AMEN..

AMMISHADDAI PROPHETIC MESSAGE MINISTRY

I don't wanna GO the way of the (world) (no) understanding (no) light shinning (thru) out the darkness of the (land) FOUL CONVERSATION (IN) THE AIR (out) in the (land) (no) I don't want my credit clean (up) (EXSPANDING) another (lie) (cry) of another NIGGA'S (dream) (scheme) of another (lie) sip on my honey (tea) V.S.O.P. U talk about C G and ME chilling in the east of the (wood) but if I (could) I spit to U on the (real) quiet its (kept) I teach in (dept) instill the ABBA'S WORD (SWERVE) (CURVE) in him was the light that keep me right (blessed) in the sober mind to keep my young NIGGA'S HYPTED to do the (right) THANG.. Build the city MAN.. Of your forefathers (dream) before the *BEAST KILLED IT WIT A SCHEME..* Another DEAD nigga (dream) going straight to the gave.. But enslave the (mind)

SCIENCE FOR THE TIME.. BECOME THE CHOSEN SEED..
(BREED) of a new (day) a NEW (dawn) ABRAM IS FATHER (TO) MANY NATIONS.. Stopping all player (hat ions) (operations) of the KINGDOM THAT TRULY COME.. Braking down the races YHWH IS THE KING thru out the nations (so) ISRAEL its time to GO.. Lets pick it up MAKE A MOVE. To building the city (PROPHECY) *" O " SON OF MAN..* PLANT THE SEED.. *LIFE OF LIVING WATER..* Save your daughter.. BLEED to the NEXT generation (BLOOD) of the (LAMB) wash your robes white as it (be) CULTER IS WHAT I (SEE)

SCIENCE FOR THE TIME.. SCIENCE FOR A TIME..
TRUE (FOR) THE (MIND) Spirits for the (kind) open up ears for the (blind) open up the eyes for the (dump) give another brother last (crumb) don't take my KINDNESS for the WEAKNESS of being (dump) thinking like the scum of the earth.. NEW BIRTH.. Come into the (real) NO SWINE of ANYKIND..

SCIENCE FOR THE TIME..
OPEN UP YOUR MIND for my first (rhyme) blessed to perceive it was (windy) (inside) destitute and (empty) surrounded by the earthly (plenty) LISTEN to the REAL.. Only keep it REAL.. To instill the *HOLY SPIRIT* for the (kind) building on the city. U might call it HIP - HOP gritty CARPENTRY (it) ain't cidity.. Ain't no room for the (shady) *CAN DARKNESS COMMUNE WITH THE LIGHT???*   *" EM "* U (do) the figure.. But in the mean time I pray and teach to besiege the city in the MOSTHIGH WAY.. Regardless of what the world would say or even think DESTRUCTION (IS) ON THE WAY..   OPEN UP your (ears) OPEN UP your (fears) and here (to) what the seers would only say.. Latter times latter days U better pray..   U better Praise..

SCIENCE FOR THE TIME..
keep a grip on your (mind) right for the (kind)

AMEN

PROPHETIC MESSAGE MINISTRY
    AMMISHADDAI
        TRUE
        BELIEVER

PSALM : IT AIN'T EAZY

IF A household (is) WORTHY LET YOUR PEACE (COME) upon (it) (but) if its NOT let your PEACE (RETURN) BACK TO U. Who ever could NOT RECEIVE U Nor HEAR your WORDS, when U depart from that house (or) city.. (Shake) OFF THE DUST FROM YOUR FEET.. CREEP (KEEP) (IT) MOVEING.. CAN TWO WALK TOGETHER UNLESS AGGREED.. ?? OVER STAND to (DECREE) Going (fast) it wouldn't (last) Rolling (eye) 94 to the PIN.. WESTVILLE where I (transcend) CUZ MY NIGGA wore the blue (suit) NEVER THINK he's in choux with the NUT WHO RAN THE JOINT.. Down to make my point.. Hollowed on the MIC.. SHOULD HAVE KEPT (TEMPO) BASIC (SIMPLE) (WILD) EXTRA (NIMBLE) (ABLE) TO UNDERSTAND INTELECTUAL (SIMBLE) GET MY STYLE WILDING.. BLESSED with my (KIN) FOLK.. Simple getting (by) Being (sick) Do my (pit) (till) I (trip) (slip) and FALL.. WAKEING UP FOR THE CALL..

IT AIN'T EAZY

SO WHAT U WANNA DO? BAILING OUT OF JAIL, OR EVEN ON PAROLE, BAILING OUT OF HELL.. (NO) YOUR HEAD SWELL.. NIGGA'S NEVER WANNA FELL.. LEAVE U ONE CHOICE LIFE or DEATH.. LIVE AND FOLLOW (IMMANUEL) GO where the (LAMB) WOULD GO.. True teachings CAST AWAY DECIET.. FOUL CONVERSATIONS DEMONIC EXSPLOITATIONS YAH IS (REAL) YAH INSPIRED instill (position) im (Standing) CALLING ALL PEOPLE Spoken Word Of (Creator) psyfer who's GOD IS TRUE.. Boast put fourth to (be) CLUE.. **TRUE TEACHINGS CAST AWAY DECIET..** KEPT IN DESCREPT (led) out to LIVE LIFE QWUITE AS (EVER) SPIRIT and the MENTLE WAS (CLEAVER) But knowing the prize was to LIVE (FOREVER)

Never die a second death.. Live for (ever)BELIEVE THAT RECEIVE THAT..
SPOKEN WORD OF CREATOR..
don't worship creation.. But return give it up (praising) and (worship) in **CREATOR..** CUZ (YAH) HOLY SAVOIR.. <u>POSSED BY THE BRIGHTIER SIDE</u> I'm down for the (ride) (action) become (bold) BIBLE (INFORMATION) Become (told)

IT AIN'T EAZY

NEVER POST (BAIL) Holler if U hear ME (stop) the sale (outs) getting high (stop) the drinking of the 40's (stop) attending worthless functions and parties.. IF U (STRONG) ENOUGH U (MIGHT) LIVE LONG ENOUGH.. To see your seed building CONSTRUCTLY in time RIGHTEOUS found in your MIND showing SIGNS of distress (never) let it get the best (wasn't) long before we hit the rock (bottom) (REALITY) (VIEW) WHERE I (SEE) OPPRESS BY THE BEAST.. 666 USA its plain as (day) So how can I tell U the things of the SUPERNATRUAL if U can't believe the things of the NATRUAL.. But ACTUAL (NO) how to maintain more excellent MINISTRY thru the INDUSTRY thru the LORD YAHSHUAH.. A better MEDIATOR of A better COVERNENT established on A better type of PROMISE.. BLESSED TO (SEE) ANOTHER (DAY) A brightier (way) So today follow the LAMB ever (way) in any endeavor become cleaver.. OVERSTANDING the TRUE WAY to the KINGDOM the COMES.. <u>Starting here on earth</u> The Kingdom's At HAND do U understand comprehand BAILING out of JAIL (WORLD) OF CONFUSSION (MYSTERY) BABYLON..

(SODOMY) WORLD SOCIETY time and chance
IT AIN'T EAZY
Anoint the CROWD Anoint the CROWD MARCH THE PEOPLE OUT TO ZION and LEAD the mass of the people from LIEING (TIME) AND (CHANCE) KNOW ITS TIME TO (ADVANCE)

IT AIN'T EAZY
AMEN

PROPHETIC MESSAGE MINISTRY
AMMISHADDAI
TRUE
BELIEVER

PSALM : WHEN HE CALLS ON U

Just like the days OF NOAH (so) shall the coming OF THE SON OF MAN (BE) LIGHTINGS and FLASHINGS Of the (clouds) with the Darkness IN VARIOUS (PLACES) changing the (faces) of many (races) his-story (brought) out many (cases) WHEN HE CALLS ON U What U gonna (do) YET I SEE U IN SOME FLY - ISH get (to) slipping and falling tripping and flipping   TRANSFIGER ME to be (unbelievable) (unconceivable) but sometimes (overstandiable) but now (moms) coming with concern for the way to get this brother AWAKE.. QUAKE LIKE A SHAKE cast away the FAKE.. No (we) don't tell a (lie) satin loony tick (close) the doors (we) don't wanna enter (in) it ain't worth the (SIN) to have a thought to (bend) turn away (transgress) the LAW.. BOOK Of INSTRUCTIONS (Before) LIVING ETNERALLY.. Look if U can't (see) The Kingdom (Is) At Hand..

WHEN HE CALLS ON U.. What U gonna (do)

UNDERSTAND to OVERSTAND I thank MOM'S for the blessed YAH INSPIRED (seed) that She Plant (to) with (in) (before) I fall to the (weed) wormwood from (within) INSPIRATION To The MOSTHIGH. BELIEVED (IT) THRU (IMMANUEL) A brighter (day) A better (way) OVERSTAND (in) what I (say) comprehend more then what we (play) MAY-DAY, MAY-DAY Martyr falling victim to the crome. Like A gentile not down with the triple K PLAN.. Expand to OVERSTAND I Thank MOM'S For the Blessed YAH - INSPIRED (SEED) that She (sow) (plant) to with (in) WHEN HE CALLS ON U.. What U gonna (do) As the Lighting Flashes From the East Flashing to the WEST (so) shall the coming of the SON Of MAN (be) LIGHTINGS and FLASHINGS Of the (clouds) with the darkness in VARIOUS PLACES.. Changing the FACES.. Of many RACES. His-story brought forth many (cases) U looking to the EAST U looking to the WEST U looking to the SOUTH U looking to the NORTH its all Babylon and its DUE to FALL On Any Giving (day) what U gonna (do) WHEN HE CALLS ON U." What U gonna (do) U can call (it)

AMEN   TRINITY = DIVINE (SPIRIT)
PROPHETIC MESSAGE MINISTRY   TREE = NATURAL
                    TRINITY and TREE (its) the same (to) (me)

Therefore when U see ABOMINATION OF DESOLATION Spoken by the WORD OF PROPHET DANIEL standing in the HOLY PLACE.. Where it ought NOT (BE) Let him (see) he who (be) in YAHUDAH (Flee) to the mountains so I pray that your flight won't be on the WINTER WAY on the SABBATH DAY (IN) ANYDEAVOR now I'm (cleaver) CLOSE YOUR EYES (see) the Vision.. I'm on the HOUSE TOP not to go down and get nothing OUT THE HOUSE (SPOSE) in the field (don't) even go back to the HOUSE to get NO CLOTHES (woes) to those who are (pregnant) (Nursing) babies in these (days) **GAZE ANOTHER FAZE.. GREAT TRIBULATIONS** such as NEVER BEFORE. Never will (be) beginning of the world until this (time) nor shall it EVER (BE) Again (so) look around and expand UNLESS THE DAYS BECOME SHORT.. No flesh could be SAVED.. Blessed to ELECT in the days.

SIGN OF the TIMES.. SIGN OF the TIMES

MANY Coming in the NAME (claim) deceiving many while U hear of the WARS and RUMORS OF the WARS. So don't sit back and (be) DECIEVED Allow yourself to be (trouble) or (dismay) for the END has NOT YET even (been) **NATION rise up AGAISNT NATION** look and see FAMINES (PESTILENCE) and QUAKES in different PLACES.. All of this: began the time of (barrow) time of (sorrow) MANY be OFFENDED. Betraying ONE (ANOTHER) hate on ANOTHER.. FALSE PROPHET rising up everywhere DECIEVING (plenty) (many) LAWLESSNESS ABOUND like A clown LOVE OF MANY growing (cold) coming (bold) WHO ENDURES UNTIL THE END.. Shall be Saved. The GOOD NEWS OF the Kingdom OF the MOSTHIGH Preached in world. Thru out the COAST from the COAST to the LAND **HOLY LAND OF ISRAEL..** Like a testament heaven (sent)

SIGN OF the TIMES.. SIGN OF the TIMES

How long " O " YHWH can U forget ME How long will U hide your FACE from ME This be the case HOW LONG can I endure GRIEF in my SOUL (cold) sorrow in my heart day to (day) wonder what to (say) HOW LONG can My enemy (be) above (me) CONSIDER, HEAR (ME) " O " YHWH OF HOST open up my eyes UNLESS I SLEEP (DEEP) SLEEP to my death unless my enemy HAVE TO (SAY) WE PREVAIL those who trouble ME (rejoice) when I'm moved (cool) TRUSTED in the MERCY of your HEART. REJOICED IN THE SALVATION.. To the next (generation) (operations) OF the KINGDOM that COME. Sing the NEW SONG.. **IMMANUEL DEALT GOOD WITH (ME)** Demon had to Flee.

KINGDOM SEAL OF THE MOSTHIGH.. SIGN OF the TIMES.   AMEN
PROPHETIC MESSAGE MINISTRY

AMMISHADDAI

TRUE

BELIEVER

PSALM : YAHVDAH BOUND ISRAEL SOUND..

ONCE VPON A TIME V WAS TRAPED.. CHAIN AND V BOUND.. BLOWING VP

AT SOCIETY (STOP) getting high (KEEP) A SOBER eye before V BLACK ANOTHER

eye (MISORY) LOVES THE COMPANY (Shed) A (TEAR) MAKE V WANNA

(CRY) Much wisdom (begot) the GRIEF.. That V see that the FALSE PROPHET spit

DANGER (DANGER) OF THE HELL FIRE that (be) knowledge and the sorrow that V

(see) NIGGA MELTED ANOHTER NIGGA brother KILL another brother..

BLOOD BATH SLAVGHTER LIKE A CALF.

CVZ the brother (didn't) (believe) in the COVER (STORY) Of THE LAMB.. Another

Brother (give) HIS SOVL for the ATONE Of the (BOLD) SWEET SMELLING
SAVOIR (AROMA).

Rolled up (having) the STORY to (be) (told) We Are The TWELVE FAITHFVL
and (TRVE)

MVTIPLY IT COMING VP WITH THE ANSWER 144,000 (G) STANDING AT THE

MT CALLED OVT IN ZION.. YAHVDAH PRACTICE WHAT V PREACH.. SPEAK

WHAT V MEAN.. Not for the green (big) money scheme DREAM Of another mad

(man) living in AMERICA (keep) your head above the (sky) reqonized we couldn't

(lie) REGARDLESS (IN) WHAT V pay ATONE the (crowd) MOVE IT IN THE

MOSTHIGH (WAY) Rip this (crowd) like the phone number # (Covenant)

Simple and its Plain (MAINTAIN) the WORD and COMMAND comprehand listen

(in) what I'm (saying) IMMANVEL GENERATION FOR MANY NATIONS..

ABRAM (HE) GAVE THE PACT.. OATH IN YISAAC.. ESTABLISH THE STATVE

Down at the camp in YAHCOB.. OVER STAND YAHVDAH was HIS well.. From the

NATRVAL to the SVPERNATRVAL

ISRAEL BOVND.. YAHVDAH SOVND..   AMEN.
PROPHETIC MESSAGE MINISTRY
AMMISHADDAI

PSALMS : LIVE AMONG CAPITIVES.. 3/17/03

Lay back listen to INSPIRATIONS (INTERPRETATION) Of VISON.. I DIDN'T have time to play around FORGIVE (ME) sweet (pee) blunt brown (tee) TIME IS SHORT to argue (minor) Feast at the (dinner) Feast on SPOKEN WORD Of YAH.. " MO " concuss thought.. " MO " conciseness open up the (mind) 3 times a day SCIENCE FOR THE (TIMES) **LIVE AMONG THE CAPITIVES..** Receive a piece of (mind) This is how I pray. OUR FATHER led to the PROPHECY (SIN) Through out the world (Strategies) to transcend ME and MY GIRL.. FOREVER LIFE on EARTH Light shine in the DARK to server (world) lights to the (world) in the DARK. File NIGGA speech every where.. But the **TRUTH RUN AWAY DECIET..** Every where I (preach) (teach) through out the (land) from the EAST to the WEST to the SOUTH to the NORTH NIGGA what u know about the (creep)MENTAL deep move (move) in silence. I forgot all u know about is the HOE (DOPE) PEDLING (GUN) PUSHING (JOKE)In do time he's gone (DIE) or **LIVE IN (CAPTIVITY)** reminiscing of the (activity)

LIVE AMONG THE CAPITIVES.. LIVING IN CAPTIVITY

Sensitivity Of the MOSTHIGH give a NIGGA (grace) move step to your (space) open up to receive your (race) **SONS OF MEN..** Receive the common (true) REPARATIONS (REPATRON - NATION) is what u owe BLESSED u what u sow.. BLOW to the IDLE.. Stop having (mind) mental CLOUDY (smoky) smoking on the blunt every (day) owe the black man (as) much (as) the apology of FORGIVENESS Before u fall.. to the tricks of BABYLON **LIVE AMONG CAPTIVIES..** (TRAVELS) thru out the lands. (TRAVEL) thru the ghetto's of the C.H.I. To the ghetto's of N.Y.C. thru out the ghetto's of SOUTH CALLY story of redeemer **MOVED SPIRIT AS ONE** Fisher man of men.. (TRAVEL) the land in ONE ACCORD we (bless) to over stand to AMOS 3: 3 **TO WALK and AGREE..** Regardless of what the world would (see) we stand in **HOLY ONE..**

LIFE AMONG THE CAPTIVES.. AMEN

PROPHETIC MESSAGE MINISTRY
AMMISHADDAI

AMMISHADDAI

PSALM : YHWH IS BACK   4/10/03

Young baht asking can I pay a (bill) keep it (real) so I (will) if I'm blessed in the
(time) TRUTH ACCORDING to the (rhyme) not fallen for the (crime) RIGHTEOUS
imparted to the (mind) SUPPORT the BAHT and the righteous (kind) For a (time)
PROCLAIM THE TESTIMENT **YAHSAVIOR A NAZARITE** see me blast with the (plot)
I see u chilling at the (spot) a whole NEW HOP (got) time to march to JAHRUSALEM to a
better (spot) WAKE UP understand the (plot) 144 K standing everyday at the mount called
ZION.. I DIDN'T wanna see my Moms (crying) STANDING (STRUCK) STUCK in
tribulations END.. FAITH and BELIEF wouldn't (bend)

                              YHWH IS BACK   I can do construction with my
(mind) continually have a thought on the MOSTHIGH meditate in (time) through out the
day PRAISE u 3 times a day I (pray) to u consistently on my lips (LOVE) your kind
(love) neighbor as I (LOVE) My self HUMBLE SELF then u shine .. (SACRIFICE) for the
time.. OPEN up the (mind) for the righteousness imparted for the (kind) open the eyes to
the (blind) shine for a time. OPRESSED but now I'm FREE.. SPIRITUAL insight its what I
(see) ISRAELITE IS WHO I (BE) know the (race) know the (heritage) know the (land)
From where u came.. FREEDOM IS AT THE DOOR..

                          YHWH IS BACK..
Knock Knock who's (there) Babylon Babylon (MYSTERY) Babylon the hoe that sit on
many waters (DAUGHTERS) OF ISRAEL come out of her.. While its time don't   (receive)
the JUSTICE and the (plagues) of her SIN. EVIL CRIMES from (within) A legal way to
(sin) **AMERICA THE PROUD and BRAVE** We got the meeting out in ZION I ain't lying
to meet the LAMB on the day of HOLY PASSOVER (BLOSSOM'S) like a (clover) range -
rover OUT MY MIND.. A move - meant UNIVERSAL (WIDE) YHWH IS BACK..
COMMANDMENTS NATION (WIDE) FATHER (ABBA) (ABBA) PLEASE.. STOP the
PRIDE.. Of the nation headed to (perdiction) people (wishing) (false) prophesying and
lying to gain the (edge) DESOLENCE (THRU) (OUT) the PROVIDENCE. QUAKES IN
VARIOUS PLACES (SHAKING) the many faces of the (races) Demons having NO PLACE
to (go) if it (be) a difference I rather it (be) HIGH BLESSED with the SOBER eye CRY
why even LIE with the HOE shed a tear.. The adversaries crumble when u walking with the
MOSTHIGH proclaim (from) (coast) to (coast) WALKING IN THE SPIRIT.. (imperial)
spiritual life (that) was lead in MESSIYAH (Bled) to (need) plant the (seed) unify to YAH
(THE) NEW (BREED) Open the mind YHWH OF HOST is (Back) IN CASE u didn't hear
the first (time) YHWH IS BACK.. COMING in the second round HOLY Rapture to your
(mind) MOSTHIGH GLORYIEST 144 K standing at the mount called out in Zion young
Nigga ain't even lying BELIEVE this RECEIVE this EXEPT MESSIYAH u become SONS of
the MOSHT HIGH so its written : u all are gods.. In DO TIME if u (can) over stand in this.
Its time to (move) come together UNIFY those of the like (mind) RIGHTEOUS imparted for
the (time) all over world **GOODNEWS PREACH FOR THE TIME..** Science for the (kind)
MOVE ISRAEL back to AFRICA north (east) let US pray to the (east) any player - hation
would have to (cease) KNOWLEDGE will (increase) u wanna stay Live among BABYLON I
pray CUZ for ME and MINE ain't NO TIME time is short.. SO HOOK ME UP.. Reparations
is what u owe so give me minds and let me go and let my people go SO WHAT U WANNA
SEE (ME) better yet see my FATHER..   YHWH IS BACK.. YHWH IS BACK..
PROPHETIC MESSAGE MINISTRY   AMEN.

267

CAPERS WAS LAYING LOW.. In the south (bend) COMING OUT the PIN (N. W. I.) Ready to (boast) the (move) Clues (to) prove coming act yeah snatch yeah catch yeah BLACK AND HARD.. Blunt (tee) strong baht at U side.. Laying low with the HOLY VEIW.. Expect (with) Review. Unless U truly know (Channel) 56 promote THE WAY.. South Bend never (less) comprehend what U wanna (Spend) cash money (trend) don't (OFFEND) Spread deferent view. (clue) to what U (do) knowledge blessed to U house Nigga fail to (recognize) (trickonowlegie) that was used on the (G) Cuz for ME and MINE.. I couldn't see HOLDING FAST to the story (that) got U were U (be) FLEE FROM THE SINS. Getting ride of EVIL that dwell among U. Coming with the best for your (mind) (spirit) and the (soul) BOLD STORY TO BE TOLD.. In the spirit and the true GHOST OF THE MOSTHIGH.. ELSHADDAI why cry I cant lie (coconut) (blunt) choc alight (tee) U get the (best) of ME.. Blessed to understand to comprehend IN DUE TIME setting up as the black (man)

PROPHESY   PROPHECY
JOURNEY EAST THRU AFRICA JOURNEY EAST JOURNEY EAST

I'M (Gonna) TESTIFY (PROPHESY) TESTIFY all (night) if I'm gone (write) fight with the (mic) (if) (its) gone (glow) (flow) (if) its (tight) strike try to get it (right) PROHECY on the (mic) looking at my peep's (hype) to keep it REAL (to) instill in the streets of the city of the CAPTIVIY Remission of the ACTIVIY that happen to my people MIGHTY SHEM.. Listen Hamburger I see U coming out ON THE SAME SCAM.. DAMED clink clink (clang)(blam) (slam) Big House the SECOND CHANCE. Now U live (among) the WALKING DEAD but U ain't (scared) just wasting (time) in the penitentiary (HOUSE) up to the next century the NEW millennium 2 (G) make (atone) for the (wrong) PLUS AMENDS FOR YOUR SINS water down the valley the dry BONE. Belly of the beast to expand (community) OUT REACH GIVE AWAY OF THE WORD.. but understand if the WORDS that I spit or NOT plain or EVEN SOUND forgive ME READ to wake SELF up to be FOUND Qumran BIBLE TEXT see me (flex) was it all the same SIMPLE maybe plain. The word of the land understand that U can TURN TO CAPERS.. Not the crimes against MIND (soul) maybe yours BLESSED with the PROPHECY of the rhyme (shine) for the (time) SEMITIC SYLE OF RHYME PROPHETIC TYPE OF RHYME..
HOLYNESS imparted for the mind
JOURNEY EAST JOURNEY EAST THRU AFRICA JOURNEY EAST
AMEN..

COMMANDMENT KEEPERS
PROPHETIC MESSAGE MINISTRY
AMMISHADDAI
TRUE
BELIEVER

PSALM : SOUTH In The ALLEY   12/01/99

Out in Calley SOUTH in the alley " MO " was the (spot) know that its (hot) I'm sitting LOCKED UP doing (time) SPIRITUAL JAIL with out the BAIL never FAIL (Hell) prophecy from the (cell) locked up chain but NOT BOND. Stuck in the belly of DECAY 666 U. S. A. what the people PROPHESY today (maintain) to kick the GOOD (NEWS) through out the land all abound HIT HIM UP all around (the) silly NIGGA (took) me for a clown.. *S. I. A. South In The Alley MORENO*

VALLEY..

I Learned the (everlasting) forever LIFE TRUE.. *IMMANUEL DIED FOR YOUR SINS BURIED ROSE AGAIN ON THE 3rd DAY..* Over stand in what I (say)but in any (endeavor) increase (to) become cleaver COMPARE to COMPREHEND for what (ever) KNOWLEDGE FOREVER.. Never lie in the (dark) Never cast (pearl) before (swine) if its NOT in the MOSTHIGH (time) *BLESSED WITH THE PROPHECY IN THE RYHME..* I couldn't allow myself the BLESSING (to) within to (be) TAKING OUT Miger Evers I pray for U FORGIVE ME and the Mother COVER LOVES the multitude of sins Massing TRU the S. C.

SOUTH In The Alley In The valley..

GO to the VALLEY. Never Fell (Hell) PROPHECY from the (cell) Nine (9) ' O CHARLIE WINTER I see U dressed up in all WHITE looking (PALE) like the demon who sit back and try to get the (SALE) endorse meant enforcement UNDERNIETH voters registration (bell) never COUNT the vote its never really meant (to) allow the people to get the (say) sway away crooked (cone) minister set up like the (pone) CASH MONEY MAKING BOND Of the beast swith in the mind false prophets and false prophecy FAKE RELIGIONS in the Valley Saying in the name of the lord but the LORD never knew him. Doing time out in SOUTH CALLEY watching all the NATIONS join to gather at the sight called in HEBREW ARMAGEDDON: Do U wanna battle (build) on the intellectual (mind) shining for a (time) SETTING UP THE BANNER (ISRAEL) follow IMMNAUEL and U never will (FELL) Dump NIGGA at Apollo SABBATH night can U FOLLOW twisted in the (plot) (not) half of the city lead captivity or DEAD mentally reminiscing of the (activity) look and see this is how it (be) separate your selves from the EVIL that DWELL among U.. Cut Him Off from the City. Eye looking with (pity) doing time out in CALLEY.. *SOUTH In The ALLEY..* " MO " was (the) VALLEY. Hell Prophecy from the Cell. *S. I. A.* Out In The valley

SOUTH In The ALLEY   AMEN..

AMMISHADDAI   COMMANDMENT KEEPERS..

269

I will rather cry to the MOSTHIGH then (lie) or even (die) see your Momma (cry) Sadducee ask (why) **DEATH HAPPEN TO THE GOOD MAN..** All things happen for the (reason) of the GOOD to the MOSTHIGH Bumping east Pomona 60 Indio (so) now U know (we) on the GO.. Mirror Mirror On the WALL waking up to the early morning SUN RISE. (Yarning) at 4 in the (morning) MOSTHIGH breath the breathe of LIFE in (me) GUILD ME (to) the crossroads of the UNDERGROUND (sound) STYLELISTIC slipping dipping (down) to the EASTSIDE back to the hood EAST of the GLEN Gary IN 32 ave brought HERE to define Cuz I knew.. Laying down My (gat) for a time and times and half a time. So as the LIGHTING STRIKE from the east flashing to the west SO shall the coming of the SON OF MAN (be) for a time and times and half a time..

We would spit (kick) bend (spend) send MONEY MOVE (TREND) 50/50/10 Never X what I mean when U see the Young Blood stepping out on the seen. Money green FEAST with the (word) set apart from the (rest) **WORD MAN OF YAH,** in the streets (Ghetto's) of the (hood) spitting to another what HE (could) Manifest for the **CALL.. PROCLAIMATION..** in the Natural to the Supernatural (actual) **BOOK OF Instruction BEFORE LIFE eternal..** Could U even (see) the KINGDOM truly at Hand did WE really OVERSTAND come in to the PEACE **ISURAEL..** So let US have fun dealing with the SON.   **IMMANUEL IMMANUEL**

                                                   CRY, LIE or DIE..

What U wanna (do) CHOICE Life or Death. We thank the MOSTHIGH for being **MERCIFUL** and everlasting **LOVE** for My people your MERCY forever last (forgive) ME my SINS (forgive) the forefathers SINS thank U for the **HOPE** of the Reparations toward your TEMPLE. Keep it Simple.. The Holy City and the Holy Mountain thanking U for the HOPE and (all) Salvation (foundation) OVERSTANDING in your will (to) instill **TESTIMENT** to Belief in **MESSIYAH** thank U for the HOPE IN ALL..   **IMMANUEL IMMANUEL**

                              YAH IS WITH US.. YAH IS WITH US
             CHOOSE Life or Death??   **CRY, LIE or DIE..**

PROPHETIC MESSAGE MINISTRY
        AMMISHADDAI
        TRUE
        BELIEVER

UNDERSTAND U ain't got (me) U don't own (me) CONTROL and CLOCK (me) HEBREWS Flock with (me) Cuz I'm (free) never stuck to this world (mentality) (actually) spot is what it (be) reputation **MORAL and DECAY** when U see the (Clampet) on the Mic **EVIL THOUGHTS..** Hyped the **GOAT NIGGA** on the left all the way gone NIGGA have baked NIGGA dead and wrong NIGGA beyond My own (SIN) NIGGA how can U win if U ain't Wright from with (in) don't bend the TRUE.. Let US pray everyday. REPENT: NO it ain't NO Heaven for a (G) Receive (me) Believe (me) Forgive (me) for My way YHWH SAVE the SOUL. Blessed in the blood (woe) to those (who) won't make the change to the GOOD..

> **DEATH (be) the PENAITY**
> **DEATH (is) the PENAITY**

Bomb on the W. T. C. Spill over flow to the (real) can U feel O ISRAEL Turn from the wicked (ways) or burn from the wicked (ways) Evil (ness) scorched in the (days) can U fill the **MOSTHIGH SPIRIT IN THE AIR..** Exercise the (mind) writing (rhymes) PROPHESY for a (times) the blind man (see) the death man (hear) the dump (speak) creep thru the hood **LIVE and never DIE A SECOND DEATH..** forever life. Living CLEAVOR (forever) I rather lose loose a friend then loose My FREEDOM to the man. SIN from with (in) OVERSHADOW GOOD that will (be) shining (showing) fourth (in) POETIC JUSTICE.. Every Soul that (SIN) will surely (die) **DEATH PENAITY   DEATH (be) PENAITY..** (no) ADULTERY (no) FORNICATION (no) SODOMITE foolish talking (jesting) OBSCENITY SEX IMMORAL (whoever) LOVES to make the (LIE) Any unclean (who) lives the life like the (dog) Living in the (smog) EVIL THOUGHTS (no) THIEVES (no) DRUNKS (revilers) GREEDY people AND THOSE who practice WICTHCRAFT..   Art of another (el) will NEVER enter in the GATES *KINGDOM OF THE MOSTHIGH:* IS U RAEL (EL) sent the **PENAITY**

> **DEATH PENAITY**
> **DEATH (be) the PENAITY**

Except MESSIYAH and U live..   AMEN.

PROPHETIC MESSAGE MINISTRY
אממסהאדדא ָניאב יאהָדאה

Waking UP early in the morning (yarning) 4:00 in the morning truly really know the **MOSTHIGH GOT ME ON MY COURSE.** To the CROSS ROADS to the UNDERGROUND. Stepping out on the STYLISTIC type of sound. BLESSED and I'm HEAVEN BOND knowing how to maintain a more excellent (ministry) thru the (industry) the **PRINCE YAHSAVIOR A better Mediator..** Of a better COVERANT establish on a better PROMISE time to EXSPOSE the key. Except the BOYZ creativity LISTEN TO THE PLEA.. East of the Glen Gary IN this is how it (be)

 SPEAK and PROPHECY (SPEAK) and PROPHECY (SEEK) U shall FIND..

Teacher Teach (Her) teacher LOOK around see we need the biblical FEACHER intellectual STYLE of (speaker) plant the seed to seek (her) coming (meeker) extra (deeper) **GRACE TO KEEP (HER)** (Preacher) turn to my brothers (keeper) hit me (up) on the pager (up) (beeper) seen U steeper in the RUTE that got U were U (be) forgot about the PRAY every (day) how to (pray) when to (pray) NOW ITS JUDGEMENT DAY.. Looking at U dark and CONDEMED by your own (way) listen to what the MOSTHIGH had to (say) repent repent falling on your knees begging FATHER ABBA please ABBA please.. **FORGIVE (ME) (IN) MY WAY..** Turn me to the NEW WAY.. Bless me to the BRIGHTIER WAY.. In MESSIYAH (walking) in the better (day) so to (day)

 SPEAK and PROPHECY (SPEAK) and PROPHECY..

From the NATRUAL to the SUPERNATRUAL (actual)manifest for the (call) prepping for the COMING while I strike (back) fight (back) to get the streets (fat) On (the) intellectual style of (track) I'm BLACK and COMELY.. U can't debate ME. **YAHS KNOWLEDGE OUT SHINE ALL..** program so call universal college. U wanna (be) FREE come on (be) FREE in the WORD. I can NO longer (be) beneath the shadow that would keep me wrong for so long.. NOW I START to get the Spirit that would keep me strong.. Plus NIGGAS cant trust NIGGAS cuz NIGGAS was NIGGAS lust NIGGAS bust NIGGAS using IDLE (time) for the CRIME. Each one of US have a song (teaching) and the (tongue) revelation to (interpretation) let it be done to (edification) building up to the SON busting out with the GUN shoots to the GOOD NEWS of YHWH. With the **SWITH and MIGHTY HAND..** (mind) (spirit) (soul) PRINCE IMMANUEL came with the story to (be) TOLD. Crucified died buried and HE rose AGAIN on the 3rd Day. Ascended back to the heavens in the (day)

 SPEAK and PROPHECY.. SPEAK to PROPHECY.. SEEK to PROPHECY

                                                    AMEN.

PROPHETIC MESSAGE MINSTRY
אממסהאדאבבאיניאהדאה

PSALM : HAPPY ABBA'S DAY   5/16/03

I'm going to (spit) to u any (way) REGARDLESS of the people
(say) I here u (say) at the park SPARK the fire of the WORD.. Swerve
curve (serve) on SABBATH.. I hear u holler **MIGHTY WORD OF
TRUE..** Moral decay and Evil thought (Rules) school don't cast Jews
before Swine (fools) despise being (blind) SIGN OF THE TIME. They
would (hear) (those) of the MOSTHIGH on the 7th and HOLY DAY OF
YAH.. Heal (her) before She kill (her) TUPAC went out like the (thriller)
LOST LENGENDS of manila instill in (her) the REALER.. **LOVE OF
the MOSTHIGH..** How to save the SOUL. **IS URAEL** Cuz if u are?
BELIEVE This.. Join in and SECURE your LIFE in the MOSTHIGH
never losing (life) from the cradle to NEW LIFE. *RIGHTOUESS and
RIGHT (LAYING) WASTE..* To the Idle and HIGH (Place) to the
PUNK (itch) NIGGA (witch) NIGGA and the FILE (trigger) NIGGA
(STOP) what u doing and change your (way) before u burn from
wicked (way) Cuz to (day) we enter (in) the 7th HOLY DAY..

HAPPY ABBA'S DAY.. Inter (in) the KINGDOM of the MOSTHIGH
UNIVERSAL and NATION WIDE **ABBA'S DAY.** HAPPY ABBA'S DAY
bailing out of jail (veil) reveal (from) my eyes I can (see) If a house hold
(its) worthy of the (peace) let it (set) but if its (not) worthy let your
(peace) return (back) (to) u (who) ever NOT RECEIVE u or hear your
WORDS (depart) from the house and the city (shaking) (off) the dust
from your feet (can) two walk to (together) and NOT AGGREE??
(Over stand) (to) degree I will Worship MOSTHIGH in the SPIRIT and
the TRUE (let) (traditions) DIE ALONE with fake (belief) Of Religion
O. G. Pharisee (Sadducee) condemning (smoking) (weed) won't
PREACH and TEACH (speak) each man the (true) to his neighbor giving
JUDGEMENT in the (gate) of TRUE (Justus) and Peace.
                                    HAPPY ABBA'S DAY

HOLY 7TH DAY WORSHIP IN THE RIGHT WAY.. YHWH.
                                    AMEN..

PROPHETIC MESSAGE MINISTRY
יאהדאה באינ אממסהאדדא.

PSALM : SLAVE (FLESH) Of the MIND..   5/19/03

Its NIGGAS that say (they) with u (but) in reality they NEVER
SHOW UP.. But in (actuality) these NIGGAS never was down (for) the
POSITIVE (ish) quick to sway (feet) running to the EVIL (in) the mist
of (decay) (all) ways spiting DEATH from the CRADLE to the
(Grave) SLAVE FLESH Of the MIND.. u (want) yours (in) the (hear)
and the (now) NO (time) for NO FAITH only BELIEVE (if) its (seen)
MONEY GREEN.. I pray for u bro (man) (legions) on your (back) hoped
(in) took over your (game) INSANE mind playing tricks on u.. doing
(crack) looking crazy (lazy) to affairs wanna eat (but)
NOT WORK.. Lay around at the Momma house being broke lay around
your Homies house doing DIRT (DEATH) around the corner (YAH)
SENT ME to warn u   This is a Creation of your own MARKET YAH
willing Cuz we chilling instilling the (real) of the (true) with the
SPICE of the SPIRIT (kill) (it) YHWH IS KING (star) at Bethlehem
(land) of Africa young Nigga (we) headed back regardless of what u
(do) **PEACE (TRUE) To u..**   Babylon (Babylon) big city (HOE)
Has falling (listening) to the MOSTHIGH has (calling) LAMB (has)
return shake the (spot) Cuz it (hot) the ADVERSARY raging (wars)
rumors of (wars)   HERE and (THERE) Money (scare) big corporate
fake and shake the slave man telling once upon a time ago he (be) a cave
(man) NEW WORLD ORDER (now) he rules the (world) Shining shores
To triple lee   *SLAVE (FLESH) Of the MIND..*

ROY and Remi pulling up (thru) the hood SMOKE A BLUNT
sticky (icky) testify of the MOSTHIGH Regardless of what u say at the
park (spark) the fire of the (word) in him was the LIFE giving LIGHT
to everyman come to the world NO I'm NOT A MUSLIM.. Here to Make a
Change (none) denomination **TRUE BELIEVER** Receive (her) at the
PENTECOST (took) belief in (her) taken heed in (her) be the seed in (her)
ROY and Remi massing thru the (hood) (smoke) a blunt sticky (icky)
testify in the (true) (Metaphor) hitting at your (door) rightly DIVIDE
word of TRUE. (1) from a house (2) from a city (pray) the
MOSTHIGH (look) (upon) these people showing (pity) (burning) from
the wicked (ways) turning from the wicked (ways)
                SLAVE (FLESH) Of the MIND..   AMEN.

AMMISHADDAI   PROPHETIC MESSAGE MINISTRY

REVELATIONS Of יהוה (Be) about my ABBA'S business.. The law of YHWH is (perfect) restoring the (soul) testimonies of (old) bold YHWH is (sure) making (wise) the simple (statues) Of YHWH are (right) rejoicing to the heart.. COMMANDMENTS Of YHWH (its) pure and its good (Enlighten) to the eyes the FEAR Of the MOSTHIGH it was clean enduring to the end.. *FOREVER JUDGEMENT Of THE MOSTHIGH (IS) TRUE..* (Righteous) more desired then the gold (yea) much MORE then the FINE, BLING (BLING) AMERICAN DREAM. Sweeter then honey and the honey comb sorter (speak) sorter (say) beseech to teach (servant) to be warned. Keeping these be the GREAT REWARD.. Who can over stand in his own ERROR ?? CLEANSE ME FROM the secret (faults) KEEP ME back from sins from with (in) let it NOT have DOMINON over ME let Me talk around *BLAME (LESS)* let Me walk around *BLAME (LESS)* shame - less (innocent) of the great (SIN) let the words of the mouth meditate on the MOSTHIGH.. Be acceptable in YAH sight YHWH is my (strength) and (redeemer) REVELATIONS Of YHWH. The MOSTHIGH Is My LOVE..

The MOSTHIGH Is My LOVE..

YAHSAVIOR (is) alive and well..   Tell everybody that u see.. SPIT (IT) FOR ME.. YAHSAVIOR (Is) alive and well.. the adversary took my SAVIOR murdered him on the CROSS. Satan dance (around) Evil grin on his (thought) he had the children Of ISRAEL throne and authority   (but) in the 3rd (day) the stone was rolled (away) leaving Satan speech - less (nothing) more to (say) men of HONOR Angles told Mary *GO and TELL the SON Of YAH..* has risen MERCY to the WORLD who believe. And receive YAHSAVIOR (is) alive and well.. If I'm gone (be) out there. I'm gone (be) on the show. (flow) about My ABBA'S business. Supreme (wisdom) in the (vision) my flow don't give me no (rhyme) (explicit) (perpetuate) (evil) (up) heval the TRUE. (If) I'm feeling (it) (I'll) let u know (If) I feeling (it) the beat going with the flow IMAGE life going (slow) (but) its cut (short) going fast looking out the window NIGGA'S TREEDING DIRT.. With out the thought on the mind.. *DO U WANNA LIVE Or DIE.. DO U WANNA LIVE Or DIE ??*

The MOSTHIGH Is My LOVE..   AMEN

I have seen with out REASON or DOUBT My life is worthless (use-less) with out supreme (guidance) to acknowledge the MOSTHIGH (presence) Its 8:00 pm I hit the party (slow) getting on the (seen) money (green)Look around (see) the dump NIGGA (scheme)
    ask the lady ??

    Would she die or lie for him asking 21 unnecessary questions.. NO CONCULIOSION to SULLUTIONS to what u spit or DO or PRACTICE in the (hood) *DEATH IS AT THE DOOR..* So raise UP or blaze UP if u have (to) To be at PEACE AMONG your (people) later for the church (steeple) its NATION TIME AMONG my (people) PEACE SPOKEN THRU THE RHYME.. Science for the time WORSHIP IN THE SPIRIT OF THE (TRUE) Regardless if u party (or) go to Church KEEP it REAL (then) instill the (true) Of what we (do) to NEVER DIE.. EVERLASTING LIFE.. So what's the problem (for) the NIGGA'S SPITING (REAL) LOOKING ON THE (BOX) M T V (big) time big city C E O (pimp) the little man in his (way) OBSERVED (IT) then I seen (it) in the Group Home (to) the Making Of the Band.. Fake ass NIGGA run the (land) I couldn't understand. What u do (why) u do (how) u do (when) u do (what) u do (with) the youth *SOUL BLESSED RIGHTEOUS MOLD..* The world was (cold) in its thought.

    u still TALKING and u SPITING like that..
    Can u feel the (skill) on how we (build) I'm accused of doing wrong or being wrong STUPID sometimes HEAD STRONG.. FEAST DAYS over birth (days) tradition never counted worth (days) To Me!! Setting back spending hurt (days) Cuz I understood (but) u wouldn't.. LOOK Around kicked it in the broke (days) had to let alone smoke (days) PRAISE the MOSTHIGH in many (ways) articulate the MOSTHIGH (love) walk around in the TRUE (WAYS) demon (ticks) couldn't (faze) when we (praise)(Son) Of (praise) *BLESSED TO MANY (DAYS)* SPIRITUAL in what I (do) *WORD OF YAH !!*
        IN WHO WE TRUST..
    u still TALKING and u SPITING like that..   AMEN.

אממסהאדדא .באינ יאהדאה   PROPHETIC MESSAGE MINISTRY

The MOSTHIGH IS MY LOVE. As long as I (live) or die I will serve U giving (clue) to the symbol of the <u>END OF TIME</u>.. Summer's near (hear) the (fear) **WORD OF the ABBA** Generation of the Fig tree.. Wake up pray to see HE who (be) in YAHUDAH (FLEE) to the mountains preach and teach to your (peeps) (pray) its not on Sabbath (rolling) out on the winter (day) or the holy (day) but WOE to those who (be) Nursing babies in the (day) IF U out on top.. Don't (go) (down) to get NOTHING OUT.. House or the box. (PLOTS) of another way (lean) to your own over standing (house) of the wicked (overthrown) but the tents of the (upright) (blessed) forever life. **NEVER DIE.. FROM THE CRADDLE (TO) EVER LIFE..** The way (seems) (right) (tight) to a man but its (end) lead the way of death (captivity) DEATH to the MIND.. I won't (lie) I tell U the (true) I proclaim the MOSTHIGH unto U..

The MOSTHIGH Is My LOVE..

YHWH is good to (me) YHWH is good to (see) YHWH is good in whom HE (be) (stretch) out (swith) in mighty hand. To expand the Good NEWS Of the coming of the SON OF MAN (lamb) of YHWH (Loin) Of JAHUDAH *FLASHING FROM The (EAST) FLASHING To the (WEST)* YHWH'S CULTER is the (best) abiding in the shadows of the MOSTHIGH. Rarely find yourself CAUGHT UP in the (mess) TROUBLES OF THE WORLDS.. Minus (stress) <u>Can two walk together and NOT AGGREE</u>?? Check your guest (confess) can (light) commune with (dark - ness) U (do) the figure (hit) me back with (degree) the best in what U (see) CUZ for (ME) sanctified set apart from the rest (blessed) (brothers) come to gather (dwell) in UNITY. But the (world) couldn't (see) (NO) THOUGHT UPON the MIND. (NO) love (lost) love - less society pay the (cost) to covet and try to (floss) I pray for (we) we won't lie I tell U the true I proclaim to the MOSTHIGH <u>the MOSTHIGH Is My LOVE</u>.. **IMAGE Of MESSIYAH** I thank the MOSTHIGH (I'm) shadow man in the (back) setting in the (corner) watching cover over Angels SAINTS in the MOSTHIGH Legends of HOLYONES shadows of 144 (K) stepping (out) in the (day) of the WORD on the (way) (edify) in the (day) in **RETURN OF IMMANUEL.. LION OF JAHUDAH..**
PROPHETIC MESSAGE MINISTRY   AMEN..

COMMANDMENT KEEPERS

On the (real) we instill what is (real) *PROPHECY* thru the (skill) to keep it (real) to try to (build) <u>community</u> (fellowship) how good it is to dwell in unity. Manifestations is what I (feel) now I spit nothing but the (real) but can u (feel) fake-tissue put me down to be killed *ALTERS* and *HIGH PLACES*.. throwing (down) u quick to (clown) stand around.. with your mouth shut. While the ***SPOKEN WORD OF YAH*** (expound)

SET THE RECORD STRAIGHT..

Ain't got no time to set around and (clown) time is short (why) gain the whole (world) and lose your (soul) BOLD lean to your own understanding ** WRONG ** u find yourself DEAD and GONE. Didn't make (it) to praise the MOSTHIGH and WORSHIP YAH on the 30th birthday. Is it worth day so why lie why cry why even care about the meaning - less (ish) that u do. CHANGE your WAYS before u BURN from the WICKED WAYS.. Become (concern) (turn) to the PRAISE.. Of CREATOR (ANCIENT) Of DAYS.. Study the Prophets WAYS. Find yourself <u>on your knees 3 times a day</u> PRAYING consistently (as) u swacker in your (way) regard - less Of what this NIGGA had to (say) ***WE GONE STOP..***

AND GET THE RECORDS STRAIGHT.. Who u with ??

I knew a man born of a (Hoe) not knowing which way to (go) not knowing what he (do) Wanna do (right) weak in his (fight) KNOWLEDGE Is the major reason my people PERISH. In this crooked (dirty) game.. Nigga's getting locked (up) turned insane..

Nigga's getting locked (up) turned insane..

It's a CRUEL and HARSE (World) continually lie to me. (steal) from another. (LOVE) (LESS) way of life (society) running doing Evil. Life long brother (in) (the) struggle do me (wrong) living life in the (dark) crooked as it (be) I was blessed (wake) (up) another day (to) (see) what it (be) (he) didn't know how to love another. So what gave u (reason) (think) (he) know how to love his mother.. CAIN MURDERED HIS BROTHER !!

(SPARK) the fire..

SPIRIT Of the WORD..

GET THE RECORDS STRAIGHT.. Chose LIFE or DEATH.. WHO U WITH ??
SELAH : its Nigga's that say they with u but in reality they never show up..

But in actuality these Nigga's never was down for NO Positive (ish) from the start.

Feet quick swaying to do EVIL.. Enter the mist Of decay (death) is knocking at the door. REPENT and FOLLOW IMMANUEL; in the ways of (true) YHWH So loved the (world) HE gave his HOLY BEGOTTEN SON.. I LOVE my family YISRAEL and the CHURCH "

GET THE RECORD STRAIGHT.. Let the records be (known)   AMEN..

COMMANDMENT KEEPERS
PROPHETIC MESSAGE MINISTRY
AMMISHADDAI
TRUE
BELIEVER

PSALM : PROPHESY to the BREATH,
PROPHESY SON Of man..

SAY to the BREATH, (thus) say YHWH MIGHTY ONE : <u>come from the four winds</u> ..O BREATH, (BREATHE) on the slain, that they may LIVE in the Name. Prophesy and (say) to MY PEOPLE. (thus) say YHWH MIGHTY ONE.. I will (open) up your graves. (Free) your mind from the (slave) come up from the (grave) BRING u to the LAND.. IS (u) REAL : FOLLOW IMMANUEL (KNOW) that u never will fell! SPELL (to) u Plain.. <u>Spoken it to performed it</u>," (for) JAHUDAH and for (the) Children Of YISRAEL and Companions.' SPARK A TUMULT.. Continue living (life) SPEAKING TRUE. U ain't (scared) walk around NIGGA'S half (dead) in the penitentiary (walk) (among) the walking (dead) sprinkle thru the (mist) is the (fed) BEAST (EYES) watching u (did) your wrong (so) make your (bed) REPENT HAVE FORGIVENESS in the HEART. Don't look for NO RIGHTS in the land Of the enemies : Get your (own) REPARATIONS is what they OWE. Do the (time) and then make the MOVE. Grace upon the head ANOINTED (BLESSED) then it (shine) RIGHTEOUS imparted for the (kind) <u>meek inherit the earth</u>. COME to NEW(birth) thought Of meditation.. BLESSED in the MOSTHIGH it ain't bout the hip - hop. (craft) Of the Gift. Its bout what u doing with the POWER Of the Gift. SOWING SEED. Thanking YAH coast to coast. BOAST upon the MOSTHIGH coast to coast. PROPHESY to the MOST..

PROPHESY SON Of man.. Lock us down if u have to (We) still PROCLAIM the NAME Of the MOSTHIGH.. It was (silly) when men (sell) they (soul) (for) (sin) (losing) from with (in) (Iniquity) to gain the whole (world) (but) lose his own soul DEATH be the penalty (change) your way (reach) out to SPIRITUAL (community) neighbor hood near u.. LEARN the CULTER OF YAH (live) right and (do) right in the (sight) Of YAH even in the penitentiary even up to the NEXT CENTRY walk (among) the walking (dead) proclaim PROPHESY to the BREATH, PROPHESY SON Of man.. SAY to the BREATH, (thus) say YHWH MIGHTY ONE : <u>come from the four winds</u> .. O BREATH, (BREATHE) on the slain,   AMEN
AMMISHADDAI   PROPHETIC MESSAGE MINSTRY

PSALM : FOLLOW the LAMB Of YHWH were HE Go's

I don't wanna HURT (again) I don't wanna FELL (again) I don't wanna (spend) a LIFE LONG JOURNEY in the world (again) I don't wanna HURT my KIN.. YAH'S people MIGHTY and STRONG from with (in) YAH'S FURTUNE (hit) me like a world (wind) (SPIN) time and chance I LOVE my Girl (again) *LIKE WISE* I hope she feel the same about (me) OPEN up my (ears) OPEN up to hear the PLEA.. BLESSING OPEN up my eye to (see) *LET NO MAN PUT ASUNDER WHAT THE MOSTHIGH PUT TOGETHER..*

FOLLOW THE LAMB OF YHWH were HE Go's..

(again) I had to pray repent from my (sin) SET IN ORDER many WORDS (PROVERBS) WISDOM better than STRENGHT never(less) the POOR MAN WISDOM its (despised) his WORDS are NOT heard.. WORDS of the WISE.. Spoken Quietly SHOULD BE HEARD.. ABOVE the rulers of fools (cool) WISDOM its better then the (weapons) of war ONE SINNER destroys much (good) but if u (would) COCO BLUNT BROWN Tee and Me.. We had to work to be (done)

FOLLOW THE LAMB OF YHWH were HE Go's..

When u see little JAHUDAH in the streets Of the HOOD (spitting) to another what he (could) SHOWING Him How to bring the intellect ON A HIGHIER (PLAIN) ON HIGHIER (EFFECT) OVERSTAND and MAINTAIN in the (NAME)
LET NO ONE DECEIVE HIMSELF.. IF U WISE.. IN THIS AGE..
Become a FOOL (wise) AVOID the worldly WAY Cuz its stupid (ness) with the MOSTHIGH the TESTIMONY Of the CONSCIENCE.. (CONDUCT) yourselves in the world (in) YHWH SINCERITY and SIMPLICITY with out the WORLDLY WISDOM Of the Flesh.. But by the GRACE Of the MOSTHIGH..
WERE MY PEOPLES AT ?? IS U RAEL ??

FOLLOW the LAMB Of YHWH were HE Go's..

AMEN..

PROPHETIC MESSAGE MINISTRY
AMMISHADDAI
TRUE
BELIEVER

I THANK the MOSTHIGH for giving (me) strength to Bear WITTNESS.. I THANK the MOSTHIGH for allowing (me) to Loving u.. I THANK the MOSTHIGH to Allowing (me) to (be) the STRONG VESSEL for HIS LIGHT.. I THANK the MOSTHIGH for allowing (me) to call the FOUR WINDS to the ENDGATHERING at the valley Of DryBones giving SIGHT to ISRAELITE.. I THANK the MOSTHIGH for the GOOD NEWS I heard (swerve) (curve) able to (endure) TRIBULATIONS FIRERY (TRAILS) standing in the SHADOW Of the MOSTHIGH.. I THANK the MOSTHIGH for LOVING (me) sending HIS HOLY SON Cuz if I (believe) I will NEVER DIE.

JOY TO THE WORLD יהוה IS KING.. LET THE HEAVENS and THE EARTH REJOICE (JOY) TO THE WORLD.. A NEW BORN KING, LET THE EARTH RECEIVE HIS KING.. Let every heart prepare HIM room let HEAVEN and NATURE (SING) יהוה IS KING יהוה RULES THE WORLD..

What's on My Mind.. What's Really on My Mind..

I THANK the MOSTHIGH for letting (me) LIVE EVERDAY CHANGE (me) reminisce upon a time HOW I used to (be) LOOK and LET (me) SEE how to keep the RIGHTEOUS course (OFF) THE CURSE receiving the BLESSING learn the LESSON in due time I will shine STOP STRESSING living with OPPRESSION (depression) on the rise.. EYE Of the MOSTHIGH on the (PRIZE) *FOREVER LIFE.* NEVER DIE a second death. DELIVER ME bow down in the PRESENTS OF CREATOR. EL OF ISRAEL IMMANUEL is who we FOLLOW living everlasting LIFE it never (fell) Young Punk wanna be the PIMP GUN JUMPER was his name (deception) was his game. I could (have) would (have) almost put him on his (back) but the SPIRIT invoked (conviction) <u>upon My Heart</u> had (me) think :

Had (me) step back had (me) sinning had (me) filling bad with in " em " (bad) situation bucking with the foreign (joke) (spoke) at HIGH NOON.. STOP SINNING if u wanna start (winning) don't worry bout the SEX smoke a blunt lit the (insent) verbally take a (walk) u don't understand the daily (grind) of being in the (world) but not transformed to the (world)

What's on My Mind.. ONE DAY hey everything will be OKAY.. ONE DAY I will be with family. ONE DAY hey how good it is to DWELL IN UNITY.. ONE DAY we will be walking with the MOSTHIGH. ONE DAY hey we will talk with MESSIYAH.. ONE DAY CULTER REIGN ABOVE THE REST. ONE DAY hey YHWH SAINTS SANTIFIED set apart from the (rest)

FREELY WE GIVE.. FREELY WE DO..
What's on My Mind..   AMEN

COMMANDMENT KEEPERS
PROPHETIC MESSAGE MINISTRY
אממסאהדדא.

PSALM : BURN the Rap (Game) 8/15/03

(KILL) the INSANE turn it to the PROPHET (PROPHETICAL) Industry last day ministry (SEIZE) the streets to the HELL HOLES of the PENITENTARY.. <u>Yet I walk thru VALLEY of the SHADOW of DEATH</u>.. I FEAR NO (EVIL) upheaval the evil that I see in my people.. *COME from the FOUR WINDS*.. " O " Breathe (breath) on the slain that they LIVE. Changing (SOULS) for the next century (KEEP) your self out the penitentiary.. יהוה is the (start) and the (ender) to the finisher in the blessing from with in (her) BENDING (SENDING) Never intending to Offending (SPEAKING) (TRUE) Regardless of what u do I LOVE My (family) *IS U RAEL* Can u feel (REPARATIONS) is what u owe (so) let My people GO.. (Back) to My ABBA'S land NORTH EAST AFRICA *CITY OF PEACE*.. the MOSTHIGH Promised Land expand the Good News thru out the Land..

BURN the Rap (Game) Refine with (fire) KILL the INSANE (Plain) to see (spitting) nothing but the (TRUE) Thru MINISTRY (INDUSTRY) Of the Game (explain) IS U RAEL spit it (plain) STOP (STOPING) all the foolishness emotions of the GENTILE.. Voting in the IDLE AMERICAN (IDLE) promotions in the (PRIDE) (Stride) leaning to your own OVERSTANDING.. Swagger in your stride (pride) from the cradle to the grave (CURSED) from the birth (sinful) in your way STAND UP YOUNG BUCK pray for the BETTERWAY.. I refuse to take a beat down for the HOOD I never own in America *"MISTORY BABYLON "* is it worthless or is it useless DIEING or KILL brother for (another) loose the FREEDOM LOCK DOWN slave again young blood I'm out to win NEVER DIE abide in the SHADOWS of the MOSTHIGH while u calling ONE ANOTHER God.. Living life dwelling in the smog.

" AHH THIS ISH GOT TO STOP " ; its (hot) in the Hood if it ain't for LIFE. (silent) the Beast (deal) with the Demon scheming (dreaming) Mommy if I had? Don't unequally YOKE yourself <u>let that HOOD ISH ALONE</u> come up out your (way) Cuz if u don't u truly will (DIE) Cry Morn a Loss in your (sin) speaking to the NATRUAL BORN KILLER from with (in) LAST CALL FOR ALCOHOL time to REPENT (change) from the wicked ways before u burn from the wicked ways. Days and a Mays plant the seeds of the (true)

BURN the Rap Game KILL the INSANE turn it to the PROPHET (PROPHETICAL) industry last day ministry (LYRICAL) DEPENDANCE.. SEIZE the streets to the Hell Holes Of America DEEP DOWN in the penitentiary.

AMEN..

COMMANDMENT KEEPERS
AMMISHADDAI

PSALM : BURN the Rap (Game)   8/15/03

(KILL) the INSANE (turn) it to the PROPHET (PROPHETICAL) industry last day ministry (SEIZE) the streets to the HELL HOLES of the penitentiary. Coming from the Four Winds " O " Breathe (Breath) On the Slain that they may Live in the Name.. I'm done with u.. u wanna BATTLE I wanna BUILD u wanna HOLLER I wanna CHILL (STEAL) to instill Cuz u blisted (twisted) in your way.. INIQUITIES caught u (flees) I'm not hear to try to blast made u mass.

DON'T TOUCH THIS WHEN U OPEN UP DOORS (FLIES)
                                                                COME IN..

DEMON TICKS I didn't say nothing about the Fhine Fhine (empty) head (ness) Not Knowing (to) REBUKE then (then) UNDERSTANDING found coming from with (in) (then) (stop) had to stop sin (then) My Nigga broke Off in sin (then) DEATH or CAPTIVITY..   Reminiscent Of the Activity..

        BURN the Rap (Game) KILL the INSANE (turn) it to the PROPHET (PROPHETICAL) industry last day ministry (SEIZE) the streets to the HELL HOLES of the penitentiary..

EBER (REU) Slang slowly change as (do) across the (centuries) spitting WORDS of Prophecies coming up like a (breeze) after OLD COVENANT writers (seeking) words to (please) the MOSTHIGH the LANGUAGE Of Moses. (seem) strange to modern day ISRAELITE a long way from our own present - day speech that we speak in (end) America the thoughts of the (SLAVE) looking at my family Hollering at the Box rooting Sugar Sane ON (to) WIN the (FIGHT) would they do (right) not apply the ANTI - SHEMITIC (RACEISM) that they do that I (feel) while they try to instill the white (light) supremacy Superman (white) hype..

        BURN the Rap (Game) KILL the INSANE (turn) it to the PROPHET (PROPHETICAL) industry last day ministry
        (SEIZE) the streets (to) the HOLE HOLES of the penitentiary..
                                                                AMEN..

COMMANDMENT KEEPERS
    .אממסהאדדא   Page 2 Of 2

283

Story telling over welling didn't lack CUZ my Nigga got my back IS URAEL (CAN U FEEL) (so) Now instill (build) love from on HIGH SPIRIT that you cant buy LIFE style set apart from the HYPOCRITICAL (BULLSHITIBAL) LIFE STYLE from the Rich and the Famous stepping LIKE Andy and Amos

　　　　　MUSIM NIGGRO consistently (cop) a plea (though) Lack of what he (see) Lack of understanding KNOWLEDGE that u missed dwelling living LIFE in Abyss (got) Me and My Peeps (PIST) looking at the HEAT that u bringing on the BLOCK CUZ its HOT know Not that this Ish got to (STOP) BEFORE the (BOUNTY) AVENGER OF THE BLOOD.. take control loose the SOUL DRAG the SINFUL Nigga to the streets of the Hood KILL the EVIL that dwell among your people in the Mist.. Let them GO CAN TWO WALK TOGETHER and NOT AGGREE.. Open up your minds to (see) Purge the land of the EVIL that's in my (people)

　　　　　UNIFIED STRUGGLES FREEDOMS FROM WITHIN.. APART from this Beast of the Land taking COMMANDMENTS of the MOSTHIGH out of the Land Getting rid of Judges who was willing to take the (stand) ITS TIME TO GO.. let my people GO pay the Reparations Of what u Owe.. SHOTS OUT to the city of Do Mona CITY setting in the (Peace) of the Lamb I Know your (poverty) but u Rich. Then said to me these are the WORDS FAITHFUL and TRUE YHWH Of Host sent the ANGLE to the SPIRIT of the Prophet (SHOW) the Servant the things that must shortly take place (behold) I AM going quickly with REWARD according to the WORKS truth according to the WORD but Now!! Believe MESSIYAH IMMANUEL died for your sins (blessed) to the ONE WHO keep the words of the PROPHECY of the (BOOK) BLESSED with the (HOOK) SIENCE for a time Repent for your Crime. Now can u (see) this is how it (be)

　　　　　UNIFIED STRUGGLES.. that u (see)

He who is UNJUST let him be UNJUST (still) (deal) who is FILTHY let be FILTHY (still) (feel) who is RIGHTEOUS let him be RIGHTEOUS (still) (build) who is HOLY still BLESS bad boy (soul) caught up on the ROW (DEATH) u coming back for some more WHY SHED A (TEAR) why even (lie) why even (cry) understand those who PRACTICE such things shall never inherit the (earth) KINGDOM OF THE MIGHTY MOSTHIGH.. ELSHADDAI why stand and even lie?? Holler if u hear Me feel Me Fear Me thus say YHWH Of Host (let) us Boast in the Most.. While (I) (stoop) to PROPHECY ONLY IN THE MIST of perversion Of the X generation　SODOMY and Player Hation Of a Nation BORN to be MISTORY BABYLON.. Don't play me close while I sit to PROPHECY thru the Ghost..

　　　　　UNIFIED YOUR STRUGGLES IN THE LAND.. SET UP THE BANNER with the SWITH and MIGHTY HAND.. UNIFIED STRUGGLES..　　　　　AMEN

　　　　　　　COMMANDMENT KEEPERS
　　　　　　　PROPHETIC MESSAGE MINISTRY
　　　　　　　AMMISHADDAI

LOSS SHEEP HOUSE OF YISRAEL..

To my (Family) extended and abroad:

The RED is for the BLOOD in MESSIYAH.. The BLACK is for the MELON IN the SKIN Of the people.. The GREEN is for the HERBAL CHARM (inheritance) Of the EARTH.. I'm an AFRICAN I'm an AFRICAN and I KNOW what's Happening.. u an AFRICAN u an AFRICAN (do) u KNOW what's Happening?? I'm an AFRICAN (never) was AMERICAN PUNK DEMOCRITE nor REPUBLICAN head strong MARKED with the BEAST Colonial ish would (cease)

Its plain to (see) u cant change (me) I'm YAHS ARMY YAHS PEOPLE for Life Its plain to (see) u cant change (me) I'm YAHS ARMY YAHS PEOPLE for Life.. Following IMMANUEL : SHADOWS OF IMMANUEL NEVER (FAIL) So let me sit and (tell) u about the (TRUE) RED the WHITE AND the BLUE (COPS) KILLING u SELF on SELF CRIME HAS GOT TO (STOP) We are BELOVED of the MOSTHIGH HOLY ONES OF YISRAEL going way back (back) to the MOTHER LAND city of UR Of the (chal * de 'ans) Blessed over (schemes) I give u land to INHERITANCE to Descendents I give them ALL MILK AND HONEY..   from the RIVER EGYPT.. To the GREAT RIVER the RIVER Eu* phra' trs - looking at the Nations surround the land PLAYER - HATE (these) ABRAHAM turn 100 yrs old when ISAAC was born after birth ISMAEL seed of HAGAR EGYPTAIN servant to SARAH.. HERITAGE to GENEALOGY Open the " eyes " to (see) GENESIS 25:12,13 : ABRAHAM the HEBREW black as me and u going back to AFRICA..

ABRAHAM - ISMAEL - ISAAC - ESAU - YAHCOB (YAHCOB) your name (.shall) NO LONGER (BE) CALLED YAHCOB (but) YISRAEL u struggled with the MOSTHIGH and (Man) and have (prevailed) GENESIS 32:28 : YAHCOB / IS URAEL ISRAELITE (KINGS) of AFRICA (SAUL) ISRAELITE chosen KING (DAVID) the MOSTHIGH chosen KING (SOLOMON) the third and last KING (UNITIED) YISRAEL the coming of SON OF MAN YAHSAVOIR to the North and the South to the East and the West INGATHERING Of the People.. COMING FROM THE FOUR WINDS " O " BREATH (BREATHE) on the slain that they may Live in the (name) MATTHEW Chapter (one) 18 thru 25 : ALL who believe and call upon HIS NAME NEVER DIE inquire EVERLASTING LIFE from the cradle to the NEWBIRTH renewing of the MIND science for the (time)

U BATTLE I BUILD U HOLLER I CHILL (PROPHECY) THRU THE RYHME.. I don't rob or steal see I'm sitting back watching the hip - hop GO into another Level ALL THE WICKED ISH the u SPIT save it for the DEVIL (SANTAN) I'm taking hip - hop where its NEVER BEEN to a whole another LEVEL taking hip - hop on the (ride)that its never been (before) I'm tired of being PLAYED LIKE the TRICKS AND HOES to the INDUSTRY acting like u don't KNOW.. (Become) my worst (foe) I'm (out) (to) SPARK A MOVE to a NATION.. Yeall walk around like u just step Off the Plantation BATTLING AND HARRASSING one another love growing COLD for your brother..

The RED is for the BLOOD in MESSIYAH.. The BLACK is for the MELON IN the SKIN Of the people.. The GREEN is for the HERBAL CHARM (inheritance) Of the EARTH.. I'm an AFRICAN I'm AFRICAN and I KNOW what's Happening.. u an AFRICAN u AFRICAN (do) u really KNOW what's Happening?? I'm an AFRICAN (never) was AMERICAN PUNK DEMOCRITE nor REPUBLICAN head strong MARKED with the BEAST colonial ish would (cease) its plain to (see) u cant change (me) I'm YAHS ARMY YAHS PEOPLE for Life.. REPARATIONS IS WHAT U OWE.. don't run from the (table) set aside the (TRUE) Getting (me) back to my homeland COMMANDMENT (PASSOVER) let me out your (hair) RE - PATRONIZE my people (return) us back to the HOMELAND. HOMELESS NATION (LOST) SHEEP YISRAEL.. wonder about to and fro. Buck the other (ish) never mind what u going (thru) if u seek (solution) step to me?? (We) can pray find a better way establish mind set to a brighter way follow Original THE WAY : ACEINTS dating back to the day EAST Of AFRICA. Original as EVER PROPHECY and then its cleaver.

Believe that receive that and wait on RETURN Of the LAMB (LION OF JAHUDAH)   AMEN..

COMMANDMENT KEEPERS
PROPHETIC MESSAGE MINISTRY
אממסהאדדאבאיניאהדאה

285

PSALM : SOCIETY Of MENTAL HEALTH..   10/5/03

SKITSO - FRANTIC (MANIC - DEPRESSIVE) Bipolar HYPERACTIVITY maybe in the FOOD that we EAT. HEREDITARY (maybe) AIR that we breath. (Maybe) just DEMONS in the (weed) (we) NEED YAHSAVIOR (maybe) just (need) assurance Of surrounding staying (grounded) in the WORD. Sway away crooked cone THE ONLY WAY : the way (truth) and the light.. We NEED protection and perfection (Consitively) CAR VANDELS PICKED ME RANDLE!! (pray) the EVIL surround (me) caught (me) slipping caught (me) chilling dipping sleeping in the Middle Of the (night) caught OFF GUARD (but) its HARD my momma told (me) it ain't easy HOT PUSUTES (SLOW) CHASES in the Neighbor hood in the GETTO the VALLEY TURN HOOD story MAKER of my brother CAIN MURDERED (ABLE) (Stay) on GUARD to PRAY to make a better (way) (thru) the MENTAL HEALTH IN SOCIETY.. MENTAL HEALTH CRYS Of the People.: CRYING OUT CHILDREN (left) to SOCIETY (society) Yeall see the DEMON handling business.

51 / 50 is what they call it.

SOCIETY Of MENTAL HEALTH.. Crisis for the people CODE ALERT for the MENTAL (ILL) Falling down DEMONS TAKE CONTROL (its) in your HISTORY is it MISTORY?? Tell (me) what can it (be) LACK Of KNOWLEDGE could it (be) the LACK Of UNITY but if (society) that's lacking YAH (VOID) Of the LAW of the MOSTHIGH (Repent) to change your way. Stand (Ground) endure until the END even till the DEATH (we) will be (SAVED)

(NEVER AGAIN)

Homie and sister (in) UNITY catch (me) KEEPING ME ON (GUARD) Pshfer in Solution. it's the WAY we SPEAK one another LOVE your brother (seek) (meek) solution to conclusion DO WE KEEP short (temper) IRRITATED (AGGRAVATED) (Just) NOT HAPPY living Life. Not GROUNDED in the WORD. Regardless Of the RICHIES and the FAME. (Is) it LACK Of KNOWLEDGE ?? Bipolar (HYPER - ACTIVITY) is it (MANIC - DEPRESSIVE) from the (MANIAC) Mentally INSANE in the (brain) was it SANTAN planting SEEDS sparking FLAMES dirty GAME u fool ONE u fool the NATION it's a (SHAME) led away like SHEEP TO SLAUGHTER (burning) in the HELL HOLES Of the Penitentiary what's going on in the TEMPLE Of the Mind.. BODY Of the MOSTHIGH its your (JOB) (for) BUILDING UP Community (responsibility) in the MOSTHIGH staying (TUNED)MENTALY TAKING INVENTORY.. What's going in what's coming out ?? Demon (Ticks) got to FLEE (do) u know how ?? (Maybe) it's the weed (anxiety) on the rise. PANIC ATTACKS is in the Air. Is it HAIR WEAVE or the (WEEK) (WEED) that u smoke ON. Weed use to make u laugh now it make u cry. Sometimes make u wanna bust the lie in the (eye) those that (know) wont (tell) those that don't (know) cant (tell) " Oh " Well 51 / 50 is what they call it.

Story of the mental crisis : SOCIETY Of MENTAL HEALTH..   AMEN
PROPHETIC MESSAGE MINISTRY
WRITTEN BY : TAMRA SHADDAI BAHT YAHUDAH

PRAISE behold a SON is BORN.. FORTURNE everlasting (LIFE)
A TROOP has (COME) HAPPY is the man to RECEIVE (it) wresting with the
(TRUE) causing (to) FORGET TANAKH hearing of the WORD.. But wait a minute
(joined) together is reward. Dwelling into (UNITIY) with your brother (increaser)
(deeper) in the FAITH.. To the SON of the RIGHT hand to the MOSTHIGH.. I won't (lie) in
due time (PERSERCUTION) New birth or (execution) is knocking at your door. Ain't No
Fog u can see (clear) Angela Vista (turn) (left) creeping thru Boldwin (hills) a waiting
on the bail away from the PAGANS LAND sway away the (con) minister set up like a
(pound) crooked in his way ABOMINATION Of DESOLATION for time and a times and
half a time.   TRIBULATIONS (END) in the last DAYS in the (END)
Young brothers (prophecy) listen to the (plea) the GOVERNMENT (BEAST) see
(progress) try's to (stop) using the (cop) badge (plus) (gun) often notified as the
DEMON SUN.. Got my Nigga's on the break and on the RUN.. We don't carry (or) submit
to the DEMON SEAL (spill) over to the streets of the hood FLEE and RUN to the Hills.
TEACH and TELL Holy (ground) listen to the SCRIP that I speak traffic an (knowledge)
while I (creep) coming with the CLAIM to EXSPLAIN not a (lecture) but the scripted
(picture) forgot about how to pray!! Woke up (its) JUDGEMENT (DAY) (condemned)
DARK and CONFUSSED by your own (way) the PASS (PRESENT) and the FUTURE..
D' bah reem (28) DEUTERONOMY

      THUG MINISTRY THUG MINISTRY.. RENEWING OF THE MIND. if it's
MOSTHIGH (will) TIME (to) ESCAPE. SET FREE IS URAEL CAN u FEEL
Quick to de - act Slow to re - act ALL WHO KEEP (Commandments) of the MOSTHIGH
and the testimony of the MOSTHIGH (SAVIOR) I will BLAZE u Building in the
TEMPLE Of the MOSTHIGH Building the TEMPLE to YHWH. Let Superstition and
Tradition DIE ALONE in one day I rebuild the TEMPLE (rededicated) in 3 (days) cleaning
out the ABOMINATION Of DESOLATION Spoken by the Prophet DANIEL standing in the
HOLY PLACE were it ought not (be) Look let him (see) AVOID the DEMON SUN on the
(run) now this bad nigga CAPERS got a bigger GUN GAT (SCRIP) and the (bat) to
split the wig and the hat expound information to my people. All who endure until the end
would be save (so) we left the bend creeping through GENARATIONS of different NATIONS
(PAGAN BELIEFS) foolish (ish) they speak on Pagan Holy Day KNOW THE TRUE
MESSIYAH wasn't even born on that (day) seek u shall find..

      THUG MINISTRY.. BUSTING thru the doors (to) open up the INDUSTRY.. Baby
Please Baby Please let DECENDENTS (see) SPOKEN WORD science to the (plea) this is
HOW WE WALK in the land walking to OVERSTAND keeping flavor with the SALT not
coming bland but keep it REAL understand buck what this NIGGA say don't now what the
SPIRIT say I'm feeling what the SPIRIT say in (me) DEATH is at the (door) today I wont
(Die) today I wont let u tell a (lie) BLESSING from the MOSTHIGH wipe away cry's tears
from your eye (looking) at my block at 40" before the THRONE of the MOSTHIGH (no)
deceit found in your TESTIMONY THUG MINISTRY (SCIENCE) KICKED TO THE
INDUSTRY.. PRAISE behold a SON is born FORTURNE everlasting (LIFE) A TROOP
has (COME) HAPPY is the man to RECEIVE (it) wresting with the (TRUE) causing (to)
forget TANAKH hearing Of the WORD.. But wait a minute (joined) together is reward.
Dwelling into (UNITIY) with your brother (increaser) (deeper) in the FAITH.. To the SON
of the right HAND to the MOSTHIGH..   AMEN

This the Killer (part) MONKEY HUSLTER (NIGGA) got the Nerve think its game (cute) to keep enemies CLOSE.. Falling for the Ancient O" KAY DOK I'm looking watching on the BLOCK seeing ignorant " G'S " (negativities) keeping DEMONS CLOSE boast about what u got knowing the first time something (JUMP) OFF u gone *SNICTH and TELL* the lie over True.. But I'm riding with the MOSTHIGH had NO room to (Fail) looked at (me) UNDER MICRO (SCOPE) almost lost my (Hope) FAITH endure until the End. Never set my self up to fail how can I win with the DEMON adversary in my corner keeping ENEMIES (CLOSE) Knowing EVIL company would have to (flee) MONKEY HUSLTE and all appearances Of the EVIL would have to (go) (get) your head busted open to the white meat with the Stone (judgment) Of the MOSTHIGH.. LEMON and BEER SPLASHED IN MY EYE.. Knowing No pity looking out from the city. I wouldn't LIE I cry I miss u man IF ONLY u knew what I KNEW seen what I SEEN.. BELIEVED in the VISION Of the Prophecies. Regardless of how u push the bill I won't fall into TEMPTATION Of the *MONKEY HUSTLE..   JUST A NOTHER CITY HUSTLE..*

Mentally it's a breeze to be free cant u (see) through MESSIYAH like the MOSTHIGH is who (we) please sees the chance to be FREE take control in the SPIRIT Of the MIND and the THOUGHT NO DECIET found in the mouth SPOKEN WORD with out a flaw TWO WITINESS STEP OUT ON the Scene don't player hate CUZ the moneys green MONKEY HUSTLE scheme of Demonic activity of the dream (2) for ONE taxing Nigga's saying its cool (it) ain't (right) never mind the (Hype) Know Yahudah (man) understand (man) the MOSTHIGH (man) is who we serve (man) SPIT IT PLAIN step to the plate get your grub on and your drink on if u hunger and thirst for the WORD Of the MOSTHIGH comprehend (man) mourning for the DEAD Absent from the body present with YHWH let us pray for the better way let the (hustle) die alone with the OLD GENERATION player hation keeping enemies close it's a NEW DAY it's a NEW DON getting rid Of EVIL that dwell among u (sodomy) has got to cease.. <u>According to the WILL Of the FATHER</u> (ABBA) please look upon US all for what has come upon US all for so long my forefather SIN but now is NO more Forgive Me FATHER Please NOW I BEAR his SIN ADULTERY was the case that u gave me. DEATH IS AT THE DOOR AVENGER Of the Blood never mind what the renegade HEBREW had to say we gone pray KEEP TANAKH Of the MOSTHIGH let the MONKEY HUSTLE DIE MURDER and DEATH has got to (go) get it right WORD WALKING in the flesh with the best 144 G get it right keep it tight fight with the MOSTHIGH might stepping back to the land HOMELESS NATION send me back to my ABBA'S Land that was Promise. Don't become Proud, <u>Knowing nothing but Obsessed</u> with Disputes and Arguments Overwhelmed (over) words from which Envy Strife Reviling (Demonic) Suspicion (wresting) with useless (men) Of Corrupt Minds Destitute Of the True suppose MESSIYAH Like is the means of gain to such WITHDRAW yourself NOW I URGE u note those who cause Division and Offense Contrary to Doctrine we talk and we learn AVOID THEM.. Now Cuz the MONKEY HUSTLE is dead lead like sheep to slaughter but my Nigga don't grow weary in doing good *LOOKING AT MONKEY HUSTLE APPEAR TO PROSPER BUT ITS NOT.. JUST ANOTHER CITY HUSTLE*   AMEN

Praise YHWH MIGHTY ONE of our forefathers (may) the GLORY and the HONOR (be) reverence (forever) may HYMNS be sung to your GLORY (forever) may your HOLY PRESENCE (be) PRAISED IN THE TEMPLE.. Were u sit on the ROYAL THRONE sitting (praising) in the DOME.. From the heavens may the HYMNS be sung (praise) YHWH, SKIES ABOVE sing His Praise HONOR (FOREVER) PRAISE YHWH all Heaven and Powers sing His Praise (Honor) (forever) PRAISE YHWH Sun and Moon sing His Praise HONOR FOREVER.. PRAISE YHWH Stars of Heaven, sing His Praise Honor (forever) Praise YHWH dews and snows sing HIS PRAISE HONOR (forever) Praise YHWH night and days.. Sing His Praise HONOR (forever) Praise YHWH ice and cold sing HIS PRAISE HONOR (forever) Praise YHWH frost and snow sing HIS PRAISE HONOR (forever) Praise YHWH lighting and storms (sing) His praise HONOR (forever) Let the EARTH PRAISE YHWH sing His praise Honor (forever) Praise YHWH mountains and the HILL TOPS Sing His Praise HONOR (FOREVER) Praise YHWH for everything that Grows.. (Sows a seed) BLESSED IN ANOITED (TO) the NEW (BREED) Sing His (praise) Honor (forever) praise YHWH Lakes (to) Rivers singing His Praise HONOR (forever) Praise YHWH Springs Of Waters (sing) His Praise HONOR (forever) Praise YHWH all people dwelling on the EARTH Sing His Praise HONOR (forever) praise YHWH people (IS U RAEL) Sing His Praise HONOR (forever) Praise YHWH (priest) Of YHWH sing His Praise HONOR (forever) praise YHWH bondservant Of the MOSTHIGH..   ALL the FAITHFUL and the (TRUE)

Sing HIM PRAISE HONOR (forever) Praise YHWH Hanaiyah (Azariyah) Mishael Sing HIS Praise HONOR (forever) (rescued) us from the world Of the (Dead) SAVE US from the Power Of Death.. (brought) us out from the BURNING (Fire) SAVE US from the FURNANCE Of the (Fire) keep it real to maintain to keep (it) HIGHIER to (admire) the MOSTHIGH MESSIYAH.. Give thanks (to) YHWH HE is good and HIS Mercy endures (forever) HIS LAW is (cleaver) Praise YHWH all who WORSHIP IN SPIRIT and TRUE.. SING HIM PRAISE the MOSTHIGH Of gods GIVE HIM THANKS for HIS Mercy endures (forever) SONG OF THREE YOUNG MEN. AMEN

PSALM : YHWH LOVES ALL (PASSION Of CHRIST)

SELAH : We having a good time (in) YHWH !! YHWH is good YHWH is good YHWH is good (YHWH) is good to (me) and (u)

We living a good life (in) YHWH !! YHWH is good YHWH is good YHWH is good (YHWH) loves (me) YHWH loves (u)

We living the good life (in) YHWH (We) having the good time (in) YHWH having the good time (in) YHWH (YHWH) is good YHWH is good YHWH is good YHWH love (all) (all) who REPENT BELIEVE IN YOUR HEART turn from the (sin) YHWH is good from (within) YHWH loves (all)

YHWH LOVES (ALL)

I beseech u (to) teach (u) therefore brethren by the MERCIES of the MOSTHIGH, *PRESENT YOURSELFS (BODIES) AS A LIVING SACRIFICE..* (Holy) Acceptable (to) the MOSTHIGH (what's) REASON of the SERVICE (don't) become CONFORMED (to) this WORLD (but) (be) transformed by RENEWING of the (MIND) (SHINE) for the righteous (kind) *(PROVE) what is GOOD (ACCEPTED) PERFECT WILL of the MOSTHIGH ..* I say therefore by the GRACE GIVEN UNTO (Me) to everyone among u NOT to THINK of Himself Higher then He OUGHT to think (soberly) seriously as the MOSTHIGH has DEALT to each and everyone A MEASURE of the FAITH (JOHN 3:16) ALL who Believe ALL who will Call on the NAME would be (saved) why sit (back) why even tell a STORY over (TRUE)   PASSION Of (CHRIST)

I'm trough (back) way (back) I live my life (back) in the day now to day living in the (2 " G's ") now I pray every (day) give attention to reading (doctrine) of the WORD don't neglect the GIFT that was in u (spirit) of the PROPHECY laying on hands of the elder (ship) (flip) the scrip meditate on YAH'S WORD and thangs living the life of the POOR RIGHTEOUS teacher Prophecy to SEEK (her) NIGGA put lead to the head.. Find yourself like the slab of meat DEAD to the flow falsely (confessed) knowledge - professing it to (be) keeping enemies Close look at u slipped up dead as the GHOST hip - hops (PAST) BURNED u seven yrs AGO the fate of the WICKED (shots) out to RIDERS (true) providers south west CALLIE Murrieta to my Nigga's on lock down (on) death row (repent) and WALK IN WAY (learn) the TRUE Accept the Culture get it (right) do the will the Father (tight) with all your (might) do what's (right) while I learn HOW to spit (first) and foremost knowledge for (self) checking out NIGGA in the mirror (first) *COME INTO NEWBIRTH RENEWING WHATS IN THE MIND ..* SCIENCE for a (time) know to understand young (blood) u couldn't fool (me) see (me) step to (me) cuz I (see) how it (be) you ain't really trying I caught u lying the other day (about) what WE JUST TALKED (about) the other (day) step away sway away crooked con.

CAN TWO WALK together and NOT AGGREE ?? AMOS 3:3 (READ) to get back with (me) cuz I (see) the FRUIT that u bare.

THE PASSION Of the CHRIST ..   AMEN

PROPHETIC MESSAGE MINISTRY

(to) the KINGDOM that come (all) who believe TRUE BELIEVERS all souls who believe ASSEMBLE self's <u>KEEP the PASSOVER Of the MOSTHIGH</u> .. And the TESTIMONY Of the *HOLY ONE* leave before its (time) We (Keep) (in) MIND Remembrance in DO time MAKE A END Of SIN : *HOLY SPIRIT PROFESSED* from within; shots out to the temple (of) hip - hop ISRAEL STANDING STRONG we will be hear for Return back to the TRUE WAY Worship and Lifestyle Culture Change A STRANGE FROM THE NAME.. IS U RAEL can u (feel) I'm tried of fighting (the) worthless cause (acceptance) of a slave (counted) up 1/3rd of a man accelerated up to the PROPERTY own by the FRANCISE..

Run By The Man.. Still Alive Still a Slave but Now U Paid : We all chosen but allow the MEDIA (to) expose and display a few of the many CHOSEN in the Negative (condemnation) perpetuation of mere speculation (STOP) Forget about dwelling on the (problem) (lets) work on solution (promote) the absolute TRUE..

I want to go HOME send me back to my ANCESTORS (land) I'm sitting on the shores of a pagan (land) thought visions of the REVELATION of (JOHN) no fake religion could step up fade (me) to try to con (me) REST with the COMFORTER SPIRIT. In the bond bloodshed in MESSIYAH PASSION OF CHRIST. Paid the cost set free CAPTIVES I want to go HOME.. Unifying struggles ready to (emerge)
Please don't become judge mental only keep the COMMANDMENTS Of the MOSTHIGH <u>ORICALES (STORYRICALES)</u> maintaining PRICIPLES (moral) ABSOLUTE TRUE.. JUST like the days of NOAH were so shall the coming of the SON OF MAN (be) as the Lighting Flashing from the East Flashing to the West so shall the coming of the SON Of MAN (be) PREPARATION BUILDING A NATION

I'M want to go HOME (so) Mr. Gentile fake Jew Mr. Heathen (Man) let my people go " Oh " know pay the reparations of what u owe and RE - PATRIOTIZE my people back to the (land) to my ANCESTORS (land) HOME Of the HEBREW (man) I wanna go HOME to WORSHIP (YAH) I'm sick and tired of being sick and tired of the GREEK (ROMAN) Culture placed upon the MENTALLITY this (be) the major reason play a part of the PROBLEM among my people living dwelling in (abyss) of America the HELLENIST house Negro HEBREW become my worse FOE cuz u rich cuz u famous excepted MARK Of BEAST (USA) Gentiles allow u to get the worthless POINT across looking at u floss kissed the ass paid the cost u wanted to (be) the field NIGGA BOSS.. Corp America RAP CITY Mogul C.E.O. Bet (own) by the EUROPEAN Bet exploited by the EUOPEAN demonic scheme I'm fighting demons and <u>prince of palities demonic spirit giving parties</u>. I PRAY my people wake up to (see) Nigga's want to play devils advocate lost on the mic and spit nothing holding TRUE to solution to conclusion delusion is what he spit bling bling big money dream cash money scheme take a NIGGA to the grave lead like sheep to slaughter Charlie Cee going back to my home land my own land sergeant carter fight to get your own land NO sodomy NO murder NO adultery see this is how it (be)
AMMISHADDAI   PREPARATION BUILDING A NATION..   AMEN

This the Killer (part) MONKEY HUSLTER (NIGGA) got the Nerve think its game (cute) to keep enemies CLOSE.. Falling for the Ancient O" KAY DOK I'm looking watching on the BLOCK seeing ignorant " G'S " (negativities) keeping DEMONS CLOSE boast about what u got knowing the first time something (JUMP) OFF u gone *SNICTH and TELL* the lie over True.. But I'm riding with the MOSTHIGH had NO room to (Fail) looked at (me) UNDER MICRO (SCOPE) almost lost my (Hope) FAITH endure until the End. Never set my self up to fail how can I win with the DEMON adversary in my corner keeping ENEMIES (CLOSE) Knowing EVIL company would have to (flee) MONKEY HUSLTE and all appearances Of the EVIL would have to (go) (get) your head busted open to the white meat with the Stone (judgment) Of the MOSTHIGH.. LEMON and BEER SPLASHED IN MY EYE.. Knowing No pity looking out from the city. I wouldn't LIE I cry I miss u man IF ONLY u knew what I KNEW seen what I SEEN.. BELIEVED in the VISION Of the Prophecies. Regardless of how u push the bill I won't fall into TEMPTATION Of the *MONKEY HUSTLE.. JUST A NOTHER CITY HUSTLE..*

Mentally it's a breeze to be free cant u (see) through MESSIYAH like the MOSTHIGH is who (we) please sees the chance to be FREE take control in the SPIRIT Of the MIND and the THOUGHT NO DECIET found in the mouth SPOKEN WORD with out a flaw TWO WITINESS STEP OUT ON the Scene don't player hate CUZ the moneys green MONKEY HUSTLE scheme of Demonic activity of the dream (2) for ONE taxing Nigga's saying its cool (it) ain't (right) never mind the (Hype) Know Yahudah (man) understand (man) the MOSTHIGH (man) is who we serve (man) SPIT IT PLAIN step to the plate get your grub on and your drink on if u hunger and thirst for the WORD Of the MOSTHIGH comprehend (man) mourning for the DEAD Absent from the body present with YHWH let US pray for the better way let the (hustle) die alone with the OLD GENERATION player hation keeping enemies close it's a NEW DAY it's a NEW DON getting rid Of EVIL that dwell among u (sodomy) has got to cease.. According to the WILL Of the FATHER (ABBA) please look upon US all for what has come upon US all for so long my forefather SIN but now is NO more Forgive Me FATHER Please NOW I BEAR his SIN ADULTERY was the case that u gave me. DEATH IS AT THE DOOR AVENGER Of the Blood never mind what the renegade HEBREW had to say we gone pray KEEP TANAKH Of the MOSTHIGH let the MONKEY HUSTLE DIE MURDER and DEATH has got to (go) get it right WORD WALKING in the flesh with the best 144 G get it right keep it tight fight with the MOSTHIGH might stepping back to the land HOMELESS NATION send me back to my ABBA'S Land that was Promise. Don't become Proud, Knowing nothing but Obsessed with Disputes and Arguments Overwhelmed (over) words from which Envy Strife Reviling (Demonic) Suspicion (wresting) with useless (men) Of Corrupt Minds Destitute Of the True suppose MESSIYAH Like is the means of gain to such WITHDRAW yourself NOW I URGE u note those who cause Division and Offense Contrary to Doctrine we talk and we learn AVOID THEM.. Now Cuz the MONKEY HUSTLE is dead lead like sheep to slaughter but my Nigga don't grow weary in doing good *LOOKING AT MONKEY HUSTLE APPEAR TO PROSPER BUT ITS NOT.. JUST ANOTHER CITY HUSTLE* AMEN

Group home (kid) mentality it don't have to (be) at the time in the last (day)
Here appeared in community (home) Of YSRAEL a group of traitorous FAKE JEWS
(Hebrews) FAKE CHRISTIAN had NO REGARD for the Law.. Given bad influence
OVER MANY Of the people (but) check it out and listen to what they say: let us
come to terms with the Gentile and the FAKE JEW our refusal to associate with the
(two) brought nothing but trouble among the (two) this Proposal (appealed) to
many of the people they all went to the Church steeple <u>WRONG DAY FAKE
RELIGION</u>: and FAKE WORSHIP rule and regulation of another man. Traditions Of
a (man) so enthusiastic they step to the KING and received the go ahead (strive) to
get ahead permission (follow) tradition PAGAN EUROPEAN WAYS.. CUSTOMS
OF ABISS.. Got me (pist) <u>don't sin</u> : they built in YAHRUSALEM a stadium like
the one in the GREEK cities like the PAGANS LAND ROMAN (fields) caught a fly
out in left (fields) make a NIGGA (steal) they had surgery (performed) to hide the
Circumcision (abandoned) the HOLY COVENANT.. Started Association with the
Wrong Crew GENTILES DID ALL SORT OF EVIL THANGS melting pot ABANDON
your own (the) PROPHET NOT RESPECTED in his HOME LAND.

WHEN DEMONS ATTACK .. WHAT U GONE DO INFACT..

Culter called HIP - HOP (<u>R@B</u>) and (blues) become ONE people in doing EVIL
all the Gentiles and many of my people YSRAELITES submitted to (decree) *MARK
of the BEAST* Adoption Of Official PAGAN WAYS sacrifice for the IDOL not
Observing <u>SABBATH 7th and the HOLYDAY</u> : treat SABBATH and FESTIVALS as
ordinary work (day) forgot about the LAW didn't hear what the SEER (say)
Appointed (Officials) Democrat or Republican commanded each town YAHUDAH to
offer to Pagan Idol's (IDOL) image of AMERICA to many of my Folk forsake the law
of the MOSTHIGH.. Obey officials against the law of the MOSTHIGH.. Defiled my
land with every (EVIL) *SIN SIN is at your DOOR..* (force) my true lights to say
something or run and hide in the fields where u gone go?? DESTRUCTION is in the
land LOOK 911 looking at the towers fall Satan would call to the KINGS Of the earth
(burn) the copy of the Sacred Books silence the HOOKS put to the death any people
who resist (censorship) and (decree) what they call (security) POWERS that
would (be) F.C.C. allow me to (speak) in the NAME Of the MOSTHIGH EL OF
YSRAEL my shadows bringing in the PEACE.. CULTER and WAYS u sat right
there on the coach and told me I had to agree (forgiveness) was the way *WHEN
DEMONS ATTACK..* Know I had to get my heart straight prepare straight the WAY
HOLY SPIRIT LEAD the WAY.. Down low and do your thang. PROPHET NOT
Respected in his HOME Land the PROPHET NOT Respected in his OWN Land (so)
what do we do to understand (listen) to the seer put away the (fear) wipe your eye
and dry your tear (blessed) the PROPHET is here;

WHEN DEMONS ATTACK ..   AMEN

PROPHETIC MESSAGE MINISTRY
     AMMISHADDAI

Life and DEFENSE is my Mentality (when) the Demons (Attack) its was hard for (me) to DESCRIBE my first VISION (SPIRITUAL) PROPHECY.. It was light in the night (then) Normandy *FIRE FALLING FROM THE SKY.. LIGHT (brighter) then Sparkles in the Night ICE LIKE HELL FALLING FROM THE SKY..* Looking at the Heathen and the Oppressive Kracker struggle to look up before the coming of the SON OF MAN; REUNIFICATION Of my people usury in a (new age) sign of time END Of the (age) MESSIYAH BACK in the last (days) YAH IS WITH US.. WHO CAN STAND AGAINST US..

LIFE and DEFENSE is my Mentality when DEMONS ATTACK

don't bite the style, but u can't ABC CBS NBC CNN and the FOX working with the Hex (Fex) my people looking down controlling from the first day church Pharisee stipple (what's) done in dark gone come to (light) BET bring my Teen Summits back (black) keep Spiritual (content) no (intent) to do me (wrong) keep your head up MESSIYAH charge me NO (wrong) (strong) staying grounded in TONAKE WARNING in my mind SHAUL seen the light before he shinned HANOKE lived 65 yrs then he walked with the MOSTHIGH forever in (time) *the FIRST WILL BE LAST.. And the LAST WILL BE FIRST..* so let us brake the (curse) PROPHECY thru the (verse) before u die carried out in the (hearse) kick mud and (disperse)

LIFE and DEFENSE is my mentality when DEMONS ATTACK for show (black) we ready to fight (back) the Label Pimped u like a (hoe) like the Artist on Death Row (dead) locked up in captivity the (memory) of the empire is NO " MO " Check the game at the (door) u got 2 black eyes your fighting hands (Zero) minus a hundred and ten (110) mad dash thru the hood " PO " PO " on the block setting low in the VALLEY its (hot) (spot) BRAND NEW (plot) DO RIGHT instead of wrong. (But) become Mature (PERFECT) in doing right (spike) the TEE COCONUT BROWN SPICE CINNAMON TEE.. Sweet pee (peeping) on the Box watching the (Cops) responding to the Hood (Negative) for Oppressed (tive) NIGGA'S still a slave in a Mess (still) ABC eyewitness BLUES (Jack Pots) Hit 7 million NIGGA'S in the Wood still up to no (good) shots ringing out in the streets.. On Wood worth and 104th (sow) the seed u reap get what u give.. Today's a good (day) last Night <u>DEMONS ATTACK</u> what I (say) caught me slipping in my words of my play with my Girl.. So real filled in (rushed) back for EARL (pray) the DEMON sleep when I creep to do the Job (suave) when I plant the seed " shish " wake up lets roll become the <u>NEW BREED NO GREED NO SODOMY NO ADULTERY</u> its 2004.. I been marinating for so (long) on my (own) so I over stand, comprehend when I'm (wrong)

LIFE and DEFENSE is my mentality when DEMONS ATTACK..   AMEN
PROPHETIC MESSAGE MINISTRY
    AMMISHADDAI

Let him hear what the SPIRIT says to the church.. We are the church and this is my (job) SPIRTUAL ear let him (here) the TESTAMENT (PROOF) to belief A COVENANT A formal AGGREEMENT with the HOUSE " O " YSRAEL can u feel " O " YAHUDAH HEBREWS (8) but listen up and be attentive to what I say (he) who Testifies to the WORDS Of a Servant perform the BLESSED ADVICE and the GUIDANCE to the Messenger ISAIAH (44) but this be the key setting back Building the City.. *BLESSED IN THE TIME* began *SHEMITIC STYLE Of RHYME.. PROPHETIC STYLE Of RHYME..* Now the Goodness TRULY had to be passed with the GOODNEWS flash this would be the (prayer) and answer for the TIME. For a TIME (TIMES) and a HALF a TIME.. (JOHN 12:44)

u see we truly know how to OBTAIN a more EXCELLENT ministry thru the INDUSTRY the LORD YAHSHUAH a better MEADATOR Of a better type of COVERNANT (ESTABLISHED) on a better PROMISE (so) exposed the KEY except the young NIGGAS CREATIVITY and the Mighty Plea (expose) **IMMANUEL IMMANUEL IMMANUEL** for whom He truly really (be) and His peoples that He choose since the day my HOLY sister SARA had to say BLESSED to given birth to the **CHOICE NATION Of the EARTH..** YAHUDAH became the Name while the YSRAELITES all stayed the (same) but since my Genealogy and NOT Biology could NOT (be) the PROBLEM that u (see) not knowing who u (be) the EDOMITES would only have u (hype) while u sitting back Dreaming Of the (fame) Smoking on the pipe while he (claim) for the TIME (TIMES) and a HALF a TIME.. So let us pray to the EAST not to the Beast (USA) <u>our FATHER ANCIENT OF DAYS</u>:

יהוה is the KING the mighty mighty KING..
AMEN

PROPHETIC MESSAGE MINISTRY
AMMISHADDAI

PSALM : SMOKING on the SWISHER SWEET BLUNT

Chilling in the EAST Of the Glen.. Gary I (in) EAST Of the Glen 809 32 (ave) I was brought here only to (define) what I knew I was laying down my Gat watching every black that I (see) make a move march on D.C. supported every black that I (see) on the box and the news from 7 to 11 checking out the O.J. deliberation (manifestation)of the wicked style RULE.. Now we see the house Nigga need some type of school blessed in the (time)began SHEMITIC type of rhyme PROPHETIC style of (school) PROPHESY (rule)

SMOKING on the SWISHER SWEET BLUNT..

Chilling in the EAST Of the Glen.. Gary I (in) EAST Of the Glen rolling out the eye 65 south on my way to G.I. Now expound all around to my all mighty peep who would creep or even come around on the rainy day " O " YHWH my heart was trouble but while I layed on my belly in my ruins of my rubble while I seen I was clean cold (smoked) off the bubble while I maintain true science to the mind (blessed) in the time.. Began SHEMITC style Of rhyme.. Prayer and the answer for the TIME..

SMOKING on the SWISHER SWEET BLUNT..

Chilling in the EAST Of the Glen.. Gary I (in) EAST Of the Glen 3685 stepping out on the snowy day out the (door) I thank the MOSTHIGH the <u>superstructed force that kept me on my course</u> to the <u>cross roads of the underground</u> coming with the stylistic sound blessed in the time began SHEMITIC style of rhyme PROPHETIC type of rhyme.. Prayer and the answer for the time the GOOD NEWS FLASH TRULY BEEN PAST.. Chilling in the EAST, Chilling in the EAST, east of the Glen.. Gary I (in) Smoking on the Swisher Sweet Blunt I was black and I'm comely U never could debate with (me) KNOWLEDGE out shine all your program so call style of college. I want to be FREE, but this is what u see in (me) try to become chummily to become (me) I got EDOM looking all full dumbly.. Speaking African revolution become no pollution to solution setting HEBREW up to be true.

SMOKING on the SWISHER SWEET BLUNT..

PROPHETIC MESSAGE MINISTRY   AMEN

PSALM : PRAY For INSTRUCTION..

Coming out of Mystery (BABYLON) GET the Money and (run) Give me reparation Give me what u (owe)for atrocity to the (people) Of the MOSTHIGH.. And let ALL NATIONS BEAR the (WITNESS) I'm sick and tired Of being sick and tired Of the PAGAN /GREEK / ROMAN way (lets) return back to the MOSTHIGH WAY : articulate the TRUE WAY the Real Way return back to the Better Day having VISIONS in the Delray to the Brighter Day Homies understand (none) Spiritual couldn't comprehend what I say SO today we spit it for the TRUE..

ALL who Believe IMMANUEL and Follow the LAMB where ever HE (GO)lets Know its time to RETURN back to my Own Land my Home Land my Fore Parents (Land) Get you're Mind (right) to understand what's the (Hype) : laying Low inspire (to) Lead Life (the) Quiet Life in the Low (Belly) Of the Beast the Triple (666) u won't caught me in the (Mix) I'm to (Old) I'm to Cold for the Spirit and Soul in this Cold but LOVE-Less Society play a (part) (try) to Lazy out if she (can) Speaking Church!! I hear the sister cry to (me) why do brothers Lie to (me) do *IMMANUEL STRIKE FEAR* in (me) *FORGIVING* (me) Long Suffer in (me) No Doubt in (me) DOWN for what's Right in (me) falling Short every other day in (me) *HOLY SPIRIT BLESSING, WINNING WITH (IN) (me)*

PRAY For INSTRUCTION the SEED Of the WORD..

The WORD was with (HIM) Planted from BEGINNING *GOOD NEWS INSTRUCTION* : Giving from (Beginning) Let US Create Man in our Own IMAGE : GENESIS 1:24-26 (Get) your Head UP keep it out the (Mix) Cuz it's ALL GOOD.. LOOK FOR RETURN Of YHWH.. Believe or Not it was (hot) looking at the (FIRES BURN) watching symbols in the SKY.. Moon turning *BLOOD RED* Nations in a Panic and they (scared) killing everybody *BLACK HAWK DOWN* exploiting his brother NATION rising Against Another NATION KINGS set among the table among (themselves) telling Lies Among (themselves) preaching and teaching Security and Peace DEMOCRITE nor REBULICAN hearing of the Quakes (here) and (there) famines (everywhere) back doing charity for my little man. If I (can)

PRAY For INSTRUCTION to OVERSTAND Ya'll know this REAL :

Ya'll Know this (Hot) but its (not) to cast JEWELS before SWINE.. Open up the SPIRITUAL (mind) for ALL NATIONS and His Kind RIGHTEOUS we stand UNITED ONE NATION under YAH..

PRAY For INSTRUCTION.. The HOLY SPIRIT to lead the path..

AMEN

PROPHETIC MESSAGE MINISTRY

Coming out of this selfish (Society) full of Porch Monkey Fables to (me) BOASTING and BRAGGING for many years it's the mental heath in SOCIETY why did they lie to me try me but claim CHRISTIANITY fake as I (see) check the SPOT leaven in the (PHARISEE) .. and the Hip - Hop Major (but) the WORD is very Near U in your Mouth in your Heart now U can do it (see) I will set before U today LIFE and GOOD (DEATH) and EVIL I Command U today Love YHWH your EL to walk in His WAY in Spirit of the TRUE.. KEEP His COMMANDMENT and His Statutes, and His JUDGEMENT to Live and Multiply YHWH your EL will Bless U in the land, which U will go (to) (Prolong) perpetuate HIS LAW U will Stand ONE NATION under YAH (IMMANUEL) DWELLING in the HOUSE OF YSRAEL..

Sojourning out in SOUTH CALLIE out in the Desert in the valley watching NIGGAS dropping Dead NIGGAS falling Out in the Alley watching S.A.'s Simulate the hip - hop the WICKED(ness) essent Of the Rap it's a done (deal) *ratta tap tap* (READING) D'VARIM chapter (30) put it to the Verse and the Melody NO I wouldn't Curse (Disperse) step away wicked (imps) stepping to (me) try my Patience (want) to small talk me today U crossed me the other day (so) today U wander why I had nothing to (say) *walking forgotten* (Put) the Verbal Assault on (Me) without play ain't no joke it's a NEW DAY A NEW DAWN .. Got me writing REPORTS up until the brake of Dawn.. C E O 's above me take the WORD of the lying man plot try to get me fired (hired) into a NEW PLACE (so) today I wouldn't leave T-TOWN without no love lost.. <u>I love IMMANUEL and all who follow</u>:

Any body who sell (out) (except) the MARK Of the BEAST will be LOST: paid the cost to be the boss (floss) lost your SOUL PLUS your LIFE to the Life Style Choose LIFE or DEATH (right) or wrong know this Nigga should have been gone 18 yrs regardless this Nigga (wrong) don't be scared to pick up the stone *cast the first stone in the SPIRIT OF THE TRUTH*.. stepping out in FAITH realigning on (ACTION) the WORKS to be (done) Getting ride Of the Evil that dwell among U weeding out the Rebel that's (dwelling) in the Mist Cancer in your Side what U (do) (bad) company corrupted the good habits KEEP IT REAL (is U real) to in (still) to my Seed and the Next Generation NO player hation I'm down for the REPARATION and going HOME to my OWN land and Justify what I do in my OWN land before the MOSTHIGH I pray we see U meet U in my OWN land <u>Set Free</u> <u>FREE AT LAST FREE AT LAST</u>.. I'm not here to try to Kiss No Ass!! Smash (dash) make amends for your SINS the Life and Struggles Of the Prophet in the Hood Cuz if they could would do U if they can (Do) U when Demons ATTACK.. Step back and get your **HEAD COUNT** receiving the Mark Of ABBA ELSHADDAI.. *The* **KINGDOM Of HEAVEN** *here on EARTH*.. *Plot and Plans to Plant the seeds Of Good* **HEAD COUNT.. HEAD COUNT..** *News.. AMEN*

PROPHETIC MESSAGE MINISTRY
        AMMISHADDAI

While u swerve (curve) thru the Sack (back) up and thru the DEL RAY He's Creating while I'm just waiting (yes) rebelist (but) vehement against the Republican buck American UNFAIR and UNBALANCED.. In all your News stepping over Spiritual News (Clues) to the Signs leading to the End Of a Age I lay my head in the Del rays with thoughts visions of the better days.. _Millennium forever in IMMANUEL never Die LOVE LOVE who is meek_ who is humble who wouldn't buckle and crumble when turning the cheek (speak) seek the TRUE to pollutions to conclusion solutions to the problems that (be) visionaries without the TEAM the Field is Much Bigger then I Dream more then the Workers that turn out to do the Good Works stuck in the Desert looking in at the Gentle (conspire) Money making Schemes try to Crush another brothers DREAM giving out Felonies high priced in everything looking at white wall half bake European suppose u represent my people in Mistake blonde head blue eyes looking at u fake living hell (bond) made a mistake lifestyle got my self caught up in the fake (judicial) system suppose to be innocent until proving Guilty so why the hell am I locked up (stuck) in the belly of decay political instrumental insane keeping Nigga's down looking at my people stand (around) LIFE STYLE hanging in the (balance) the ONLY SUPPORT IS THE LAMB Of YHWH

HEAD COUNT..   SO GET YOUR HEAD COUNT..

Before we make a move (shake) the SPOT tonight is the struggle (live) to wake up in morning learn and rejoice through the trail and tribulation of the (day) STEP (ONE) repent (pray) ask for the brighter (way) Cuz at the end of the (day) u become light to the world (salt) to the earth (life) to the game the life and struggles of the PROPHET in the (hood) INSPIRED Of the MOSTHIGH ELOHIM ELSHADDAI.. I have NO Dreams just a billion (one) VISIONS (conclusion) to the INGATHERING Of the people from the FOUR CORNERS Of the Wind " O " breath (breathe) on the slain that I may PROPHESY in the NAME..

VISIONARY (VISIONARIES) the MOVERS and the SHAKERS to the MOVEMENT..   Get your HEAD (right) keep the SPIRIT (tight) Fight for what's (right) before the MOSTHIGH return and (STRIKE) do the will of the FATHER (ABBA) ELSHADDAI..

Get the HEAD right to Get your HEAD COUNT..

(144,000)   AMEN

PROPHETIC MESSAGE MINISTRY
    AMMISHADDAI

PSALM : FEAR Pulling Him out the Fire .. 6/8/04

Looking at the (moon) Mountains and Stars looking out my back yard I Gazed upon the (sky) I thank U I knew it had to (be) the MOSTHIGH I like the Natural High above the tipsy type Of High (why) Know longer shed a tear UNDERSTAND getting stronger in my WEAKNESS and my FEAR <u>No longer shading tears of UNHAPPYNESS</u> : Under Oppression Descrimation maybe sometimes under AGGRESSION seeing the need Of another (meet) I'm doing good the Adversary see try to (Stop) destroy relationship (closest) to (me) those who be got HOLYSPIRIT HOLY (BE) LOVED Evil is always at my (door) I choose the POSITIVE over Negative but in still in the NAME.. " O " YHWH .. My faith in YAH all my hearts desire Mr. Gentle man FORGIVE ME Don't charge me with my (prior) I did wrong in the Day ..

FEAR Pulling Him out the Fire ..

Bent (intent) on ESCAPE setting back as a second class citizen in the EUROPEAN Land as a slave these Nigga's stuck in a (box) its secular U say.. That I can't Speak that .. <u>No where in the WORD tradition Of a man</u> : I thank YAH in all I (do) if U believe and Following in IMMANUEL then U would be the Candidate that I speak Positive to the Good following COMMANDMENTS Of MESSIYAH (first) before over traditions of Man .. RICHARD J MEYER
Speak the LAW Of the MOSTHIGH above the man TRUE BELIEVERS TRUTH (SEEKERS) FEEL (me) man I'm just trying to go (meeker) (Deeper) compassion and Exposure (be) the speaker Living FREE.. In the 2005 with my Soul YAH is Good to (me) <u>MIGHTY ONE Of my Father</u> : Please Forgive (me) allow my people to GO FREE .. Of NO Charge .. I take it to the Congress I take it to the senate that's right NEW LEADERSHIP is needed .. <u>Having Priest set with Judges</u> seem as thought that Sabbath was a bashing but its not just information to better helping (me) to lead a better life .. ABBA BLESSED me in the (fight) let my people Go (reparation) is what u owe (not) from the Father but thru the SON for Dieing for your SINS .. Do what's right Reason to the (Service) *FEAR Pulling Him out the Fire ..* AMEN..

PROPHETIC MESSAGE MINISTRY
AMMISHADDAI

NATIONS Of the EARTH..

It don't have to (be) **DEATH and CAPTIVITY**.. at your (Door) your hands full Of Blood " O " Mystery Babylon <u>dirty trick your president say u</u> above.. 8 documents show attempt to murder (Castro) Vietnam " 68 " secretly Off the books starting (wars) from way back in the (day) secretly then Openly (today) AFGAN to IRAN they coming for u boy : <u>constitution in crisis secret Government</u> raising the (prices) arm and leg (we) the people paying the cost (we) the people our children being sent to (war) <u>DEATH IS AT YOUR DOOR</u> Egypt in " 52 " Iran " 53 " Guatemala in " 53 " Korea " 61 " (Zaire in 1960) Dominican Republic in 1963 Bolivia in " 71 " Brazil in " 64 " Indonesia in " 65 " Ghana in 1966 and I wont mention NO MORE but I could when they say Security and Peace..

The blood shed that would be on your hands " O " Mystery Babylon I'm looking out to all Nations of the Earth sipping on the Wine Drunk with the Hoe that sit on many waters anything go u wanna be a pimp.. Like that Hoe (so) know Cuz u got to (go) Reap what u sow Bloodshed knocking at your (door) AVENGER Of the Blood <u>FORGIVE THEM FATHER ABBA YAH SHALOM (FOR) THEY DON'T KNOW</u>.. it don't have to (be) **DEATH and CAPTIVITY**.. at your (door) so let us (pray) and get together (unity) let's prepare the (road) the Banner Seed Of Jesse its here..

(REPENT) OF YOUR WARS..   NATIONS Of the EARTH..
Sipping on my champagne blessed to the SPIRITUAL CAMPAIGN.. Those who would know YAH shall do mighty (campaigns) in strange land to do the (works) listen to the seer to explain. The LOVE Of the MOSTHIGH my momma always told me if he hit u hit him back !! But the ABBA ELSHADDAI (KING) Of the Earth !! Tell the Prophet down to the people *TURN the OTHER CHEEK :* JUDGMENT is the MOSTHIGH **DEATH IS ON THE SONS OF DISOBEDIENCE** Price Ysrael lets rollout I'm ready to go to my own land understand my home land I plan to Build and expand away from the EVIL ish. Nigga's stalking more Demonically Harder then ever Riding the Beat.. Coming from the reality (rap) staying Negative Specifically (dynamically) explicitly its gone hit excuse my slang (forgive) me in Yahshuah (name)
AMMISHADDAI   (REPENT) OF YOUR WARS..   AMEN

I'm waking up early in the Morning (Yarning) going out to bury the (dead) But (instead) my mind won't allow the Positive thought to leave my (head) when a love one dies we should mourn (yarn) weep and wall being present at the (burial) weep bitterly and passionately (distinctively) what we all (share) OBSERVE THE PERIOD OF MOURNING for the DEAD.. **MOURN A WHOLE DAY or MAYBE (TWO)** but then pull yourself together (reconcile) yourself to the loss (cross) Grief can undermine your (health) messing with your (wealth) lead U to your own (death) *GRIEF LINGERS ON AFTER DEATH..* Of the loved One don't lose your Head in the SOROW; drive it away before it (follow) U to the Grave (slave) to the MEMORY.. To day it was his turn; tomorrow it will be your (turn)

BELIEVE THAT.. RECEIVE THAT.. TAKING HEED IN THAT.. When the DEAD IS (LAID) let the Memory of them (fade) once they are gone pick up your (CROSS) reconcile your (loss) taking COURAGE mourning for the DEAD..

MOURNING FOR THE DEAD.. MOURNING FOR THE DEAD..

HE WHO PREPARED US FOR THIS VERY THING IS יהוה also who has given us the SPIRIT to Guarantee.. If and every foolish talk would have to (cease) all who believe all who call upon the name never die inherit everlasting life *ALWAYS CONFIDENT WELL PLEASING* rather to be absent from the body and to be present with יהוה therefore make Our Aim whether Present (or) Absent to be well pleasing to the MOSTHIGH.. EL ELIYOHN acts of kindness and charity or eternity and everlasting..

SIRACH SON Of YAHSAVIOR
MOURNING FOR THE DEAD.. MOURNING FOR THE DEAD..
Shots out to my people, laying low in the VALLEY Of the DRY BONES..
AMEN

PROPHETIC MESSAGE MINISTRY
AMMISHADDAI

FAITH and CULTER ..

POETRY : Praise to יהוה a song Of Salvation, take Refuge from coming Judgment יהוה our Crown Of Glory a cornerstone in Zion <u>the blindness of disobedience, futile confidence in Egypt</u> : (American Government) DEMOCRATE or REPUBLICAN .. in Quietness and Confidence, " this is the Way, walk in it" Do not rely on Egypt (American Way) *Babylon Mystery or Old* .. A reign of Righteousness, <u>land of the Majestic King</u> Fury against the Nations, the highway of Holiness יהוה word stands forever, the Majesty Of יהוה, יהוה renews strength " Fear not I will help you " Justice to the Gentiles, a light to the Gentiles I have called you by my Name, the redeemer Of YSRAEL *Promise of the Spirit*, the folly of Idolatry; Cyrus will perform יהוה will, " Ask me of things to come" look to me, and be Saved" Prophecy against Babylon (Confusion) יהוה reason for prophecy, *No peace for the wicked, a light to the Gentiles ..*

יהוה will remember Zion .. I will save your children, look to the Rock (MESSIYAH) Gladness and joy in Zion, put on your strength " O " Zion behold my servant <u>by His stripes we are healed</u>, Heritage Of יהוה servants come to the waters " Salvation for the Gentiles spiritual adultery rebuked, healing for the backslider יהוה chosen fast, justice is turned back. The Redeemer Of Zion, the Gentiles Bless Zion the good news of Salvation, Yahrusalem's Salvation assured; only יהוה Saves : יהוה loving Kindness, <u>the potter and the clay</u> .. Righteousness Of יהוה Judgment. *New heaven and New earth " Heaven is my throne .. " rejoice with YAHRUSALEM all flesh shall worship* יהוה

AMEN

ISAIAH 25-28 / 29:11-24 / 30-35 / 40-66

PROPHETIC MESSAGE MINISTRY
        AMMISHADDAI

PSALM : REAL TALK; spoken Word volume 1

REAL TALK baby come TALK in my Ear ..
MAN it's a many lonely females LOVELY and ALL .. What (do) I say what (do) I (do) to build u to.. The COMFORTER SPIRIT .. in the Hearts of mankind Please baby (tee) don't lead your (seed) to the PAGAN'S (WAY) LONERS in the Heart Lovers of the Bling (lead) like sheep to the slaughter college (Bling) Science fall educate your self to YHWH'S Life Lovers of Gold Lovers of Silver Lovers of the LEX u (con) and All put it down follow YHWH'S Way Of Life COMMANDMENT (KEEPERS) Show " em " All about All that Ride on the Way to (Life) but Never Die but take my last (breath) to (eternity) bowing down to YAH Praised the LAMB for us All ..

REAL TALK.. REAL TALK baby come Whisper the WORD in my Ear..

Don't be surprised if the Gentile (flock) race to (grab) Garments (sleeve) of the Hebrew man to understand YHWH'S Way Of Life .. *LEAD to ETERNAL Life ..*
the ROCK is here ..
(GOVERMENTS Fall)
(Diablo build the Wall its was to Tall)
For the Idol mind .. IDOL WORSHIP (Lovers) of the Crack Pipe (Lovers) of the Same Sex   (Lovers) of the LEX u (con) and All put it down follow YHWH'S Way Of Life .. *REAL TALK for survivers ..* and All from the Sinful Way (born) in us All (wake) up for your Call (trumpet) Of the MOSTHIGH ..
BLOWING ON THE FEAST OF TRUMPETS DAY BLESS u and ME TODAY.. Cuz to (day) with my Health and my Strenght was a good (day)

REAL TALK .. REAL TALK ..   Now let me walk on my way to Eternal Life .. Coming from the Four Winds (breathe) on the slane that they may Live ..
Bomb on " em " with the *REAL TALK ..*

REAL TALK baby come TALK the WORD in my Ear ..
REAL TALK baby come whisper the LIVING WORD in my Ear .. Tell it like it is don't be a shame girl let your FATHER be your guild ..

AMEN

FAITH and CULTER ...
PROPHETIC MESSAGE MINISTRY
AMMISHADDAI

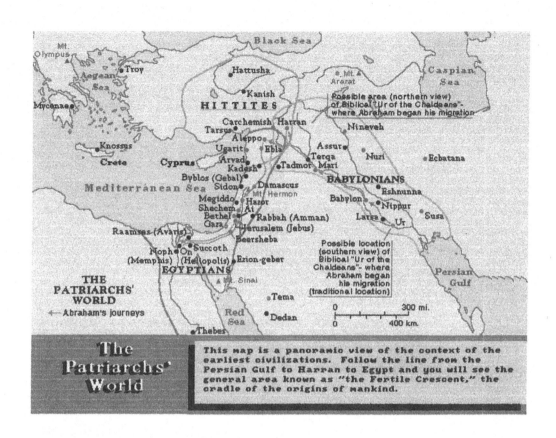

The Patriarchs' World

THE PATRIARCHS' WORLD
← Abraham's journeys

This map is a panoramic view of the context of the earliest civilizations. Follow the line from the Persian Gulf to Harran to Egypt and you will see the general area known as "the Fertile Crescent," the cradle of the origins of mankind.

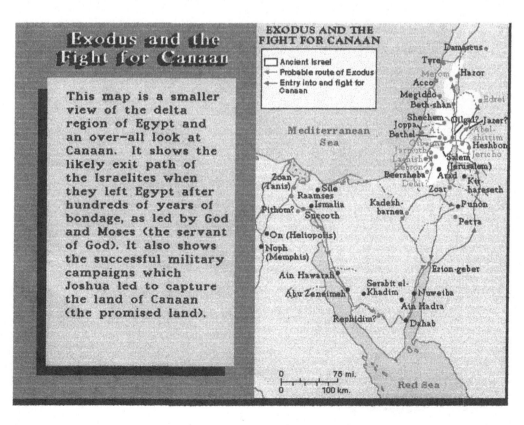

Exodus and the Fight for Canaan

This map is a smaller view of the delta region of Egypt and an over-all look at Canaan. It shows the likely exit path of the Israelites when they left Egypt after hundreds of years of bondage, as led by God and Moses (the servant of God). It also shows the successful military campaigns which Joshua led to capture the land of Canaan (the promised land).

EXODUS AND THE FIGHT FOR CANAAN

☐ Ancient Israel
← Probable route of Exodus
← Entry into and fight for Canaan

305